ROMAN

ROMAN

by Polanski

Pan Books
in association with Heinemann

First published in Great Britain 1984 by William Heinemann Ltd
First published in paperback 1985 by Pan Books Ltd,
Cavaye Place, London SW10 9PG
in association with William Heinemann Ltd
9 8 7 6 5 4 3 2 1
© Eurexpart B V 1984
ISBN 0 330 28597 1

Printed and bound in Great Britain by
Collins, Glasgow

ACKNOWLEDGMENTS

So much time and energy has been put into this book by so many people that it feels like a cooperative venture, almost like the making of a motion picture. I want to express my heartfelt gratitude to:

Edward Behr for his infinite patience, for listening to days and days of tapes, and for putting it all together.

John Brownjohn for helping to polish it all.

And to Peter Gethers for giving it the final touch.

ILLUSTRATIONS

The author wishes to offer his thanks to the owners and photographers who have permitted him to reproduce their work, as indicated in brackets.

to my friends,
past, present and future

ONE

For as far back as I can remember, the line between fantasy and reality has been hopelessly blurred.

I have taken most of a lifetime to grasp that this is the key to my very existence. It has brought me more than my share of heartache and conflict, disasters and disappointments. It has also unlocked doors that would otherwise have remained closed forever.

Art and poetry, the land of imagination, always seemed more real to me, as a boy growing up in Communist Poland, than the narrow confines of my environment. From an early age, I realized that I was not like those around me: I inhabited a separate, make-believe world of my own.

I couldn't watch a bicycle race in Krakow without picturing myself as a future champion. I couldn't view a movie without seeing myself as the star or, better still, the director behind the camera. Whenever I saw great theater, there was no doubt in my mind that, sooner or later, I myself would hold the center of the stage in Warsaw or Moscow or even – why not? – in Paris, that remote and romantic cultural capital of the world. All children entertain such fantasies at one time or another. Unlike the majority, who soon become resigned to their lack of fulfillment, I never for a moment doubted that my dreams would come true. I had a naïve, simpleminded certainty that this was not only possible but inevitable – as preordained as the drab existence that should by rights have been my lot.

My friends and family, who used to laugh at my wild aspirations, came to regard me as a buffoon. Ever eager to

1

amuse and entertain, I assumed the role with good grace. I never minded. There were times when the obstacles in my path were such that I needed all the fantasy I could muster, simply to survive.

On a January evening not long ago, at the Théâtre Marigny in Paris, one of my childhood dreams was more than fulfilled. Attired as Mozart in an eighteenth-century frock coat and powdered wig, I was about to make my stage entrance in a dual role, as director and costar.

The first-night audience – a blend of politicians and film stars, celebrities and socialites – was the kind that columnists like to describe as 'glittering.' Though pleased and flattered by their interest, I was far more conscious of the many old friends who had come to give me moral support, some of them from halfway around the world. Their presence meant that I mattered to them, that I did, after all, have a family in the widest sense.

The play was Peter Shaffer's *Amadeus*. Throughout, the Venticelli, the 'little winds' or scandalmongers, preface and punctuate the action of the play like a Greek chorus. As I waited in the wings, listening to their serpentlike whispers, I seemed to hear a medley of voices from my past. Some belonged to those who had nagged and chided me for daydreaming, others to those whose encouragement had helped make my daydreams come true.

At that moment the line between reality and fantasy was not only blurred but less perceptible to me than ever before. The two had at last become one.

When my cue came, I went onstage and performed with the same ease and lack of inhibition as I had for my friends in childhood. Yet, as I lived out the last tragic phase of Mozart's life, my daydreams returned. It dawned on me that there was a theatrical thread running through my life, with its triumphs and tragedies, joys and sorrows, intense love and unimagined grief. In the same way, I found it hard to distinguish between the half-seen faces beyond the footlights and the ghosts of the past. It was almost as if I were performing for all my friends

2

and loved ones, past and present, living and dead.

Amadeus drew to a close. The lights went up; the audience gave us a standing ovation, stamping and cheering. Curtain call followed curtain call. Still in a daze, I walked the hundred yards from the theater to a nightclub that had become a regular haunt of mine over the years. Light-headed with champagne, I found that the distinction between past and present continued to elude me as our first-night party hit its stride. It became confused in my mind with similar gatherings in London, New York, Los Angeles, and – most recently – Warsaw.

I had directed and played in a Polish version of *Amadeus* immediately before starting work on the Paris production. Because our Warsaw run was closely followed by the military takeover, few of my Polish friends had managed to attend the French premiere. Even my father, who always came to my openings, had been unable to leave Krakow.

The 'war,' as we Poles called it, cast a long, grim shadow over what should have been a joyous highlight in my career. In Warsaw, our first night had been a very special occasion, attended by many who had influenced me and made me what I was. Seeing them again – talking about the past and visiting places I hadn't set eyes on since childhood – brought memories flooding back.

A child's perception of things has a clarity and immediacy unmatched by any subsequent experience.

My own earliest memories are of Komorowski Street in Krakow, where I lived when I was four. Above each entrance was an Art Nouveau animal – elephant, bison, hedgehog – carved in stone. The mythical beast at No.9 was a hideous hybrid – part dragon, part eagle. When I was a child, the house had not long been built and smelled of fresh paint.

There were two apartments on the third-floor landing. Ours was the one on the right: a small, airy, sunny place, modern except for its traditional tiled stoves. The two main rooms overlooked quiet, middle-class Komorowski Street. The rear of the building faced a bustling market. Those were

3

the days when peasant women still came to the door with butter and eggs, their own farmyard aura mingling with the fragrance of the fresh loaves of bread brought in by the baker's delivery boys.

My mother was a very orderly person. Everything in our apartment was spick-and-span. The one untidy place was in the side wall of the balcony where we had a closet crammed with junk, including a mysterious contrivance. My father claimed it showed him when I was lying. Since I already half believed in the existence of such a device, the fact that we owned one worried me beyond belief. The domestic lie detector came into play whenever I was suspected of concealing the truth. It wasn't until much later that I identified it as a defunct, discarded bedside lamp of extremely peculiar design.

Although my father wasn't a wealthy man, I went short of nothing. Yet I was, in many respects, a demanding, difficult, and petulant child with a tendency to sulk and throw tantrums – a spoiled brat. Why? Perhaps because of the long fair hair – which I loathed – that led grown-ups to mistake me for a girl. Or perhaps it was my response to those who laughed at and mimicked the Gallic way I pronounced my *R*'s; I had been born in Paris the year Hitler came to power and spent the first three unremembered years of my life there, acquiring a French accent that stayed with me until the age of five or six. Last but far from least, there was my very name itself. Anxious to invest their child with a French cachet, my parents had registered me at birth as 'Raymond,' which they erroneously assumed to be the French equivalent of Roman, a common enough Polish name. Raymond, unfortunately, is unpronounceable by the average Pole save as 'Remo,' and I was so enraged and embarrassed by this outlandish appellation that I sloughed it off as soon as possible. Thenceforward, except to doting relatives and sarcastic schoolmates, I was either plain, straightforward Roman or Romek, the Polish diminutive.

I always had to do things my way. As my father was to tell me, interminably, in later years, I used to fly into a fury if he held me while riding on a subway escalator, stamping my feet and turning puce with rage. The same thing would happen if he tried to deprive me of his precious camera, which I towed around on a string like a toy car.

My feelings were easily hurt. On August 18, my fifth birthday, Aunt Teofila gave me a splendid crimson fire engine with rubber tires, telescopic ladders, and a removable set of firemen. My family and their assembled friends were deep in conversation – the party was more for them than for me – so, left to my own devices, I decided to examine the toy more closely. Having removed the rest of the crew, I tried to lift the driver out of his seat. The miniature figure broke off in my hand; it was a fixture. Horrified, I secreted it in the nearest stove. When the grown-ups finally decided to pay me some attention, they noticed that the fire engine was driverless. I feigned ignorance, but my mother unerringly found the missing figure. The chorus of indulgent laughter that greeted my misdemeanor was more hurtful than any scolding would have been.

All these scenes are remembered somewhat haphazardly but they are incredibly strong and vivid. With no preconceptions to measure them against, a young mind, fresh and uncluttered, absorbs impressions eclectically, at random.

Another such memory lingers, of the day some Galalith was delivered to our house – a sample crate of a new color for my father's small plastics business. He owned a workshop that molded the substance into ashtrays and all kinds of ornamental knickknacks.

My father set to work opening the crate with me looking on. After a while I, too, began attacking the nails with a claw hammer. 'Thanks,' he said sharply, 'I don't need your help.' I was cut to the quick. He took a slab of shiny red Galalith from its bed of wood shavings and held it out as a peace offering. I was sorely tempted to take it – it looked and smelled alluring in the extreme – but shook my head and turned away.

My father often hurt my feelings in little ways. He never

5

hurt me physically, though, even when I broke the household's one taboo: I was strictly forbidden to touch his pride and joy, the massive Underwood typewriter on which he composed his business correspondence at home, typing impressively fast. I was, however, allowed to stand beside him and watch, and he encouraged me to pick out the letters on his keyboard. That was how I learned my alphabet.

It was lucky I did, for I was removed from kindergarten on my very first day for saying, *'Pocatuj mnię w dupę,'* to a girl in my class – or was it to the teacher herself? I must have overheard the phrase from one of my uncles. It means 'Kiss my ass.'

My disgrace left me spending a lot of time at home, alone except for Annette and our maidservant. Annette was my teenage half sister, my mother's daughter by her first husband. She was a movie fan, and we sat through many an afternoon together in half-empty Krakow theaters, watching movies of which I understood nothing. My earliest screen memory is of an American musical in which Jeanette MacDonald, attired in a vaporous white gown, descended a staircase to the strains of 'Sweethearts.' I recall this so vividly because I was dying to relieve myself. Annette, who refused to miss a minute of the film, told me to pee under the seat.

I was never bored. There was always something worth watching from the windows on either side of the apartment. In any case, it was difficult to be bored in a city like Krakow, with the trumpeter up in St Mary's church tower sounding his ritual fanfare on the hour, Wawel Castle, the Vistula River, and the climactic event of the year, the great summer festival known as Wianki.

The latter loomed so large on my horizon that I would spend days, with Annette in tow, combing the riverbank for a spot that would give us the best possible view of the fireworks and pageantry, floats and processions of decorated barges. Wianki, which went back to pre-Christian times, commemorated the legend of Princess Wanda, who had jumped to her death from Krakow Castle rather than marry a German king. At dusk, down the river so close to where we lived,

6

floated hundreds of wreaths adorned with lighted candles; the princess's death was reenacted by a white-clad girl who leaped into the Vistula from a make-believe castle mounted on a barge. It was a fairy-tale occasion, culminating in a huge display of pyrotechnics that took my breath away. To me, fireworks were magic. I couldn't wait for them to start, couldn't bear them to end.

There was winter magic as well. The sparklers fizzing on our Christmas tree mesmerized me with their cascades of silver fire – miniature fireworks in our own home! That, together with the taste of dried raisins, figs, and walnuts, went to make up my first remembered Polish Christmas at 9 Komorowski Street. Snow, too, became part of that Christmas when Uncle Stefan bought me a pair of skis and I tried them out for the first time, eagerly but unsuccessfully, on the white banks of the Vistula.

My memories of my mother are both vivid and hazy. I recall the sound of her voice, her elegance, the precise way she drew thin lines over her plucked eyebrows, the equally careful way she applied lipstick to alter the shape of her upper lip in keeping with contemporary fashion, and the mean little face of her fox fur, which savagely bit its own tail. I recall her naturalness when I once walked into the bedroom and saw her naked. Many people later told me she was strikingly beautiful. She was also, as the war was to show, resourceful and proud. I like to think that my own obstinacy and resilience are inherited from her.

I remember one summer my parents had rented a country chalet in a mountain resort with the impossible name of Szczyrk. It was, in retrospect, our last truly carefree, happy time together. It was also my first real contact with nature. The countryside was a dream, heavily wooded and hilly. For a long time afterward I thought all forests had to grow on hillsides.

My parents were in the garden with some friends, engrossed in a game of cards. I watched them from a distance, horsing around in a deck chair, fiddling with it till it collapsed with me on top, my fingers trapped in the wooden framework. My predicament left me embarrassed and guilty. I'd been warned not to play with the deck chair and didn't want to draw attention to myself, but the pain was excruciating. I blacked out. When I came to, a doctor was bending over me. 'You were turning blue,' my mother said.

My sixth birthday coincided with our holiday at Szczryk, and my mother had invited some children over for a tea party. They arrived early, while I was still on the pot. I heard my mother telling them, matter-of-factly, 'Romek's on the throne.' I longed for the floor to swallow me up, pot and all – how could she betray me like this? – and refused to emerge. My mother pretended that 'being on the throne' meant something quite different: that I was king for the day because of my birthday. She invented a whole game based on my new title, but nothing would induce me to join the others.

Krakow is enclosed by Planty, a circular park where the old city walls used to be. Once, while my father and I were strolling there, we came across a hawker selling prints which, when folded in a certain way, transformed the faces of four men into the likeness of a pig. To judge by the small crowd clustered around him, the hawker was doing a roaring trade. My father told me that the cartoons were of Hitler, Himmler, Goebbels, and Göring. He explained who they were and why the Nazis represented a threat to our country.

These names began to crop up more and more often. It was symptomatic of a new tension in the air – of fears that war was imminent. All over town, novel forms of activity could be observed: trenches were dug in Planty Park; windows and storefronts crisscrossed with adhesive antiblast paper. My family held a series of conclaves – hours of earnest discussion from which I was excluded. The upshot was that my father decided to give up the Komorowski Street apartment and rent a hideout in Warsaw, much farther from the German-Polish border. Meantime, while awaiting developments, we were to move in with my grandmother and my two unmarried uncles, Stefan and Bernard. Apparently the situation had become so grave that it seemed safer to concentrate the family under one roof.

My grandmother's apartment in Kazimierz, Krakow's only approximation to a Jewish quarter, was in total contrast with our former home – a huge, dark place approached by way of a moldering courtyard. The tiled stoves were not white, as in our own apartment, but vast baroque affairs with elaborate ornamentation.

Each room had its own particular smell. The tang of my grandmother's pomade pervaded the bedroom she had turned over to us, which had an ornate brass bed and a dressing table with a triptych mirror. The bathroom smelled of drains and ancient plumbing. It had an old-fashioned bath with a shiny copper boiler. My two uncles' skis were kept in there, too. The bedroom they shared was strictly out of bounds to me. The living room, which they used as a workroom, reeked of mothballs from the skins they made up for the furrier who employed them.

My grandmother's name was Maria. My parents and uncles called her Mother, but to me she was Granny. I adored her. She was quite small, with gray hair done up in a bun, and habitually wore black. Because she had insisted on giving up her room to us, she slept in the kitchen. This, until I started going to a proper school, was where I now spent most of my time. I found it an endless source of entertainment and fascination, but not just because of my grandmother's inexhaustible patience, her readiness to play with me and answer my quick-fire questions. The kitchen contained a big carved dresser, a pair of scales that lent itself to an infinity of games, and jars full of mysterious syrups and homemade jams. On the windowsill stood a smaller gauze-covered jar containing only water, and on the gauze reposed a bean. Sprouting from the bean were wispy white roots that grew perceptibly longer, day by day, and seemed to have a life of their own, like some exotic tentacled sea creature. Although my grandmother had meant to teach me how vegetables grew, I found the sight more horrifying than educational.

One Sunday my mother took me, as usual, to play on the banks of the Vistula. It was exceptionally hot that summer of 1939; but the river always provided a welcome breeze, and butterflies danced there in the shimmering sunlight. One of them looked different from the rest – big and brown, with patches of blue. Capturing it in my sailor-boy hat was an incredible feat. Uncle Bernard put it to sleep with ether and mounted it on a cork. He said it was a Queen's Page – a real collector's item.

The day after I had made this memorable catch, panic seized the family circle. Our emergency plan was put into effect. My mother hurriedly packed our bags and announced that she was taking me to Warsaw with Annette. Because all our household effects were stored in Krakow, my father decided to stay on there with his brothers, at least for the moment, to see how things shaped up. My fatalistic grand-mother refused to budge – whatever happened.

War had broken out, but no war was going to rob me of my prize possession. My mother wanted to leave the butterfly behind. Such was my fury that she relented and offered to pack it, but I wouldn't have that either. We finally departed for the station, loaded down with luggage: I carried my mother's hatbox, my school lunch box, my teddy bear – and my Queen's Page pinned to its cork.

It was the first time I had been separated from my father and the first time I had traveled by train at night. Some drunks in our third-class section started pestering my pale and harassed mother, so she paid for a second-class supple-ment and moved us into another car.

My father believed we would be safer in Warsaw, where our new abode turned out to be an unfinished suburban apartment house. The place was quite as spotless as our Komorowski Street apartment, but with one major dif-ference: apart from a fold-up bed and a mattress, it was completely unfurnished. This hardly mattered, since we started spending all our nights, and some of our days, in the basement.

The regular wail of the air-raid sirens brought our fellow residents – total strangers to us, one and all – rushing down, panic-stricken, to stake out their claims in the cellar. What with babies screaming, old people grumbling, and women having hysterics, absolute pandemonium reigned. Our refuge was airless – hot, muggy, and rife with frightful rumors that the Germans were about to use poison gas. Warsaw residents had proper gas masks; latecomers like us had gauze pads moistened with some foul-smelling chemical.

The real torture, during those nights below ground, was not being allowed to take off my shoes because my mother feared we might have to run for it. Mesmerized by the flicker of candlelight, I slept fitfully in her arms, clutching my teddy bear, dozing and waking by turns until the all-clear sounded. At this, family groups would pick up their gas masks and trudge back upstairs, only to race down an hour or two later when the sirens started wailing again.

As the air raids got worse, we ran short of food. We also ran short of money. There was no word from my father. My mother, who came from a well-to-do Russian family and was considered to have married beneath her, had always had a maid in Krakow. But now, surprisingly, she proved endlessly resourceful, scavenging for food like everyone else.

She returned from one of her daily excursions with a sackful of sugar mixed with grit because she had scraped it up off the street. After melting the sugar in a biscuit tin, she strained it to remove the grit and baked a whole batch of delicious little cookies, some of which we sold for ready cash.

Another time she came back with a bucket-sized can of pickled cucumbers. We ate nothing else for several days. At first we enjoyed them, and the briny water tasted good. It only gradually dawned on us that this diet aggravated our thirst at a time when drinking water was in short supply. We had been warned to fill the bath and every container we could lay our hands on. When the taps ran dry, it became my job,

11

and Annette's, to line up for hours with pots and pans at distribution points.

Sometimes, when my mother went out, Annette and I would panic, fearing the worst. 'Let's sleep,' Annette said. 'Time passes quicker that way.' And it did.

I always waited for my mother to return with tremulous, heart-pounding anticipation. One evening, hearing footsteps, I rushed to open the door – and in walked four people I had never seen before: a bombed-out couple and two children. Without a word, they proceeded to bed down in our tiny hallway. My mother came back to find the apartment crawling with strangers, but there was nothing she could do.

For me, there were advantages to being unsupervised for the first time in my life. I started playing around the bomb craters with other boys. I found the tail fin of a German bomb and lugged it home – another trophy. I made a gruesome discovery in a nearby street: a dead cart horse. Examining it more closely the next day, I saw that a hunk of meat had been sliced off its hindquarters. More excisions appeared the day after that – gaping holes in the decomposing carcass. We discussed this, the three of us, and decided that however hungry we became, we would never resort to rotting horse-meat.

Something much more distressing met my eye when one day I strayed farther afield: Marooned on the fourth floor of a bombed, wrecked shell of a building, a lone dog was howling and whimpering. No one took any notice. I was irresistibly drawn to this sight, begging complete strangers to rescue the animal. They brushed me aside and walked on.

Several days later I was playing on our vacant lot when I noticed someone squatting on his heels, watching me intently. It took me a while to recognize my father, he was so gaunt and unshaven. He held out his arms, and I ran to him. He hugged and kissed me. His beard prickled. Right away I started wailing – showing him how well I could imitate an air-raid siren.

It was good to have a father around again, especially since he got rid of our uninvited guests. Now, as the four of us huddled together on the floor, he told us about his travels.

To escape the oncoming Germans, he and my two un-married uncles had joined the mass exodus and trekked east to Lublin on foot. My third uncle, David, who was married to Teofila, a baker's daughter, made the journey there in his in-laws' horse-drawn delivery van. The Germans were already in Lublin when the brothers arrived, so they had to hide. They eventually split up, my uncles returning to occupied Krakow, my father joining us in Warsaw. Our emergency plan had been a complete miscalculation. Instead of staying put in Krakow, which had seen no fighting at all, we had headed straight for the very epicenter of the war.

I wouldn't let my father out of my sight. I took him to see the dog, whose whimpers were growing steadily fainter. He shrugged. 'What can we do?' he said, but I couldn't put it out of my mind. The next time I passed the spot there was no dog.

Soon afterward I saw a solitary Polish armored car driving along a ruined street, its crew haggard and exhausted. The same afternoon, holding my father's hand, I watched serried ranks of Wehrmacht infantrymen march through Warsaw shoulder to shoulder, spruce and toylike in their gray-green uniforms. I was fascinated by any kind of soldiers, even Germans, but my father squeezed my hand hard and said, 'Swine, swine!' under his breath.

TWO

The first Jews came to Poland from Prague and Germany early in the eleventh century. It was Kazimierz the Great who, three hundred years later, invited the Jews to Krakow from other parts of Europe and bestowed upon them great privileges and opportunities. He saw them as economic pump primers who would turn Krakow into a commercial center rivaling the major cities elsewhere in Europe.

By the time World War II broke out, Krakow's 60,000 Jews had lived cheek by jowl with the rest of the population for more than 500 years and were fully integrated. Although there was a predominantly Jewish quarter, where my grandmother lived, nothing remotely resembling a ghetto existed because – thanks to King Kazimierz and his successors – Krakow's Jews had enjoyed full rights of citizenship from the very first. They had played an important role in the city's development, contributing not only to its commercial growth but also to its reputation as a cultural and intellectual stronghold, with the world-famous Jagiellonian University, magnificent Renaissance architecture, flourishing theaters, fine art galleries, and prestigious publishing houses.

One question is always asked whenever the 'Final Solution' crops up: Why did the Jews allow themselves to be slaughtered during World War II? Why weren't they aware, from the outset, of what was in store for them; why didn't they grasp the truth earlier and rise en masse against their oppressors?

The main reason why their apprehensions were only gradually and belatedly aroused was that the Holocaust had yet to come. It was outside any known frame of reference. Pressures built up slowly and did not at first seem more than mildly threatening. The Germans' method was to lull people into passivity, to foster a sense of hope, to persuade the Jews that things couldn't possibly be *that* bad.

My own feeling was that if only one could explain to them that we had done nothing wrong, the Germans would realize that it all was a gigantic misunderstanding.

What happened to my family is a perfect illustration of the way the 'Final Solution' worked.

Superficially life resumed its normal course after our return to Krakow, yet nothing was quite the same.

I started school. It was just around the corner, and I didn't like it. School meant sitting in rows and filling up exercise books with *Ala ma kota* ('Ala has a cat'). I don't think I got much farther than that because after I was enrolled for only a few weeks, Jewish children were suddenly forbidden to attend. That was all right with me because the tedium of it all would have been unendurable except for a gadget the teacher sometimes produced. This was an epidiascope used for projecting illustrations onto a screen in the school hall. I wasn't at all interested in the words or even the pictures it projected, only in the method of projection. I wanted to know how the gadget worked and constantly examined its lens and mirror or held up the proceedings and made a nuisance of myself by masking the beam with my fingers.

I also found I could draw: not the usual childish scrawls but quite sophisticated drawings with a semblance of perspective. The portraits I made of my family were recognizable. I also remember sketching a pretty good likeness of a German soldier in his teutonic helmet. The only thing I wasn't able to copy, for some reason, was one particular Star of David. The two triangles that made up the star were interlaced with great complexity. I had plenty of time to study this pattern, however. From December 1, 1939, onward, my family had to wear strange white armbands with the Star stenciled on them in blue. I was told it meant we were Jewish.

My parents had never practiced their religion. My mother was only part Jewish, and both she and my father were agnostics who didn't believe in religious instruction for children. Now, being Jewish meant that we couldn't stay where we were.

We moved yet again – not voluntarily, as at the outbreak of war, but under compulsion. We didn't have to move far. Our resettlement, which proceeded without fuss or threats, was handled by the Krakow municipal authorities, not by the Germans. Though permitted to take only as much as we could carry, we found our new quarters no worse than the old except for over-crowding. Our allocated ground-floor apartment, on Podgorze Square, on the far side of the Vistula, was bigger than my grandmother's but shared by several families. Granny was no longer with us. She had been assigned a diminutive room at the other end of Krakow's new 'Jewish area.'

My parents, my sister, and I now occupied two rooms in a cavernous L-shaped apartment with lots of windows and a view of a red brick church. There were several shops nearby, and food could still be bought.

This was the first phase. We could come and go freely, and I played with Polish, not just Jewish, kids. The only reason my father didn't buy us a Christmas tree that first winter was that he preferred not to draw attention to himself.

Soon afterward Annette took me to the window and pointed. Some men were at work on something right across the street. It looked like a barricade.

'What are they doing?' I asked.

'They're building a wall.'

Suddenly it dawned on me; they were walling us in. My heart sank; I couldn't stop crying. This was our first real sign that the Germans meant business. Workmen also bricked up the main entrance and windows on one side of our apartment house, blocking our view of the square and the church. The bricked-up side now formed a continuation of the wall, so a new entrance had to be knocked through on Rekawka Street,

16

with steps leading via the basement to the large dark hallway. It all meant that what was once a pleasant outlook – a quiet street leading into an open square with trees – had now become a cul-de-sac bounded by an expanse of red brick neatly topped with scalloped concrete crenellations.

A main road cut our new metropolis in two. There was a barbed-wire fence on each side of this busy thoroughfare. Residents of the ghetto could watch the traffic go by, just as they themselves could be seen by those who used the road, but the road itself was out of bounds to us – off limits and inaccessible. To enable people to get from one part of the ghetto to the other, a small footbridge was built.

Despite our confinement, it would be wrong to think that fear dominated our lives throughout this preliminary phase. I had some good times, too, in those first few months, playing with my sled in the snow, swapping postage stamps, mixing with other boys.

It was on Rekawka Street that I first learned about sex. With other kids I scoured the streets, picking up odds and ends. Our loot included some small rubber tubes like deflated balloons, which we found in doorways and gutters. These, said a boy in our group, were condoms. Grown-ups used them to avoid having children. He explained that to make babies, a man entered a woman with his penis. In some bewilderment I pondered this revolutionary notion. Was this the only way babies came, or was there a combination of circumstances? I had always been told that babies were delivered by a stork.

My companions looked scornful. I argued that one room in our Rekawka Street apartment was occupied by a woman who was unmarried and lived alone but had a baby just the same. Didn't this imply that the stork was involved? The others weren't so sure after all.

I reverted to the subject a few days later, with the same group. I'd had an inspiration. Once inside a woman, I said, you didn't just keep it there, you moved it back and forth. I was made to feel naïve; of course you did, I was told.

During these early months the ghetto was – despite periodic bouts of terror – a self-contained town where people went courting, got married, and even entertained. In addition to its own Jewish police force, or *Ordnungsdienst*, the local administration, or *Judenrat*, its makeshift health service and social workers, the ghetto boasted a small restaurant and a shabby, open-air café cabaret with a band in which accordions predominated. Two friends of my father's, the Rosner brothers, belonged to this ensemble. The wall of the café was adorned with a mural; it depicted a Hassidic Jew, in traditional garb, being checked by a Polish policeman, while from the tails of his long black coat protruded the head of the goose he was smuggling into the ghetto. I attended the birthday party of young Richard Horowitz, aged three, the Rosners' nephew, and cakes and hot chocolate were provided for us children. Richard, a temperamental little brat, refused to drink his birthday cocoa.

Though peaceful enough, these weeks were marked by small but ominous turns of the screw. My father's beloved Underwood typewriter was confiscated. Not long after the wall was completed, all Jewish families had to hand in every scrap of fur in their possession. They stood in line for hours. My mother surrendered her fox; my grandmother, her fur collar.

One night we heard screams issuing from the stairwell. We promptly switched off all the lights, and my father crept out to see what was happening. He tiptoed back with the news that Germans were in the building. He had seen a woman being dragged downstairs by the hair. We sat and waited, the room lit only by the glow from the stove. Idly I licked my finger and drew a swastika on the wall. My father angrily wiped it off.

I was always being urged to visit Granny. Sadly my relations with her were not what they had been. I found her questions a bore. She was forever asking me about my parents. Was all

18

well with them? Were they quarreling? Her inquisitions probably reflected genuine, justified concern, but I dismissed them simply as prying chatter. I'd ceased to be her pampered baby. I couldn't wait to terminate our tedious sessions and get back to the first special friend I ever made.

Pawel – I never did get to know his last name – lived next door to us. He was around twelve years old, a motherless orphan billeted with a foster father who didn't love him, beat him continually, and made him look after his baby sister all day long.

Because of Pawel's household duties, I couldn't play with him all the time. I knew he led an appallingly unhappy life – the kind I'd only read about in children's books – but he didn't let it get him down. Brown-haired and tall for his age, with a strong, handsome face, he was a smart kid with an extraordinary capacity for absorbing and marshaling facts.

Pawel was my joy – my first real companion and compensation for an increasingly constricted and fear-ridden existence. This close relationship with someone outside my family circle was an educational as well as an emotional awakening. I'd always had a craving for practical information of all kinds, and Pawel could supply answers to everything: not the sort of dismissive, grown-up answers that left my curiosity unsatisfied but genuinely scientific explanations about the nature of electricity, how cars ran on gasoline, what kept planes in the air. He had made a perfectly good electric bell out of two coils of varnished copper wire and a trembler. Together we embarked on the construction of a simple battery-operated motor. I used to draw a lot of eccentrically designed airplanes, and he patiently explained why they would never fly, teaching me elementary principles of aerodynamics picked up from God knows where. Even today, whenever I see a strange aircraft like an AWACS plane or a space shuttle, I wish I could say to Pawel, 'You see, old friend, weird shapes *can* fly. . . . '

I had just been visiting my grandmother, and was impatient to get back to Pawel, when I received a foretaste of things to

19

come. At first I didn't know what was happening. I simply saw people scattering in all directions. Then I realized why the street had emptied so quickly. Some women were being herded along it by German soldiers. Instead of running away like the rest, I felt compelled to watch.

One old crone, at the rear of the column, couldn't keep up. A German officer kept prodding her back into line, but she fell down on all fours, groveling, whining, and pleading with him in Yiddish. Suddenly a pistol appeared in the officer's hand. There was a loud bang, and blood came welling out of her back. I ran straight into the nearest building, squeezed into a smelly recess beneath some wooden stairs, and didn't come out for hours.

I developed a strange habit: clenching my fists so hard that my palms became permanently calloused. I also woke up one morning to find that I had wet my bed. There was nothing I could do to conceal this disaster. I was fiercely scolded, but the next night the same thing happened again. It became an almost invariable occurrence. I used to fall asleep, dream that I'd wet my bed, and wake to discover that my nightmare was an unwelcome reality.

Hoarding was forbidden. We had been warned in advance that the ghetto would be searched for illicit stocks of food. As bad luck would have it, my mother had just baked some rolls, and these became an object of controversy. She wanted to crumble them up and flush them down the toilet, but my father persuaded her to put them in a hatbox and hide it on top of a wardrobe.

In came a tall German officer in peaked cap and glossy riding boots, escorted by a soldier and a civilian from the *Judenrat*. He started talking to my mother in German, then went with her to inspect the kitchen. My father and I just sat there, not daring to move. The officer returned, followed by my mother. We thought the inspection was over, but he lingered, smiling faintly, circling the room like a bird of prey, picking up my teddy bear and swinging it by one leg, looking the place over. Suddenly, with the tip of his swagger stick, he reached up and flicked the hatbox off the top of the wardrobe. He picked it up, opened it, and scattered the rolls all over the floor.

He laughed. Then he started swearing and barking at us in German. Finally, still swinging my teddy bear, he strolled out of the room. That was all, but my mother was angrier than I had ever seen her. 'I told you we should have gotten rid of them,' she hissed at my father. 'I feel as if I'd choked on the damned things.'

My mother beat me once, quite hard – I can't recall why. It was the only time she ever raised a hand to me, and it was probably for some very good reason. In retrospect, the stress of ghetto life must have been well-nigh unendurable. It accounted for my parents' rows and their little, nagging, carping unpleasantnesses to each other. Although I didn't know it at the time, my mother was pregnant, an additional source of strain and anxiety. My own worst fear at this time was that my parents might split up. That thought, which worried me almost more than anything else, may well have contributed to my bed-wetting.

Some stretches of the ghetto perimeter were enclosed by a barbed-wire fence, not a wall. From one particular position near the fence that flanked the main road, we could watch the weekly open-air film shows staged by the Germans in Padgorze Square for the inhabitants of Krakow. These shows included newsreels and propaganda films of Panzer units in action or Wehrmacht troops parading down the Champs-Élysées. Their purpose was to impress upon the Poles that the armies of the Third Reich were invincible. Every so often, during breaks in the proceedings, the following words were flashed on the screen: 'JEWS=LICE=TYPHUS!' We must have looked pretty bizarre to the people on the outside: a little cluster of faces peering through the barbed wire, craning to catch a glimpse of these macabre drive-in movies. I even used much of my stamp collection to pay a boy who

21

owned a toy projector to show me, on a dirty towel, some orange-tinted scenes of early silent movies.

The part of the ghetto that had no wall, only a fence, included some rising ground – open scrubland with a few rocky outcrops. This was where I used to go sledding, that first winter of the war, and this, too, was where, without my parents' knowledge, I now began sneaking out of the ghetto.

It was like walking through a mirror and emerging on the other side – entering a different world complete with street-cars and people leading normal lives. Everything seemed sunnier, brighter, brisker, more prosperous. For the first time I saw the wall from the outside, and it didn't look the same. The inner surface was plain, rough brick; the exterior made quite a decorative impression with its stippled cement finish and scalloped, Oriental top.

I was not alone on my first excursion. Two other boys came with me, one my own age, the other much younger. We interrogated the little one: What would he say if asked where he lived?

'I'd say I live at Rekawka Street, number ten.'

That did it. We sent him straight back and headed for our chosen destination, a shop that sold stamps. I knew it well, having spent some pocket money there before the wall went up. It was near the church. The woman behind the counter eyed us curiously. 'You boys are from the ghetto, right? Aren't you taking a bit of a risk?' Although I pretended not to know what she meant, I never went back there again. Being on the outside was a great adventure, but my experience in the stamp shop showed it to be dangerous as well. It wasn't until I was back inside the ghetto, after slipping through the wire again, that I felt entirely safe.

My father had made plans for my survival should he and my mother both be taken away. Having a lot of friends and acquaintances in town, he found a couple, Mr and Mrs Wilk, who were prepared to help me. I was not to live with them but they agreed to find a family who would take me in. I was fortunate in not looking Jewish – one of the factors that

22

persuaded the Wilks to look after me. The other factor was money. My father made this arrangement in the early days, when ghetto laborers could still move around unescorted, and it cost him plenty – all the family jewelry and his life savings.

My youngest uncle, Stefan, married a very pretty, Aryan-looking girl, Maria, who had forged papers enabling her to live as a Pole outside the ghetto. She must have paid off a guard because she once managed to slip in and visit her new husband. While there, she taught me how to make the sign of the cross and the basic Catholic prayers – further protection if I had to make it on my own.

On my preliminary visit to the Wilks' my mother accompanied me. She was employed by the Germans at this period, outside the ghetto – as a cleaning woman at Wawel Castle, headquarters of the Governor General of Poland – and had a pass that entitled her to come and go on her own. The idea was that I should get to know my way to the Wilks' so I could go back there as soon as they found a place for me.

I returned there quite soon after that first visit. The ghetto was a rumor mill, and rumor had it that the Germans were about to mount a major deportation raid. The Wilks found a family who agreed to take me for 200 zlotys a month. They lived on the outskirts of town, in what was almost country-side. I never knew their name, but the man of the house was a cooper who hammered away at his barrels in a yard. The nights I spent under his roof were nightmarish, not only because I was among strangers but because I dreaded wetting my bed if I fell asleep. Willing this not to happen, I stayed awake. This didn't last long, however. After only a few days, Mr Wilk came to pick me up. The cooper's wife said I couldn't stay there anymore – the neighbors were getting suspicious. I was happy to go back to the familiar and, in my mind, secure ghetto – but the 2,000 zlotys that were paid on account were never returned. Neither were the two little suitcases with all my belongings.

When I returned, we were moved to another house on the far

side of the main thoroughfare, only a short distance from where my grandmother lived. The Germans had regrouped the survivors in a smaller area that became, as time went by, an overcrowded slum. Rekawka Street now lay outside the ghetto's reduced perimeter. The Germans didn't bother to build a new wall; our diminished ghetto was enclosed by a barbed-wire fence. Pawel was gone: taken away with the earliest batch of deportees. For the first time I understood the meaning of a broken heart.

In our new abode, a huge, old-fashioned apartment with high ceilings, we shared a room with a young couple and their little boy, Stefan. The father was an architect, and our families soon became friendly. Also sharing our quarters was a smelly old man with an equally smelly dog called Fifka. My sister slept in a room next door, partitioned off from the other occupants by a wardrobe.

Stefan was four or five years old with curly blond hair and an overly serious face. He had a whole collection of toy cars and told me that when he grew up, he wanted to be a racing driver – or a car. He said a lot of quaint and endearing things like that. We played together nearly all the time, and he became to me what I had been to Pawel; the eager recipient of all sorts of information.

Not long after this latest move my father learned that another raid was imminent. My mother took me out, on her pass, to the Wilks'. When the time came for me to go back, it was my father, not my mother, who collected me on his way from the factory in town where he was employed as a metalworker. He had bribed a guard to let him quit work early and was returning to the ghetto without his armband. When Mrs Wilk handed me over to him in the street, he hugged and kissed me with surprising intensity.

As we were walking back across the Padgorze bridge toward the ghetto, he started weeping uncontrollably. At last he said, 'They took your mother.'

I said, 'Don't cry, people are watching.' I was afraid his tears might advertise the fact that we were Jews, unescorted and off limits. He pulled himself together. Then, near the entrance to the ghetto, we joined a group of returning workers.

My mother's disappearance affected me far more deeply than Pawel's, but there was no doubt in my mind that we would be reunited. Our immediate concerns were: Where was she being held? How were they treating her? Was she getting enough to eat and soap to wash with? When would we receive a letter from her? We didn't know – not then – about the gas chambers.

Stefan's parents had also been deported in the latest raid, so my father took him under his wing. Though saddened by the disappearance of our loved ones, we continued to play together. There were plenty of things to play with – although the Germans had picked through everything of value – among the personal possessions abandoned by people who had already been taken. Stacked at one end of the communal bathroom in our crowded tenement was a whole heap of such relics – suitcases, books, family snapshots – and among them was a child's scooter. This I appropriated. A woman who recognized it stopped me in the street. 'That's not your scooter,' she said sternly, and made me put it back.

It is *now*, I thought, but didn't have the nerve to say so.

Again came rumors of another raid, and again I was sent to stay with the Wilks. After a couple of days with them, however, I ran away. Raid or no raid, I wanted to be with my father.

I walked up to the ghetto entrance and asked to be admitted. A Polish police guard waved me away but he let me pass when I told him I lived inside.

It was a hot, sunny day. The streets were empty. The entire neighborhood was deserted except for two armed SS guards strolling leisurely in the distance outside the barbed-wire fence. The silence had an ominous quality. Something, I knew, was dreadfully wrong. I ran through the stinking hallway to our room. There was no one there.

Feverishly I toured the places where I thought my father might be. My grandmother's room was empty and in chaos. The stationer's shop around the corner, another likely place, was also deserted, the door wide open. Everything inside was as neat and undisturbed as if the owner, a friend of my father's, had just stepped outside for a breath of air. I ignored the paints and crayons and sparklers – whole cartons of them, there for the taking. I checked the till to see if it contained any money. If so, there was a chance that the owner would be back. It was empty.

I panicked. Everyone I knew had disappeared. I needed to find people – total strangers even. The silence was unendurable.

The first grown-ups I met were standing in the street, guarded by Polish militiamen. Inside some of the houses searches were still in progress. I could hear boots pounding floorboards, voices shouting orders in German. 'What should I do?' I said to the grown-ups nearest me.

One of them asked where I lived.

'Over there. But what's going on?'

Someone else said, 'If you know what's good for you, get lost.'

But I didn't. If I stayed, I thought, I would somehow link up with my father.

An SS officer emerged into the street. Plump and school-masterish-looking, with pebble lenses, he was holding a sheaf of papers in his hand. Some of the prisoners started pleading with him. He ignored them, preoccupied with his paperwork, then had us marched off to Plac Zgody, the square where the main gate was. Here we found a mass of other prospective deportees. Some were standing idly, some squatting on their heels, some sprawled on the cobblestones, some weeping. They had been held there for the last two days. This was the biggest raid so far.

Threading my way through the dense crowd, I came across Stefan wandering around by himself. Although he could give me no definite news of my father's whereabouts, I was glad of

26

his company. I continued my search with him, peering this way and that, questioning strangers, elbowing my way through the throng. The scale of the deportation terrified me, and so did the thought of getting caught up in it. I realized how foolish I'd been to return. Somehow or other, we had to get out. Stefan, with his blond hair and appealing little face, might prove our salvation.

A senior SS officer rolled up, ensconced in the sidecar of a motorcycle combination. Surrounded by a bevy of deferential subordinates, he started giving orders. I explained my plan to Stefan, who spoke a little German. I rehearsed him: He was to go up to the officer and request permission for the two of us to go home, just to get some food – we would be right back. Then, if the officer said yes, we would try to cross the wire.

When it came to it, Stefan's nerve failed him. Near us, guarding the assembled ghetto inmates, stood a young Polish militiaman. He was only one of many posted at intervals around the herd of deportees. I went up and tried out our story on him. He must have seen through it but pretended not to. His nod of assent was barely perceptible. We started running. 'Walk slowly,' he growled, 'don't run.' We walked.

I knew the way: through a courtyard, along various alleyways, up one side street, down another. At last we reached the boundary – the barbed-wire fence that separated the ghetto from the rest of Krakow. There was my familiar little gap in the wire and no guard in sight.

'Go on,' I told Stefan. I was used to crawling through, but he was frightened. 'Go on!' I urged him, but eventually I went first and waited for him, cursing the time he took. He scrambled through the tiny gap, and there we were, out on the other side. It was like a dream. We walked slowly away from the wire like ordinary children out for a stroll. We neither looked back nor exchanged a word until we heard the rumble and clang of streetcars. Then, for the first time, we glanced at each other: We'd made it.

Our arrival at the Wilks' was almost an anticlimax. All Mrs

Wilk said was 'What's this? *Two* little Jews this time!' Stefan was such an endearing child that he soon charmed her out of her anger.

As soon as the dust had settled after this latest raid, we returned to the ghetto. I was reunited at last with my father, who had since moved into the room formerly occupied by my grandmother. Granny had been taken away. So had my sister, Annette. From now on, my father shared Granny's old room with Stefan and me.

These were the final weeks of the Krakow ghetto's existence. We children were now put to work in an institution, part factory, part orphanage. We received one meal a day and an hour or two of schooling. The rest of the time we made paper bags – folding and gumming sheets of brown paper for hours on end. Stefan was with me. Being so little, he found the hours long and the work demanding. His bags were a gooey mess, but he never cried.

On the day the Krakow ghetto was finally liquidated, March 13, 1943, my father woke me before dawn. Taking me to Plac Zgody, to a blind spot just behind the SS guardhouse, he coolly snipped the barbed wire with a pair of pliers. He gave me a quick hug, and I slipped through the fence for the last time. Stefan had to stay behind with the other children; there was no one to take him in on a permanent basis.

When I got to the Wilks', however, the door was locked. No one was home. I wandered around for a while, uncertain what to do. Then, glad of any excuse to rejoin my father, I headed back to the ghetto.

Just short of the bridge I saw a column of male prisoners being marched away by Germans with guns at the ready. They were the last surviving inmates of the ghetto, and among them was my father.

He didn't see me at first. I had to trot to keep up. The marching men were attracting plenty of attention; many people turned to stop and stare. Still trotting, I tried to catch my father's eye.

At last he spotted me.

I gestured, turning an imaginary key to illustrate my predicament.

He dropped back two or three ranks with the tacit assistance of others in the squad, unobtrusively changing places with them so as to be farther from the nearest guard and closer to me. Then, out of the corner of his mouth, he hissed, 'Shove off!'

Those two brusque words stopped me in my tracks. I watched the column recede, then turned away. I didn't look back.

THREE

Tylko swinie siedza w kinie! ('Only swine go to the movies!')

According to this resistance slogan daubed on the walls of Krakow's movie theaters, I was a double-dyed pig. I soon knew every shiny wooden seat in every single one of the city's theaters. Movies became my ruling passion – my sole escape from the depression and despair that so often overwhelmed me. My guide and companion on these outings was a boy named Mieczyslaw Putek, or Mietek, as I called him, a tall, dark, taciturn youngster of my own age. Mietek and I were inseparable, if only because I lived in one room with him and his parents.

Shortly before curfew on the day my father was marched away, the Wilks had come home and found me waiting for them on the street. After keeping me with them for only one night, however, they dumped me on the Puteks. I was once more farmed out at a profit as Roman Wilk, the son of an imaginary relative deported by the Germans.

Boleslaw Putek, Mietek's father, was a janitor, and the building he looked after was a good place to hide in. Who, after all, would have dreamed of looking for a small ghetto fugitive in an apartment house entirely requisitioned for German officers and their families?

I had no papers of any kind. Luckily Mietek never asked me embarrassing questions, like why I didn't go to school. I often wondered why not. Perhaps he knew all along but discreetly refrained from saying so.

My first real taste of freedom, as Roman Wilk, was riding the Number One, a small, old-fashioned streetcar that half-circled Planty Park. I had been on it before the war, with my parents, but Mietek showed me what a real ride was. The front section, being reserved for Germans, was to be avoided at all costs. So was paying the fare. The best way to travel free was by riding outside on the couplings and jumping off before the stop.

My father's original payment to the Wilks entitled me to a small allowance of pocket money. Most of this went on the movies, but movie seats were dirt cheap, so a little went a long way. I lapped up every kind of film from operettas like *Gasparone* to a circus romance with the Tonnelli Brothers, two acrobats in love with the same woman. 'The world's too small for both of us,' said one of them. This, I thought, was the ultimate in sophisticated dialogue.

Mietek often came with me, partly for want of anything better to do and partly to keep me out of trouble. When he was in school, I went on my own. When my pocket money ran out, I would stand and gaze at the lobby stills. One actress in particular took my fancy, a statuesque blonde called Marika Roeck. I daydreamed of marrying her someday, though I was aghast at the thought of what my father would say to his son's marrying a hated German. I later discovered that she was Hungarian, so I needn't have worried after all.

The luxurious Swit movie theater was a Germans-only establishment off limits to Poles. I talked Mietek into pretending we were German children. He slapped down the money for two 'third-class' seats – the ones nearest the screen, which were our favorites – without a word. We sat through a German version of *Puss-in-Boots* with actors disguised as animals and no Polish sub-titles. Listening to Mietek's recriminations as we rode home in the streetcar, I realized that we had risked our lives for a thoroughly lousy film.

I met a slightly older boy named Krupa, which in Polish means 'lump.' Krupa, who didn't go to school either, sold the *Krakauer Zeitung*, the only authorized newspaper. He showed me how I, too, could make some money. Stacks of

31

unsold papers were left when the official vendors had finished their stint. A middleman took his cut on these leftovers by reselling them to 'pirate' newsboys at a premium, so the only way to make a profit was to short-change customers or angle for a tip.

Meanwhile, movies were becoming an absolute obsession with me. I was enthralled by everything connected with the cinema – not just movies themselves but the aura that surrounded them. I loved the luminous rectangle of the screen, the sight of the beam slicing through the darkness from the projection booth, the miraculous synchronization of sound and vision, even the dusty smell of the tip-up seats. More than anything else, though, I was fascinated by the actual mechanics of the process.

My ambition was to build myself a projector of sorts. What I had in mind was a simplified version of the schoolroom epidiascope – a box with a lens at one end. I got a lens from a flashlight. Now I needed a box. I searched the neighborhood trash cans without success. One morning I hitched a ride on a garbage wagon back to the main dump. There, after scavenging for hours, I found what I was looking for: a small tin tea caddy colored red and gold. Next, I needed to cut a square in one side and a circle in the other. For want of any better tools, I used a hammer and a nail. It was a noisy business.

Mietek's aunt, Janka, a good-looking nineteen-year-old, was visiting that day. She'd never liked me much, so she relished telling me to quit hammering.

'I'm making a projector,' I said.

'I can't help that,' she snapped, and made a grab for it. I wrestled with her, using foul language picked up on the streets. She threw my tin out the window. When I went to retrieve it, she locked me out of the building. My tools were inside. After ringing and ringing to no effect, I disconsolately roamed the streets and met up with Krupa. To annoy Janka, we jammed the doorbell with a matchstick and ran away.

'I'm going to report that little bastard to the Germans,' Janka told her sister-in-law that evening. Mrs Putek talked her out of it, but it was clear that the Puteks were finding me

32

an increasing risk as well as a nuisance. I never did finish my projector – they decided to get rid of me, to put a safe distance between me and Krakow. Accompanied by Janka, who was now in a slightly better mood, I boarded a train so jam-packed with peasants that we had to stand pinned against a toilet door all the way there.

We got off at a small station called Przytkowiece, I carrying my suitcase and Janka a bundle containing food. We walked and walked along a narrow dirt road, under a sun so hot I thought I was going to faint. I had no socks, and my blistered heels started bleeding.

Our final destination was Wysoka, a little village where I was to lodge with a couple named Buchala. Wysoka wasn't a village at all, strictly speaking, but a country crossroads with a church, a school, and a combination grocery store and post office. The Buchalas lived a couple of miles away in a tiny farmhouse on the side of a hill, almost hidden by trees. I still missed my parents dreadfully, and this, my third move in as many months, should by rights have aggravated my gnawing sense of deprivation. It was the countryside that saved me. My one previous contact with nature had been that brief summer vacation before the war. Now I was discovering a new world. It was like starting life afresh.

The Buchalas, who were wretchedly poor, owned a hectare – two and a half acres – of land and kept a heifer. Much older than his wife, Mr Buchala was a simple soul, gruffly inarticulate and rather stupid. He was a cobbler, but the villagers must have known he was an appalling craftsman, for orders were few and far between. Most of the shoes he made were for his own family. The pair he produced for Marcin, his elder son, were so big that the toes curled up, making him look like a circus clown. Mr Buchala was a cobbler in the sense that he owned the tools of the trade, just as another peasant farmer in the village was known as the barber and functioned as such – with similar results – because he happened to own a pair of hair clippers.

Marcin, little taller than I despite his sixteen years, was simian-looking and almost as doltish as his father. Jaga, twelve, was a retarded, drooling girl. Only little Ludwik, two years my junior, was entirely normal.

The whole family revolved around Mrs Buchala, a strong, scrawny, energetic woman whose head scarf was as much a part of her as her amiable, gap-toothed grin. She was the civilizing influence that made everything bearable. She was also the real head of the family, deeply religious but without cant, kind and sensitive but almost as illiterate as her husband. Her kindness to me was all the more remarkable in that the Puteks rarely paid her anything for my keep; most of my father's unofficial trust fund had seemed to vanish en route.

The day began with her singing, as she kindled the fire, 'When comes the dawn, all living creatures render thanks unto thee, O Lord.' It would have been unthinkable to start a meal without first making the sign of the cross.

Outwardly the setting in which the Buchalas lived was idyllic – a region of rolling hills sprinkled with cottages with blue-tinged whitewashed walls and thatched roofs. In reality their life was an unending daily fight for survival. They grew wheat, rye, and potatoes, so our staple diet consisted of salted boiled potatoes and a species of gruel, sometimes made more palatable – when the family could afford it – with a little milk. Baker's bread being too expensive, Mrs Buchala baked her own – a kind of coarse, gritty rye. The rye was ground by hand on a primitive millstone that might have been a relic of the Middle Ages.

Buchala himself was a natural drone who spent most of the day sitting on his bed, puffing at a blackened pipe. It was Mrs Buchala who ran the farm. They never quarreled except when tobacco-planting time came around. Mrs Buchala refused to allow her husband more than a minuscule corner of their precious field, and he was always pressing her for more. That was his only luxury: home-cured tobacco finely chopped on his cobbler's bench.

There was more to eat in summertime. The Buchalas had a semblance of an orchard, and the woods were full of mushrooms and berries. Then we used to gorge ourselves on cherries and plums. I would also stave off my pangs of hunger with a surfeit of unripe green pears – with dire consequences.

The outside privy was right alongside the manure heap. Night soil was spread around the fruit trees, cow dung on the field. Flies were kept at bay – more or less – with saucers of juice from the poisonous red- and white-spotted mushrooms which I became quite expert at finding in the woods.

What with the heifer, the manure, the human excrement, and our own unwashed bodies, the prevailing smell must have been overpowering. Although I was never seriously ill at Wysoka, I always had boils on my legs, was covered in insect bites, and had to be regularly deloused with kerosene. Such washing as we did was done in the cowshed, to which I would duly retire with my pitcher and basin, careful never to expose myself. In Poland only Jews were circumcised.

Behind the barn was a well. There was no rope, just a long pole with a hook on the end, so drawing water was quite an art. This was Marcin's job. The Buchalas were afraid I'd make a hash of it and lose their bucket.

I wasn't aware at the time quite how poor the Buchalas were. I thought all farmers lived as they did. The five of us were cooped up in a space little bigger than the kitchen of our Komorowski Street apartment, I in a sort of cubbyhole behind the cowshed, the rest of the family divided between two tiny rooms where they slept, cooked, and ate and where Mr Buchala sometimes made shoes.

Marcin spent part of the time away, working as a farm laborer. Jaga had just enough intelligence to help with the household chores. Ludwik, the only bright one in the family, attended the village school. I didn't, of course, not having any papers. This meant that I did an extra-large share of the work around the farm.

As time went by, I assumed a number of responsibilities. The heifer was mine to look after, and I would take her out grazing all day, preferably on other people's land, learning where the best patches of grass were and keeping a weather eye open.

When harvesttime came, the whole village joined in. The men brought their own scythes with them. I was too small to wield one – in any case, Mrs Buchala was afraid that people might start asking questions about me – but I did go stubble cutting with the other children and helped with the threshing, beating the ears of rye with a flail. I also did my share of housework and potato peeling. I learned to make rope out of hemp, fed the chickens and rabbits, and played with the cat.

As winter gradually approached, the landscape underwent a transformation. There were spectacular new colors, mostly reds and golds, and unfamiliar country smells. Everything looked different. I woke up one morning and saw frost on the grass. Still later snow fell overnight, and the silent hills were shrouded in white.

It was during this cold weather, with the countryside at its bleakest and strong winds whistling through the leafless trees, that I saw, a long way off, a man making his way toward me in the snow. He looked familiar; for one delirious moment I thought it was my father, released from the concentration camp and coming to fetch me. Then, as he drew nearer, I saw that he didn't resemble my father in the least. When he was out of sight, I burst into tears and, swept up by my new faith, began praying fervently with my well-learned Catholic verses.

Christmas came, and with it another novel experience. Nothing had prepared me for the way the Buchalas entered into the spirit of the occasion. Marcin cut down the biggest tree that would fit inside the house, and we adorned it with precious decorations saved from one year to the next – tinsel, paper cutouts, gilded walnuts – as well as apples, candles, and little star-shaped cookies. Our special Christmas fare included a rabbit and a piece of bacon.

One day the first car ever to enter Wysoka got stuck in the mud with two German soldiers inside. The villagers laughed at them but helped them extricate it. None of the Buchalas except Marcin had ever seen a car before. Ludwik hadn't even seen a train. I took him on the long walk to

Przytkowiece station to show him his first one. I expected him to be dumbfounded when it came puffing in. Although he thanked me politely afterward, it would have taken an earthquake to impress him. He didn't know what electricity was either. I kept explaining to him how one could light up different rooms in a house at the flick of a switch. He didn't believe me.

We went on another long trek for another purpose, this time accompanied by Marcin. Mrs Buchala was convinced that the family's heifer was in season. The animal didn't actually belong to them. They looked after it on the understanding that they could have any milk it provided. In fact, it provided them with great expectations and nothing else.

We duly took the heifer to be serviced at a farm some miles away. Once she had been tethered to the contraption used on such occasions, the farmer led out a monstrous great bull. Marcin grinned lewdly and asked if we wanted to watch.

Ludwik and I said no. I had seen animals copulating before and was curious about sex in general, but that bull scared me out of my wits – I felt sorry for my friend the heifer. We sat and waited in a ditch beside the road. When Marcin finally called us over, he was looking glum. 'She didn't want to,' he said.

Dusk was falling by the time we set off on the long walk home. Marcin, with enormous gusto, started telling stories about travelers being pursued by goblins. I was torn between fear and curiosity, eager to see a goblin just once.

Although I played with other boys from the village, I never got really close to them. We weren't interested in the same things. Once they threw me into a duck pond to teach me to swim. I scrambled out, pretending I'd almost drowned, but they only laughed.

It was soon after this that I came across some moldy old papers and mouse droppings inside a trunk left behind by Mrs Buchala's eldest sister, a schoolteacher. There was a dog-eared copy of a Catholic magazine entitled *The Soldier of the Immaculate Queen*, full of accounts of miracles, bleeding stigmata, and edifying tales of divine retribution visited on sinful children. I also found *The Song of Roland*. Though practically illiterate, I struggled through every word. So the first book I ever read was a twelfth-century French epic poem translated into baffling archaic Polish.

Living about a mile away was a farmer's daughter named Julia, who must have been eleven or twelve. Her family owned a whole herd of cows, and I used to go there for milk. Because I regularly volunteered for this chore, a joke was born: 'Roman's sweet on Julia.' I would set my greasy cap at a rakish angle before leaving the house – a gesture copied from older boys – but was always too shy to talk to her.

While making one of these trips during the autumn, I heard voices calling in the distance. Turning, I saw a peasant driving a horse and wagon far behind me. There were two German soldiers with him. I walked on quickly.

The next day I was picking blackberries in a lane in the same part of the woods. I heard a whistling sound, followed, a split second later, by a sharp crack. I peered around and saw, about 200 yards away, the same horse and wagon with what looked like the same German soldiers. One of them was lowering his rifle. I dropped my tin mug of blackberries and ran as fast as I could, then hid in the bracken until it was dark. I never discovered why the soldier took a potshot at me, and I never told anyone, not even Mrs Buchala.

Soon after that, the Germans organized their first population census in the area. When Wysoka's turn came, Mrs Buchala arranged for me to spend the night at another village. The house she took me to was larger than hers but occupied by only one person, a woman in her twenties, big and full-bosomed, with braided blond hair. Kind and motherly in manner, she gave me a supper of potatoes and sour milk, even a piece of sausage. There was only one bed – a huge straw mattress with a mountainous eiderdown – in a room full of religious prints.

When bedtime came, the woman put on a nightdress, and I realized that we would be sleeping together. I was conscious of her warmth, her bigness, and her not unattractive odor. She fell asleep fairly soon – or appeared to – and cuddled me as I had cuddled my teddy bear in the past. The difference in our sizes was almost as great. Although I couldn't muster the courage to return her embrace, I was aware of a vast, soft expanse of flesh, and part of me wanted to squeeze it out of curiosity.

The interminable walk back to the Buchalas was the low point of my life in the country so far. It was a cold, windy day, and my loneliness was intensified by the bleak and deserted landscape. I felt that no one wanted me, that there was no reason for things ever to change. When I reached the Buchalas' house, tired, depressed, and slightly bemused, Mrs Buchala didn't appreciate my need for affection and reassurance. She simply said, in a matter-of-fact voice, 'You're in no state to eat now – you'll only be sick. Wait awhile.'

Fed up with her and everyone, I retorted, 'I'm not hungry anyway,' and went off to bed, where I cried myself to sleep.

Winters at Wysoka were a joy in one respect because I learned how to ski – after a fashion. My duck pond tormentors showed me how planks could be bent into skis and pieces of barrel hoop used as bindings. Hazel branches served as ski poles.

The hill that ran down to the village from the Buchalas' field made an ideal ski run, and we raced down it all day long. We were all self-taught. Utterly unafraid, we headed straight for the foot of the hill. Our only means of braking was to put our ski sticks between our legs and sit on them. I guessed there must be some way of turning but never found out what it was.

Our notions of how the war was progressing were hazy in the extreme. Anyone found in possession of a radio was severely punished, so all our news came by word of mouth. We did get to hear about the Warsaw ghetto uprising, but the Buchalas had a stereotyped conception of Jews in general. They

39

couldn't believe that people whom they saw as cringing and despicable, speaking with comical accents and interested only in money, were capable of rising in arms against the Germans. It was different later on, when the Polish Home Army launched its abortive Warsaw insurrection. Then they were eager for news and proud of what was happening.

During my last summer with the Buchalas I came to realize that the war was going our way. I was out picking myrtle berries on one of those really hot, windless afternoons when the air is filled with insect noises. Gradually the hum of the bees was overlaid by another sound: deep, throbbing, swelling in volume, blotting out everything else.

Looking up, I saw a swarm of aircraft flying in formation high above. They could only be Allied bombers. My heart overflowed with exultation. I lay back in the grass and feasted my eyes on the spectacle.

Then other sounds superimposed themselves on the persistent hum – popping noises preceded by puffballs of smoke in the sky. A bomber was hit, and I saw several parachutes blossom in quick succession. One of them floated straight toward me, and for a long, long moment I thought, hoped desperately, that it would land within a stone's throw. Then it drifted away behind some trees and was lost to view.

My whole soul went out to the airmen. I would have given anything to be able to help. I longed to find them, to hide them at the Buchalas', but I wasn't even allowed to visit the spot where their plane hit the ground.

That Flying Fortress raid, which destroyed the synthetic oil and rubber complex at Monowice in August 1944, was a harbinger of changing times, for me as well as the Germans.

By now food was becoming really scarce, and the Buchalas simply couldn't afford to feed me anymore. The other problem was that the Germans started fortifying a range of hills not far from Wysoka, using POW labor. Almost overnight the area was swarming with field gray uniforms. It was time for me to return to Krakow.

FOUR

The German occupation of Poland ended for me as it had begun, in an air-raid shelter. This time, however, the atmosphere was very different.

The mood in Warsaw in 1939 had been one of hysteria and panic; now, back in Krakow with the Puteks, jubilation reigned despite our fears of what the final days might bring. Besides, Mietek's father was still the janitor of the requisitioned apartment house, so our air-raid shelter – specially built for the German residents, who had just been evacuated – was one of the safest in Krakow.

We knew the Germans were losing the war because daylight raids had become more and more frequent. Although our basement shelter resounded to the thunder of bombs and gunfire, a carnival spirit prevailed there. Apart from a handful of neighbors, our companions belowground were strangers who had been caught on the street and taken refuge with us. Among them was a flamboyantly dressed, heavily scented redhead who looked like a high-class tart. Some of the men seemed to be on familiar terms with her, perhaps because they'd met her in the line of business. There was also a rather distraught white goose, part mascot, part emergency food supply, which got under everyone's feet. Mrs Putek said it would be eaten only as a form of thanksgiving once the Germans left.

There was plenty of noise inside the shelter as well as out. Someone kept playing a German cabaret hit, over and over again, on a phonograph, and much badinage went on between the unattached males and the redhead, who haughtily declined to join them in the cellar's deeper recesses. A great deal of vodka was consumed. When the battle showed no signs of easing or ending, we cornered the goose and pinned it down on a washboard. One of our next-door neighbors, a big, burley warehouseman, took careful aim with an ax. The head dropped off, blood spurted everywhere, and I felt sick. The carcass was plucked, stripped, and made ready for the pot.

We might have remained in the cellar indefinitely had not fists started pounding on the iron door. It was a sinister sound, all too reminiscent of German house searches in the past. Sure enough, a voice yelled in German, 'Open up, you swine!' When an ashen-faced Putek complied, there stood Mr Jozek, the janitor from next door, beside himself with joy and vodka, shouting, 'Come on out, you stupid assholes – they've gone! It's over, I tell you!'

All the strangers promptly dispersed, and we abandoned the shelter for the third-floor apartment which the Puteks had 'liberated' after the German exodus. There the grown-ups plied themselves with brandy and champagne from stocks left behind by the former occupants. 'Say what you like about the Germans,' proclaimed Mr Jozek, 'at least they got rid of our Jews for us.'

Someone went out onto the street and brought back our first Russian soldier. He wasn't one of the heroic figures I later saw in Soviet war films, but a flat-faced, snub-nosed, bewildered-looking Slav with a threadbare uniform and a mouthful of metal teeth. He had no rifle, only a cleaning rod. I sat beside him while Mrs Putek served him up a huge plate of goose stew. He ate ravenously, all the while urging me to do likewise. '*Kusbay, kusbay!*' he kept saying – 'Eat, eat!'

For the first and perhaps the only time in Polish history, Russians were made welcome in Poland. During those first few days almost all Polish families did as the Puteks had done and ritually shared the last of their food with them.

Within a few weeks, however, we began to regard them with a more critical eye. Theirs was a desperately poor army, not averse to rape, with a passion for wristwatches and any

42

loot they could take back home with them.

My memories of this period, as I roamed the streets without fear of arrest for the first time in years, are of the incredible confusion that followed the Soviet entry into Krakow. The weather was raw; the dirty snow turned to sludge; our shoes and clothes were permanently sodden. Red Army convoys were forever getting snarled up, with officers shouting, drivers cursing, trucks revving, and Poles watching this new display of martial might openmouthed. Not all the vehicles were carrying military equipment. I have a vivid recollection of Zim trucks piled high with wardrobes, sideboards, closets, carpets, and mirrors, and of fat, ill-favored female soldiers perched on top, stolidly guarding their loot.

As we became more familiar with the Red Army units that crowded into the city, I realized how the Russians had made a virtue of necessity: their Zim trucks had crude wooden chassis, but the engines were indestructible; their boots were made of cheap felt but kept out the cold; their knapsacks were plain canvas bags with webbing straps at the base which, when tied around the neck of the bag, formed effective shoulder straps.

Soviet soldiers were kind to children, not only sharing their rations with them but also – at the height of the famine that swept through Krakow in the weeks immediately following the German withdrawal – operating mobile soup kitchens. Food was virtually unobtainable, and I came closer to starving then than at any other time in the war.

The Russians brought their ideological pageantry with them – not just billboard portraits of Marx and Engels, Lenin and Stalin, but huge plaster of Paris busts of them as well. They also erected obelisks adorned with red stars and inscriptions extolling the heroism of their soldiers. It all seemed designed to appeal to children, and it did. Without understanding what communism was about, I became a convert.

I rushed to see my first Soviet film. The language sounded strange, after so many years of German sound tracks, and the plot was also outside my experience: a heroic Red Army

43

soldier trapped behind the German lines, tapping out messages in Morse to his headquarters.

No sooner had the Germans evacuated Krakow than the entire population began scavenging on a grand scale: for food, stores, clothing, and – inevitably – weapons. For months and even years after the war many Poles went around in discarded German uniforms. They had nothing else to wear.

I became a specialist scavenger. Primarily interested in anything that went off with a bang, I joined a gang of local children who collected and bartered anything from bullets and manually operated air-raid sirens to Wehrmacht insignia and badges of rank.

Opposite the Puteks' apartment house was a barracks that had been, throughout the war, a German military depot. We swarmed all over the premises, bearing off anything of interest. Our hauls included rifles, pistols, and boxes of ammunition. Before long a Red Army sentry was posted at the entrance to keep looting within bounds.

His presence didn't put a complete stop to our activities. The depot contained an inexhaustible supply of straw overshoes for protection against the snow, and these we removed in vast numbers under the benign gaze of the Russian sentry, who didn't know that inside them we had secreted ammunition, flares, dismantled weapons, and other forbidden treasures.

German flare cartridges made admirable fireworks. The trick was to bore a hole near the base, insert a fuse, light it, and retreat at speed. I had once lit a flare in the middle of a deserted street when a Russian soldier wobbled out of nowhere on a bicycle and spotted the burning fuse. He teetered uncertainly, wondering whether to skirt it on the right or the left, and finally fell off, swearing, when the flare went up.

I ran away. Not far, though. I was caught and taken to the police station. A body search revealed the presence of a grenade detonator in my pocket. I was in bad trouble. I gave the police a false name and address, afraid they would take me there to check up on me, but they didn't bother. They let me go.

We were not the only youthful pyromaniacs in town. On a vacant lot on the outskirts of Krakow a rival gang lit a fuse attached to several crates of cordite and ran for cover. Not far enough, though. The resulting explosion, which could be heard for miles, made a crater several feet deep and killed the whole bunch.

We went to inspect the scene. A man was carting something away in a wheelbarrow. It was covered with an old sack. 'You want to see my son?' he said quite unemotionally, and lifted a corner of the sack. 'There's a leg missing,' he added. 'If you find it, let me know.'

Later, while exploring the area, we came across part of a boy's leg, grayish and caked with dirt. It was a long way from the crater.

This dampened my ardor, but not sufficiently. Determined to try out a German hand grenade, I pulled the pin and lobbed it over a wall. I knew the delay was only a few seconds. Minutes passed, but nothing happened. Perhaps it was a dud, I thought. I hesitated a little longer. Just as I was rounding the wall to check, it exploded. That cured me.

Mietek didn't accompany me on these forays. The Puteks had decided that I was a bad influence. My partner in crime was Krupa, the Lump. Now that there were no newspapers to sell, looting had become his new trade. Most of my finds were in some way related to my passion for fireworks, but I did unearth some German rubber stamps, which, though of no use to me, greatly interested a couple of Polish black marketeers who bought them for a surprisingly large sum. I wondered why they needed them, but not for long.

In the wake of liberation there was no legal currency, and the first new banknotes were now being issued: 500 zlotys per person on production of a *Kennkarte*, or German identity card. The Third Reich eagle on the card was snipped out with scissors as a form of receipt. My rubber stamps must have enabled the black marketeers to forge quite a number of identity cards. I gave the proceeds of this deal to Mrs Putek to

45

buy food. Having eaten the last of the rabbits we'd been raising, we were now reduced to eating the hoarded crusts we'd fed them on.

Clothes were almost as much of a problem as food. My own getup at this time was practical but eccentric. I'd found some workmen's dungarees. Because the trouser legs were far too long for me, I folded them back so they doubled as socks, protruding above the ankles of my oversize hobnailed boots. Although this arrangement was hard on the feet, I prided myself on my vaguely military appearance.

The Germans were to leave me with one enduring memory. Late one night – it must have been after twelve – I got up for a pee. I heard the drone of an airplane as I switched on the bathroom light. Blackout regulations were still in force. It occurred to me that I ought to lower the blind; but the window looked out onto an airshaft, and I couldn't be bothered. Just as I was about to go back to bed, I was hurled through the bathroom's frosted glass door. I landed outside in the passage, stunned and deafened.

The air was thick with dust. I couldn't see it – the whole apartment was pitch-black – but I could feel it in my nostrils. We called to each other in the darkness and were reassured: everyone was safe. Then we started groping our way down to the shelter, half-afraid that the stairs might have been blown away. I didn't notice till we got there that I was bleeding profusely; my left forearm had been deeply gashed by a sliver of glass – so deeply that a flap of flesh was hanging loose. I pressed it back into place, and Mrs Putek bandaged me up. The next morning I spent hours waiting in line at the outpatients' department of the local hospital. In my naïveté, I was sure I'd been responsible for Krakow's only German air raid since their departure. There had been three bombs in all, one on the former German depot, one on the waste ground where I'd tried out my hand grenade, and one on the building next door.

Immediately after the liberation I saw some things that not

only appalled but shamed me. German corpses had been left behind in the streets, and these the Poles defiled, excreting on them or propping empty vodka bottles between their legs. Several weeks after the liberation I witnessed another harrowing scene. A German officer, who had doubtless hidden to avoid capture by the Russians, was being led down the street on a string, with his hands tied behind his back. His captor kept prodding him with a stick while other Poles walked alongside, jeering, kicking, and spitting at him.

While rooting around in a deserted garret, I came across a cache of cheap Bakelite figures – fairy-tale characters like Snow White. Krakow's best-known toy shop, Filous, had just reopened, so I took the woman owner some samples of my find. 'How many do you have and how much do you want for them?'

'I've got lots,' I said, and pointed at the window. 'I want that.' I came away with my first epidiascope. It was just a glorified cardboard box with a lens and a bulb holder, but it worked perfectly well. I played with it constantly. Nobody could understand my interest in such a gadget, not even Mietek.

His parents, meanwhile, had washed their hands of me. Provided I didn't get them into trouble with the neighbors or the authorities, I was left to run wild. Then, one day, just as I was really beginning to enjoy my untrammeled existence as Roman Wilk, I heard the dread cry 'Remo!' My uncle Stefan had spotted me on the street.

Of the trio of uncles on my father's side, two were now to play a prominent – and largely unwelcome – role in my life. Stefan, the youngest, had spent most of the war hidden in a room in Krakow, looked after by his wife, Maria, whom he'd married in the ghetto and who, on the strength of her Aryan appearance, had managed to obtain some false identity papers. The middle brother, David, husband of Teofila, the baker's daughter, had survived deportation by becoming a *Kapo*, or concentration camp trusty. Bernard, the eldest and my favorite, was not as fortunate. We were soon to learn that

47

he had been killed – clubbed to death, ironically enough, by a *Kapo* wielding a chair leg.

Uncle Stefan, who seemed pleased to see me, insisted that I leave the Puteks and come to live with him. I was more resigned than enthusiastic. Much of what I had been through in the preceding four years I was unable to communicate to anyone, least of all to him. I became an eleven-year-old boy again, subject to family discipline and restraints but deprived of the contentment a real family would have given me. My move revived memories of my father and mother, for whom Stefan and his wife were very poor substitutes indeed. I so resented being treated like a child that I began to look back on my years in the Buchala household with something close to nostalgia.

Not having been able to attend school. I was regarded as a bit of a freak. Uncle Stefan was appalled by my backwardness and tried to get me enrolled, but a cursory test revealed my total ignorance of Polish literature and history, let alone algebra and geometry. His verdict: 'You might at least have tried to learn *something* in all these years!'

Uncle Stefan's years in hiding had taken their toll on his nerves, and he wasn't the most even-tempered of men. Although he had retained a sense of humor, I found his sarcasm wounding. For all of Aunt Maria's kindness, it became painfully clear that I was a burden to them both – an illiterate orphan whose future was one big question mark. I was forever being lectured when I failed to perform my allotted duties – like cleaning Uncle Stephan's shoes – to his full satisfaction. Uncle Stefan seemed to have a lot of shoes.

What aggravated my general depression was that as time went by, we all became tacitly convinced that my parents would never return. Millions of deportees never did. The handful that had survived, however, were starting to drift back. It was a tragic time for most families but an exhilarating one for the happy few. Scenes of wild rejoicing could be observed outside the railroad station when camp survivors, still in their striped prison garb, were reunited with their nearest and dearest. I recall watching many such emotional

48

reunions, many such tearful embraces, and wondering when I, too, would see my parents again. In protest against the injustice of it all, I spent more and more time alone in Uncle Stefan's apartment, projecting picture postcards on the wall with my beloved epidiascope.

It was there, high up on the sixth floor, overlooking the town, that we heard of the German surrender. Flares and tracers lit up the sky as Russian and Polish soldiers loosed off their weapons. Aunt Maria's sister had brought her Polish soldier boyfriend to a little celebration dinner. I urged him to blaze away, too. He stepped onto the balcony, cocked his rifle, and fired, then handed it to me. I reloaded, squeezed the trigger, and was sent reeling back into the kitchen by the unexpected kick.

Gradually Red Army propaganda displays gave way to Polish government posters carrying announcements of all kinds. Various organizations were being founded or reconstituted. In my need to belong to something – anything – I joined the Boy Scouts. Filling out the application form, I wrote. 'Wilk, Roman.' I hesitated when I came to the space beside 'Religion,' then put 'Catholic.' It wasn't just that my real religion might have debarred me from membership. Roman Wilk, Catholic – that's who I felt I was.

My small size and lack of uniform set me apart from the rest. After my first outing with the troop my feet hurt so much I knew I had to have some proper shoes. I didn't want to ask Uncle Stefan, but one of his friends advised me to try the local Jewish relief organization. Roman Wilk, Catholic, felt somewhat uneasy about this. 'We help only Jewish children,' I was told.

After detailed questioning I came away with a magnificent pair of brand-new black rubber-soled boots. Unfortunately they fitted so well that I couldn't wear my trousers as socks anymore, so I simply folded up the surplus and went sockless.

My relations with Uncle Stefan went from bad to worse.

Eventually Aunt Toefila took me to live with her and Uncle David. They and their seven-year-old daughter, Roma, shared a large but crowded apartment with the Horowitz family – a whole bunch of them. There were young Richard and his parents, a daughter called Niusia, the two Rosner uncles who had played in the ghetto café orchestra, and another couple.

Richard was one of the very few children to have survived deportation from the Krakow ghetto and the only one to have survived the transit camp that followed. His father had hidden him in a latrine cesspool, neck-deep, while the other children were being rounded up for liquidation. Curiously enough, his ordeals hadn't changed him a scrap; he was just as spoiled as he had been on the day of his birthday party in the ghetto, throwing tantrums and refusing to drink his cocoa.

Regina Horowitz was a typical Jewish mother, warm, resilient, and vital – a tower of strength. She always lit candles on Friday nights, and for the first time in my life I found myself in a household where Jewish rites were observed. It was a strange and unfamiliar experience. Jews were still very reluctant to practice their religion in public – a great deal of anti-Semitism still existed in Poland. Several pogroms took place at this period, at least one of them in Krakow.

Uncle David had reopened his shop, which sold sanitary ware and plumbers' supplies. Business was brisk, thanks to the postwar demand for new housing, so I was enlisted to help serve behind the counter. I immediately became an expert salesman and thoroughly enjoyed myself until Uncle David started a sideline. Having bought up a batch of celluloid identity card holders, he sent me off to sell them on the street. I resented hawking them around on a tray and disliked the humiliation of proffering unwanted goods to indifferent passersby. All that compensated me for those wasted hours was that I chose a spot outside a photographic shop filled with secondhand home movie projectors.

This was the period when UNRRA packages started arriving. They were like missives from some far-off planet. The Horowitz apartment abounded in Lucky Strike cigarettes, jars of instant coffee, cans of condensed milk, and corned beef. We children marveled at the lemonade crystals and chewing gum, the candy bars and DDT powder.

When the grown-ups were out, I led Roma and Richard in putting on theatrical shows, tipping a big wardrobe on its side to make a stage and dressing up in our elders' clothes. We also adopted a stray puppy. Within days, all three of us were truly in love with it. Then the animal disappeared. Uncle David went through the motions of helping look for it, but Niusia told us he'd drowned it in the Vistula, simply because he thought the apartment was already too crowded.

Once, to punish me for some piece of mischief, Uncle David administered a methodical beating. I had to drop my pants and bend over a table while he used the buckle end of his belt on me. I had to count the strokes while he drew blood. Then he ordered me to thank him and, when I refused, beat me some more. It was the *Kapo* routine – the Germans' way of maintaining discipline in their camps. The sound of the blows, mingled with my cries of pain, struck terror into the other children. Although Aunt Teofila did her best to make up for this incident, it permanently alienated me from all my uncles and aunts.

Whether or not I derived some stimulus from the sight of my own naked body, stripped for bathing after years spent in households where baths were unknown, I discovered masturbation. It gave me some inkling of why grown-ups made such a fuss about sex. The trouble was, I believed it to be an invention of my own, so its pleasures were marred by a profound sense of guilt. I prayed to God, less in the hope of resisting temptation – that, I knew, was too much to ask – than as a kind of talisman designed to preserve me from temptation in the first place. When I prayed, I still prayed as a Catholic.

*

51

Alone in the Horowitz apartment, I built myself a crystal set from instructions I'd found in a book and bits and pieces picked up in the flea market. When it worked, and I heard a Polish voice issuing from the remnants of the old loudspeaker I'd converted into an earphone, I summoned the old man who lived across the landing, and he listened, incredulously at first, then ecstatically, to the program I'd picked up. The Horowitzes were less impressed. Nobody showed any interest except young Richard, who parlayed my achievement into one of his own: he prevailed on his father to buy a proper radio set. It was a real sensation and we sat there listening to it night after night.

Out of the blue, a returning survivor from Mauthausen delivered a note from my father. Although I couldn't remember his handwriting, and the whole thing seemed too good to be true, I carried the note with me everywhere I went. Taking advantage of his welcome news, Uncle David tried to break it to me that my mother wouldn't be coming back. I listened, but at heart I didn't believe him.

Then, one evening, on returning home from the shop, I heard a voice in the kitchen – a strangely familiar voice. It was my father, drinking vodka with Uncle David and looking, if anything, younger than when I had last seen him. I hurled myself into his arms with a cry of joy, and he hoisted me onto his lap. No one had held me like that for years. Despite my overwhelming happiness, I felt awkward – too big to be dandled on any grown-up's knee. For some reason, I couldn't tell my father about the Puteks, the Buchalas, and my years at Wysoka. I wanted to put them out of my mind, and I was too shy even to attempt to explain how I'd felt – how I'd longed for him and my mother.

He didn't mention her, nor did I. He clearly fought shy of unlocking the grief inside me, and I, afraid of what his answer would be if I put the fateful question, preferred to leave it unasked. It was a long time before I learned the truth: that she had died in a gas chamber only days after being taken away. Even at this late stage I nursed a lingering hope that everyone was wrong and that she would return.

My sister, Annette, had survived Auschwitz. She met my father in one of the processing camps. Rather than return with him to Poland, she had gone to live in France.

Where my father himself was concerned, I felt reassured. He looked far fitter than I would have expected after seeing so many newsreels of liberated concentration camps. Tanned and crewcut, he had been well fed by the Americans and was wearing U.S. Army fatigues. Curled up on his lap that first night and recalling photographs of concentration camp victims with swollen joints and skeletal limbs, I could hardly believe there wasn't something wrong with him and imagined from the feel of his legs through his denims that they must be mere skin and bones. Besides, I knew that many survivors had returned, outwardly in good health, only to fall sick and die within days or weeks.

From one angle I was right to be suspicious of my new-found happiness. My father stayed with us for only a few days. Then he was off again, on a variety of business ventures, and when he came back to Krakow, he wasn't alone. He turned up accompanied by a stylish young woman with dyed auburn hair.

Many years have passed since then. Wanda, whom he later married, came to look on me as a son as time went by. At first, however, her resentment of me was as strong as mine of her. I regarded my father's liaison with her as an unpardonable betrayal of my mother. I despised what I saw as Wanda's superficiality, her pretensions, and the way she queened it over the rest of the family. They bitterly resented her, too, so I was torn between my dislike of Wanda and my natural loyalty toward my father.

But my father's reappearance was more than an emotional landmark: from the time he returned, I never lacked for material things. I even started dressing better and receiving more pocket money than most other boys of my acquaintance. Since I stubbornly refused to go on living with any of my uncles and aunts and since my relations with Wanda were so bad, my father found me a series of lodgings in town. I now had someone to turn to. There were no more beatings, no more stints as a street trader. Most important of all, my father employed a tutor to help me catch up on my neglected education and found a school prepared to enroll me.

FIVE

In Class 5A I found myself sitting next to a lean, handsome youngster with a sardonic expression and a shock of dark hair flopping over his eyes. We got talking in the two intermissions. It was only when the bell rang for morning break, and my new acquaintance rose to join me outside in the yard, that I noticed he had a limp. At the end of the day, having discovered that we were near neighbors, we walked home together as a matter of course.

Piotr Winowski and I became close friends despite our very different backgrounds. He was a scion of the middle-class Warsaw intelligentsia. His father, a violinist, had been killed during the war. His mother, who owned a restaurant and a patisserie, was an ultrasophisticated society woman who prided herself on knowing all the right people. Heavily made up and elegant in a rather flashy way, she was grossly overweight and a martyr to liver trouble. Piotr himself had suffered from some kind of bone tuberculosis in early childhood. His limp was the result of an operation that had gone wrong, leaving the right leg considerably shorter than the left.

He was a highly intelligent, destructively critical boy with a lively, probing mind. He did not, however, share my practical bent. He had no urge to excel, no conventional desire to succeed whatsoever, though a little effort would easily have enabled him to do so. He despised all forms of ambition, derided his teachers, refused on principle to do any homework, and was spoiled to death by his mother. His chief enjoyment lay in practical jokes, mimicking others, and play-

55

ing the buffoon. He was also one of the finest natural actors I have ever met. We fed on each other's fantasies, stimulated each other by drawing, to an increasing extent, on our common passion for the movies. I discovered Winowski's love of the cinema when the entire school was taken to see a prewar film about the Polish national hero Tadeusz Kosciuszko. The theater was packed with children, and we couldn't decide which we hated more: the noisy audience or the mediocre film. The same afternoon we went to see Errol Flynn in *Robin Hood*. That, we agreed, was more like a movie.

At this time foreign films were flooding into Poland after a five-year wartime hiatus. Winowski and I started going to the movies more and more often, sometimes twice a day. Our tastes ran at first to swashbuckling tales of adventure – we saw *Robin Hood* again and again. Really good movies always drew big audiences. When we were in funds, we bought tickets from scalpers, sometimes turning scalper ourselves to make the price of two seats for a later performance.

We both began collecting usherettes' programs containing stills and synopses of individual movies. Because we could seldom afford programs as well as seats, we went scavenging for them in trash cans out behind the theaters. In the course of one of these expeditions we came across a few frames of discarded film. This chance discovery prompted us to look for more, and we started collecting offcuts in earnest. No one else was told of this activity or invited to share in it. Who, after all, could have been expected to understand that sifting through a trash can and finding a snippet of celluloid was like retaining a little of the essence of some movie, like hanging onto a dream? When Winowski's interest waned, as it ultimately did, I continued prospecting on my own. Many old prints were in very poor condition, and projectionists tended to perform drastic surgery on them when repairing breaks and splicing them together. My most extensive collection of offcuts came from *Snow White and the Seven Dwarfs*, which must have been in particularly bad shape.

As time went by, the two of us became more discriminating in our film taste. We paid many visits to Carol Reed's *Odd Man Out* and the Laurence Olivier version of *Hamlet*. Inspired by the latter, which I saw at least twenty times, I read all of Shakespeare's plays in Polish and tried to imagine how they, too, would look as films. I also read a book called *On the Silver Screen*, which answered many of my long-debated questions about filmmaking. I was particularly struck by the book's description of the director, the man in charge, whom it likened to the captain of a ship. Not even the producer was allowed on the sound stage when the red light came on.

When clowning around, Winowski and I got our main inspiration from American slapstick comedies and Disney cartoon characters, which Winowski could imitate to perfection. These provided the raw material for our gags. One of our ambitions, for instance, was to remove the grand piano from Mrs Winowski's drawing room and deposit it in the street. This daydream, which we never put into effect, was lifted from a film in which Laurel and Hardy contrive to transport a piano across a rope suspension bridge in the Alps, all the while pursued by an ape.

Winowski had a genius for devising scary scenarios. His mother could never fathom our passion for Napoleons, pastries topped with enormous dollops of pink whipped cream. She didn't know that they served us as weapons in a game invented by her son. Armed with a Napoleon apiece, we would shut ourselves up in the pitch-black hallway of the Winowski apartment, sometimes with a couple of other boys, and stalk each other. The winner was the one who managed to creep up, undetected, and shove a Napoleon in another boy's face – or, better still, crown him with it.

The two of us were always at the bottom of our class. Drawing was the only subject I excelled at. I got good marks in geology and biology, passable ones in Polish language and literature, and that was it; the rest of my marks were abysmal. My reasons for doing well in geology and biology were twofold. First, they entailed a lot of drawing, and secondly, we were taught them by a female martinet who kept us in order; during her classes we remained as quiet as mice. Since Winowski and I did practically no homework, we dreaded being called on to answer her questions. Several times, having attended roll call, we hid behind the coatracks to escape this ordeal.

In other teachers' classes we both engaged in varying degrees of hooliganism. It was during religious instruction that Winowski really went to town. Father Grzesiak was a ruddy-cheeked priest with pale blue eyes, stubbly hair, and the face of a bewildered peasant. Winowski did some truly terrible things to him. He would start cleaning the blackboard, then surreptitiously grab the volleyball from the closet beside it and embark on a lightning game behind the priest's back. Far worse was his tripwire routine, which he referred to as bearbaiting. To get Father Grzesiak moving in the required direction, he would punctuate his remarks by twanging a steel comb, plucking a tine at the end of every sentence. When Father Grzesiak charged in the general direction of this infuriating sound, he would trip and fall flat on his face. Getting to his feet, the unfortunate man would clasp his hands and roll his eyes heavenward in silent prayer. Then he would lash out at the suspected culprit, pulling his hair and cuffing him about the head. He almost invariably picked on the wrong boy.

Instances of exceptionally outrageous behaviour were entered in our conduct books, which we were sometimes instructed to take straight home for our parents to countersign. On one such occasion Winowski indulged in a kind of theater of the absurd. He waited for his crime to be recorded and left the room. A bare two minutes later, having forged his mother's signature in the toilet, he returned the book to Father Grzesiak with the utmost deference and ceremony. The priest went berserk and grabbed him by the ear, but even this was grist to Winowski's mill. He surrendered himself to further violence by clambering onto the school bench, then onto the desk itself, enabling Father Grzesiak to get a better grip.

For all his execrable behavior, Winowski whetted my intellectual appetite. Before we met, most of my reading

58

matter had been limited to Karl May adventure novels. I was now introduced by him to Knut Hamsun's *Hunger*, John Knittel's *Via Mala*, Axel Munthe's *The Story of San Michele*, and a lot of other good books.

My friendship with Piotr Winowski also taught me a lot about Poland, the war, and our new regime. A member of the Armia Krajowa, or Polish Home Army, his father had been one of the non-Communist resistance fighters who waged a heroic struggle against the Germans, only to be wiped out during the Warsaw uprising when the Russians encouraged them to attack the Germans and then left them in the lurch. It was at Winowski's home that I first heard about the AK, as it was familiarly known, and about the heroism of the 'Free' Poles who had flown with the RAF and fought at Monte Cassino.

The Communist regime, at this time, was beginning to rewrite history in a ludicrous attempt to persuade the masses that only the Communist-led resistance movement had been effective, whereas the AK had been nothing but a gang of bourgeois traitors. What happened to the Winowskis was an insight into Communist methods. Because of the housing shortage, Mrs Winowski was compelled to take lodgers. The couple who moved in were party activists with influential local connections, and it didn't take them long to spread themselves in the Winowskis' spacious 'bourgeois' apartment. My friend and his mother were confined to two rooms, which put an end to our Napoleon fights. It was entirely consistent with Winowski's character that this Communist invasion of a liberal, middle-class home should have filled him with wry and morbid satisfaction. It furnished him with plenty of material for wickedly apt impressions of his mother suffering at the hands of her tenants.

One thing I couldn't share with Winowski. His limp precluded him from joining the Boy Scouts, and my new school troop – No 22 – was becoming the focal point of my life. Now that my father had bought me all the paraphernalia a Scout could possibly need, including a magnificent Polish cavalryman's horsehair knapsack, I no longer looked like a tramp.

At the end of my first year in school Troop No 22 went off to summer camp. It was a glorious experience – my first real holiday and my yardstick, ever since, for anything memorably enjoyable. Everything about it, even the way we got there, spelled adventure. The war-shattered Polish railroad system was still reduced to carrying passengers in cattle wagons, and that was how we traveled. Not all of the way, though, because one of our many stops en route was marked by an incident that left me profoundly ashamed.

With one other boy, I was detailed to mount guard over our belongings while the rest of the troop lunched in the station restaurant. My companion slept while I stood sentinel outside. Idly at first, but then with mounting alarm, I looked on while a locomotive shunted some freight cars back and forth. Even as I watched, it reversed down a track that converged with our own. I wanted to run and warn the driver that he was on a collision course, but my fear of ridicule got the better of me. The inevitable happened. With a slow, long-drawn-out grinding of metal, the locomotive plowed into our stationary cattle wagon and crushed it. My slumbering companion jumped out of his skin.

I couldn't forgive myself for not having raised the alarm. To have done so would not only have turned me into a hero but spared us the rigors of a protracted journey. The derailment sentenced us to a two-day wait, followed by a long truck ride, in the course of which I was violently carsick. My lack of initiative indirectly earned me a nickname that clung for several weeks – to wit, Puker.

Our final destination, a place called Bytow, west of Gdansk in former Prussian territory, more than made up for the delays and discomforts of the journey. We pitched our UNRRA-supplied tents on high, wooded ground near a lake. The countryside was spectacularly beautiful – like Wysoka at its best, but with congenial company thrown in. Our month under canvas, which was intended as a form of survival course, was the most exciting episode in my school career.

Our troop leader, whom I hero-worshiped, was an AK veteran named Lech Dzikiewicz. Tall, rangy, and grave-faced, he came from a long and aristocratic line of army officers. Under his command, we carried out our duties to the letter. These included taking turns in the field kitchen. One day the acting cook left so much sand in our potatoes – from washing the pots and pans in the lake – that we started slinging them at him. Nothing happened until muster parade that evening, when Dzikiewicz dramatically announced, 'Food was thrown at me today.' There was a stunned silence. 'It was meant for the cook,' he went, 'but you might as well have thrown it at me. You must be taught a lesson.'

Dismissed, we turned in and went to sleep, but not for long. Roused by bugles in the middle of the night, we dressed and paraded in pitch-darkness. The seniors then proceeded to put us through our paces, drilling us on the parade ground and chivying us across country till dawn. No sooner had we collapsed inside our tents, exhausted, than reveille heralded another full day's training. It was tough, character-building stuff, but none of us resented this parody of military life. We took pride in belonging to a really rugged troop and never held a grudge against our Scoutmasters for treating us as they did. On the contrary, we derived a kind of masochistic enjoyment from the whole experience.

Another night, while two of our sentries were asleep on duty, some girls from a Guide camp across the lake made off with our flag. They added insult to injury the next morning by marching over to us and ceremoniously returning what they had taken. We responded to this abject humiliation by mounting a commando raid in which I was privileged to take part.

Our punitive expedition had all the ingredients of a military operation. After landing by boat in the middle of the night, a dozen strong, our invasion force split up. One detachment went for the girls' flags, the other for their tents. These we collapsed by pulling out the pegs, then carried out a high-speed withdrawal. As we reembarked, checking our numbers to ensure that no one had been left behind, we could hear bugles blaring and whistles shrilling above a chorus of indignant squeals.

But summer camp was memorable for another incident, one that changed the whole direction of my life.

Campfire singsongs and skits set the customary seal on our day. Too shy to contribute in the past, I made up my mind to brave the possibility of ridicule and join in. My knockabout improvisations with Winowski and capacity for mimicking others, by endless hours at the movies were now to stand me in good stead.

One evening I volunteered to deliver a comic monologue I remembered from a session with my first troop. The flickering campfire provided just enough light for me to see the expectant faces of my audience. I was conscious of the lake shimmering below, the breeze rustling in the lofty oaks around me. As I launched into my act, my inhibitions seemed to melt away.

It was a set piece, couched in broad mountain dialect, about a doddering old peasant who describes the series of calamities that befall him when he inveigles a couple of tourists into taking a ride in his horse-drawn cart. 'It was a fine day,' I began. 'The birds were tweeting, and I had a good horse.' To my surprise, no one heckled or catcalled from the outset; indeed, ripples of delighted laughter ran around the campfire as I got into my stride.

It was a once-in-a-lifetime sensation: the discovering of a natural talent capable of giving pleasure to others. An under-size thirteen-year-old, and even younger in appearance than my years, I felt a sudden surge of self-assurance as I realized how completely in command of myself I was. I knew, while still in the midst of my act, that this was what I wanted to do: to perform for others, to evoke their laughter, to be a worthy and legitimate focus of attention. Overnight I became Troop 22's head of entertainment. I was in constant demand from then on, organizing, directing, and starring in all our Boy Scout shows.

I had discovered my vocation.

62

SIX

The Merry Gang was a children's radio program that put out Communist-flavored soap opera twice a week. Discounting a couple of adult actors, the voices were those of real children.

One day an announcer invited listeners to visit the studio, which was still housed in the old prewar radio station. I ran all the way to Lubicz Street and roamed the premises, enthralled. Some children were rehearsing around a microphone in a glass-walled booth. I paused to watch them.

Two grown-ups had been discreetly observing me. One of them, a woman in her forties with dark hair streaked with silver, asked what I thought of the program.

'It stinks.'

They both laughed.

'Really?' The woman's tone was polite but patronizing. 'Why?'

'The kids don't sound natural.'

'Think you could do any better?'

I said yes.

They asked me to recite something. Instead of a poem, which was probably what they expected, I gave them my mountain peasant's monologue. Halfway through, I could sense that interest had taken the place of condescension. I was hired on the spot and told to report for my first rehearsal in two days' time.

I became a permanent member of the *Gang* and was paid my first professional fees. They were negligible but they did lend another dimension to the theatrical games so dear to Winowski and myself. Most of my earnings were spent on a

Kodak box camera that I used to shoot stills of our fanciful tableaux.

Although I was inordinately proud of becoming a radio voice, none of my classmates ever listened to the program. They found the story line childish, the message boring. Even Winowski failed to share my enthusiasm. Only Mrs Horowitz was impressed.

My disembodied voice became our main source of contact, for it was around this time that I moved out of the crowded apartment we were all sharing. I couldn't stay on there indefinitely. Now that my father had returned to Krakow, it was up to him to provide for me. He had rented a small place for himself and Wanda, whom he planned to marry. There was no room for me, and it was clear, in any case, that Wanda didn't want me under the same roof. That suited me fine – the feeling was mutual – but it upset the rest of the family when my father moved me into a furnished room. Once again I'd been dumped on strangers. To console me, my father bought me an American waterproof wristwatch and Wanda presented me with a bicycle. Things were no substitute for the love I craved, but at least the new arrangement enabled me to enjoy my father's proximity without having to submit to his constant scrutiny. I now had a little room of my own.

My landlady was an old woman called Mrs Sermak, practically toothless and always dressed in black. Her daughter and a war-orphaned niece shared a bed in the room next to mine. Old Mrs Sermak slept in the kitchen of her tiny apartment. Hers was a deeply religious working-class home, singularly drab and joyless. No form of communication was possible between me and the three female Sermaks; we had nothing in common on any level.

The woman who'd patronized me at the radio station turned out to be in charge of *The Merry Gang*. She was Maria Billizanka, a party member and the wife of a distinguished physicist. She also ran the Young Spectators' Theater, at which several children from her radio show had already appeared as guest performers. Together with Renek Nowak, another new recruit, I was soon roped in. Renek was supporting his mentally disabled mother so he truly needed the money. In addition to his artistic activities he kept busy wheeling and dealing in the flea markets. My first stage appearance was as a chorister in a period vaudeville show. It was nothing great – just a walk on part. The lead was played by a boy of my own age called Jurek Zlotnicki. He had starred in *Frontier Street*, a film about the Warsaw ghetto, and was the first person I'd met with real screen experience. I admired him tremendously. Quite unlike my father, who regarded my new activities as a waste of time, Zlotnicki's parents devoted themselves to nursing his career.

Maria Billizanka had very definite views on the handling of child actors. She wanted no stars, no overinflated egos. She insisted that we take our schoolwork seriously and not regard ourselves as a race apart. 'Go out of here and do your homework,' she would exhort us, but I couldn't tear myself away from the theater. I explored it from greenroom to gantry and, when I wasn't needed for rehearsals, hid and watched them from the balcony. I made a nuisance of myself trying out costumes and wigs, experimenting with makeup and Plasticine. This lent a new dimension to my practical jokes. I played what I believed to be a wonderful prank – scaring an elderly actress out of her wits by moaning horribly in the greenroom toilet. She opened the door to find me slumped on the floor with blood pumping from a realistically slashed wrist. Even Winowski was impressed when I pulled the same trick on him and showed him how it was done.

Billizanka started holding auditions for the lead in V.P. Katayev's *The Son of the Regiment*, the story of a Russian peasant boy – the mascot of a Red Army combat unit – who gets captured by the Germans. They try to extract information from him about the Soviet order of battle, but in vain. The boy captive's regiment launches a counterattack, and thanks to the little hero's intelligence-gathering while in enemy hands, the Germans are resoundingly defeated. Renek Nowak and another boy alternated in a minor role. I got the lead.

I was working with real professionals – people who could give me guidance and teach me my craft. Josef Karbowski, who directed the play, was a well-known figure in the Polish theater. My costar, Antoni Rycharski, who played the Red Army captain, gave me lots of valuable advice and my first real insight into the world of the stage. Rycharski, an exceptionally talented actor, had one disastrous failing: an alcoholic, he could never be relied on to show up sober and had been known to pass out and miss performances altogether. His drink problem made for tension on the stage, and many was the time I reeled under the impact of his vodka-laden breath.

The Son of the Regiment was a huge success with fantastic reviews. It was chosen to compete in a Warsaw festival of Soviet plays. This thrilled the entire company, not so much because it was an honor as because it meant a visit to the capital. Everyone was relieved when Rycharski turned up at the station stone-cold sober. He soon discovered the restaurant car, however, and had to be carried off the train on arrival. After that members of the company were detailed to watch him in turns.

I found Warsaw quite unrecognizable, which was hardly surprising. The city where I'd spent the first few weeks of the war no longer existed. Whole swaths of it had been flattened after the ghetto uprising. Another, much larger part of the capital had become a battlefield during the 1944 uprising that ended in the annihilation of the Polish Home Army. Finally, not long before the Germans moved out, Hitler had given orders that Warsaw be razed to the ground. The surviving inhabitants had been deported or driven out, and demolition squads had destroyed what remained of the city, building by building.

After the war the Polish authorities decided to rebuild the old part of Warsaw exactly as it had been. This task was only just beginning when our visit took place. There were mounds of rubble and construction sites everywhere. We were accommodated in one of the few buildings still standing, the Bristol Hotel, where I shared a room with one of the adult actors.

For him, as for the rest of the company, our trip to Warsaw presented an opportunity to have some fun. The ruins were haunted by numerous prostitutes nicknamed *gruzinki* ('rubblers') after the scene of their professional activities. My roommate brought one of them back to the hotel because he didn't fancy screwing her on a pile of bricks. I was promptly told to move in with Renek Nowak because he wanted to share her with another actor. Not a little shocked, Nowak and I discussed this at some length. How, we wondered, could two men screw the same girl?

We returned to Krakow with our pictures in the paper. A substantial cash prize went with the kudos we'd won. Years later Billizanka told me that the prize had been awarded to me, but that her aversion to boosting youthful egos had prompted her to share it out among the cast.

The prize money would, in fact, have come in very handy. Wanda's new bicycle had been perfect for transporting me around town, but it wasn't long before I started getting ambitious. Bike riding had become a passion. I invested in some dropped handlebars and a set of lightweight wheels, but my efforts to convert the machine into a proper racing bike proved abortive. All the items I needed were hideously expensive, Western-manufactured components which could not be satisfactorily modified to fit my roadster frame. Because Mrs Sermak wouldn't let my bike past the door, I spent hours tinkering with it on the gloomy landing outside her apartment, up to my elbows in grease.

My attentions at this time were not focused solely on radio, the theater, and bicycles. At long last, my new way of life brought me into contact with some real, live girls. I was vastly attracted to one who played in Hans Christian Andersen's *Snow Queen*, the production that followed *The*

Son of the Regiment. She was blond and sweet-faced, with a complexion like a peach. On New Year's Day Jurek Zlotnicki threw a party at his parents' home. It was my first experience of a party complete with girls, music, and dancing. We also played games like postman's knock, and the winner was entitled to kiss his partner. I took my *Snow Queen* girl out on the landing. In slow motion I applied my lips to hers, and we stood there swaying awhile. When the party broke up, I walked home on air, knowing I'd just lived through the most joyous moment of my life. Only one thing haunted me: although I'd held the girl in my arms, I couldn't recall the feel of her breasts against me and cursed myself for not making a mental note of the sensation.

Thanks to all these novel distractions, my school grades further deteriorated. Winowski and I walked a tightrope. We were just good enough to move up with our class at the end of the year, but ours were the lowest grades of those who did. Then Father Grzesiak took his revenge.

I came home one day to find him deep in conversation with Mrs Sermak. It was exceptional for teachers to visit their pupils, so my heart sank at the sight of him. Mrs Sermak disappeared into the kitchen, and the priest started interrogating me. He wanted to know all about my past.

I already had an inkling that he regarded me with suspicion because of something that had happened in church one Sunday. Catholic prayers I could recite by heart, but the ritual of confession was a mystery to me – I didn't know the proper words to use so I never confessed. Realizing that it was a heinous offense to take communion unshriven, I'd been horrified when Winowski gave me a surreptitious tug that landed me on my knees beside him in a row of boys awaiting the wafer and chalice. On reaching me, Father Grzesiak pointedly passed over me as if I didn't exist, then went on to the next in line. Now he fixed me with his beady blue eyes.

'Who exactly are you?' he asked. 'Where were you baptized?' I mumbled something about living in the country during the war. 'Where?' he insisted. 'What was the name of your parish priest? Tell me, and I'll write to him.'

I ducked his questions and retired to my room. Grzesiak followed me, superciliously noting the picture of the Black Virgin of Czestochowa above my desk. In the absence of a Winowski to cut him down to size, he pursued his inquisition to the bitter end.

'You're a little liar,' he said finally. 'You've never been baptized at all.' He took me by the ear and led me over to the mirror. 'Look at yourself. Look at those eyes, that mouth, those ears. You aren't one of us.' On that note he flounced out of the room. My mind was in turmoil. Being Polish was more than a question of religion or registration; it was like belonging to a select club. In quest of an identity I could take pride in, I'd falsified my membership form. I had sinned by omission in failing to disclose that I was Jewish, not out of shame, but because, after my Wysoka years, I tended to regard myself as a Catholic. Now my sin had found me out.

I was enraged that the priest should have discussed me and my family background with Mrs Sermak; I felt it was none of his damned business. Worse still, I suspected that he might have been tipped off by none other than Winowski for the sheer fun of it. He had once seen Mrs Horowitz light the Friday night candles. I never found out.

As soon as Grzesiak had gone, I took another look at myself in the mirror. I didn't look Jewish, with my fair hair and up-turned nose, but I did look undersize and puny for my age. My face I couldn't change, my physique was another matter. I took a pillowcase and went straight downstairs to the street, where I filled it with some cobblestones left behind by some road workers. From then on I engaged in daily weight-lifting and body-building sessions, determined that no one should humiliate me in the same way again.

Like many youngsters growing up in Communist Poland, I was not unnaturally torn between Catholicism and Marxism. The effect of Communist propaganda on the young was considerable – after all, the Red Army had liberated us from German occupation – but something of Mrs Buchala's simple faith had lingered with me. Now that Catholicism wore the face of Father Grzesiak, I turned my back on it.

At fifteen I had reached the stage where Polish children either transferred to a lyceum, which prepared them for admission to a university, or went straight to a vocational training school. My previous grades were far too poor to qualify me for the former, though Winowski just scraped into a place. Having always been interested in mechanical things, I delighted my father by obtaining a grant to study at the electrotechnical department of the Krakow Mining Engineers' College. However, I realized almost immediately that I was in the wrong place. Physics and chemistry were a bore; mathematics was largely incomprehensible. The only two subjects that really appealed to me were electricity and technical draftsmanship.

Meanwhile, my newfound craze for athleticism had found an additional outlet. As Winowski and I drifted apart, I drew closer to Renek Nowak, who shared my love of cycling as well as acting. Together we joined the Cracovia Sporting Club and embarked on a grueling training program designed to equip us to compete in road and track events.

Whenever my machine was in working order, I pedaled for distances of up to 200 kilometers a day on the Krakow-Zakopane road. Cycling developed into a passion that threatened to eclipse my interest in the theater. I felt capable of achieving great things, but only if I had a genuine racing bike. Discreetly sounded out on the subject, my father didn't respond. Though generous in many other respects, he declined to finance what he regarded as a futile and dangerous pastime.

When the racing season opened in the summer of 1949, I was keen to notch up sufficient points to make my mark in the Cracovia Club, even, perhaps, to earn a place on one of its official teams. My times were good, especially on the track, but mechanical breakdowns had already cost me several important training sessions. I discussed this problem at interminable length with Renek Nowak and another friend,

Marian Skalny, who trained with us. Marian was a good all-around athlete who enjoyed competing in most forms of sport. One day, while I was watching him play tennis at the municipal stadium, a young man got into conversation with me. Later, when Marian joined us, we sat in the bleachers and talked cycling – the summer vacation's series of racing fixtures, my machine's shortcomings, my general predicament. The young man, a total stranger to us both, sympathized with me. It seemed he knew of a prewar racing cycle in mint condition and could let me have it for a mere song. In postwar Poland 'prewar' was synonymous with the best that money could buy. My heart leaped at this proposition. Providence, I felt, had sent Janusz Dziuba my way.

I should have known there was something fishy about his offer, but I couldn't resist it; besides, he had such an honest, open, ordinary face. By selling my two racing wheels in the flea market and adding the proceeds to my meager savings, I could get myself a proper racer. We plied Dziuba with questions. Although he clearly knew nothing about cycle racing, his description of the machine made me covet it even more, however shady its origins might be. It was kept in an old lady's attic, he said – just where, he wouldn't tell me.

A few days later, when I called at the address I thought he had given me, nobody seemed to have heard of him. Then, by sheer coincidence, I bumped into him at the flea market and eagerly inquired about our prospective deal. Was it still on? Yes, he told me, I was to meet him next Thursday in Freedom Square. I duly sold my wheels, and on June 30, the eve of the summer vacation, I waited for him near the offices of the UB – Poland's equivalent of the KGB. Marian, who had qualms about the deal, was with me.

Dziuba showed up later, carrying something wrapped in newspaper. He drew me aside.

'Who's that?'

'What do you mean, who's that? You met him the other day. He's all right.'

Dziuba's evident annoyance at my having brought a friend

71

along reinforced my suspicion that the bicycle was stolen property. I felt guilty, but it was too late now – I'd sold my wheels.

'Where is it?' I asked.

'In the bunker.'

I knew this landmark well, though I'd never been inside. The Germans had built it during the war – an air-raid shelter in the park across the way, visible from above as a grassy mound about a hundred yards long. The concrete ramp that led belowground was regularly used by visitors to the park as a makeshift privy. It was a dank, dark, foul-smelling place. Even if the racer was stolen, I thought Dziuba was carrying caution to extremes.

It had started to rain. A uniformed park attendant and a man with a bicycle – not a racer – were standing near the mouth of the ramp, engrossed in conversation and oblivious of the weather. I itched to get the whole transaction over, but Dziuba wouldn't move. We stood in the lee of a building across the square till the men had gone.

'You stay here,' Dziuba told Marian as we started toward the park. He made his way down the ramp, carefully avoiding the turds. 'Those pigs would shit anywhere,' he said. He took a screw of newspaper and lit it, holding it above his head like a torch, then walked ahead of me. The tunnel appeared to be empty.

'Where's the bike?' I asked.

He said it was around a bend. His improvised torch gave a final flicker and went out. The darkness was total except for a glimmer of light from an air vent not far off. I was slightly ahead of Dziuba now and feeling my way along the wall.

Quite suddenly I felt a tremendous shock. It was a familiar sensation, and at first I thought I'd touched a live wire. Then I realized that I was lying on the concrete floor, that someone had hit me on the head. I thought my assailant must have been hiding ahead of me, waiting in a recess for me to pass, until I felt Dziuba crouching over me and heard his voice. 'Where's the money?' he whispered. The words swelled and faded like a distant radio signal.

'Marian's got it.' I lied.

He turned me over and found the wallet in my hip pocket. Then he ripped the watch off my wrist – my father's treasured present – and ran for it.

I staggered to the air vent. There was a mound of dirt on the floor beneath. I scrambled up it and, standing on tiptoe, clung to the sides of the opening. Marian was staring down at me, aghast. '*Jesus-Maria!*' he said. 'He really fixed you.'

'He took the lot,' I blurted out.

Marian said, 'Wait here!' and sprinted off.

I hauled myself up through the air vent. It was still raining. Looking down, I saw that the front of my shirt was sodden with blood. A woman in a beige trench coat caught sight of me. She came closer, emitting little birdcalls of distress. She turned nasty when I thrust her aside and she saw the bloody imprint left by my palm.

I could taste the blood now – taste it and feel it running down my face. But I didn't care. My only thought was how to explain the loss of my watch to my father.

While I was debating this problem, a big old-fashioned garbage truck pulled up beside me on the road that skirted the park. Marian was perched on top with one of the crew. 'Romek!' he called, beckoning furiously.

Another man, who was standing on the step of the cab, hauled me aboard. I found myself sitting next to Dziuba. The driver hemmed him in on the far side while the man on the step discouraged any attempt to escape on my side.

The driver had seen me emerge from the air vent, bleeding like a pig. That and the sight of one man chasing another had been enough to make him drive around the park and intercept the fugitive. Dziuba ran full tilt into the truck; he hadn't even struggled when they grabbed him. Now, looking as if he wouldn't hurt a fly, he tried to hand me back my wallet and watch.

'Don't take them,' the driver said quickly. I didn't.

Once inside the police station, Dziuba started clowning

73

around – giggling and hopping on each foot when told to remove his shoes. He was also relieved of his belt.

Over a basin in the precinct washroom I took stock of the damage. There were several deep gashes in my scalp. After cleaning myself up as best I could, I asked a policeman if I was free to leave. 'Sure,' he said, 'in an ambulance. You're going straight to Emergency.' I did my best to protest but was too weak to be particularly effective. I asked Marian to tell Mrs Sermak I'd had a cycling accident – nothing serious. En route to the hospital an ambulance man started asking questions and filling in forms. I was getting woozy by now: I could remember the name of the street where I lived but not the number, the month of my birth but not the date itself.

At the hospital they X-rayed me. Then, despite my protests, they shaved my head. It hurt like hell. After being stitched up, I was put in a crowded ward. The doctor said I'd been hit five times, which surprised me: I couldn't recall anything but that first, numbing blow. I would have to stay in the hospital for a couple of weeks at least, he said. I was lucky not to have a fractured skull.

Just how lucky, I realised only when a detective later came to interview me. There'd been no bicycle, of course, just a stone wrapped in newspaper. I asked what Dziuba would get. The detective drew a finger across his throat. I thought he was having me on. 'For hitting me over the head?' I said.

The detective smiled grimly. 'Be thankful you've got a thick skull, boy.' Dziuba was a wanted man – a triple murderer. He'd already bludgeoned people for less than the value of a watch and a pair of racing wheels.

I was relieved when there was no talk of conspiring to receive stolen goods. My one remaining worry, as I lay there, was how my father would react to this latest debacle. He already regarded me as an utter failure, saw no future in the theater, was appalled by my school grades, deplored my interest in cycle racing.

Now I'd gone and lost his watch.

74

SEVEN

There were no recriminations, as it turned out. When my father and Wanda came to see me, they were less disapproving than emotional – relieved at my narrow escape from death at the hands of a ruthless killer. My own preoccupations were more down-to-earth. I could hardly hope to win any races that summer with a wheelless bicycle.

My father, who insisted on my convalescing somewhere well away from the scene of recent events, arranged for me to spend a quiet, comfortable vacation at Rabka, a Polish mountain resort. After escorting me there in person, he left me to my own devices.

I stayed at one of Rabka's numerous boardinghouses – quite a prewar establishment, with most of the amenities of a small hotel, including a bridge room for adults and a games room for their offspring. Among the guests were several youngsters of my own age. Although most of them belonged to what remained of Krakow's upper middle class, I became an honorary member of their set. They regarded me as something of a celebrity, partly because of my success in *The Son of the Regiment* and partly because of my connection with the notorious Dziuba, whose trial was just about to open. My youth had exempted me from being called as a witness – the evidence against him was damning enough in any case – but my personal appearance was a graphic reminder of what he'd done to me. Rather than expose my shaven skull and unsightly scars, however, I concealed them beneath a turban-like bandage.

It was thus attired, while playing with my newfound

friends in the games room one day, that I first saw the girl whose name still conjures up a vision of innocence, youth, and beauty in my mind – a vision untarnished by the passage of time.

Krystyna Klodko was fourteen, a slender girl with the sort of fairy-tale face that seems lit by some inner radiance. She had small, high breasts and moved with a dancer's grace. I watched her, instantly entranced, as she greeted and was greeted by my companions. They all appeared to know her, and it was clear that she shared their social background. Although she was staying elsewhere in Rabka with an uncle and aunt, Krysia, as she was called, became a regular visitor to our boardinghouse and a regular participant in our communal activities.

One of the games we played was that old favorite, postman's knock. My passion for Krysia had not gone unnoticed by my boardinghouse friends. One of them, seeing how smitten I was, kindly played matchmaker by cheating in my favor. As if in a dream, I found myself entitled to claim a ritual kiss from the object of my platonic adoration. I wanted to take her by the hand but I didn't dare to. So we just walked side by side into the lobby adjoining the games room. Darkness had fallen, and the lobby was bathed in moonlight. Tentatively at first, I put my arms around the girl. To my mingled delight and trepidation, she responded. Her mouth was soft and warm. Our kisses did not have the violence or naked passion of lovers' kisses, but they were real enough.

During the days that followed Krysia and I swam together, walked together, talked together for hours on end. She was the first girl I'd ever had a proper conversation with – the first I found I could talk to without any tongue-tied diffidence. In her gentle but intellectually stimulating company I became aware of the gaps in my education. She and her friends seemed to know so much about so many things other than movies and the theater.

By the time I left Rabka I was head over heels in love, even though Krysia and I had done no more than kiss, hold hands, and talk. She'd given me her address in Krakow, but I couldn't summon up the courage to call on her. Poland was still an orthodox Catholic country with narrow views on boy and girl relationships, and it would, for example, have been unthinkable to expose my beloved to the disapproving gaze of Mrs Sermak. A daydream took shape in my mind: once I got my bicycle back into running order, I would cruise the street where she lived. When we met, I would pretend it was a chance encounter. But our reunion remained a daydream. I never saw Krysia again, though she was never far from my thoughts for months, even years.

The detective had been right about Dziuba. He was duly sentenced to death and hanged. My hair grew back, covering the mementos I carry to this day, and I started working in the theater again. I was growing a little tired of being treated like a child by Billizanka, and when Renek Nowak suggested that I join him as a regular member of the Groteska theater company, I agreed on the spot, even though I knew it would play havoc with my studies.

The Groteska was a puppet theater with a fine reputation. Though primarily aimed at children, its shows were no knockabout Punch and Judy affairs, but a sophisticated blend of puppetry and live acting. In *The Tarabumba Circus*, I not only operated the puppet clown, Gagatek, but, when he made his exit, reappeared as his living replica and stepped down into the auditorium. After a certain amount of byplay, I startled my diminutive double – now operated by someone else – by coming face-to-face with him onstage.

The Groteska's director was Wladyslaw Jarema, an eccentric perfectionist and admirer of British theatrical traditions who was forever quoting an aphorism – coined, I believe, by Gordon Craig – to the effect that the best theater is one with no actors. Jarema, who fundamentally abhorred children, put on children's shows only to keep his municipal grant. He attracted a number of dedicated, talented designers and actors who looked on their work with him as a valuable apprenticeship. Their salaries were always in arrears, but they grumbled and left it at that. The atmosphere of the

Groteska was quite unlike that of the Young Spectators' Theater. Renek and I were treated like adults, and in this new environment my Boy Scout principles started going by the board. A lot of vodka was consumed backstage after rehearsals, and parties were regularly held in the lobby of the theater itself.

On New Year's Eve the Groteska company held open house for a crowd of friends. Food and drink abounded, and papier-mâché animals from *The Tarabumba Circus* were disposed around the balcony like human spectators of the festive scene. A great deal of sexual activity was going on in the unlit parts of the theater. My fellow actors had fixed me up with a date. She was a busty brunette of eighteen, and full of initiative – a very sexy number altogether. 'Show her the animals,' urged my leering colleagues, and she promptly took me in tow. Clearly she was a party to the plot. Even I realized that once upstairs, I would be expected to do more than show her a collection of papier-mâché puppets. Halfway to the balcony my nerve failed me. To the girl's derision, I made some lame excuse and ran out on her. By the time I got back to my lodgings I regretted it. My platonic love for Krysia was strong; but so were the sexual tensions of a sixteen-year-old boy, and I could have kicked myself for passing up a sure thing.

My move to the Groteska was putting an end to any ambitions my father might have entertained of having a successful mining engineer for a son. My theatrical activities had led me to skip more and more classes, and when the time came for the rest of my year to move up, I was told to stay put. Being held back was more than a disgrace; it sentenced me to an additional year at a school I didn't like and made the prospect of matriculation seem infinitely remote. Failure to gain my *matura*, that precious and indispensable piece of paper, would not only deny me admission to a drama school – my secret goal – but render me liable to the draft.

Desperately casting around for some way of catching up, I

enrolled in an extramural course especially designed for people who, like me but in many cases far older, had been deprived of a formal education by the war. The Communist authorities, who disapproved of such private initiatives, were thoroughly obstructive. Refused premises of any kind, we started meeting at a fellow student's apartment. This, however, was raided in our absence by the UB because our classes were suspected of being antigovernment get-togethers masquerading in educational guise. The whole experiment foundered.

At a loss for a school and with time on my hands, I sought refuge in sport. I took up fencing. My interest in skiing had never waned either, even at the height of my cycle racing craze, and I had developed into quite an accomplished performer. The Cracovia Club's skiing section was relatively new, so juniors capable of times as good as mine could expect to be regularly selected. I began to nurse serious skiing ambitions and ate like a horse to boost my weight for downhill events. In Communist Poland, sports represented a rare outlet for individualism – one of the few ways a person could hope, if selected for a national team, to travel abroad and see the enchanted West. At the same time they were strictly state-controlled. It was symptomatic of the political climate that sporting and athletic clubs were restructured at this period, becoming centralized and deprived as far as possible of their regional associations. The Cracovia Club, with its suspect Latin name, became the Krakow branch of the Textile Workers' Club.

But Stalinism was tightening its grip in other ways. My father, a small, struggling entrepreneur, was harassed by government inspectors and crippled by penal taxation. The Winowskis, already restricted to the use of two rooms in their own apartment, now found themselves banished from the kitchen, though their Communist lodgers magnanimously allowed them to use the toilet. Mrs Winowski's restaurant was nationalized without compensation, and she feared that her tearoom would go the same way. She now spent most of her time in bed, bemoaning the depredations of the Communist regime.

Soviet films, plays, and books served to emphasize Poland's complete dependence on its 'fraternal' neighbor. I went to the theater whenever I could. The socialist-realist propaganda plays were so abysmally tedious that in order to keep theaters filled, workers, peasants, and soldiers had to be bused there in droves and locked in to prevent them from slipping out halfway through. By contrast, some of the visiting Soviet companies were stupendously good in classical revivals. Polish productions were mostly adaptations of Goldoni, Lorca, Chekhov, and Gorky. However, Shakespeare, too, received an occasional airing. I went to see a production of *A Midsummer Night's Dream* and there was a stunning performance by the young actor who played Puck, Tadeusz Lomnicki. His inventiveness, his impish giggle, his stage presence really overwhelmed me. It was the first time I was conscious of seeing a great actor at work and it was especially inspiring to me because Lomnicki was quite short. From then on, I followed his career from afar, envious of his talent and success.

My own generation reacted against the Stalinist climate in the only ways open to us. We listened to the Voice of America and the U.S. Armed Forces Network, with its continuous output of jazz, and dressed as provocatively as we could. The official term for us was 'hooligans.' The staid citizens of Krakow called us *dzolerzy* or *bazanty* ('pheasants'), and being a Pheasant entailed a lot of scavenging in the flea market – a lot of expense, too.

Shoes were all-important. The most sought-after had no toecaps. Black leather was the conventional material, though blue suede was even more highly prized. Ankle-tight trousers were surmounted by long-skirted plaid or corduroy jackets with ski-jump shoulders. Shirts had to have shallow, wide-angled collars. Most of us doubled the ends under or, if we had mothers or girlfriends who could sew, got them to stitch

the points back permanently in imitation of the Edwardian
roué look. This was accentuated by a tie with a huge one-
color Windsor knot. My own particular pride and joy was an
American fishtail, ultra-wide, part yellow and part maroon,
with a stylized rose in the middle.

Hair was worn upswept at the front and brushed back into
a 'duck's ass' behind. Really conscientious Pheasants topped
off this creation with a cloth cap set at a jaunty angle and
bulging at the back, where it had been padded with newspaper. Before entering one of our haunts, it was customary to
spit on our hands and slick our greasy wings of hair. When
fights broke out, café floors would be littered with rolled-up
balls of newspaper from Pheasants' caps.

I learned my Pheasant lore from Adam Fiut, who headed a
neighborhood gang. The son of an undertaker whose business had so far escaped nationalization, Adam was a tough,
handsome 'hooligan' and the despair of his parents. In return
for his tutoring, I kindled his interest in movies and the
theater.

Attired in Pheasant gear, I haunted places that offered a
glimpse of the West – a whiff of the exotic world that by now
seemed so much more attractive to me and my friends than
the drab monotony of Communist Poland. Among these
places was Krakow's so-called Press and Book Club, a
library-cum-reading room where one could buy a cup of
coffee and browse through not only a handful of politically
acceptable foreign newspapers like *L'Humanité*, the French
Communist daily, and *Les Lettres Françaises* but also sports
magazines like *Miroir-Sprint*, with its full-page pictures of
cycling aces such as Louison Bobet and Hugo Koblet.

Still in search of some educational establishment that would
enable me to retrieve my lost year and obtain the school-
leaving certificate essential for admission to drama school, I
met a Book Club habitué who was studying at Krakow's
School of Fine Arts. I'd vaguely considered trying my luck
there but dismissed the idea as far too ambitious. This high

school had an elitist reputation, and I doubted if I had the requisite ability. My acquaintance at the Book Club persuaded me otherwise.

Having spent the summer vacation of 1950 accumulating a portfolio of drawings – anatomical studies and architectural designs – I presented myself at the school and submitted them to the director, Wlodzimierz Hodys. I waited outside his office, dressed as conservatively as I could manage. I could see into a studio where a tall red-haired student was making a plaster mold of a bull's head modeled in clay. As he worked, he sang a wartime Red Army song. Although I felt a certain awe of someone so obviously at home in the prestigious establishment I was hoping to join, some impulse made me break the ice. 'Those Russians,' I said, 'they certainly know how to write songs.'

Instead of snubbing me, he looked up with a smile and said simply, 'They do indeed.'

That was the sum total of my first conversation with Jan Tyszler. A moment later I was ushered back into the director's office and informed that I had been accepted as a second-year student.

Enrollment at the School of Fine Arts transformed my attitude to work. At long last, I was passionately keen to do well. I couldn't wait to get to school in the mornings, reveled in almost every aspect of our syllabus, and discovered that I'd been unduly modest about my talent for drawing. I was not only as good as my classmates, I was considerably better.

Much of the credit for my newfound diligence belonged to Hodys himself, whose lectures on art history were stimulating in the extreme and inspired me to read widely on the subject. Hodys was an anomaly in Stalinist Poland - an autocrat who ran his school like a personal fief. He had a high-pitched, affected voice, made even more distinctive by a strong Lwow accent. We were scarcely conscious of his homosexuality, even though he was a bachelor who took in some of his favorites as lodgers. We made fun of the way he walked and talked without realizing that we were aping

82

homosexual mannerisms. But nothing, not even his foibles and favoritism, detracted from his brilliance as a teacher.

I soon became better acquainted with the third-year student I'd accosted on the day of my interview. Jan Tyszler came from a Wroclaw family so desperately poor – his mother was a widow – that Hodys got him a small grant and permitted him to live in a hostel normally reserved for students of the Krakow Art Academy. Although he was one year my senior, we had an immediate bond. To my surprise and pleasure, I found that he fully shared my enthusiasm for the cinema as well as my passion for photography. We spent days taking photos, then nights developing and enlarging them.

Very few foreign films were filtering through the Polish censor's net at this frigid stage in the cold war, but those that did were like a draft of some heady wine from far-off climes. One of them, *Sans Laisser d'Adresse*, a slight, sensitive comedy set on the Left Bank in postwar Paris, was a special favorite of Tyszler's and mine. Its haunting theme song, '*La Fiancée du Prestidigitateur*,' sung by Juliette Greco, became our mood music and signature tune – something that seemed to conjure up all the magic we missed in our own bleak surroundings. We whistled it endlessly.

It was Tyszler who got me promoted to his own class. He kept insisting that I was wasting my time where I was and that it might be worth asking Director Hodys to move me up. I was too scared to risk a rebuff, but Tyszler had no such qualms. He buttonholed Hodys on the stairs one day, told him I felt competent enough to join the third year, and obtained his assent on the spot. Hodys's decision was typical of him – the act of a benevolent despot whose word was law, undertaken without consulting any member of his staff.

During this period, a whole new world opened up to me, one that was forever to alter my perceptions and thought processes.

The government allowed only the official art and literature of social realism to be taught in Polish institutions, but at my new school some teachers were less concerned with politics than with art. They introduced me to the writings of

Witold Gombrowicz, which led me to the works of Bruno Schultz, which in turn led me to Kafka. Although the syllabuses ignored any other movements – up until this time I had never even heard if Impressionism – the teachers had their own system of overcoming such restrictions. They would leave an open book – filled with cubist or surrealist reproductions, not officially sanctioned – lying around in a conspicuous place. Any interested student soon found his or her way over to study such tantalizing forbidden fruits.

It's difficult to imagine but it was a shocking and incredible concept to take in: artists could deliberately distort reality for the sake of pleasure.

The School of Fine Arts was coeducational – one of the few such establishments then in existence – and this, too, was a novel experience for me. I started dating a first-year student named Hanka Lomnicka, not least because she was the younger sister of the actor I so much admired. She even resembled Tadeusz in a very feminine way, with her tousled fair hair and heavy-lidded blue eyes.

My relationship with Hanka was, at first, easy, uncomplicated – and chaste. We went to movies, poetry readings, museums. We also necked a lot. I liked her, and although she never supplanted Krysia Klodko in my thoughts – whenever I went out with Hanka, I felt I was somehow betraying my grand passion – we became almost a couple, not only enjoying each other's company, but taking it for granted.

Given a suitable place, we would almost certainly have gone to bed together. I had left Mrs Sermak's depressing apartment and moved to less supervised lodgings, but I couldn't take Hanka back there – certainly not to spend the night. Hanka's mother disapproved of me for some reason; that meant I wasn't around her home very much. Then, one day, she told me her mother was going to Warsaw for a few days, so she'd have the apartment all to herself. She said she'd cook a dinner for me. In teenage parlance of the day, this was a veiled invitation to come spend the night with her. When I showed up, however, Hanka changed her mind and wouldn't let me stay after all. Stung and disappointed by this first taste of feminine inconsistency, I walked out. I avoided her for as long as I could. When we eventually met, I told her it would be better if we didn't see each other anymore. She cried, but I was adamant, so she began dating Piotr Winowski instead.

He and I were now in different schools; as a result we had been seeing less of each other. He and Hanka had met while we were still dating. When Hanka took up with him, I saw even less of him than before. Renek Nowak, always the purveyor of such gossip, told me that Winowski was very much in love with Hanka. Nowak added, cattily, that Hanka's mother approved of Winowski as much as she had disapproved of me. I now got the impression that out of embarrassment at dating my former girlfriend, Winowski was deliberately avoiding me.

One day, though, there he was, waiting for me outside the art school. He wanted to break the news to me that his mother had died, carried off by obesity and cyrrhosis of the liver. Neither of us knew what to say. Then, as we were walking down the street together, he suddenly burst out laughing. It wasn't callousness, just a spontaneous reaction to the absurdity and unfairness of life in general. In a fair and rational world, mothers didn't die, leaving their sons with predatory Communist lodgers, legal entanglements, and little or no money. 'They're closing in fast,' he told me. 'You mark my words, they'll grab her room before the bed's cold. Meanwhile,' he added briskly, 'let's have ourselves a party.'

What was left of the Winowski apartment was so crammed with the remnants of their former affluence that it took Nowak, again, to point out to me in a sneering aside that the famous Winowski piano we had once hoped to slide down the stairs was gone. As a token of his love, after his mother's death, Winowski had given it to Hanka, who took piano lessons but had no instrument of her own. With the bashful reserve of youth, neither Winowski nor I ever referred to this gift.

I had rejected Hanka, but my circle of female acquaintances was widening. Nowak introduced me to a girl who had seen me on the stage and wanted to get to know me personally. She was only fourteen, he said, but 'a great lay.'

I was three years older but didn't look it. I'd reached the stage where I desperately wanted to get laid. In my mind, I would only grow to normal height once I started having sex, but I was certain that because of my size, no girl would even look at me. I saw no way out of this dilemma.

My new acquaintance, however, was different from Hanka: slim and very pretty and even more sensual-looking. She seemed to like me. Certainly, no girl had ever before given me that bold, knowing, come-hither look. At our first meeting we must have exchanged banalities, but her signals were unmistakable. Had we been older or less inhibited, we would have acknowledged a strong mutual physical attraction and made love. But I felt a little awkward. I really wanted my first time to be with someone I was in love with. While I was attracted to this girl, there was no sense of involvement. I was determined, however, to end the suspense and made my plan for the May Day parade.

When we met, that May 1, 1950, I suggested that instead of watching the parade, we go home together. She agreed. With the preparedness worthy of a former Boy Scout, I'd borrowed the key to Winowski's apartment. Once upstairs, we made for his mother's old room.

The girl complained of the heat.

We could always take our clothes off, I suggested.

She complied in a flash, which rather put me off. Why so obvious, I thought; why so ostentatious? Suddenly, for the first time in my life, I found myself alone with a naked girl. She was dark-haired and extremely pretty. As we kissed, I noticed that one of her eyes was blue, the other hazel.

I led her over to the bed and undressed, too. I had my condoms ready; they'd been burning a hole in my wallet for ages. In our group, making love 'bareback' was considered the height of irresponsibility and an invitation to disaster. The girl settled herself beneath me in a practiced way, pulling me down on top of her. All of a sudden I pictured Mrs Winowski breathing her last on this selfsame bed only days

86

before. Recalling her ample form, her garishly painted lips and flabby powdered cheeks, I froze.

'What's the matter?' asked the girl.

'Know something?' I said. 'Let's do it on the floor.'

I could tell I'd scored a point; she thought I was kinky. I tugged an old plaid blanket off a moth-eaten, broken-springed armchair and, more by luck than judgment, spread it out in front of a tall gilded mirror propped against the wall. Thus my first real experience of sex was with a fourteen-year-old girl in front of a mirror that reflected all there was to see.

She must have sensed my inexperience. 'Was that your first time?' she asked afterward. I sniggered as if to underline the absurdity of the question, but she shamed me by saying, gently, 'What a pity – I thought it was.' Then we made love again.

It was a case of first time lucky. I didn't lose my virginity to some fat old prostitute, as so many of my Krakow classmates did, but to a young girl far more experienced than myself – a girl who made love purely because she liked me and enjoyed sex.

We dressed and went downstairs. I felt exhilarated but still uninvolved. More than anything else, I wanted to be alone. When she put her hand on mine in the streetcar, the intimacy of the gesture embarrassed me. The St Mary's trumpeter blared the hour. 'God,' I exclaimed, 'it's late – got to dash.' I kissed her lightly on the cheek and jumped off.

I roamed the streets awhile, savoring a mixture of emotions: curiosity satisfied, expectations not entirely fulfilled. By the time I got back to my lodgings exhilaration had yielded to disenchantment. I looked at myself in the mirror. There had to be something different about me. If there was, I couldn't detect it, yet I saw myself with the eyes of someone who'd made it at last.

The girl and I met several times after that. We made love on each occasion, quite uncomplicatedly, almost wordlessly, wherever we could find a secluded spot in some park or shrubbery. Then I started dating other girls, lost track of her, and now I don't even remember her name.

EIGHT

One Sunday morning in 1950 I noticed that the inhabitants of Krakow were behaving oddly. Everyone was out on the streets, perfect strangers were accosting one another, little knots of people standing around. From their faces, some feverishly animated, others stunned and ashen, it seemed that a calamity had occurred.

It had. Overnight the government had declared all existing Polish currency worthless. Millions of people suddenly had their savings wiped out; the few remaining small entrepreneurs, my father among them, found themselves ruined once more. Not having any savings at all, I wasn't personally affected. But this arbitrary measure signaled the start of a new era – a process that was to transform Poland into one of the most repressive police states in Eastern Europe.

Krakow, with its wealth of cultural tradition and its cosmopolitan atmosphere, was a particular thorn in the side of the new regime. The Communist authorities resolved to change its character by expanding and industrializing it. They decreed the construction of the Nova Huta steelworks, a monstrous plant on the city's outskirts.

As the face of the city changed, so the authorities strove to bring about a transformation in the attitudes of its people, especially the young. This they did by stepping up recruitment into the ZMP, or Communist Youth League. Most of my fellow students joined the school branch, largely for opportunistic reasons, but my own disaffection from communism was now so complete that I steered clear of it. Our branch secretary was supposed to be elected, but Hodys, with characteristic disregard for anything but his personal inclinations, had assigned the job to one of the minions who lived under his roof.

It was at this stage that Hodys went sour on us. Just as Tyszler and I had benefited from his autocratic whims, so we now began to suffer from them. Quite simply he developed an aversion to us both. Perhaps he had tired of us; perhaps he realized that we were unsuitable material for domination and too high-spirited to become entirely dependent on him. Whatever the reason, and despite our status as his most promising third-year students, he began to cut us down to size. Instead of singling us out for praise and attention in class, he snubbed us, deliberately ignoring our raised arms when we volunteered answers to his questions. He started picking on us for trivialities, accused us of damaging furniture and fooling around. His manner, which had been amiable to the point of unctuousness, became brusque and dismissive.

Tyszler was the first to bear the brunt of this transformation. An older student at the hostel where he lived had been systematically stealing from the other inmates. Tyszler caught him in the act and worked him over. A few months earlier Hodys would probably have commended him; now he severely reprimanded him for causing trouble. Tyszler blotted his copybook still further by daring to criticize the way the secretary of the school's ZMP branch had been appointed.

One of Hodys's many eccentricities was to make us turn up at school an hour early to hear him give readings from the German Romantic poets – in the original. Only he could have indulged in such a whim. Nineteenth-century German poetry had nothing whatever to do with our syllabus, but his enthusiasm for it was such that we regarded these extra sessions as a harmless fad – a small price to pay for his spellbinding lectures on the history of art. We continued to tolerate them until the eve of the official Easter break, when he requested our presence at a reading from Heinrich Heine at 7:00 a.m. the following day.

Tyszler, who declared that Hodys had finally flipped, cut the reading and went off to Wroclaw to see his mother. The next time I saw him, after the break, he was quietly packing his belongings. When I asked what was up, he said he'd been expelled.

Dumbfounded, I left the classroom and knocked on Hodys's door. He couldn't have meant it, I thought. If I explained how poor Jan was, how much his visits meant to his widowed mother, what a good sort he was, and how seriously he took his work, Hodys would surely reinstate him. It was a vain hope.

'Get out of here!' Hodys shrilled. 'You're no longer a student of mine!'

I returned to the classroom in a daze. Gradually the truth sank in; I had been expelled, too.

If Hodys had sentenced me to death, the effect on me would have been little less shattering. It was as if an abyss had opened at my feet. After years of frustration and inadequacy I had found myself at last. Art school had been a source of pure joy to me. Now, that paradise was lost. My sense of injustice and deprivation was so keen that I seriously contemplated suicide. I had reached a dead end. Without a school-leaving certificate, I couldn't hope for admission to a drama school or any other institute of higher education. Somehow or other, I had to obtain my *matura*.

After searching around for another school in midterm, I eventually found one at Katowice that would take me on as an extramural student. It was a sad caricature of the art school I'd left, with a poor reputation, lamentably low standards, and second-rate teachers, many of whom were drunks. I was grateful, nonetheless, for the chance to get my high school diploma.

Staying with some friends of Wanda's near Katowice, I slaved for several months, but my bad luck held to the last. To avoid any charges of favoritism or collusion during the *matura* exams, the head of the matriculation board was always imported from elsewhere. This year Katowice's choice had fallen on none other than Hodys. It was a hellish week, the week of the final examinations, but I passed. Hodys, who couldn't resist one last act of spite, delayed countersigning my certificate until I went to Krakow and confronted him in his office. He signed the document and tossed it across his desk without a word, without even deigning to look at me.

By now, however, Hodys had ceased to matter. I was about to act in my first real movie, and not even he could do anything about that.

I owed it all to *Son of the Regiment*. A group of Lodz Film School students were making their diploma film on location some two hours from Krakow, where a huge dam was under construction, and they needed me for a small part.

The Lodz Film School supervisor, Antoni Bohdziewicz, who hired me for the picture because he had seen me onstage, told me to stay in Krakow until sent for. The date he had given me came and went, and still I heard nothing. Scared that he might have forgotten all about me, I turned up unannounced.

It was late afternoon when I got there. The hotel was filled with the bustle and organized turmoil that only a film crew generates. Actors and technicians were returning from the set; camera equipment, lights, and props were being unloaded; the production room teemed with people, all of them apparently engaged on business of the utmost urgency. 'We're running late,' Bohdziewicz told me. 'We're way behind schedule. That's why we didn't call you.' I must have looked crestfallen because he quickly added, 'You may as well stay now you're here.'

Someone else said, 'He can share my room.' He was a Jewish-looking fellow with horn-rimmed glasses and a bald head pink with sunburn. His name turned out to be Jerzy Lipman, and he was in his final year at Lodz as a student cameraman.

Like all Polish films of the time, *Three Stories* was an insipid propaganda exercise about ZMP youngsters exposing spies and saboteurs and building socialism. That mattered

91

little, though. What mattered was the opportunity I got to watch a real film in the making, to soak up Lipman's patient expositions when I picked his brains in our room at night, to get the feel of a film crew on location, to look while our production manager, Ignac Taub, an unshaved figure with shoes untied and laces trailing, riffled through papers, answered the phone, made snap decisions, fixed my salary, and simultaneously flirted with a pretty production secretary. Above all, I was consorting with those mythical figures, Lodz Film School students in their graduation year. One of them was Andrzej Wajda.

The irony of the situation, in view of Wajda's subsequent rise to fame, was that *Three Stories* had originally been planned as *Four Stories* – a quartet that would enable four teams of students to demonstrate their competence within a feature-film framework. The first three teams had already run away with so much screen time that none remained for Wajda's contribution. This left him hanging around the set with nothing to do, and some of his enforced leisure he devoted to showing me the ropes. Like Bohdziewicz, he had seen me act in the past and was an ex-student of the Krakow Art Academy, which gave us something in common.

Bohdziewicz may not have been the world's greatest director, nor did he leave any memorable films behind; but he was, indisputably, one of the greatest teachers Lodz ever had. His students hero-worshiped him, and it was easy to see why. Though he was casual and relaxed, humorous and low-key, his rapport with them was extraordinarily stimulating. He was there to supervise a film being made by others, but when the time came for my own first appearance on the set, he took me personally in hand and coached me in the two lines the script assigned me in my minor role as a peasant boy.

I found it all so very different from playing the lead in *Son of the Regiment*, so much more intense. Striving for naturalism onstage was one thing; doing so outdoors with a camera goggling at you, with lights and reflectors and swarms of people hovering in the background, required another kind of nervous voltage altogether. For me, that first time on the set was an awakening. I knew beyond a doubt that these were the people I wanted to be with from now on. I wanted to lead their kind of life and talk their language.

I wouldn't have dared, at this stage, to apply for admission to the film school itself. Lodz was a prestigious establishment – the only one of its kind in the country – but an indirect means of getting there in the end might be to realize my long-harbored ambition of entering the Krakow Drama School. I already knew several people there, two of whom were acquaintances from the fencing club. They were an inseparable but oddly matched pair: Bobek Kobiela, a hook-nosed, ungainly comic, and Zbigniew Cybulski, big, dark, and handsome, with a dramatic intensity that gave a foretaste of the reputation he was soon to gain as one of Poland's most promising young actors. They both encouraged me to believe that I would sail into the drama school.

Krakow Drama School was administered by Vice-Rector Tecza, whom I had known since my days with the Young Spectators' Theater. Although his acting experience had been confined to bit parts, he wielded great influence because of his longtime party membership and staunch adherence to the official line. Undeterred by the recollection of one or two altercations with him as a child actor, I decided to apply for admission.

Candidates were required in the first instance to memorize and recite two poems of their own choosing. Together with Adam Fiut, the undertaker's son, who by now fervently shared my acting ambitions, and a stage-struck acquaintance of ours, Jerzy Wasiuczynski – fat, bald, and a born comic – I set about preparing for this ordeal. Taking advantage of my previous stage experience, I coached them – and polished my own performance – in the course of long rehearsals, most of them held at Fiut's home.

We got through the preliminary audition, which narrowed the field from several hundred to around fifty, without difficulty. This qualified us for the intermediate stage, a week's intensive teaching and assessment by drama school staff members, who helped us prepare for the final examination,

93

which consisted in the recitation of two set passages of verse, one contemporary and the other classical. We persevered with our out-of-hours rehearsals, sometimes on the banks of the Vistula or on the grounds of Wawel Castle, in the company of two other short-listed candidates, Marek Szyszkowski and Maria Nowotarska. I was now unofficial coach to a group of four.

On the day of the final examination, I went through my paces confidently. More prone to stage fright than I, but fortified by the thought of all our hard work together, my 'students' felt they stood at least a fifty-fifty chance. My own success they took for granted; so did I.

The list of acceptances was duly posted. All their names were on it; mine was not. If anything, they were even more flabbergasted and miserable than I was myself. Vice-Rector Wlodzimierz Tecza told me that I had been rejected because of my size; there weren't enough parts for people of my build. 'Only if you measure talent by inches,' I retorted – just the sort of cockiness that had spelled my undoing. But underneath the bravado, I was devastated.

One hope remained, and that was a slim one. Warsaw had a drama school but that was even more politically conscious than Tecza's establishment. Emphasis was laid on a sound proletarian background and membership of the ZMP, but I decided to apply nonetheless. Although the drama section had already held its final examination, a few extra places were reserved for late applicants. As it turned out, the drama section wouldn't even consider me. That left the vaudeville section – a more likely prospect but, to me, a rather degrading one. I auditioned for that and was turned down again.

Two fat men were standing in the corridor near the board on which the results had just been posted. They were recruiting for yet another establishment – hailing each unsuccessful candidate like a couple of fairground barkers. 'Cheer up,' they said breezily, 'there's always room for you in our outfit.' Their 'outfit' proved to be the circus school at Julinek, a one-horse town not far from Warsaw. I made a note of their particulars.

By now I was getting really desperate. Unless I was accepted by some institute of higher education, I would be drafted in the following fall. After nearly three years' service as an army conscript I could kiss my acting career good-bye. Hoping against hope, I applied for admission to Krakow University.

In Poland, as in all Communist countries, the points system laid considerable emphasis on a candidate's political record and devotion to the Marxist-Leninist cause. 'Administrative merit,' meaning membership in Communist youth organizations, could count for as many as five points; 'social work,' for four; 'parental merit,' alias impeccable working-class origins, for two; other miscellaneous political virtues, for three. Supreme academic excellence scored only seven points; other factors, fourteen. The odds against my making the grade on any basis of assessment were long indeed.

To make matters worse, my checkered school career had left me without a document called an *opinia*, or testimonial affirming my political reliability and general merit. To obtain one, I went before a special board at Krakow City Hall. Seated across the green baize table, chairing the committee that was about to examine me, I found the party apparatchik who had been *personalny*, or head-of-personnel-cum-political commissar, at Billizanka's theater. He had known me for years. Although he had no reason to be hostile, I detected a certain coolness in his manner. I came away with the sealed envelope I was supposed to present to the university authorities. I couldn't resist opening it.

'This candidate is keen to enter the acting profession but was turned down,' I read. 'The board does not recommend he pursue his studies any further.'

I decided to dispense with the document, but I was still determined to get into the university by hook or by crook.

Because there were usually far more vacancies than applicants for the PE course, and because my devotion to physical fitness made the prospect not too uncongenial, I entered my name. I was turned down flat. That reduced me to the most abject of last resorts, Russian language and literature – the least popular of all courses and, consequently, the one with the largest number of vacancies. I was turned down again.

Like a rat in a trap, my mind scurried around in search of another opening. Remembering the circus school, I sent in a formal application. I intended to become a film director, I wrote, 'so sooner or later I'll end up in a circus anyway.' Successive failures had made me strangely resilient. I derived a sort of masochistic pleasure from the thought that if I made it in the end, I could boast of having launched my career as a circus hand.

Winowski and I discussed my dilemma over vodka and raspberry syrup in the one remaining, cluttered room of his apartment he was still allowed to use.

Winowski's plight was even worse than mine. Thanks to his low grades and 'bourgeois' social background, the lyceum had expelled him. Broke, he had taken a job as a lathe operator at the Nova Huta steelworks. There he got into more trouble by leaving his lathe unattended for the five minutes it took him to down a beer in the canteen. By the time he returned, his deserted lathe had manufactured a whole cocoon of metal shavings. He was interrogated, accused of sabotage, threatened with jail, and fired. Now he was unemployed, without resources or prospects of any kind. His limp exempted him from military service, but he tapped his head when I spoke of joining the circus school. I went into my Galician Jew routine. 'Anyssing iss besser zan army,' I insisted.

With four other deferment seekers, I stood at attention, stark naked, before some officers seated at a table covered with a red cloth. They examined records of my 'social origins' at considerable length. The presiding colonel noted that I had never joined the ZMP. He asked for details about my capitalist father.

He was really more of an artisan, I told them, with a workshop employing half a dozen men who manufactured belts and handbags out of leatherette.

'What's the name of his establishment?' demanded the colonel.

My heart sank. 'Er, *Gentleman*,' I replied, mispronouncing the firm's name to make it sound less English. The members of the board were vastly amused.

I explained that I was seeking deferment in order to go to the circus school. That evoked more mirth. 'Are they so short of clowns?' someone asked.

The colonel conferred with his brother officers. After leafing through a book of rules and regulations, he informed me that circus schools were not among the educational institutions for which deferment could be granted.

That really sealed my fate. Only an act of God could prevent my being drafted in a few months' time – that or some initiative on my own part. Sooner than go into the army, I thought, I would flee to the West.

I set about planning my escape with the same misguided ingenuity I had devoted to building a racing cycle. My original plan was to cross into East Germany by river and canal. The wall did not exist then, so my chances of sneaking into West Berlin seemed fair. I proposed to construct a primitive form of one-man submarine, disguised to resemble a waterlogged crate and driven by a pedal-powered propeller. After much research and experimentation I abandoned this idea because it presented far too many technical problems.

Next, I thought of getting to Bornholm, a Danish island in the Baltic some sixty miles from the Polish coast. I sold my cycle and invested the proceeds in a kayak. After training on the Vistula for most of the winter, however, I realized that I would stand no chance at all unless the sea was as calm as a millpond.

By now my call-up date was imminent. There was nothing to do but to make myself scarce. Ditching my kayak, I left Krakow for Katowice. Some of the trains that stopped there, I knew, went all the way from Moscow to Paris. What was left of my savings went on renting cheap hotel rooms, shared

97

with half a dozen others as broke as I, and buying snacks at Katowice station. I haunted the platforms day after day, studying timetables, watching the trans-European expresses come and go. Having identified the cars that went as far as Paris, I started taking brief rides in them to see if they offered any suitable hiding places.

The one I settled on called for the construction of a false ceiling outside a toilet door – a plywood box large enough to contain me but so well tailored to fit the available space that it looked like an integral part of the car's interior. As long as its external surface blended with the rest of the paneling, it might pass undetected. Many short reconnaissance trips were needed to get the measurements right, take color samples, and make wax imprints of the angles to be matched, which were irregular owing to the car's curving roof and tapering conformation.

During one of my surreptitious visits to Krakow – surreptitious because I'd led my father to believe that I was already in the circus school and I didn't want to risk being spotted – I went to see Adam Fiut, the only friend who'd been initiated into my escape plan. It was then, while glancing out of a window over-looking the undertaker's yard, that I caught sight of Piotr Winowski.

He was in terrible shape – gaunt and pallid, his clothes filthy and almost in rags. He told us that he was now working underground in a Silesian coal mine. He no longer had anywhere to live in Krakow because his lodgers were in sole occupation. With the blessing of the laws now in force, they had taken over the whole apartment. His mother's tearoom had also gone, expropriated by a workers' cooperative. He had come to Krakow to ask them for some compensation, but they had thrown him out. Now he was returning to Silesia completely broke, without even the price of a rail ticket.

We shared what money and food we had and talked until the small hours. Winowski gave us a humorous account of the one bright spot in his gloomy existence, a Silesian game-keeper's wife who shared her bed and board with him when her husband was away in the woods. He could still joke about his misfortunes, still make us laugh as much as ever, but there was an aura of doom about him. That night we slept three to a bed, Adam, Piotr, and I, though Piotr's incessant coughing didn't give us much rest. In the morning he left. It was our last sight of him. He died in Silesia not long afterward – why and how, we never discovered.

I had to abandon the false ceiling idea. The car I'd planned to install it in was suddenly withdrawn from the trans-European service. After more long hours of observation I now pinned my hopes on a French car that regularly stopped at Katowice on the Moscow-Paris run. It was new and elegant in appearance, with a toilet halfway down the corridor.

This time my chosen place of concealment was in the toilet itself, above a low, paneled ceiling which presumably masked the plumbing. To curl up inside there, I needed more than one helper. I discussed the matter at length with Adam Fiut and Jerzy Wasiuczynski. Although complicity in an attempted escape might have earned them a long term of imprisonment, they volunteered to help. Neither of them ever mentioned the risks involved; that made me doubly appreciative of their readiness to do so.

The three of us boarded the car at Katowice, Adam and Jerzy carrying a bottle of vodka with which they planned to celebrate my escape.

Almost immediately we hit a snag. The ceiling panel had never been removed before, and the screws were thick with paint. Our screwdrivers couldn't get a grip on them, and the harder we tried, the more often they skidded off and scratched the surrounding paintwork.

Adam remained ice-cool throughout, but Jerzy, who was keeping a lookout in the corridor, started celebrating my escape in advance. Sweating in the overheated car, he announced that he needed a few nips of vodka to fortify himself. 'You're getting out of here,' he said. 'We're staying.'

We eventually removed enough screws to enable us to prize the edge of the panel down and peer inside. Although I could just have squeezed into the recess, we'd run out of time. Adam and Jerzy would never have been able to screw the panel back before we reached the border checkpoint. In any case, it was so badly scratched that even a perfunctory glance would have aroused the suspicions of frontier police accustomed to carrying out ultrathorough inspections.

'It's no use,' I said. 'Let's screw it up again and get out of here.' We barely had time to do so before the train pulled into the station on the Polish side of the border. That night, while traveling back to Katowice, we all got thoroughly drunk.

It wasn't quite the end of my escape plans. If all else failed, I thought, I would try to cross the border on foot. But by now I'd run out of money, so I went to see my father. We weren't on good terms at this time and hadn't seen each other for months. I pretended to be on a brief vacation from my mythical circus school. Wanda was out when I arrived, and he had to leave for a business appointment before I could get around to asking for money.

I was all alone in his apartment, brooding on my fate, when the phone rang. It was Jerzy Lipman, the cameraman whose room I'd shared during the filming of *Three Stories*. Andrzej Wajda was making his first full-length film, he said, and he had a major part in it for me.

NINE

Those who have never lived under Communist rule can have little conception of what the Polish film industry was like when Wajda, then twenty-seven, embarked on his first full-length film just after Stalin's death.

It wasn't an industry at all in the Hollywood sense. It had no private capital of any kind. All filmmaking was party-approved and subsidized by a branch of the Ministry of Culture, and it was the government and party that decided how funds should be allocated. A film's success wasn't gauged by box-office receipts; what mattered was its ideological content and political message. To a large extent this state of affairs persists today. Only during the 1956-57 thaw and the heyday of Solidarity was there a free choice of subjects, and even then some themes were taboo – for instance, the story of the non-Communist resistance movement and the AK's Warsaw uprising in 1944.

In the early 1950's state control was absolute. Screenplays were vetted by bureaucrats before production funds were released. Supervisors ensured that directors stuck to their scripts, and no film was released prior to an all-important board meeting known as the *kolaudacja*. This comprised a formal screening of the finished product, followed by a debate between its makers and the relevant party and ministry officials, who had the last word. It was they who decided whether or not a film was to be released, who decreed cuts and changes in dialogue. It was not uncommon for whole chunks of a film to be reshot by order of the authorities.

Prewar Poland had maintained a small but improving

output of films, mostly cheap, mediocre drawing-room comedies too amateurish for export. Even if the films themselves were poor, their standard of acting and musical scores were quite good. During the late 1930's, however, a small group of filmmakers founded a cooperative called START. The shorts it turned out were distributed alongside foreign films and subsidized by means of various tax concessions.

When the Russians invaded Poland from the east in September 1939, seventeen days after Hitler's incursion from the west, a number of Polish filmmakers were pressed into employment on Soviet war and propaganda films. Later, when the Russians fashioned a Polish army out of the prisoners they had taken in 1939, several Polish directors and cameramen were attached to it as combat film unit personnel. This was so in the case of Stanislaw Wohl, the outstanding Polish cameraman of his generation, and Jerzy Bossak, one of Poland's finest documentary directors. In the wake of the German retreat in 1944, members of these Polish film units returned to their native land, where the Russians set up a military film studio in Lublin. Such was the small band of survivors that founded Poland's postwar film production units.

They included some extremely competent people, notably Aleksander Ford, a veteran party member who was then an orthodox Stalinist. Others, like Wohl and Bossak, did their best to campaign for artistic originality and freedom, standing up to party hacks and ministry bureaucrats at considerable personal risk. The real power broker during the immediate postwar period was Ford himself, who established a small film empire of his own.

When Wajda's first film was being planned, the party and ministry apparatchiks responsible for the cinema were no different from their colleagues in other branches of government. The men and women who controlled and supervised the Polish film industry had scaled the party ladder at the cost of their souls; anything original or unorthodox, any story told in a novel or unconventional way, aroused their suspicions. They were not only among the dumbest representatives of

Polish society but obstinate into the bargain, owing their jobs to the tenacity with which they opposed anything new and unfamiliar and, thus, potentially dangerous to the regime. Their devotion to the drab conformity they sought to impose on Polish films was a reflection of their personal drabness.

All devotees of the cinema yearned to see a Polish film that would depart from the jejune, conventional propaganda clichés foisted on the public by the system. We had been sufficiently exposed to foreign imports to know that films could be made in a different way. Wajda, with the fire of youth and a painter's eye, set out to break the dreary official mold.

The film that had prompted my summons to Warsaw, *A Generation*, was, superficially at least, no different from dozens of earlier Polish movies about the wartime resistance movement. If Wajda's script had departed from the accepted norm, the authorities would never have let him make it.

What was different was his telling of the story. This became apparent at the very start of the film, with its spectacular opening long shot, which overlooked the Warsaw slum where most of the action was to take place and, after exploring it in minute detail, culminated – without a single break – in a close-up. There was a deliberately stark newsreel quality about the Nazi occupation scenes, together with unmistakable traces of Italian neorealist influence, but there was also something quintessentially Polish about *A Generation*. Thanks, too, to a cast of characters that were a cut above the usual propaganda stereotypes, it was unlike any film that had ever been made in Communist Poland.

All I gathered, when the call came through, was that the picture had a part in it for me. I had been dimly aware, before the phone rang, that Wajda was making a film in Warsaw, but that was all. I wasted little time in my father's apartment after that. Returning from his business appointment to be informed that I was off to act in a film in Warsaw, he called me a damned liar. Although I couldn't altogether blame him in view of my previous evasions – not to mention the sheer coincidence of my having been there when the call came through – we had a flaming row. I eventually walked out and slammed the door behind me, determined never to see him again. Not even having the price of a rail ticket, I expertly dodged the conductor on the Warsaw train.

The crew and cast had assembled at a small hotel. The first person I met was Ignac Taub, production manager on *Three Stories* but now promoted to the status of executive producer. 'Ah,' he said, 'you've worked for us before, haven't you? What did you get for *Three Stories*?'

I told him.

'A pittance, dear boy, a mere pittance. You were robbed. Tell you what. I'll double it. What do you say to two hundred forty zlotys a day?'

It was the lowest rate he could possibly get away with. I might have held out for more, but it never crossed my mind. To me, it was enough that I found myself part of a team that included several old friends and filmmakers whose talents I admired. Jerzy Lipman was now Wajda's cameraman, Zbigniew Cybulski had joined the cast, and I finally got to know my longtime idol, Tadeusz Lomnicki, who was playing the male lead. I refrained from mentioning that I'd had an unconsummated affair with his sister.

A Generation was a young people's film – at thirty-two, Lipman was older than any of us, including Wajda – and a new experience for all concerned. Discounting *Three Stories*, none of us had been involved in a full-length film before.

The atmosphere on the set reflected this youthful enthusiasm. During the shooting of *Three Stories* I had relished the sheer novelty of being around while a film was in the making. In the case of *A Generation* we all realized that Wajda was attempting something original. Because he was no remote, autocratic director, but a man who liked to work with his cast and crew as an integrated team, he was always inviting suggestions, discussing ideas and alternatives. It was fascinating to watch him at work and make a contribution, however modest, to the creative process.

I hung around, whether or not I was wanted on the set, as I had in my old theater days. By this time I had read everything

I could find on the subject of filmmaking, and I was just as interested in lighting, camerawork, sound recording, and special effects as in acting.

The same went for Jerzy Lipman. Aside from being a fine cameraman, he prided himself on his talent for pyrotechnics. No bomb blast could ever be loud or spectacular enough for Jerzy. He was ecstatic when an explosive charge went up with such force, during shooting, that actors and camera crew alike were showered with dirt and debris – even when a piece of debris lacerated his own bald pate.

It was unusual, in those days, to go to Wajda's lengths in creating truly authentic settings, and some of his scrupulous attention to detail rubbed off on me. Other directors seldom shot interior scenes on location; they used studio sets. That wasn't good enough for Wajda, who wanted his windows to give a view of the actual surroundings. His composite set of the central character's house was built in the middle of a genuine slum, and there was a near riot when the carpenters came to dismantle it; the local inhabitants wanted to move in.

A Generation suffered badly from prerelease problems. The *kolaudacja* was a stormy one. Some scenes had to be reshot to reinforce their ideological content; others, including a spectacular fight scene between Cybulski and me, were cut altogether. The *Generation* ultimately shown and admired around the world was a pale shadow of Wajda's original version.

That spring of 1953 all Poles were being issued with new identity cards, which they had to collect from their local police stations. From my point of view, this posed a threat. I knew that if the military authorities were on my track, they would have notified the Siemiradzki Street station in Krakow, where I was registered. If I went there, I might be picked up; if I didn't, my failure to report might spark off an investigation into my whereabouts.

In June I eventually plucked up the courage to go collect my card, telling myself that if an attempt were made to draft me on the spot, I would take to my heels. After consulting his files, the duty officer handed me my new ID card without a word. It was inscribed: 'Occupation: Student.' I never discovered how or why I had slipped through the bureaucratic mesh, but it was good to be able to lead a normal life again, at least for the next twelve months.

This meant that I could resume my existence in Krakow openly and under different auspices. Fortune seemed to be smiling on me at last. I was summoned to Lodz to undergo a screen test for a major part in a film about a cycle race, and I got it. This picture, *The Enchanted Bicycle*, was scheduled to be shot the following summer.

Until now, with the exception of a few special friends like Fiut, Winowski, and Tyszler, most of my companions had been theatrical small fry or cycle racers and skiers. Before long, however, I found myself mingling with an entirely new circle of acquaintances.

One chance contributor to this change in my social life was Professor Antoni Bohdziewicz of the Lodz Film School, who had supervised *Three Stories*. Bohdziewicz not only did his best to look like an Oxford don but had all the finest attributes of the breed, including a genuine and disinterested liking for any young people in whom he discerned seeds of talent. He used to look me up whenever he visited Krakow, and we often toured the flea market together in search of trendy foreign gear unobtainable elsewhere.

Although the municipal authorities had moved this hive of black-market activity farther and farther away from the center of town in an effort to discourage people from patronizing the place, it remained as popular as ever. One day, while Bohdziewicz and I were inspecting the wares on display at a clothing stall, he nudged me and murmured, 'That's an interesting face.' I followed the direction of his gaze and saw a handsome, dandyish young man, plus girlfriend, picking over the merchandise on a neighboring stall. We struck up a conversation, and it proved to be my entrée into a world of unfamiliar but congenial attitudes.

Wiezlaw Zubrzycki was a Krakow graduate in art history. Cultivated and widely read, he nursed the sort of contempt

106

for the modern egalitarian world invariably displayed by aristocrats whose old order had collapsed around their ears. Utterly and outrageously candid about himself, he was a Catholic intellectual and avowed political reactionary. Through him I started meeting the remnants of the Krakow nobility, who lived in crumbling mansions or cluttered apartments, selling off the last of their family heirlooms now that all their estates had been seized. Their manners were those of a bygone age. They habitually spoke French and talked of Western Europe as if it were still a part of their daily lives.

Thanks to my film earnings, I was probably better off than most of its members, the majority of whom were broke, and I was always buying them meals. Looking back, however, I think they accepted me because of our common attraction to all that smacked of the West. They were not only older but far more culturally immersed than I was. Their superior knowledge and sophistication dazzled me. I found that I not only shared their enthusiasms but had arrived, quite independently, at similar conclusions about the state of our country. My political views had come full circle even before I met them. Unlike a lot of my previous acquaintances, I had shed no tears at Stalin's passing. I realized that there must be something very wrong indeed with a regime that imposed such absurd restraints on individual freedom. My new friends, who were dissidents to a man, reacted against the drab, conformist tyranny of communism in a variety of ways. They displayed their contempt for authority by taking a keen interest in contemporary Western literature and music, notably jazz, by baring their souls in a very un-Polish manner, and even by engaging – almost as a matter of principle – in homosexuality. They likewise felt that deliberate idleness and excessive drinking were blows struck for freedom.

One such free spirit studying art history at Krakow University was Piotr Skrzynecki – a wit, a hippie before his time, and Communist Poland's worst-ever student cadet. He kept us in stitches with accounts of his running battle with the military authorities. University students were obliged to

107

devote one day a week to military training and attend a long summer camp. Piotr got a doctor to diagnose his trouble as 'a strong psychical aversion to firearms.' He was finally exempted from further attendance when he climbed a tree in camp and refused to come down until discharged. Piotr's 'aversion' was understandable in that his father, a colonel in the Polish Army, had been captured and shot by the Russians after they had invaded Poland in 1939, under the terms of the German-Soviet pact.

In company with Piotr Skrzynecki and others like him, I devoted long afternoons to idle café chitchat and longer nights to endless debates on aesthetic, cosmopolitan, 'reactionary' topics. The setting for our discussions could not have been more atmospherically suitable. Wieslaw Zubrzycki lived in the tower room of a weirdlooking neo-Gothic mansion designed by his architect father. Here it was that we drank and smoked and talked for hour after hour, largely about our obsession with the West.

It is almost impossible to convey the extent of that obsession at a time when Poland's isolation was so complete. There were no newspapers or magazines to serve as a link with the outside world, and almost no films, but one of my long-standing passions to survive this period was the theater.

With Adam Fiut, I started going ever farther afield – to Warsaw, even to Poznan – whenever there were shows of more than routine interest to offer. Anything that transcended the commonplace attracted us like a lodestone. We made pilgrimages to see the Berliner Ensemble, for example, and were utterly bowled over by the brilliance and originality of Bertolt Brecht's productions.

We had abandoned the Pheasant look by now, but not some of the rough-and-ready ways that went with it. When we failed to get tickets for the Peking Opera, we scaled the outside of the Jan Slowacki Theater, via a drainpipe, and got into the upstairs foyer. Nabbed by some attendants, we were hauled before the theater's legendary director, Ludwik Solski, then in his nineties. Despite his awesome reputation, he treated us with surprising indulgence. 'After risking their necks like that, these lads deserve to see the show,' he decreed – and lent us his private box.

At Poznan, the management proved less accommodating. Tired after our long train journey, we got there after curtain-up. We pleaded with the manager to let us in on the ground that we were drama students. When he refused, we sneaked in anyway and found ourselves some seats in the upper circle. He spotted us and had us ejected.

Adam lay in wait for him after the performance. 'That's for the seats,' he said, and punched him on the nose. The manager fell to his knees, groggily groping for his glasses, and Adam took off.

'Let's get that son of a bitch!' I shouted, pointing and sprinting in the opposite direction, and a posse obediently followed me on a wild-goose chase. Adam and I, who had employed this routine in the past, met up at the station later.

Unless he had already been successfully indoctrinated, any normal young Pole developed a craze for jazz during the Stalinist period. It was not only a window onto a completely different world but a form of protest, for American jazz was officially decried as a product of 'putrid imperialism.' There were some remarkably fine jazz musicians in Krakow, mostly students who met for weekend jam sessions the venues of which were advertised by word of mouth. Though never raided, these sessions were held clandestinely, in classrooms or 'safe' apartments, and devotees paid substantial sums to hear their idols perform. Different groups essayed different styles. There was bebop, New Orleans, and Dixieland, but the most popular groups were those that emulated the Modern Jazz Quartet. Gradually, in the years following Stalin's death, jazz became more respectable; during those summer months in Krakow it was still banned, and illegality added a touch of spice to every jam session.

When winter came, I reapplied myself to skiing. One day, during a major downhill race for women, I witnessed a really bad accident: one of Poland's most promising Olympic hopes, a girl named Kika Lelicinska, collided with a tree and fractured her spine. Her coach elbowed the ski patrol aside and insisted on taking her down himself. He lost control, and his toboggan, with Kika strapped to it, careered downhill, crashing into tree after tree. She sustained further fractures and ruptured her spleen.

Kika, who spent several months in the hospital, was never able to race in major competitions again. She happened to be part of my charmed circle of new friends – a budding sculptress, still at the Art Academy, who restored old paintings as a sideline. She had an impish face, short brown hair, and an athlete's body – broad-shouldered and slender-waisted – with skier's thighs and small but powerful hands. I had never met anyone like her. She was two years my senior, tough, tomboyish, and mordantly witty. Her nickname for me was the Brat. When awarded damages for her skiing injuries, she promptly spent almost the entire sum on throwing a wild party. 'Here goes my spleen,' she toasted.

Finally, after yet another long night of talk and vodka in Zubrzycki's neo-Gothic garret, Kika and I made love while the others slept. When morning came, we took off together. We breakfasted at a milk bar, then idled away the rest of the morning in a public library, looking at art books. Kika became my regular girlfriend. We never actually lived together, but I used to spend the night at her place whenever her mother was out of town.

Entering into this love affair, we realized, Kika and I, that we had the same approach toward personal freedom: she felt there was nothing wrong with either of us having an occasional affair with someone else. When two people in love saw a lot of each other, she said, their relationship went beyond the initial sexual attraction. The ties that formed between them were far more important than physical love. Enforced monogamy, whether in the man or the woman, subconsciously created resentment and wrecked the relationship. I had very little experience myself but instinctively felt the same way.

It was Kika who introduced me to the delights of sailing. I spent some idyllic weeks with her during the summer of

110

1954, camping out in the forest of the Mazury lake district and learning the rudiments of boat handling from her friends – a tight little yachting fraternity with its private recognition signals, esoteric jargon, and contempt for landlubbers. My affection for Kika came to embrace Mazury as well, one of the most beautiful parts of Poland, with alternating stretches of mat green forest and sparkling blue water. I enjoyed every moment of that glorious summer until summoned to report for work on *The Enchanted Bicycle*. Leaving Kika and Mazury was such a wrench that I almost failed to show up.

The two or three months I spent on this latest assignment gobbled up the rest of the summer. They also taught me that filming could be hell as well as heaven, that not all directors and crews were like Wajda and his team. The personnel was as mediocre as the picture itself turned out to be: an ideologically slanted piece whose message was that collective effort was all and individualism counted for nothing.

At the same time my growing experience of the filmmaking process and widening acquaintance with those involved in it served to render the idea of my applying for admission to the Lodz Film School less farfetched, less remote from the realms of possibility. Bohdziewicz, whom I consulted, was gently encouraging. 'What have you got to lose?' was the gist of his advice, so Zubrzycki and I put our names down.

We were only two out of several hundred applicants for the three different courses: directing, camerawork, and production management. After a preliminary interview by a woman professor who narrowed the field to eighty or ninety, Zubrzycki and I were summoned to Lodz itself for a two-week series of tests and examinations. We had to travel there at our own expense but were housed in dormitories and boarded free of charge.

Several candidates withdrew before the first week was up. Thanks to my erratic schooling, I fared badly in written tests on subjects such as Marxism-Leninism and the history of the working-class movement, but my stage and screen experience, as well as my time in art school, gave me a distinct

111

edge in other respects. I was in my element when it came to art history, and even more so when we had to write a short script and devise scenes to be acted out by members of our study group.

The examinations seemed to drag on forever. Outside school hours I saw little of my fellow candidates, Zubrzycki excepted. Most of my spare time was spent with people I already knew from the film world – senior Lodz students who treated me as an equal because I'd been on location with them. This exempted me from the hazing they traditionally meted out to young hopefuls like me. I was also fortunate in having a friend at court in the shape of Bohdziewicz, who helped offset any adverse effects that may have been produced by my bumptious manner and deficient political consciousness. He apparently summed me up to the examiners as 'A little wild but shows promise.'

When it was all over, the names of the successful candidates were posted on the notice board. Of the eight selected for the student directors' course, three came from Krakow. I was one; the other two were Zubrzycki and Majewski, a School of Architecture graduate. It was quite a triumph for our hometown.

There was a wild party in Lodz that night. My father was overjoyed when I phoned him the news. For the first time in my life I hadn't let him down.

TEN

Lodz was a dump. Everyone thought so. Its textile and chemical factories belched smoke day and night, sprinkling it with soot and augmenting the universal grime which, together with diesel fumes, peeling walls, and broken windows, has always seemed to me the very essence of an industrial city in a Communist country. It was so devoid of charm – so unlike Krakow – that my elation at having been accepted by the film school was tempered with doubts about my ability to stick it out for five whole years.

Largely built during the Industrial Revolution, Lodz was laid out in blocks, New York fashion, with streets intersecting at right angles. The only thoroughfare with metropolitan pretensions was Piotrkowka Street, which boasted a Grand Hotel and a few department stores. In any other city Piotrkowka Street would have been called Stalin Avenue in compliance with a general directive, issued in the heyday of Stalinism, to the effect that all main streets in all Polish cities were to be renamed in honor of the 'Great Benefactor.' This omission was no tribute to passive resistance on the part of the city fathers; although 'Main Street' happened to be the name of one of the shabbiest alleys in town, they had obeyed the directive to the letter.

That Lodz should have become Poland's film center was a quirk of history. With the Polish capital in ruins after the war, the government had reestablished the film industry in the nearest provincial city capable of housing it, and there it remained. Similarly, when a national film school was founded, common sense prescribed a site where studios and offices already existed. A nineteenth-century mansion, once the property of a textile magnate, was requisitioned for the purpose, and the first course opened there in 1947.

However much of an extravagance a film school might have seemed in a country as impoverished and war-ravaged as Poland, its existence was formally justified by an inscription in the entrance hall, under a medallion portrait of Lenin. 'To us,' he was quoted as saying, 'the cinema is the most important of all art forms.'

The school was a remarkable place for several reasons. Given our postwar lack of resources, it was lavishly equipped and heavily staffed. The staff-student ratio was, in fact, worthy of a luxury hotel – teachers and technicians outnumbered inmates – and nearly all the personnel were first-class. The building itself housed two projection rooms, photographic laboratories, cutting rooms, sound recording facilities, a library, lecture rooms, a canteen, and, last but not least, a bar. The latter, situated at the foot of the broad main staircase, was the school's epicenter. It was here, whether jostling for drinks at the counter or perched on the stairs like birds in an aviary, that we congregated between classes to argue, swill beer, fight, and – sometimes to our cost – compete to see who could jump from the highest step and land without breaking an ankle. There were facilities at the school for parties and Saturday night dances, and the mansion's spacious grounds contained a pond in whose murky waters we swam, either by choice or – when pushed – involuntarily. Junior students, who slept in an annex or were scattered around town in hostels, looked with envy on the seniors, whose status entitled them to share comfortable rooms in the school itself.

Lodz was run on the principle that since its inmates were there to be turned into filmmakers, they should gain as much practical experience as possible. They were consequently sent to work for considerable periods as apprentice film editors and lab technicians at the Film Polski studios in town. In the course of their five years student directors were required to make at least two one-minute silent shorts, a ten-

or fifteen-minute documentary, a dramatized film of the same length, and, finally, a 'diploma' film that could run for even longer. Opportunities for further filmmaking were almost limitless, however. Student cameramen, who were allocated a certain amount of raw film purely for practice purposes, could readily be prevailed on by student directors and production managers to collaborate in turning a mere exercise into something more elaborately structured. Students in their senior years often worked as assistant directors on films in production, and there was always someone making a film at the school itself who needed volunteer actors and scriptwriters.

During our first year most classes were common to students of all three categories, so the freshmen combined to form a large and widely assorted group. They ranged from two student cameramen – Andrzej Kostenko, with whom I became very friendly, and Kim, a North Korean who seldom opened his mouth – to Henryk Czarnecki, a student director whose curiously ingratiating manner and efforts to be chummy left most of us cold. I saw less of Wieslaw Zubrzycki than in the old days, especially since he spent a lot of time at home in Krakow and neglected to turn up for important classes. Now that he had joined it, he took a rather condescending view of the school and its inmates, whom he tended to regard as peasants.

But my circle was not confined to freshmen. Because of my previous involvement in films, I knew and consorted with a lot of senior students, either in their school quarters or at the Grand Hotel, whose Malinowa Restaurant and Mermaid Bar were favorite haunts of the Lodz filmmaking fraternity. Some of these seniors were preparing a feature film to be called *The End of the Night*. Though tripartite like *Three Stories*, it was far less propagandistic and better integrated. The influence of *Rashomon* could clearly be detected in its well-structured account of a 'hooligan' incident as seen through the eyes of three different characters. Adam Fiut and Zbigniew Cybulski were both in the cast, so I was doubly delighted when the student syndicate not only offered me a

115

part as well but took me on as an assistant director.

Working on *The End of the Night* brought me into contact with a highly colorful character named Marek Hlasko, who had written some dialogue for it. Though not a member of the film school, he was on friendly terms with a number of the older students and already enjoyed quite a reputation as a self-taught writer with an uncanny gift for narrative and dialogue. Marek's reputation extended beyond the purely literary, however. A born rebel and troublemaker of immense charm, he often bragged of his experiences as a truck driver and posed as a proletarian. He could be found most nights in the Mermaid Bar, brawling or looking for a brawl.

The Lodz Film School's odd blend of permissiveness and strict academic standards was to some extent personified by its rector, Roman Ozogowski, a party appointee but an inoffensive, puny little man with a docile and tractable nature. There was no daily roll call, no monitoring of lecture attendances, and students didn't even have to remain in Lodz all the time. They were, however, required to take end-of-term examinations and keep an index, or permanent work record, which had to be endorsed by their teachers every semester. Courses on the history of the cinema were also obligatory, as, of course, was the inescapable schooling in Marxism-Leninism. During our first year, however, we concentrated on the very foundation of our craft: still photography. We spent hours in the basement lab, busying ourselves with enlargers, developing tanks, and dryers. It was assumed that we knew nothing whatsoever about photography. Having owned a still camera since the age of fourteen, I felt frustrated. I itched to make a movie, but first I had to demonstrate a command of the principles and practices of still photography. This was such an essential part of our curriculum that anyone who failed to make the grade was automatically flunked. Despite his intellectual brilliance, Zubrzycki fell short of the required standard and was asked to leave.

116

At the end of my first year I produced quite a creditable portfolio of photographs. Most were of misty Krakow street scenes and children at play, but I also included some still lifes with nudes in the background, using Kika and Majewski's girlfriend as models.

Throughout our time at Lodz, and even while at the still photography stage, we absorbed an endless stream of movies. In use all day and sometimes till late at night, the projection rooms were always thronged with students. Some would be watching films directly relevant to their courses; but others were playing hooky for sheer interest's sake, and many was the time when some studentless teacher would open the door and bellow for the missing members of his class. Films were our meat and drink. We gorged ourselves on the great world classics, which were shown again and again, discussing, analyzing, and criticizing them *ad infinitum*.

We were able to see many films that were not accessible to the general public, even in the tough Stalinist period. All we needed was a requisition slip, countersigned by three members of the staff, to get the projectionist to show us the movie of our choice. If it wasn't available in Lodz, the National Film Archives would forward it from Warsaw. And though very few foreign films were actually bought for distribution and general release, many were sent to Film Polski on approval, and these, too, were screened for the benefit of our privileged little community. Word would spread whenever some film of outstanding interest was in the offing, and we all would do our best to squeeze into the school theater.

Our seniors were much impressed by the early Soviet cinema, whereas the class immediately above ours was more receptive to the Italian neorealist school. My classmates and I were far more bowled over by *Citizen Kane*.

It wasn't like anything else I'd ever seen. Gregg Toland's camerawork, with his extensive use of wide-angle lenses, brought the viewer right inside the set – one was seeing ceilings for the first time. Technique apart, it was as if Orson Welles had made the film with an audience like us in mind. The epic quality of the narrative, the originality with which

117

the story of a man's life was told, broke completely new ground. It was a new cinema language, full of implications and allusions.

This was even truer of Kurosawa's *Rashomon*. It exerted the same kind of pull on me as *Citizen Kane*, but for different reasons: the notion of the relativity of truth, seen through the eyes of three different characters, was made for the cinema. No other medium could have done it that well.

Another screen landmark was Buñuel's *Los Olvidados*. Here it was the violence, the realism, the unambiguous appeal to the emotions that bowled me over. Many of my film school friends dismissed it as sensationalism, but I felt it compared with the best kind of raw, naturalistic literature.

As the film school's reputation grew, many foreign students joined us. When I first arrived, however, the only foreigners there apart from Kim, our taciturn North Korean, were some Bulgarians. They were an exuberant, boisterous bunch. They chased every girl in sight, held chili-eating contests, and were always wheeling and dealing on the black market. Their main aim in life was to remain in Lodz for as long as possible. None of them had any desire to return to his native land.

The most flamboyant of the Bulgarians was Kola Todoroff, a senior student cameraman. I was desperately eager to make a movie, and he had been assigned to make an exercise film in color, so I talked him into turning it into a dramatized short instead of wasting his raw color stock on something routine. Having persuaded our teachers to grant us the necessary leave of absence, we traveled to Krakow at our own expense. It was there, as a totally inexperienced novice, that I directed my first motion picture.

Todoroff and I worked out the logistics of it all – the shot-by-shot storyboard and location schedule in the flea market and on Krakow's streets – with the intention of postsynchronizing the film back in Lodz. I also enlisted the enthusiastic support and participation of Adam Fiut, now a second-year drama student.

As well as director, I was star, producer, wardrobe mistress, continuity girl, and makeup man. The film, which I called *The Bicycle*, was all about my brush with death in the Krakow bunker. Wanda's nail polish made excellent blood.

The night before shooting started, I was more apprehensive than I could ever remember – almost as if making up for the stage fright I had never felt in the theater. While waiting for dawn in the student hostel where Todoroff and I had found beds, I endured sleepless hours of bowel-churning terror. At the same time my anxiety was pleasurable, almost ecstatic. Every shot was firmly imprinted on my mind, but I couldn't help inventing scenarios of failure, wondering what would happen if the rented convertible cab we needed for traveling shots failed to turn up, or the police prevented us from filming in the flea market, or Kola got his exposures wrong and we returned to Lodz with a load of blank negative.

Strangely enough, when we got down to work on that very first morning, my anxiety vanished and I felt perfectly at ease. I soon learned two lessons, though. Having planned to shoot early in the morning, when the streets were deserted, I discovered that although the light seemed adequate to the naked eye, the light meter wasn't registering the minimum exposure necessary. Filming at dawn proved impossible. My second discovery was how cumbersome even a skeleton crew could be when it came to shooting on location. Setting up the camera and moving from one site to the next took far more time than I'd allowed for.

In the end, all our work came to nothing. *The Bicycle* was developed at the Film Polski lab in Warsaw. It was a low-priority job, however, because the documentary center's resources had been fully mobilized to handle footage shot by Polish and Soviet crews covering Poland's major event of the year, the Warsaw-based International Youth Festival. Their films of this ideological jamboree, developed in Warsaw, were dispatched to the Soviet Union for editing. Thanks to some idiotic mix-up, so were our rushes of *The Bicycle*. Only the first batch of negative ever came back. The excellence of its color and camerawork, not to mention Adam Fiut's performance in the role of Dziuba, made the loss of the remainder doubly frustrating. I almost wept at my inability to complete what might have been quite a notable effort on the part of a first-year student director.

The festival itself was some consolation, prefaced as it was by much excited talk about the tens of thousands of foreigners converging on Warsaw. Its themes were peace, international understanding, and freedom for the oppressed colonial peoples of the world. Those who attended it were members of Communist youth organizations, but their political affiliations didn't worry us. In any case, a lot of them came along purely for the ride.

Such was the thrill of meeting youngsters from beyond our own well-guarded borders that we felt – Communists or not – they must be far more interesting than the Communists in our midst. They included Indians, Africans, and Asians of every hue. Never having seen a black face before, some of Warsaw's inhabitants were so intrigued that they tried to touch their skin to see if the color would rub off.

The festival opened during the summer vacation, at the end of my first school year. Kika and I arranged to meet up in Warsaw, determined to make the most of it and we had the time of our lives. Ballet and theater companies, orchestras, choirs, and folk ensembles from all over the world combined to produce the broadest conceivable spectrum of shows and concerts. The majority of seats were allotted to members of the Polish *nomenklatura*, or Communist establishment, but Polish reverence for foreign visitors was so extreme that we managed to get into a lot of shows by pretending to be French. The one time I got some tickets legitimately, things went wrong.

Instead of embarking on a conventional theatrical career, Kobiela and Cybulski had devoted themselves to organizing a student company, the Bim-Bom Theater, in Gdansk. They made a tremendous hit at the festival by putting on a sophisticated, satirical review full of mime and poetic metaphor. The show was booked solid, but Cybulski gave me a couple of complimentary passes. When I flashed our tickets at the door, the bouncer waved them aside and insisted that the house was full. There was a scuffle. He ripped my shirt, I hit him, and someone called the police. I was hauled off to the local station, Kika marching staunchly at my side.

Marek Hlasko caught sight of me being led away. 'What's up?' he called.

'Forget it,' I said, knowing how he tended to behave on such occasions. He came along anyway, loudly protesting what a farce the whole thing was.

I was hustled into the station by my police escort, leaving Marek and Kika outside. I could still hear Marek volubly dismissing the affair as a joke and announcing, with supreme conviction, that he would fix things. The desk sergeant eyed me distastefully. 'What have we got here,' he grunted, 'another hooligan?' I wasn't charged, just told to sit on a bench and wait. The place was full of drunken youths.

Ten minutes later my escort reappeared. 'Out,' he said, pointing to the exit.

Marek was strutting around on the sidewalk with Kika, manifestly pleased with himself. 'See?' he said. 'Now you can write your memoirs: "How I Survived the NKVD Dungeons." ' He put his arms around the cop who'd released me and hugged him fondly. 'You can thank Ziutek here. Now you're going to buy him a drink.' Marek's self-assurance never ceased to amaze me.

I went off to buy a bottle of vodka, and we found ourselves a secluded spot among the bomb-blasted ruins of Warsaw's old quarter, parts of which were still uncleared. It was a perfect night, warm and balmy, with a moon the size of a dinner plate. Marek continued to strut and hold forth and strike poses while Kika and I and the policeman perched on a mound of rubble. We all got plastered. I went off to fetch another half liter. When I came back with it, the other three were singing a Red Army marching song, con brio.

The policeman took a long pull on the bottle and addressed himself to Marek. 'You're an educated man,' he said thickly. 'You can tell me: Is there a God or isn't there?'

Marek, standing there with the moonlight glinting on his black leather jacket, glared down at him. 'Ziutek,' he said, 'if there is a God, he's a rotten old whore who watched what went on at Auschwitz and Hiroshima – who saw millions of innocent people murdered – and what kind of God is that? No, my friend, there isn't any God.'

The policeman nodded torpidly. 'Mmm,' he said. Then a thought struck him. 'But in that case, who made the world?'

I don't recall how Marek dealt with this transcendental question because I passed out almost immediately afterward. On that note, the festival and my summer vacation ended.

My second year at Lodz was even happier, if anything, than my first. I'd moved by now to an unfurnished room in town, bright and sunny, and fixed it up with a big bed and wall-to-wall bookshelves. The greater social freedom it gave me went hand in hand with greater intellectual satisfaction. I had my first official encounter with a movie camera. My preliminary school exercise, *Murder*, was a one-minute short in which a man, visible only from the chest down, slinks into a bedroom, deliberately stabs a sleeping figure with a pocket knife, and slinks out again. The theme of my second short, *The Smile*, which ran for two minutes, was set for me by my supervisor. It showed a voyeur, played by Todoroff, peering lecherously through a bathroom window at a naked girl drying herself. Almost caught in the act, he retreats. When he sneaks back for another look, all he sees is an ugly man brushing his teeth. The man, who catches sight of the voyeur in the bathroom mirror, turns and gives him a toothy grin.

I also applied myself to theory as well as practice. I started taking a more vocal part in our ceaseless staircase debates on the nature and theory of the cinema, once coming to blows with a fellow student over the merits of a recent Polish film we'd seen. Most of our arguments centered on the dichotomy between form and content. We discussed the subject endlessly, both in and out of class, and always ended by talking in political as well as aesthetic terms. This was because 'formalism' rated as a cardinal sin in Communist eyes, and there were constant wrangles over which directors allowed form to predominate over content and how hard it was to maintain a satisfactory balance between the two. Theses written by students in their graduation year were full of such aesthetico-ideological jargon, which I found fascinating but, at the same time, sterile and inconclusive.

The relative importance of form and content was brought home to me in an unexpected way. One day Cybulski turned up in my room with a briefcase full of film and told me to get hold of a 16 mm projector. The school didn't have one – another of its unusual extravagances was to employ nothing but professional 35 mm equipment – but I managed to extract one from a private source. We closed the shutters, hung a sheet on the wall, and the show began.

It was a collection of silent, scratched, and battered old porno films dating from World War II, almost certainly of German origin, which Cybulski had unearthed in Gdansk. All the porno clichés were there: the man peering through the keyhole watching a girl masturbate, the ugly seducer having sex in socks and suspenders, the couple surprised in mid-fornication and the lover hiding in a closet while the husband takes up where he left off. They were pathetic pieces of work, badly filmed, ill lit, and out of focus, but we watched them spellbound. Pathetic or not, they were sexually titillating. More than that – not that I ever dared produce them in evidence at a film school debate on the subject – they were proof that content could triumph over form!

There was only one aspect of the Lodz curriculum that filled me with dread. It was a condition of their deferment that under-graduates had to spend every Wednesday doing military training. I abhorred Wednesdays, not just because I hated all things military but because of the waste of time involved. You couldn't skip cadet corps parades or fool around in them. They were run not by the school but by the Defense Ministry, whose coercive powers were absolute. Any student performing unsatisfactorily was referred to a draft board and packed off at once to start his two years' national service.

Students from the Lodz Film School, Art School, and Drama School all were trained by the same unit. Its com-

123

manding officer, Major Karwiel, wore a Polish uniform but was one of the many Russians seconded to the Polish Army. Any impression that he might be Polish was dispelled by his thick Russian accent and naïve habit of signing his name in Cyrillic characters.

'Discipline will be maintained at all times,' he would bellow. 'I'll make a fucking army of you yet!' I detested having to don my scratchy, oversize uniform and boots, detested the exercises, the mindless drill parades, and the fieldcraft that seemed such a travesty of my Scouting days, detested even more the interminable boot-polishing and rifle-cleaning sessions at the end of the day. Most of all, I despised the element of indoctrination – the automatic assumption that the West was our enemy. We were taught to identify 'enemy' insignia and badges of rank, which were invariably American. If ever war broke out between the Soviet bloc and the West, I wanted the West to win.

I naturally kept such thoughts to myself. The film school was tolerant and unorthodox by current standards, but we were nearing the end of the grimmest, most repressive phase in Poland's postwar history. Although we didn't know it, we were on the brink of a liberal thaw. This transitional phase had a tragi-comic impact on some of my fellow students.

The ever-affable Czarnecki was still trying hard to be popular with our crowd. It took us quite a while to discover that he was not only a card-carrying Communist but an informer to boot. The truth about Czarnecki emerged one night when we got our Korean student drunk. It was Kim's birthday, so we persuaded him to let his hair down for once. Although Czarnecki attended the party and even contributed some of the liquor, he turned us in the next morning. Possibly afraid that some other informer might report his presence at this rowdy and reprehensible binge, he went to the school authorities and blamed Andrzej Kostenko for organizing it. Kostenko, a student cameraman in his junior year, was expelled. When permitted to return a year later, he had lost all seniority and had to start the course again from scratch. Once we knew Czarnecki for what he was, we habitually called him Traitor – as in 'Pass the salt, would you, Traitor?' To judge by his amiable acceptance of the nickname, he might almost have regarded it as an accolade.

Far more bizarre than Czarnecki was a character named Wieslaw Arct. A genuine ideologue who could stand up and speechify for an hour at a stretch, Arct was such a committed Communist that some of the senior students thought he must be crazy. Deciding to play an elaborate practical joke on him, they doctored his radio to enable them to cut in on programs and broadcast announcements of their own. This they proceeded to do in a fiendishly methodical way, planting stories when they knew he was listening. One of their bogus news flashes, which purported to come from Radio Free Europe, alleged that counterrevolutionaries inside the Lodz Film School were plotting to overthrow the regime.

Already showing distinct signs of dementia, Arct went over the top and launched an immediate investigation of his own. After vainly trying to mobilize the teaching staff, he burst in on Bohdziewicz and accused him of being in league with the conspirators. Quite unmoved by his ravings, Bohdziewicz phoned the nearest mental hospital and had him committed.

Arct's insanity should have been universally evident, but it wasn't. Two other students, also party members, warned Bohdziewicz that he couldn't commit a loyal Communist and get away with it. They backed off when he reached for the phone and asked if they wanted him to call another ambulance.

Two months later Arct escaped from the hospital and returned to school as if nothing had happened. He redoubled his attendance at lectures and party cell meetings and started bossing people around again. He was persuaded to resume his treatment only when a doctor from the hospital begged him to return on the ground that he was badly needed there as an organizer. Even while inside, Arct had engaged in political and social work and founded a patients' football team.

Discharged as cured and 'normal' a year later, he resumed his studies. Such was the clout conferred by party membership that even a person as obviously deranged as Arct – especially one who owed his hospitalization to excessive ideological zeal – could expect to be readmitted to the school without question. He continued to attend cell meetings, though he no longer chaired them. He soon started throwing his weight around, too, and showing renewed signs of mental imbalance.

Although the Polish thaw of 1956-57 had yet to come, conditions gradually eased following the Khrushchev disclosures. This process was heralded by a more liberal tone in the press, which even printed some covertly anti-Soviet editorials. Censorship was relaxed, and party hard-liners began to lose their grip. Before long the whole country was in a ferment. At the film school, students were quick to react, burning their party cards and ransacking the filing cabinets where confidential character assessments were kept. No one made a move to stop us, so we read them aloud. To our vast amusement, we learned that the film director Andrzej Munk, when a student, had been classified as 'potentially dangerous,' guilty of 'cosmopolitan tendencies,' and 'a gastronome.' The *personalny* in charge of these records was downgraded to canteen manager, a job he performed with the success and enthusiasm of one who has found his vocation at last. He even took to raising pigs in the school grounds.

Arct and Czarnecki made a perfect adjustment to the new situation. When we eventually got hold of the text of Nikita Khrushchev's famous speech denouncing Stalin's crimes, it was Arct who read it out to the assembled school, and when students and factory workers held a mass meeting at a Lodz football stadium to determine future policy, one of the principal speakers was none other than Czarnecki, our resident informer and party spy.

I couldn't help myself. As soon as Czarnecki sat down, I ran to the microphone and presented a thumbnail sketch of the orator the crowd had just been applauding. I told them what he really was. The moral, I said, was that those who had bossed and ill-treated us in the bad old days were trimming their sails to the wind of change.

126

Though quite extempore, it was a fluent little speech. By the time I finished my several thousand listeners were seething with fury. Czarnecki escaped a lynching only because the rally's organizers smuggled him out of the stadium. The next day a delegation of workers and students was appointed to go to Warsaw and lobby the new Party Secretary, Wladislaw Gomulka. On the strength of my speech, I was chosen to represent the school.

We never did get to see Gomulka. After hanging around the Central Committee building for hours, we were addressed by a senior member of the Politburo. 'Never fear, comrades,' he assured us, 'we'll do what needs to be done.' I relayed this assurance to my fellow students, but that was my first and last direct involvement in politics. The whole episode left a bad taste in my mouth. I realized how easy it was, under the existing system, for opportunists to parlay public disorder into the beginnings of a political career.

As for Arct, his troubles were only just beginning. He now looked upon me as an ally and wanted, in his deranged way, to help champion the cause of liberalism. He burst into the rector's office. 'You're an oaf, a weakling,' he told Ozogowski. 'You couldn't run a barnyard. Look at Polanski. *There's* an organizer for you! *He* ought to be in charge here.' Ozogowski had him committed again.

A week or two later he sent for me. 'Poor Arct seems fond of you,' he said. 'He's in the hospital and asking to see you.' I was just on the way out but he added, 'Oh, yes, and he wonders if you'd mind bringing him some sausage.'

I paid Arct a visit. He looked a mess – black eye, swollen lips. Some fellow patients had roughed him up for trying to wrench a crucifix off the wall. He was quite demented. 'There are two kinds of people in here,' he whispered hoarsely, 'Communists and Catholics, but the Communists are just Catholics in disguise.' He wolfed the sausage I'd brought him with ravenous appreciation.

Gomulka's first few months in power gave promise of better times ahead. Apart from increasing the flow of foreign films,

127

books, and plays, they brought a greater measure of personal freedom. For the first time Poles with relatives abroad could apply for passports to visit them. I had been corresponding since the war with my sister, Annette, who was now married and living in Paris, so I got her to vouch for me. This was the first step on the long road toward obtaining a passport.

It was many months before the authorities issued me one of these coveted documents. I carried it around everywhere, taking it out from time to time and reverently turning it over in my hands like some precious jewel. Even the vile-smelling glue under the cloth cover seemed redolent of freedom and adventure. Possession of a passport entitled me to buy all of ten U.S. dollars for expenditure abroad. It also enabled me to buy an air ticket to Paris, but a canny friend advised me to spend the extra zlotys that would cover a flight to Nice as well, just in case I was able to catch a glimpse of my Mecca, the Cannes Film Festival.

I threw a little party before I left. In the small hours, aware that my friends were watching me curiously, I tossed a few clothes into a suitcase. Snapping it shut, I picked it up and headed for the door. 'See you around,' I said. 'Me, I'm off to Paris.'

ELEVEN

The Paris I knew was the Paris of Marcel Carné, André Cayette, and Jacques Becker, but particularly of Jean-Paul Le Chanois' *Sans Laisser d'Adresse*, the film that had so enchanted Tyszler and me at art school. To the aristocrats and intellectuals of Krakow, as well as to film school students and all young Poles of my age and outlook, Paris was the hub of the civilized world.

Wonderment overcame me as I stood in the arrivals hall at Le Bourget, watching the baggage handlers unload my cheap suitcase. To one who came from a country where anyone sporting a tie and a clean shirt was assumed to belong to the ruling bureaucracy, they looked exceedingly well dressed. My sense of wonderment increased aboard the airport bus that whisked me from Le Bourget to the Invalides terminal, through brightly lit streets that seemed to be paved with gold. At Les Invalides I extravagantly took a taxi. As I rounded the Place de la Concorde, its fountains and illuminations had all the magic, all the ethereal beauty, of the Christmas tree sparklers of my childhood.

Annette and her husband had been waiting for me to make this trip for almost a year, but my love of the dramatic dictated a surprise entrance. When I finally knocked on the yellow door of their second-floor walk-up at 100 Rue de Charonne, unheralded, unexpected, and long past their bedtime, I caused a predictable and gratifying sensation. To Annette, her husband, Marian, and their daughter, Evelyne, I must have seemed as exotic as any creature from outer space. Although we'd corresponded and exchanged snapshots, I wouldn't have recognized Annette if I'd passed her on the street. After a couple of hours' family chitchat, I camped on a pullout bed in the living room of the tiny apartment.

On my first ecstatic morning in Paris, with a pounding heart and a plan of the city in my pocket, I made the long trek on foot from the Rue de Charonne to St-Germain-des-Prés, where most of *Sans Laisser d'Adresse* had been set. For all my movie-gleaned impressions of Paris, the sights and sounds of the place itself were a revelation. I had come straight from one of the drabbest of the Soviet satellites, where well-stocked shops and elaborate window displays were a distant memory. Even the Rue de Charonne, in what was by Parisian standards a shabby working-class district, seemed infinitely prosperous – so abounding in riches as to be scarcely credible. What seemed most surprising of all, to one whose visual memories were almost exclusively of postwar Poland, was the infinite variety of the goods on sale, their wide range of shapes and colors. Shops sold not just one brand of any particular item, as in Poland, but an indescribable profusion of makes and designs. Already predisposed in favor of the West, I marveled at it all.

Although I had very little money to spend, Paris was my oyster. I explored a different part of the city each day, methodically working my way through its museums and art galleries. Annette and Marian took me to one or two good plays and some of the cheaper Pigalle night spots. They also gave me the wherewithal to buy Métro tickets and plug the gaps in my film education.

I haunted the Paris Cinémathèque to see all those films which had failed to reach Poland, absorbing so many in such a short time that I felt my spell in Paris should really count as a credit in my film school index. I was especially fascinated by two actors who had yet to be seen on Polish screens: James Dean and Marlon Brando. What they accomplished was what I instinctively wanted and strove for in a performance – naturalism or, rather, a form of mannerism so original that it made their characters seem real. In Poland all acting suffered from conventions bred by generations of traditionalism. Here was something completely new. Brando through cool casualness, Dean through sheer tension and neuroticism brought something completely new to the screen.

Although Annette's husband wasn't an Orthodox Jew, I underwent another brief immersion in the kind of close-knit Jewish family atmosphere I'd last known when lodging in Krakow with the Horowitzes. Annette and Marian took me to delicatessens, where I ate kosher food for the first time in ages, but most of the time I went off prospecting on my own. I haunted the discotheques in St-Germain-des-Prés, kept an eye on the Sorbonne posters advertising student dances, starting going to them and staying out till all hours.

I also met Gesa. She was taking notes in front of a Matisse in the Musée de l'Art Moderne. God knows how I screwed up the courage to accost her in my halting French, but I asked her if she was an art student. One thing led to another, and I ended by going out together.

Gesa, a very pretty blonde of around seventeen, was a German girl visiting Paris with a party from a Hamburg architectural college. Ours was one of those lightning affairs that blossom best between two strangers who meet abroad and never get a chance to discover their points of difference. Aside from a common interest in art, our only real bond was Paris itself, and I suspect that much of our mutual infatuation may have been based on linguistic misunderstandings.

Paris is a city made for walking, and on one of our late-night strolls, after gate-crashing a student dance at the Beaux-Arts, I showed Gesa around Les Halles. This particular quarter of Paris used to have a night life all its own. Only a few minutes' walk from the Louvre, its narrow streets were carpeted with cabbage leaves and vegetable refuse of every description. Its stalls and shops and warehouses, all deceptively small and cramped in appearance, were a staging post for most of the food consumed in Paris and the north of France. Any driver who lost his way and landed up in Les Halles could count himself lucky if he took less than a couple of hours to extricate himself from a mass of trucks unloading anything from sides of beef to lobsters and rounds of Gruyère.

The cafés, bars, and restaurants of Les Halles got into their stride late at night and kept going till breakfast time, when some of the smaller establishments closed. Restaurants bursting at the seams, traders and middlemen vociferously haggling, porters bustling to and fro – all these items of local color made Les Halles a favorite haunt of wealthy Parisians painting the town. They would round off the night there at dawn, spooning up onion soup and rubbing shoulders with some of the roughest, toughest, hardest-drinking characters in the French capital.

But Les Halles was more than a food market. It had been a prostitutes' stamping ground ever since medieval times, and there they paraded all night long – hundreds of them in every conceivable permutation of age, shape, size, race, and hue. Les Halles was amply equipped to satisfy two forms of hunger, gastric and sexual.

I asked Gesa if she'd care to spend the night with me. The answer was yes, but that left another hurdle to be cleared. None of the sleazy Les Halles hotels would accommodate a pair of genuine lovers; theirs was strictly a short-time operation.

We headed east. Somewhere just past the Boulevard de Sebastopol, I found a slightly more respectable establishment. I paid in advance and was given a key, led Gesa upstairs with my arm around her waist, unlocked the door, and switched the light on. Then I switched it off again, fast. The room was so squalid I couldn't bear to look.

Just then Gesa whispered, 'It's my first time.' She must have sensed my surprise because she took me gently by the hand and led me over to the bed.

We became even more inseparable after that. Paris in the spring is as kind to lovers as every sentimental ballad claims, and we roamed it hand in hand until at last, like all good things, our springtime idyll came to an end.

I received a polite but firmly worded communication from

132

the new dean of the directors' faculty at the Lodz Film School, Jerzy Bossak. Its gist: unless I returned without delay, I would be expelled.

Gesa's vacation was also drawing to a close, and I was determined to spend at least one night with her in less sordid surroundings. I stretched my financial resources to the limit by taking a room at a second-class Left Bank establishment proudly calling itself the Grand Hôtel de Lima. There, in a room with turquoise walls, azure curtains, and a yellow bedspread, we made love till the sky began to pale.

We crept out of the hotel very early that morning. Gesa's coach was leaving at seven-thirty. She sneaked into the student hostel where she was supposed to be staying, emerged with a suitcase, and joined her sniggering class-mates aboard the waiting coach. We didn't speak. I felt bereft when she waved and the coach pulled out. We'd promised to write and see each other again, somewhere, sometime, but the prospect seemed pretty remote.

That set the seal on my Paris interlude. Only one thing remained to be done before I returned to Poland: I simply had to drop in at the Cannes Film Festival, if only to be able to brag that I'd been there.

Andrzej Wajda's second film, *Kanal*, was being shown that year, so he was there with the Polish delegation. I asked the conductor on the airport bus from Nice where the festival offices were. At the Croisette, he told me, gesturing vaguely. I picked up my cheap suitcase and got out, looking less like an aspiring filmmaker than a penniless immigrant. Cannes hit me right between the eyes – palm trees swaying in the sea breeze; flags of all nations fluttering from the Palais du Festival; giant billboards proclaiming the films on offer. I found my way to the information bureau and learned that the Poles were staying at the Hôtel Martinez. I hadn't known where the Croisette was, let alone the Martinez. When I finally located the hotel, I toyed with the idea of strolling around the lobby till I happened to catch sight of Wajda, then faking a chance encounter – 'Hello, you here, too?' – but time was too short. I called his room from the reception desk. 'Andrzej,' I said, 'what's cooking?' There was a pause.

'Who is this?'

'What do you mean, who is this?' I said. 'It's me, Romek.' That worked just as well.

Wajda gave me lunch and took me to the festival showing of Ingmar Bergman's *The Seventh Seal*. Underacted, with sober camerawork and almost deadpan dialogue, it had levels of complication which I didn't fully understand – at least not at that first screening. Bergman seemed to follow the principle that anything too easy to grasp is flat and boring. His remarkable talent was that he could leave his audience with the feeling that if they hadn't fully grasped the complications, it was their fault. Whatever one didn't understand, one gave Bergman credit for.

There was one last cinematic treat in store for me. While waiting for a bus to the airport, I realized that only a taxi would get me there in time to catch my plane. Also waiting for the bus that never came was an elderly Frenchman with a mane of white hair, accompanied by a younger woman. We agreed to share a cab. He introduced himself with French formality. 'Abel Gance,' he said. 'And this is my assistant, Nelly Kaplan.'

I'd thought that Gance was dead. Did he realize that at the film school we knew his work by heart, along with that of René Clair and Jean Vigo, that he figured in our history of film course as one of the greatest innovators of all time? I was too shy to tell him so. Instead, I introduced myself with equal formality: 'Polanski, student, Lodz Film School.' We barely exchanged another word before splitting the fare and going our separate ways.

Back in Lodz I was the student-fresh-from-Paris. My sartorial splendor – drip-dry shirts and a pair of drastically pointed black shoes – proved it. Everyone was eager to hear about the cars, the girls, and the films, in that order. I inflicted endless impersonations of James Dean and Marlon Brando upon my friends and acted out the movies I'd seen. For nights on end, I was the star attraction.

My friends were not alone in wanting to hear about Paris. I was visited by a UB plainclothesman who demanded details of my time abroad. Had anyone urged me to stay on in Paris? Had I been contacted by the editors of the expatriate periodical *Kultura?* I hadn't, as it happened, but I made a mental note to get in touch with them as soon as I got another chance of going to Paris. They sounded like my kind of people.

My closest friends at the film school now were two student cameramen, Andrzej Kostenko, reinstated after his year's rustication, and Andrzej Kondratiuk, a good-looking youngster with curly hair and wild blue eyes, whose ultimate ambition was to direct. Another regular member was Michal Zolnierkiewicz, a tall, gangling architect and one of the ugliest men I've ever seen, with a huge nose, no chin, a Panlike beard, and a nervous, asthmatic titter. Improbably enough, he was forever surrounded by pretty girls and kept us all in hysterics with tales of his unlikely sexual escapades. Yet another indefatigable raconteur was Jerzy Kosinski, a social science graduate with jet black hair and a passionate interest in photography. Finally, there was Wojtek Frykowski, whom I first ran across at one of the student dances of which I was a zealous organizer. Because he was a notorious troublemaker and hadn't been invited, I wouldn't let him in. We nearly came to blows, but the next time we met, at a bar in town, he thrust a glass of vodka into my hand. It was the prelude to a long friendship.

Wojtek, with his broken nose and slightly crooked mouth, had the macho looks of a nightclub bouncer. He was one of the few members of our set with a car of his own and money to splash around. His father, one of the last small textile printers in town, was always crossing swords with the authorities but had contrived to remain in business. Although he had a degree in chemistry and was an Olympic class swimmer, Wojtek preferred the company of 'hooligans' and film school students. Beneath his tough exterior, however, Wojtek was good-natured, softhearted to the point of sentimentality, and utterly loyal.

135

Another, rather different member of our circle was Kuba Goldberg, a graduate of the film school who had cut quite a dash there despite ducking every filmmaking test throughout his five-year course. A witty, snappily dressed elf of a man with prematurely wrinkled features, Goldberg emitted quite an aura for one reason only: having attracted the attention of Andrzej Munk he had been appointed his personal assistant.

Munk, an early graduate of the school, was not only the most talented director then working in Poland but one of the most endearing, amusing, and charismatic figures in the Polish film industry. He had first made his mark as a documentary director, and an early film of his about pit ponies retired from the mines and discovering the joys of nature – frisking timidly, half-blind, like puppies on their first excursion from the maternal dog basket – was one of the most moving documentaries I'd seen. Poland had two independent filmmaking centers, Lodz for fiction and Warsaw for documentaries. At this time, though soon to start making fiction films, Munk was based in Warsaw and came to Lodz only to teach. Extremely convivial and great fun to be with, he enjoyed the company of his juniors, and a few of us were privileged to become his friends; I often stayed with him and his wife when visiting Warsaw. In spite of his ultraconservative appearance – heavy horn-rims and a civil servant's taste in gray suits – Munk was a born swinger. We reveled in his sense of humor, his cosmopolitanism, and his outstanding talent.

Back at Lodz, however, where he ran the documentary course, the teacher took precedence over the friend and boon companion. When, he asked, was I going to show him the documentary all students had to complete in their third year? I submitted several outlines, but he rejected them all on the ground that they were more fictional than documentary. At last I suggested organizing a school dance and making it the subject of my documentary exercise. Munk pronounced this a pretty uninspired idea but told me to go ahead.

The film I had in mind was a practical joke on the grand scale – one which, even by local standards, was bound to cause a stir. Practical jokes were part of the school tradition, as Munk well knew. While studying there, he himself had been an acknowledged master of the art. It was Munk, together with his buddies Kuba Morgenstern and Wadim Berestowski, who had carried the hazing of candidates to new and unprecedented lengths. Every year, when a fresh batch arrived, they took over a classroom and converted it into a doctor's consulting room. Complete with girl students disguised as white-clad nurses and props such as stethoscopes, a weighing machine, and surgical gloves, Munk solemnly examined the applicants one by one, irrespective of sex. He made them strip, touch their toes, and answer a variety of embarrassing questions about their sex lives.

I had done my modest best to perpetuate the Munk tradition. I would slip combs or condoms into bowls of stew in the school canteen, then wait to savor the moment when my victims discovered these weird and incongruous objects in their lunch. I fixed pretty female freshmen with a catatonic stare as they ate, keeping it up until embarrassment made them push their food away and leave the table – whereupon Kostenko added insult to injury by gobbling up the remains. I once inserted a carp in one of the developing tanks – they were, of course, situated in the laboratory darkroom – and the whole school rang to shrill screams of terror from an unwitting girl student. That little caper triggered a full-scale investigation.

I had also staged more elaborate set pieces. On one occasion, I faked a violent row with Majewski. Seemingly oblivious of our surroundings, we pursued our shouting match along the corridor, down the stairs, and into the office of the rector's hunch-backed secretary, Nina. A bunch of fellow conspirators tried to keep us apart – or pretended to – but the drama ran its course. While Kostenko went down on his knees, begging him not to do it, Majewski pulled out a pistol and shot me. I slumped to the floor, oozing stage blood. Nina fainted.

My most complicated hoax enjoyed the cooperation of the rector himself and a student interpreter. The school received a steady stream of distinguished visitors, mostly foreign scholars whose lectures tended to be excruciatingly boring. I spent hours making myself up as Professor Auguste Picard, the celebrated but eccentric undersea explorer. His visit had been announced, and the rector's car met me at the station. I had prepared a lengthy address in fractured French, relating the denizens of the deep to the art of cinema, the bathyscaph's observation window to the camera lens, and our interpreter even had a Polish translation ready. Someone blew the whistle, however, and I regretfully had to cancel my 'visit' at the very last moment.

The documentary exercise I was now planning aimed to use one such elaborate practical joke for purposes of *cinéma vérité*. At this period 'hooliganism' was rife throughout Poland. Bored with their lives and denied anything worthwhile to do in their spare time, young people lurked in alleyways and side streets, preying on passersby for no logical reason: hitting them if they stepped on a chalk line; snipping off their ties; harassing and bullying them just for kicks. Lodz had a number of such gangs, many of whose members I knew. One of their favorite pastimes was to find out where parties or dances were being held, then gate-crash and break them up. My film was designed to capture a rumpus in progress.

I duly organized an open-air dance on the school grounds. My fellow students thought I was going to film them having a good time; only the camera crew knew different. Contacting a well-known gang of 'hooligans,' I invited them to arrive halfway through and do their stuff. They were to mingle unobtrusively at first and only make their presence felt by degrees.

Some of the buildup effect was spoiled by overeagerness on their part. No sooner were they over the wall than they started throwing punches, wrenching girls away from their partners, pushing students into the pond. My single camera crew struggled to shoot as much of this concentrated action as they could, barely managing to get enough footage before the dance turned into a shambles. I called my test piece *Breaking Up the Party*.

It wasn't the teachers so much as the students who were furious with me afterward; indeed, I thought I detected a faintly humorous undertone in the reprimand I got from Dean Bossak. Munk, who was hardly entitled to take a stern line, insisted that my film constituted a genuine documentary exercise as well as a joke in poor taste. The disciplinary committee, which had considered expelling me, let me off with a warning.

I was always on the lookout for any chance to make extra-curricular films. Maciek Kijowski, a student in the cameramen's faculty, had to shoot some film for exercise purposes, so I persuaded him to use his allotment of stock on a fully structured short and let me direct it, as I had with Todoroff in my first year.

I already had some very definite ideas about shorts. I'd seen enough of my fellow students' work to know that the main pitfall in composing a short was to make it look like an excerpt from a full-length film. Cartoons and documentaries proved that even very short films could tell a convincing story with a beginning and an end, but to do the same with actors required a different approach. Sounds had to be used as punctuation, dialogue kept to a minimum or dispensed with altogether. As far as I was concerned, a realistic theme was out. Though hung up on surrealism, I also wanted to convey a message. The short I aspired to make would have to be poetic and allegorical yet readily comprehensible.

All these conclusions were the product of instinct, not conscious deliberation, and my primary mental image was equally irrational: two men emerging from the sea with a grand piano. It was ludicrous, absurd, and quite in keeping with our zany practical jokes. Aside from carrying a piano around, the two men don't do anything exceptional. They try to enter a restaurant, take a streetcar, check in at a hotel. They are ridiculous, innocuous creatures, but their strange burden earns them rejection and persecution wherever they go. The grand piano idea may have stemmed from my boyhood games with Winowski. The only problem, I decided, was that a piano might encourage the wrong kind of symbolic inference; it might suggest that the men's rejection was that of artists by philistines, whereas I wanted it to be general. In the end, I settled for an old-fashioned mirror-fronted wardrobe like those found in third-rate hotel rooms the world over.

Aware that there was to be a competition for experimental shorts at the 1958 Brussels World's Fair in a few months' time, I went to see Stanislaw Wohl, the dean of the cameramen's faculty, and boldly announced that I wanted to direct a prize-winning entry. The trouble was, my project called for a seaside location and would thus be unusually expensive for a student short. I submitted my shooting script of *Two Men and a Wardrobe*, complete with a storyboard illustrating every shot. As soon as he'd read it, Wohl instructed the production office to allocate the necessary funds.

Sopot, our choice of location, was an 'in' resort near Gdansk. Shooting there was like making a film at St-Tropez in midsummer, and I and Andrzej Kostenko, whom I'd enlisted as my assistant, were thrilled to be the center of attention in such surroundings. The place was crowded with vacationers – so crowded that filming on the streets soon ceased to be a thrill and became a nightmare. What started out as a ten-day schedule dragged on for three weeks.

Being wholly in favor of typecasting and thoroughly averse to using professional actors, I'd recruited two principals who supplied the absurd physical contrast I needed: little Kuba Goldberg, with his wizened face, and a fourth-year student named Henryk Kluba, who was prematurely bald.

Most of our crew squeezed into the same small rented apartment and set to work with a will. At first, the atmosphere hummed with enthusiasm. Little by little, however, my principals got sick of toting a wardrobe around. Both had other commitments and were eager to get away. Henryk complained that the beard I'd made him grow had earned him insults while commuting by train to see his girlfriend in

Gdansk – some fellow passengers had called him a dirty Jew – and that it was blighting his love life. Little Kuba pranced around, egging him on, daring him to get rid of the loathsome appendage. 'All right,' Henryk said, '*you* do it for me.' Unimpressed by this charade, I watched while Kuba – who happened to be shaving himself at the time – transferred some lather to Henryk's face. Then, to my horror, he actually shaved a couple of inches off one cheek. I shook him till his teeth rattled and swore I'd strangle him if he tried it again. As it was, we had to shoot Henryk from one side only for several days to come.

Although we were falling behind schedule, there was no hope of extracting additional funds from the school. We managed to hang on to our camera car, but I had to start paying for our meals out of my own pocket.

When it was all over, I took the product of our labors back to Lodz and started editing. I already had my sights set on someone capable of providing *Two Men and a Wardrobe* with the right musical backing – something cool and offbeat enough to underline the absurdity of my characters' predicament – but was wary of asking him to work on something as insignificant as a student's apprentice piece.

Jazz had become respectable as the thaw progressed, and young Poles everywhere were flocking to concerts and festivals. One of the biggest box-office draws was a group headed by Christopher Komeda. Originally a doctor of medicine, Komeda had developed into Poland's leading jazz pianist and composer. Aware that he hadn't yet worked on a film and hoping that the prospect might appeal to him, I got in touch. He turned up accompanied by his wife, Zofia, who did most of the talking. Komeda himself, red-haired, bespectacled, and afflicted with a slight limp – a legacy of polio in childhood – just sat there and listened. He seemed almost standoffish at first, as cool as his music. When I got to know him better, I realized that his reserve was a symptom of profound shyness, a veneer that masked the gentleness and high intelligence of the man beneath.

I ran the rough cut and waited apprehensively for

141

Komeda's verdict. His wife spoke first, as before, but there was no doubting his enthusiasm. Having seen the film, even in an unfinished state, he liked it sufficiently to write the catchy, lilting accompaniment that contributed so much to its atmosphere.

Then I showed the finished product to Wohl and Bossak. They helped me enter it for Brussels without even getting clearance from the Ministry of Culture – some measure of the relaxation that had set in since the thaw began. I took the cans to Warsaw and airfreighted them to Belgium.

I was listening to the radio when the news came through. The gold medal had gone to an animation film made by two Polish graphic artists. The bronze medal, said the announcer, 'has been awarded to R Polanski, a student at Lodz Film School.'

My medal from Brussels caused quite a stir in Lodz, and *Two Men and a Wardrobe* became the first school short to be commercially released in Poland. Invited to Brussels to receive my award, I traveled there under Ministry of Culture auspices – quite a change from my first trip abroad – and took the opportunity to pay a brief second visit to Paris, where Annette and Marian welcomed me like a conquering hero.

Things were looking up for me in all sorts of ways. I acquired a brand-new status symbol – a Peugeot motor-scooter purchased 'black' from someone who'd bought one after waiting months for the indispensable government voucher, then resold it to me at a premium. On the professional front, partly because I was considered a bright young prospect and partly because of my improving knowledge of French, I landed a coveted assignment.

Claude Guillemot, a budding director from France, had been invited to Lodz as an exchange student, and the school appointed me his assistant. This gave me a firsthand insight into the French approach to filmmaking and developed my taste for all things Gallic, including the records of Georges Brassens, which were very popular with my French associate.

Guillemot was staying at the Grand Hotel, of course, and

142

one day, while sitting in the lobby with him and Kuba Morgenstern, who was also staying there on an assignment, I saw a girl walk over to the reception desk and pick up her key. She was spectacularly beautiful, with huge eyes and a ripe, sensual mouth. Her figure, shown off to perfection by a simply cut dress with horizontal stripes, was just as spectacular.

'Who's that?' I asked Morgenstern.

A girl from a film in production called *Eva Wants to Sleep*, he said – Barbara something-or-other. Apparently she'd gotten the part after entering her photo for a competition in a movie magazine.

My avid interest wasn't lost on Morgenstern because he took pity on me and introduced us a few days later. The girl's name was Barbara Kwiatkowska.

TWELVE

There had already been a number of girls in my life. I was seeing less and less of Kika. I was still writing to Gesa, but our chances of actually meeting again were slim. Lodz itself had pretty girls by the score – aspiring actresses, ballet and film school students – and having my own pad in town gave me plenty of scope for entertaining and getting to know them.

But Barbara, or Basia, as her friends called her, wasn't the type of girl to embark on a casual affair. Although she had trained at one of the state-run schools that turned out dancers and musicians for folk ensembles, she came of peasant stock. Despite her glorious looks, she was strangely insecure and gauche in manner, with a rustic habit of clapping a hand over her mouth when she laughed – almost as if aghast at her own temerity in laughing at all. Shy and reserved for an eighteen-year-old of such outstanding beauty, she didn't at first regard me as a serious candidate for her affections. She liked me well enough to go around with me on a platonic basis, but that was as far as it went.

My designs on Barbara weren't exactly furthered when the school picked me for another plum assignment, this time as assistant to Jean-Marie Drot, a well-known French TV director. Drot was visiting Poland with a camera crew to make a series on our country's cultural and artistic heritage, a task for which he was eminently well equipped. His knowledge of art was encyclopedic, and working with him was an education in itself, not only culturally and intellectually but socially, for Drot was a *bon vivant* with a taste for all that life had to offer in the way of wine, women and good conversation. Yet enjoyable as it was to tour the country with him for weeks at a time, I pined for Barbara. We corresponded regularly, but letters were a poor substitute for Barbara herself.

Whenever I did manage a trip to Lodz, we spent time together in cafés or at my place, drinking wine and listening to Georges Brassens records inherited from Claude Guillemot. Barbara held a special fascination for the opposite sex; everyone ran after her. Perhaps because we weren't yet involved with each other, I was one of the few people she confided in. She told me she was having an affair with a prominent filmmaker – a married man – and that it was unlikely to come to anything. Just because I was her confidant, however, there was no certainty I'd ever become her lover.

One night she phoned me from her hotel in an emotional state – something to do with her affair, I gathered. I said I'd come at once. She was in tears when I got there, so I did my best to console her – gave her a hug and told her to cheer up. Thinking a change of scene might help, I installed her on the pillion of my Peugeot motorscooter and took her to my place. As we talked, far into the night, I detected a spark of feeling in her manner toward me. At long last, I diffidently suggested going to bed together.

She refused. Having expected little else, I was careful not to seem put out or do anything that might prejudice a subsequent change of mind. I offered to drive her back. The night was crisp and fine, with a canopy of stars overhead, so we decided to walk. At some stage we paused to talk. She must have seen the stark frustration in my eyes because she suddenly said, 'Let's go back.' Once in my room she stripped and got into bed – just like that.

Barbara was one of the most beautiful girls I'd ever seen. She had dark blond hair, almost brown. She had an almond-shaped face, great, long eyelashes, a tiny, upturned nose, and a slender, muscular body. We made love again and again, but I was aware, even so, of a kind of reticence in her. Although she was sensual, her sensuality fought a losing battle with something else in her nature. Barbara never gave herself completely in the act of love – and certainly not to me on our first night together.

I still recall the pang I felt when she slipped out of bed that dawn and stood looking down into the street, naked. I'd never seen such utter perfection before, but my pride at having possessed it was alloyed with the realization that I might never again experience the same passionate intensity, that I might, if only through sad force of habit, begin to take her for granted. Throughout our relationship I strove to encourage her in the belief that sex could be a source of joy. Looking back, though, I suspect I always got more out of it than she did.

Retrospection is one thing, actuality another. Feasting my eyes on Barbara's flawless back as she stood at the window that morning, I felt on top of the world. She had an early call, so I drove her to the studio on my scooter. I did so with characteristic panache, and elation made me even more reckless than usual. Halfway there, not having felt her arms around my waist for a while, I glanced over my shoulder. She wasn't there. Somewhere along the way, in the course of one of my more hazardous maneuvers, I'd lost her.

She was waiting on the sidewalk, unhurt and wearing her wonderfully childlike, innocent village maiden's smile. The next day she called me again. I picked her up and took her back to my room. A few days later she moved in with me. Being a couple – Romek and Basia – was a marvelous feeling. Our relationship didn't impair my work. On the contrary, it gave me a new equilibrium, a fresh impetus – just what I needed when I came to draw up my plans for my diploma film.

My subject was one of those outwardly dull and uneventful lives that never make the average person think twice. The idea stemmed from a short story in a newspaper about an elderly attendant in a public lavatory who has a mystical vision. To me, a lavatory attendant's life seemed to epitomize vacuity, drudgery, monotony. Nobody would ever look at an old crone in a public lavatory, with her pathetic saucerful of coins and her vacant, impersonal air, and conceive of her having had a life imbued with passion and drama.

Such was the genesis of *When Angels Fall*. I wanted the film to convey an impression of breadth despite its twenty-odd minutes' duration. Above all, I wanted it to be romantic almost baroque in style – a film readily interpretable by its audience as the daydream of an old woman nearing the end of her life. Old people fascinated me. I'd always felt that the old were even more deserving of care and attention than the young. They were so helpless, so resigned, so ignorant of life despite their accumulated experience and proximity to death.

In need of an elaborate Art Deco set, I approached a Krakow Academy student, Kazimierz Wisniak, whose work I knew and admired. Together we designed the public lavatory for *When Angels Fall*, molded its *fin de siècle* ceramic urinals in plaster, and assembled it on the school's sound stage. Modeled on a lavatory in one of Krakow's historic squares, it had a roof of frosted glass tiles, set flush with the sidewalk, through which those inside could glimpse the tide of humanity flowing overhead, the shadows of anonymous feet coming and going.

When Angels Fall was a portrait gallery of friends. Acting ability still mattered less to me than physical appearance, so I chose nonprofessionals as opposed to mannered actors schooled in the academic Polish theatrical tradition. Andrzej Kondratiuk played the old woman's soldier son, Andrzej Kostenko, a homosexual looking for a pickup; Kuba Goldberg, the electrician who comes to read the meter. Barbara was the old woman in her youth.

For my principal character, I used an inmate of a home for the destitute. She was over eighty, and her face had just the right blend of senile resignation, apathy, and residual good looks. Her expression was gentle and absolutely vacant. She accepted my offer without fully understanding what her role entailed. On the set she was undemanding, passive, unaware of what she was doing there. I extracted a performance from

147

her by purely technical means. There was only one snag: her jaw shook continuously. Though useful in some scenes, this tremor became obtrusive in others. I discovered that she lost it at once when given candy to suck, so from then on we fed her candy nonstop. 'What'll you do with the money?' I asked her when shooting ended. Buy some sugar, she said – the institution always kept them short of it, so she'd buy some of her own. Nothing else? She pondered the question for a long time, and her jaw started trembling again.

'No,' she said eventually, 'just some sugar.'

Not for the first or last time, I overran my schedule. We had to do a certain amount of shooting on location – street scenes in Krakow and a battlefield sequence near Lodz. When we came to shoot the latter, I recalled Lipman's creative pyrotechnics in *A Generation* and tried to emulate them. Like him, I almost brained myself with flying debris. Postproduction work took forever, partly because I'd used black and white for the narrative sequences and color for the old woman's visions of the past. The music, of course, was written by Komeda.

I showed *When Angels Fall* to the school board, which gave it a mixed reception. The members liked it, but not as much as *Two Men and a Wardrobe*. This set a pattern for the future: critics have always preferred my penultimate film to my latest. Although *When Angels Fall* was accepted as a diploma film, it didn't earn me a graduation certificate. To complete the course, students had to write a thesis. This I never did. I volunteered to write something practical – a comparative glossary of cinematic terms in Polish and French – but the school authorities declined to accept such a theme. What they wanted was the sort of thing most students turned out: a highbrow dissertation with some such title as 'Formalist Tendencies in Eisenstein's Work.' In later years, with varying degrees of malice, Polish film critics were to claim that I was merely a Lodz dropout.

Another reason for my failure to write a thesis was a sudden influx of work. Thanks to Jerzy Bossak, I was hired full-time by Kamera, one of the more prestigious 'autonomous production units' established after the 1956 thaw, largely in consequence of proposals drafted by Bossak himself, who was Kamera's artistic director as well as dean of the directors' faculty at Lodz. These new units stimulated film production because, although full financing still required authorization from the Ministry of Culture, they were free to develop projects, commission screenplays, and hire directors. Andrzej Munk, who was to direct a Kamera production entitled *Cross-Eyed Luck*, gave me an assistant director's job with special responsibility for crowd scenes.

Cross-Eyed Luck was a Polish satire that could never have been made during the Stalinist period. Too parochial to win the international acclaim it deserved, it recounted the trials and tribulations of a chronic unfortunate – a sort of latter-day Job condemned by fate to suffer under any regime to which Poland was subjected, whether prior to World War II, during the German occupation, or after the Communist takeover. Some of the comedy was visual slapstick, but most was caustic social and political comment.

The script had been built around the comic talents of Bobek Kobiela, who had since split up with Cybulski and quit the Bim-Bom Theater, but Munk was stuck for a really pretty girl to play the part of a sexy little bitch who seduces everyone in sight, including her private tutor. Though shy of suggesting Barbara, I finally did so. The success of her first film, *Eva Wants to Sleep*, had made her something of a star – a kind of Polish Brigitte Bardot.

'I know she's good-looking,' Munk said, 'but who's going to do her acting for her – you?'

'No,' I said. 'I could direct her, though.'

Eventually, after more fruitless auditioning, Munk not only hired Barbara but took me up on my facetious suggestion and told me to direct her scenes. I so much wanted her to give an outstanding performance I overdid it. I was scathing in my criticism and, not wanting to appear soft in public, made her repeat her lines again and again – so much so that Munk felt I was bullying her. He took over from me. When I found I couldn't watch without butting in, he threatened to

149

bar me from the set. He couldn't, in fact, have done so indefinitely because I had a brief acting role in the picture: I played a new tutor who, after the hero – Kobiela – has been fired, seduces the girl himself.

Because of all the work that was coming our way, Barbara and I were often separated for days or even weeks at a time. She was much in demand after *Eva Wants to Sleep*. As for me, aside from my duties as Munk's assistant, I was juggling half a dozen balls at once: playing minor film parts; writing for a movie magazine; working in a dubbing studio. We were still very much in love – I was, at least – but it didn't prevent me from having one-night stands when Barbara was away or I was on the road. I was attracted to other girls, and when I got the opportunity to do so, I slept with them. The frustration of remaining faithful at all times led, I still felt, to subconscious resentment. From my own point of view, these brief affairs didn't impair our relationship in the least.

Then came a welcome opportunity to spend some time together. *Eva Wants to Sleep* earned Barbara an invitation to the San Sebastián Film Festival. Since *Two Men and a Wardrobe* was also to be shown there, I wangled an invitation for myself.

Barbara went down big with some Spanish producers, who pressed her to sign a contract for several films. I balked at the idea. This was the zenith of the Franco era, and the political atmosphere was stifling. As I saw it, no worthwhile film could be made in such an environment. I was very much a youthful devotee of *l'art pour l'art* and quite indifferent to financial considerations. The very thought of making a film exclusively for money struck me as obscene.

Barbara, whose naïveté extended to politics, was disappointed by my veto. Although it irked her that Spanish policemen patrolled the beaches with tape measures, checking the dimensions of swimsuits and arresting bikini-clad girls, and that our unmarried state had raised eyebrows in San Sebastián, where we shared the same hotel room, she failed to understand my objections to her working in Spain. Privately she may have sensed that they were selfish as well as

150

artistic. One of my reasons for not wanting her to make movies in Spain was the prospect of being without her for weeks and months on end. I was self-centered enough to be hurt that she would even consider the idea.

We quarreled, though not for long, and I finally got my way. Barbara turned her Spanish offers down. Before heading for home, I took her to St-Jean-de-Luz and on to Paris for her very first holiday abroad. She was so happy just to be there, so utterly feminine in her reactions, so childishly delighted by all she saw, that my heart melted. I felt closer to her than ever before. Later on I realized that this summer excursion had been the apogee of our relationship.

Now that I was an established member of the Kamera group, I itched to make a full-length film of my own as soon as possible. I went to Bossak and sounded him out. He asked if I had a particular theme in mind. No, I told him, nothing concrete, except that I was determined to use the Mazury lake district as a setting. Mildly encouraged by his response, I went away and set to work on an outline.

My diploma film had been deliberately, theatrically baroque. I wanted my first feature film to be rigorously cerebral, precisely engineered, almost formalist. It started out as a straightforward thriller: a couple aboard a small yacht take on a passenger who disappears in mysterious circumstances. From the first, the story concerned the interplay of antagonistic personalities within a confined space. Though stagy, the notion of isolating three people from the world lost its theatricality when the setting was a sailboat.

I wrote a short treatment and submitted it to Bossak, who liked it enough to suggest my developing a full screenplay in collaboration with Kuba Goldberg. I signed my very first film contract with Kamera and we started work together. We didn't get very far. Kuba, who was on the lazy side, contributed little.

Then Jerzy Skolimowski appeared on the scene. Skolimowski, whom I'd met through Komeda, had started out as a jazz groupie, fixing the lights for Komeda's ensemble on tour. A university student, amateur boxer, and published poet, he was also a film school aspirant who happened to be visiting Lodz for the two-week entrance exam. At my suggestion he took a look at what Kuba and I had so far produced. Head and shoulders above his fellow candidates in talent and originality, Skolimowski faced the examiners during the day and burned the midnight oil in my room thereafter. Our duo became a trio, and the fee, which amounted to 24,000 zlotys, was eventually split three ways.

Skolimowski was a stimulating and inventive collaborator. He snatched every moment he could spare to help me develop the screenplay, toiling nonstop into the small hours while moths flew at us out of the hot summer night. His contribution to *Knife* was a major one. It was he who insisted that the action, originally spread over three or four days, should be compressed into twenty-four hours. Once Skolimowski joined us, Kuba's role became restricted mainly to typing, swatting moths, and fetching us cold drinks. After Skolimowski had left, I continued to hone the screenplay into shape on my own. Bossak and Jozef Krakowski, Kamera's administrative chief, were highly enthusiastic about the finished product and submitted it to the screenplay vetting board at the Ministry of Culture. My expectations were at a fever pitch – preproduction had actually started – when the board rejected it on the ground that it lacked social commitment.

As if to demonstrate that troubles never come singly, my relationship with Barbara turned sour. After attending the International Youth Festival in Vienna as an official guest, she returned from Austria but didn't rejoin me in Lodz, nor did she get in touch. I heard she was staying in Warsaw but couldn't find out where. Then a friend broke the news: Barbara was having an affair with Lech Zahorski, a well-known graphic artist. Apparently they'd met in Vienna.

Although it came as a shock, I was conscious that the fault lay with me. I hadn't been an easy partner. I was very much the Polish male chauvinist, selfish and domineering, and our relations had been strained by my persistent attempts to educate Barbara in the ways of the world, which must have become unbearable in the long run. I took the train to Warsaw and went looking for her. I didn't confide in anyone, not even Andrzej Munk, but he must have guessed what was wrong. To take my mind off things, he said, why not go see the movie showing next door to his apartment in Warsaw's old quarter? It was Orson Welles's *Othello*. I went but walked out within minutes, too preoccupied with my personal problems to take anything in. After sweating in a phone booth for an hour, calling everyone I could think of, I finally learned that Barbara would be catching a train to Lodz late that afternoon.

I went to the station and waited. Sure enough, Barbara turned up, escorted by a suave, elegant-looking man of mature years. They held hands and kissed tenderly as they said goodbye. Leaping aboard at the last moment, I made my way to her compartment. My abrupt appearance startled her, and a highly emotional scene ensued. I said I understood her reasons but found her conduct sly and furtive. She started crying.

Once in Lodz, I took her up to my room. We talked the situation over and spent the night together. I realized that she was genuinely torn between two people – infatuated with Zahorski but still attached to me. She went back to Warsaw for a few days, ostensibly because she 'had to be alone' then returned to Lodz and announced that Zahorski needed her. 'I'm his last love,' she told me dramatically.

After yet another spell in Warsaw, Barbara returned to Lodz to make a movie, and we drifted back together. She was so influenceable that whoever was around stood the best chance of exercising his will over her. Besides, we had been together for a full two years, and she was used to me. Desperate to keep her, by any means, including marriage, I proposed. She found this gesture so unexpected, so intriguing perhaps or even touching, that she said yes. We became man and wife in a short civil ceremony on September 9, 1959.

Wadim Berestowski, the veteran practical joker, now working as a director in Lodz, got together with our friends and organized a wedding-night party.

It was such a wild, drunken affair that all who were there still speak of it with awe. My buddies from the film school turned out in force, as did most of the people I'd worked with in films. Komeda and the rest of the jazz fraternity played till they dropped, and prodigious quantities of food and drink were consumed.

We started doing impromptu turns with whatever we could find in Berestowski's apartment. When someone unearthed a Hula-Hoop, I played ringmaster and made Jerzy Lipman jump through it. Someone else draped the hoop in toilet paper and set fire to it, greatly enhancing the act's dramatic effect.

It wasn't long before our revels attracted the attention of the police. Taking advantage of Barbara's star status, we sent her out on the landing to placate them. She not only succeeded but invited them in for a drink. 'Miss Basia,' they said, 'we'll be back. First, we have to deal with those assholes on the other floors who complained about the noise.'

We burlesqued grand opera, silent movies, bullfights. No Polish party is complete without a cabbage stew called *bigos*, and this began to feature prominently in our clowning – *bigos* as snow in a Polish movie, *bigos* as snow on the stairs with me skiing down them. We sent Kuba Goldberg to the moon: he crouched on one end of a makeshift seesaw – an ironing board – two of us landed heavily on the other, and tiny Kuba sailed into the air, to be miraculously caught by friends on his return to earth. Later he passed out. Gravely concerned about his premature wrinkles, we gave him a face pack of *bigos*. Other people started passing out, too, and we swathed them in toilet paper. They lay there like Egyptian mummies till someone set them ablaze, when they instantly sprang to life. By morning Berestowski's apartment was littered with bodies, prone and supine.

I did my best to forget about the inauspicious prelude to our marriage. Although Barbara had deceived me, I couldn't entirely blame her. There was a peculiarly passive streak in her nature – a refusal to face facts. I used to tell her she was

154

like the bankrupt who takes refuge from the bailiff in a closet and gets carted off with the rest of the furniture. Barbara tended to take the line of least resistance, but that, I realized, was part of her appeal.

We had been together for so long before actually getting married that our new status was no big deal; we just continued living in my room. Barbara was no housekeeper, didn't cook, and in any case we had no kitchen. But in various ways there *were* changes. Our friends, for one, started treating us differently. One couldn't help being moved by a wedding ceremony, even in the drabbest, most bureaucratic surroundings. And it was nice to introduce Barbara and be able to say, 'This is my wife.'

One day, after we'd been married several months, the front page of a Paris daily splashed a photograph of Barbara captioned 'Who is this beautiful stranger?' The accompanying story explained that a French film director, Robert Menegoz, had spotted the girl's photograph in a magazine feature on the Vienna International Youth Festival and was determined to 'discover' her for a role in his next film. Anyone able to supply information about her was invited to contact Ulysses Productions, a French film company.

Jean-Marie Drot sent me the clipping from Paris. As soon as I received it, I put a call through and was referred to the company's PR man, Yvon Samuel. 'I'm the husband of the person you're looking for,' I told him.

Although I'd suspected that the whole thing was an elaborate hoax, Samuel's questions were quite to the point.

'How good is her French?'

'*Elle parle rien*,' I replied, idiomatically but ungrammatically conveying that she didn't speak a word.

'Fine, fine,' he said. 'How soon can you come to Paris?'

Suppressing an urge to say we were as free as air, I said we might possibly make ourselves available in the next few weeks. Then came a call from Pierre Roustang, the producer. Barbara, he said, must be sure to bring lots of 'romantic' dresses with her.

'I don't speak French, and I don't have any romantic dresses,' Barbara protested.

'Then you'd better start learning and get some,' I told her. I'd embarked on a new career – that of Barbara's husband.

THIRTEEN

On Christmas Eve 1959 Barbara and I endured a wretchedly
bumpy flight to Paris – two young Polish innocents hoping to
make their mark in the world's most sophisticated capital.

We bounced around over Le Bourget in appalling weather
for an hour after the seat belt signs had gone on. I felt airsick
enough to want to die. In a rare display of tenderness and
concern, Barbara squeezed my hand till it hurt.

Still queasy, we found Pierre Roustang waiting for us at
the airport in his Citroën DS, accompanied by Yvon Samuel.
Attacked by motion sickness again on the drive into Paris, I
couldn't have imagined a less promising start to our venture.

Roustang took us to have drinks with Jean-Louis Trintignant, his male lead. Behind all the formal French *politesse* and
somewhat stilted words of welcome, I could sense that something was wrong. The truth dawned when Samuel drew me
aside.

'I thought you said she spoke French?'

'I didn't.'

'You did – you said, "*Elle parle bien.*" '

'I said, "*Elle parle rien.*" '

'Oh.'

I didn't discover until years later that they nearly called the
whole thing off then and there. Despite a crash course from
me, Barbara's current knowledge of French didn't run to
much more than *bonjour* and *merci beaucoup*.

Installed at last in the Hôtel Napoléon, near the Étoile,
where we were to stay for the duration of shooting, we
bounced experimentally up and down on the outsize bed,

157

played with the massive brass faucets in the marble bathroom, and marveled at the array of room service and valet buttons, the complimentary flowers and fruit. We weren't to know that Robert Menegoz's film *The Thousandth Window*, an eminently forgettable comedy financed by a pressure group eager to improve the rather tarnished image of France's real estate developers, would sink without trace.

Barbara's role was that of a Polish student living *au pair* in the home of a Parisian suburbanite – Pierre Fresnay, the veteran French actor – who clings to his tiny house in defiance of a real estate company's efforts to evict him, thereby preventing the completion of a major housing development. The love interest was supplied by a romance between Barbara and Trintignant, cast as the corporation architect, and the set was a mock-up villa surrounded by towering apartment houses.

The financial backers couldn't have read the final script, which was scarcely designed to enhance their reputation. After the first private screening Roustang was led away by white-faced men in expensive suits, and sounds of a furious altercation drifted into the projection room.

Roustang himself was to play a prominent part in my life for the next few years. A rotund, balding man with gold-rimmed glasses and a distinctly parsonical manner, he had an aristocratic wife, a Jesuit brother, a luxurious Paris apartment, a house in the country, and servants, secretaries, and hangers-on galore. He took the greatest pride in his brand-new Citroën, which one day was bisected by a falling plane tree, under our very eyes, outside his home on the Boulevard Richard Wallace. Before becoming a producer, Roustang had run an advertising agency that handled films recommended by Catholic associations. When we first met, he was at the zenith of his career and sat on an influential Catholic film vetting committee. He wound up turning out soft porn.

Although Barbara's fee was a mere $1,000, Roustang treated us quite generously where expenses were concerned, if only for publicity purposes. Barbara and I were temporarily in great demand. Yvon Samuel did a thorough PR job on us. He arranged for us to appear in fashionable night spots where *paparazzi* were always on hand, and Barbara, who was photographed *ad nauseam*, made the cover of *Cinémonde*. I was her constant escort – her interpreter, manager, coach, and morale booster. Her initial insecurity was such that she never wanted me to leave her side.

Though totally committed to Barbara's success, I was bursting with such suppressed and unfocused energy I could hardly keep still. I was desperate to achieve something on my own. I quickly recognized that her film was trash but couldn't do more than look after her while it lasted. Fortunately she picked up French fast and began to show signs of greater self-assurance. One day, while we were killing time in a restaurant on location in Touraine, waiting for the rain to stop, she started retouching her makeup. Roustang, who was sitting beside her, watched the process with an appreciative eye. On impulse Barbara turned and playfully applied some lipstick to his mouth. The result so tickled her that she improved on it with some eye shadow. Slowly but surely she made him up as a woman. Roustang just sat there, submitting to this treatment with utter docility. The effect was startling and disturbing.

Whether or not he nursed a secret passion for Barbara, as his entourage claimed, Roustang certainly buzzed around her like an amorous but inhibited bumblebee. When shooting ended, he invited us to stay on in Paris at his apartment. He also presented Barbara with a cuddly black poodle puppy. This unusual gift, which we christened Jules, became our pampered child.

Roustang asked me to subtitle his film in Polish – merely, I suspect, as a pretext for giving us some money. We took advantage of our spurious opulence to entertain friends from among the Polish community in Paris, which had recently been swollen by newcomers who, like us, were making the most of the thaw and its relaxations on foreign travel. These included Cybulski and Kobiela, who turned up in France with no visible means of support. They were rescued from starvation by a fellow Pole named Andrzej Katelbach, who had settled in France after having served with the Free Polish forces in Britain during the war. A huge, sloppy, boisterous bear of a man in a baggy suit, Katelbach owned a plastic flower factory. Charitably he gave Cybulski temporary employment on the flower production line. Kobiela turned out stems.

Barbara and I were in a quandary now that her film assignment had ended. Should we return to Poland or contrive to stay on in France? Roustang's interest in us, his Polish protégés, waxed and waned by turns. He seemed enthusiastic when I outlined the plot of *Knife in the Water* and said he wanted to make it in France. At his suggestion I embarked on a French adaptation with the help of Jurek Lisowski, the finest living translator from Polish into French and vice versa. But by the time it was finished Roustang had inexplicably gone cold on the project.

We weren't in a hurry to go home, either of us; but our visas would soon expire, and our funds were getting low. Nor could we stay at Roustang's apartment forever. There was a certain awkwardness about being his permanent houseguests. On top of that, we had rather alienated him by signing Barbara up with an agent, Lola Mouloudji, who promised her a big career in the West. Even if he didn't have another movie part for her, Roustang resented being deprived of his status as Barbara's patron.

Lola Mouloudji persuaded the Italian director Gillo Pontecorvo, who had come to Paris in search of a female lead for his next picture, *Kapo*, to give Barbara a test. Pontecorvo was the first Western Communist intellectual I'd come into contact with. Despite our political differences of opinion, I found him charming and brilliant, with a keen sense of humor. He took to me, but he took to Barbara even more; in fact, he was enchanted by her. Unfortunately his producer wanted someone with a name, so the part went to Susan Strasberg.

I'd made a number of friends among the Polish expatriates who worked for *Kultura*, the dissident literary review I'd been questioned about by the UB in Lodz. With them we

160

discussed our future. Zygmunt Hertz, *Kultura*'s business manager, urged us to stay on in Paris by hook or by crook. Other friends rallied around, notably the Lisowskis, Jurek and Hanka, who solved one of our more immediate problems by inviting us – and Jules – to move into their tiny studio apartment until we could find a place of our own. There we led a happy-go-lucky, cheek-by-jowl existence for several weeks, sharing household chores and whatever money we could borrow or scrape together. Jurek, big and warm-hearted, and Hanka, an exuberant, good-looking brunette, could not have been more helpful or hospitable. Meanwhile, I vainly tried to interest French producers in my little-known self and even less known script for *Knife in the Water*.

After discussing our predicament yet again with Zygmunt Hertz over beers at the Café de la Paix, we took the plunge and applied for what the Polish authorities termed consular passports, which enabled Poles to live and work abroad but to visit Poland freely. They proved so hard to obtain and involved us in so much red tape that I almost went back to *Kultura* and volunteered for political exile. As a last resort I requested an interview with our ambassador, Stanislaw Gajewski, who took it upon himself to grant us two of these coveted documents. But for Gajewski, my career might have taken quite a different turn.

Our other problem, money, was more intractable. Although Paris was dirt cheap in those days, we couldn't live on air. With the aid of a loan from Lola Mouloudji, we relieved the congestion in the Lisowskis studio apartment by renting a little furnished walk-up near the Gare de l'Est, in the unfashionable Tenth Arrondissement. While I persevered in my attempts to woo French producers, we subsisted on borrowed funds and the hospitality of our widening circle of show business acquaintances. One of them was Betsy Blair, who invited us to a lot of free meals at her Left Bank apartment. There I met Karel Reisz, Lindsay Anderson, and sundry other members of the British movie avant-garde. I also became friendly with a young French actor, Claude Berri, who was playing opposite Betsy in a

Paris stage production. Heated intellectual discussions alternated with party games at Betsy's gatherings. When they broke up late, as they often did, the Métro would be closed and we couldn't afford a cab, so we walked. Jules had to accompany us everywhere because he howled if left on his own and drove the neighbors to distraction. Still a puppy, he whimpered as we trudged along the Boulevard de Sebastopol until I picked him up and carried him the rest of the way home.

Even an official invitation to the 1960 Cannes Festival aggravated our financial problems. Barbara went as a member of the cast of *Cross-Eyed Luck*, a Polish entry, but our government wouldn't pay her fare from Paris, let alone mine. The festival organizers met the cost of bed and breakfast for one at the Hôtel Martinez. Had I registered as Barbara's husband, I would have had to pay a substantial supplement; as her 'lover' I stayed there gratis. A Polish hotel would have been far less broad-minded and accommodating.

This trip to Cannes was quite an improvement on my last fleeting visit. I reveled in the stacks of hyped-up promotional blurbs that appeared with the Martinez's free breakfast every morning, not to mention the vast range of films to choose from. I accepted every invitation we received except those that might have involved me in paying a share of the bill.

At one cocktail party I was accosted in Polish by a thickset man with the face of an Assyrian potentate. 'You have a very pretty wife,' he said.

I expressed my appreciation of his appreciation and asked what brought him to Cannes.

'I'm a producer,' he said. 'My name is Spiegel.'

Sam Spiegel was already something of a legend. I took to him at once, not least because he'd deigned to make small talk with a nonentity.

But it wasn't Spiegel who took our destinies in tow after *Cross-Eyed Luck* had failed to make an impact at Cannes. A Polish-born wheeler dealer named Leo Lax dreamed up some ambitious plans for us both. He invited me to lunch with Sammy Siritzky, one of France's leading distributors.

Over lunch I outlined the plot of *Knife in the Water*, which seemed to kindle Siritzky's interest. Afterward Lax and Siritzky played a round of golf. Desperate to go on selling my film, I plodded from hole to hole and watched them as they swung and putted with agonizing deliberation, wholly intent on their game. Golf struck me as one of the dullest pastimes ever devised by man.

When *Cross-Eyed Luck* flopped, Barbara's hopes of a major contract faded, but Leo Lax was still full of grandiose talk as he drove us back to Paris in his Cadillac convertible. He would make her a star, he promised.

A few days later he summoned us to read the contract he'd drawn up. It bound Barbara to him for seven films, and the advance on signature was a paltry $400. We were so broke, we nearly took it. Barbara would have signed her own death warrant without reading it first, but I wanted Lola Mouloudji's advice. Not even having the price of a Métro ticket, I panted all the way to her office with a copy of the document. She took one look at it and said, 'Are you insane?' That was the last we saw of Lax. Thanks to another loan from Lola, we survived.

Then the tide began to turn. René Clément, the celebrated French director, had just made a star out of Alain Delon with his hugely successful *Purple Noon* and was about to use him in another picture. He now asked to meet Barbara. Lola insisted that she look just right for the occasion in a sexy, snappy little dress.

With the remains of our cash, Barbara and I picked out a dress at the Galeries Lafayette – pink, low-cut and girlish, with thin shoulder straps and a flared skirt. Then, with Barbara proudly clutching the bag containing her new acquisition, we rushed to call Lola from a phone booth on the ground floor. Lola announced that Barbara was to meet Clément in the bar of the Hôtel Lutétia at eleven the next morning. Overjoyed, Barbara flung her arms around my neck. That was when I became aware she wasn't holding the bag any longer. 'Where's the fucking bag?' I squawked. It was gone – stolen. Barbara burst into tears. Mournfully we took the escalator to the subway station beneath the store. Down on the platform our suspicious eyes X-rayed every Galeries Lafayette bag in sight. We now had neither dress nor money. My rage transferred itself from the thief to the French in general – to the snooty coiffeur who wouldn't set Barbara's hair unless she let him cut it as well; to the supercilious neighborhood grocer who sneered because we always bought the cheapest brands; to every callous, arrogant, sarcastic, cocksure Parisian I'd ever met.

Once again our Polish friends rallied around. Hanka Lisowska lent Barbara a suitable dress. I delivered her to the Hôtel Lutétia and waited in a café across the street. When she rejoined me an hour or so later, her expression said it all. She'd gotten the part. The one condition, reluctantly accepted, was that she drop her unpronounceable Polish surname. From now on she was to be Barbara Lass.

By our standards, Barbara and I had become rich overnight. I'd been hankering after a car for ages, and she sanctioned the extravagance.

I could sense, as I walked into the showroom, that none of the Mercedes salesmen considered me a genuine prospect. I was shabbily dressed and looked ridiculously young for my age, and I knew it. The knowledge made me bristle. Condescension yielded to servility when I leveled my finger at a Mercedes 190 convertible and said, 'I'll have one of those – in red.' I made the down payment in cash.

Even when delivery time came, the salesman tried to take advantage of my youth. An established customer had chosen the same color and wanted immediate delivery. Would I mind waiting another couple of weeks? The salesman added that he'd make it worth my while by throwing in a radio free of charge. 'No,' I insisted, 'I want it right now.'

We settled our debts and moved to a more comfortable apartment at 5 Rue de Bérite, on the Left Bank. Jules started eating fresh meat instead of canned, and Barbara left for Rome to work on Clément's picture, *Quelle Joie de Vivre*. I went to work, too, but on something less ambitious.

At this period, shorts could be a paying proposition in

France. For the benefit of budding filmmakers, the Ministry of Culture not only stipulated that every program must include a short but awarded prizes to the best ones. Jacques Brunet, a French Canadian producer whom I'd met while working with Jean-Marie Drot, agreed to back a short of mine because he couldn't afford to underwrite a feature film like *Knife in the Water*.

Mercifully the financial vicissitudes that beset this undertaking have become a faded memory. I'd secured the services of a tiny studio in one of the seediest quarters of Paris. It was only thanks to the owner of this studio, Claude Joudioux, a former electrician, that the film was made at all. When Brunet flitted off to Canada and his checks started bouncing, Joudioux had no choice but to let me complete it on his premises.

The Fat and the Lean was in the same genre as *Two Men and a Wardrobe*. I played a skinny little browbeaten servant and hired Katelbach to play his fat and domineering employer. Although Katelbach had never acted before, he was such a boisterous, roistering extrovert I felt sure he'd do justice to the part. One casting problem remained. A goat played a prominent part in the action, but animal-renting outfits were prohibitively expensive. One day, while scouting a suitable location at Meudon, near Paris, we came across a flock of goats whose owner made cheeses and hawked them around the neighborhood. We hired one of his animals, which, though cheap, turned out to have very little camera sense.

Just as I was about to finish shooting, Komeda and his group arrived in Paris for some concerts. This was a wonderful stroke of luck. He wrote the music – free of charge – and rehearsed it in our new Left Bank apartment, using a piano rented for the purpose. The entire group camped there, and their nocturnal jam sessions caused friction with the concierge.

With angry tenants complaining about the noise, problems of direction with Katelbach and the goat, and lack of finance, I had my fill of troubles. Because I was technically a visitor to France, my name couldn't appear in the credits as sole director, so the editor, Jean-Pierre Rousseau, was billed as codirector. *The Fat and the Lean* won a quality prize and became a hit with cinema clubs, but it did little to further my career.

No sooner had Komeda left than another friend from Poland arrived. Andrzej Kondratiuk turned up just as I was about to pay Barbara a visit in Rome, so I took him along in the Mercedes. Jules came, too, of course.

Barbara was living in a luxurious penthouse, rented for her on Via Po, and was thoroughly enjoying her new life-style. Kondratiuk and I moved in and were soon sampling the delights of Rome ourselves. Gillo Pontecorvo, who was much in evidence, took us to all the right places. At Otello and the Caffè Greco, his regular haunts, we found ourselves rubbing shoulders with countless expatriates from the U.S. movie world. At this period Rome was not only the center of the European film industry but almost an extension of Hollywood. When we visited Cinecittà Studios, which were booked solid, the sets from *Cleopatra* were still in place.

One of the expatriates I met was Alicia Purdom, the Polish-born wife of American actor Edmund Purdom. Alicia seemed to have no special reason for being in Rome other than a taste for the *dolce vita*, but the reason became clear when she confided that she'd had an affair with a rising young U.S. politician named John F. Kennedy. It seemed that, at the outset of Kennedy's presidential campaign, some hard-faced men had called on her, handed her some money, and strongly advised her to leave the country. Through Alicia, who was a dedicated swinger, I made the acquaintance of such reigning celebrities as Stewart Granger and John Derek.

Rome was an exciting place but its charms began to pall. Searching around for something to do while Barbara was on the set, Kondratiuk and I started writing a script for a short. We didn't know where, how, or when it would be made, but we called it *Mammals*.

When the Clément assignment ended, Barbara and I decided to spend Christmas in Poland, courtesy of our new passports, which allowed us to come and go as we pleased.

We took it easy for the first few days. It was good to be back in Krakow, with its snow-mantled churches and misty little streets filled with hurrying figures muffled up against the cold. It was good, too, to see my father and Wanda again after these two years abroad. We had all, in our various ways, grown up, and Wanda started becoming motherly. They'd seen little of Barbara but now easily succumbed to her charm. Leaving her with them, I paid a visit to Lodz.

It was like old times. We sat in the Mermaid Bar: Kondratiuk, Kostenko, Frykowski, the chinless Zolnierkiewicz, and I. 'What about *Mammals*?' Kondratiuk said suddenly. 'Why don't we go ahead and make it anyway?' Our script had been turned down by a state production unit specializing in shorts. Off the cuff, Frykowski volunteered to finance the film. We estimated it would cost around 90,000 zlotys to make. Frykowski, who was still flush at the time, could easily afford to put up half that sum. Kostenko, who'd just inherited some money from an aunt, offered to underwrite the balance. We drew up a contract on a paper napkin.

'This,' I said, 'must be Poland's first-ever private production since the war. Frykowski – producer; Kondratiuk – co-writer and cameraman; and Kostenko – assistant to director Polanski'.

Private ownership of 35 mm equipment and raw stock was illegal, but we had to get around the regulations somehow. We lit up a cigar apiece and strode into Wohl's office at the film school, puffing ostentatiously. He complained that we were smoking him out. The cigars were mandatory, we retorted; we were producers, after all.

Wohl made a school-owned Arriflex available to us, and Frykowski, who took his producer's duties very seriously, bought some surplus 35 mm stock from a crooked lab technician. We loaded our equipment into two cars and headed for Zakopane.

Mammals, the last of my shorts, was shot in the snow; all the action takes place against a pure white background. The film is a succession of visual gags. Far away in the empty white expanse a dot appears. Gradually it turns into a sled and two men, one pulling, the other being pulled. They engage in an unremitting power struggle, each bent on getting the other to haul the sled. The devices they employ in this duel for dominance range from compassion and emotional blackmail to physical coercion.

As in cartoons, the props appear on demand. Perhaps the most effective visual gag occurs when one of the men, pretending to be injured, starts bandaging himself. The bandages melt into the snowy landscape until they render him completely invisible. In the end, the sled is stolen by a sausage salesman – a tiny part played by Frykowski. Thereafter the antagonists continue their journey on foot, each trying to induce the other to carry him.

My *Mammals* twosome were Michal Zolnierkiewicz and Henryk Kluba, who'd graduated from the film school since *Two Men and a Wardrobe*. Michal's height and conspicuous ugliness made him a natural for the role of the dominant partner. For all his amateur status, though, he was as hard to handle as any temperamental superstar. He suffered from hallucinations brought on by an inordinate sex drive. 'Hey!' he'd say, pointing to a figure on the horizon. 'Just look at that fantastic chick!' It was the postman, trudging toward us through the snow.

Michal was also a compulsive talker, starting as soon as he woke in the morning and keeping it up till he fell asleep, with disconcerting suddenness, at night. Then he would begin snoring – and how. Michal's snoring was no series of intermittent grunts and snorts but a deep, continuous, throbbing roar that shook our rented farmhouse – all night.

I finished shooting just in time; the snow was disappearing fast. With the film in the can, a new set of problems arose. Because we had made it illegally, there was no way we could get the negative processed other than by slipping it into a lab as part of someone's official production. Kostenko was entrusted with the rushes.

I collected Barbara and Jules and set off for Paris. I had a distinct feeling I would be back very soon.

FOURTEEN

I was right. Encouraged by further improvements in the political climate, Bossak soon got in touch and suggested giving *Knife in the Water* another try. I tinkered with a few scenes, adding some snippets of dialogue designed to impart a trifle more 'social commitment,' and Bossak resubmitted my freshly typed script to the Ministry of Culture with a strong intimation that I'd been toiling to remedy its deficiencies for the past two years. This time the screenplay committee passed it for production.

Leaving Jules in the care of Andrzej Katelbach and his wife, I got into the Mercedes and headed for Poland alone. Barbara was already making another film in Rome – *Licantropo*, an Italian werewolf drama.

I arrived to find that the Kamera production unit fully shared my delight and excitement at the prospect of making *Knife in the Water*. Thrilled that I was about to embark on my very first feature film – my ordeal by fire – I naturally enlisted the services of some old friends and associates. My two assistant directors were Andrzej Kostenko and Kuba Goldberg. Jerzy Lipman, who'd tutored me so patiently back in the duys of *Three Stories*, came in as my cameraman. To Wojtek Frykowski, a very strong swimmer, I promised the job of lifeguard for the waterborne sequences.

I started casting. For the middle-aged journalist husband I settled on an experienced stage actor named Leon Niemczyk, who was handsome and slightly mannered in a way that suited the part. I originally intended to play the young hitchhiker myself, but Bossak dissuaded me. Any director making his first feature film was vulnerable to criticism of all kinds, he stressed, so combined responsibility for screenplay, direction, and one of the three parts might lay me open to charges of egomania. Rather than court the hostility of critics, I eventually picked someone straight out of drama school, Zygmunt Malanowicz, a tormented young Method actor with the right kind of looks. Casting the journalist's wife proved more difficult.

In all three cases I formed a mental picture of the physical type I required, then set about finding someone to fit it. Of the three, the wife's appearance was the hardest to match. Eva Krzyzenska, whom I'd seen in Wajda's *Ashes and Diamonds*, was the only Polish screen actress who approximated to what I had in mind but she wasn't interested in working with a novice director, so I decided to look for a nonprofessional. The young woman I needed had to look plain and unremarkable when clothed. At the same time she had to look unexpectedly, ripely voluptuous in a bikini. Jolanta Umecka, whom I spotted while prospecting at a municipal swimming pool in Warsaw, seemed to satisfy both these requirements. On the strength of a screen test I gave her the part.

The two key production men were not only new to me but as different from each other as chalk and cheese. Jurek Laskowski, a poker-faced ex-army captain with a prodigious capacity for hard liquor and a richly military turn of phrase, had worked on *Cross-Eyed Luck*. Stanislaw Zylewicz was a dapper Kamera executive with a tiny Adolphe Menjou mustache, an affected manner, and a voice to match. A thorough dandy, he was so anxious to avoid staining his slacks with sweat on location at the height of the summer that he lined his waistband with a toilet paper cummerbund.

Second only in importance to the cast and crew was the large houseboat that became our floating home for several months in the summer of 1961. I insisted on renting this in the knowledge that it would make for greater efficiency and mobility while shooting on the Mazury lakes, quite apart from being cheaper than a score of hotel rooms. Normally used to accommodate army engineers, it was a primitive craft with two rows of cabins, a galley, and a dining room. Our skipper Captain Kijek, was a Polish merchant navy veteran so dour that I never once caught him with a smile on his face. In addition to Frykowski, we carried a complement of boatmen, drivers, and kitchen staff. Zylewicz, our executive producer, was too grand to live on the houseboat. He installed himself and his production office in a hotel ashore.

Since the bulk of the action in the film took place on the water, a whole flotilla was required: the sailboat itself, a sleek-lined eleven-meter yacht; a floating camera platform; an electricians' boat; and motorboats for towing and transportation. Lake winds made shooting a maddeningly slow business. The sun would be on one side, but then we would have to tack – swing around to catch the breeze – and the light and shade would change accordingly. Background continuity was another chronic headache. Cloud patterns could change dramatically midway through a series of shots, forcing us to start again from scratch or switch to another scene. More often than not, as we were towed back to the houseboat in the evening calm, we would see the trim figure of Zylewicz standing on the stern deck, awaiting our return. 'How many meters?' came the ritual cry. Sometimes the answer would be 'None!'

Even discounting wind, weather, and the natural hazards of filming afloat, *Knife in the Water* was a devilishly difficult picture to make. The yacht was quite big enough to accommodate three actors but uncomfortably cramped for the dozen-odd people behind the camera. When shooting aboard, we had to don safety harness and hang out over the side. Lighting a scene, even in stable weather conditions, presented major problems. It required great ingenuity to mount lamps in the rigging and great skill to maneuver the generator boat – which had to follow our every change of tack – without snapping the cables that linked it to the yacht.

The cast presented problems of their own. I realized, for the first time, that every actor requires a different directorial approach. Leon Niemczyk was relatively easy to direct; I

171

only had to show him what I wanted and he did it. With Malanowicz, the youth, I quickly found that conventional direction was counter-productive. I had to use a sort of Stanislavsky approach with him, building up an atmosphere and coaxing him into the angry young rebel he was supposed to be. He had to do it for real, on his own terms and in his own way.

But my real cross, both on set and off, was Jolanta Umecka, my swimming pool discovery. For one thing she couldn't swim. Frykowski attempted to give her a crash course but it was no use; we ended by hiring a double. As for her acting, the problem wasn't merely inexperience – that I'd taken for granted. What exasperated me was having to direct someone who couldn't remember her lines or where to put her feet, or when to take off her sunglasses, in the simplest of takes. More irritating still was Jolanta's utter passivity. The naturalness and artlessnees that had so impressed me at first sight turned out to be manifestations of a genuinely bovine temperament.

We tried gentle persuasion and infinite forbearance. Then we were goaded into rougher tactics designed to jolt her out of her zombielike state – all to no avail. In the end we resorted to foul language, not for meanness's sake, but to shock her into some kind – any kind – of response. In the scene where she thinks the youth has drowned, she is startled to see him reappear and pull himself aboard. We did take after take and got nowhere. Finally, Kostenko hit on the idea of firing a flare pistol behind her back at the appropriate moment. That did the trick. By this time we were in a state of complete frenzy. 'Well, did that help, you bitch?' I yelled.

'Yes,' she said serenely, 'it helped.'

We had yet another problem with Jolanta: she started putting on flesh at an alarming rate. The sexy Jolanta of the early takes threatened to become unidentifiable with the chubby Jolanta she was fast becoming. Something had to be done. Kostenko and I took her jogging, hauling her along by a belt attached to her wrist when she flagged. We ordered the cook to serve her smaller helpings and no seconds, but it did no good.

We soon found out why. Jolanta was a secret glutton who hoarded bread, apples, and sausage beneath her bunk. It was Laskowski who discovered the awful truth. 'Kit inspection, sir!' he barked, laying out the fruits of his research on her blanket.

I thought she might be less obsessed with food if she had some sex. This became a recurrent topic of conversation among the men on board, but no one volunteered to sacrifice himself for the common good. The only person who betrayed a flicker of sexual interest in Jolanta was Zylewicz, who, for all his prim and precious ways, had lecherous inclinations. He kept tweaking her bikini top during rehearsals: 'I see it more like this' – tweak, tweak – 'a shade fuller here, a fraction tighter there.'

Jolanta's ravenous appetite developed into a standing joke. On one of our morning trips to the set Frykowski took a small piece of Styrofoam from a rip in a life jacket and started munching on it. Anything to do with eating was guaranteed to attract Jolanta's attention. With his mouth full, Frykowski explained that the stuffing in our life jackets was a form of emergency ration. We all followed his example and chewed on bits of Styrofoam. Jolanta took a piece, chewed it, and swallowed. Grimacing at its taste and texture, she gamely said, 'I'm sure it's very nourishing.'

Outside distractions added to my difficulties. My first brush with the press came early on. A reporter from *Ekran*, a movie magazine, spent a day on the set, joined us for dinner aboard the houseboat, and was treated to a hotel room ashore by Zylewicz. He seemed innocuous enough, but the piece he wrote was a straightforward hatchet job. Entitled 'For Whom and for What?,' it told of extravagant living aboard a luxury yacht and fleets of expensive cars, all provided by the Polish taxpayer. The story made such a disastrous impact that Bossak and Krakowski came to investigate in person. Although they saw right away that the allegations of extravagance were absurd, Bossak made me change the prop car from a Mercedes to a Peugeot. So, to avoid 'provoking' the Warsaw *nomenklatura*, many of whom drove around in Mercedes sedans, I had to reshoot the exterior sequences using a Peugeot; the interior scenes, for which a Mercedes had been used, I reluctantly left as they were.

Because the shooting schedule was so tough, we kept up our spirits by letting off steam after hours – at night and on Sundays. We all drank quite a bit, played outrageous practical jokes on each other and on any unsuspecting victim we could find, and even, on occasion, wound up in a brawl or two.

On August 18, my birthday, the cook, an ex-fighter, stopped shadowboxing long enough to bake me a cake. When called on for a speech, I rose from my place at the head of the table and launched into a long, mock Shakespearean tirade on life's injustices. Deliberately mistiming a histrionic gesture, I ended up with icing from the cream cake all over my hands. Little Kuba Goldberg entered into the spirit of the act and started licking my fingers like a dog. Captain Kijek promptly left the table.

We adjourned by boat to the tavern where we did most of our weekend drinking. Here we installed ourselves in the 'consuming room,' as Polish bars were bureaucratically termed. A poetry reading was in progress in the room next door. Overcome with vodka and emotion, one of our young electricians rewarded the poet with some loud, appreciative remarks. 'The words are beautiful; it's all so beautiful,' he kept saying, over and over again, until the audience turned on him. When he refused to leave, they started manhandling him.

This assault on a member of our crew couldn't be tolerated. Frykowski picked up a chair and broke it over an assailant's head. Then, without giving his stunned victim a second glance, he pulled up another chair and sat down again. It was all over in seconds. The man he'd hit was the skipper of the pleasure steamer *Chopin*, which we badly needed to shoot some scenes from. After that he took some persuading.

But behind all the light relief lurked constant anxiety. I brooded about the weather, worried about our slipping schedule, became aware of an undercurrent of unease among the staff, cast, and the crew.

Then came two blows in quick succession.

We returned from a day's shooting to be greeted with the news that Andrzej Munk was dead. I couldn't accept that I'd never see him again; it was my first confrontation in a very long time with the tragic and instantaneous disappearance of someone close to me. We learned that a truck had collided head-on with Munk's little black Fiat on the Warsaw-Lodz road. As he would have wished, we toasted his memory in the tavern that night, telling anecdotes about him, recalling his innumerable hoaxes and outrageous sense of fun. Kuba Goldberg, who could take it no longer, retired to the washroom to weep. Equally overcome, I joined him there.

A policeman walked in and relieved himself. 'Hey,' he said, catching sight of us, 'what's going on here?'

Between his sobs, Kuba blurted out, 'Why don't you piss off and leave us in peace?' The policeman summarily arrested him for 'insulting a representative of the state.' I tried to intervene and was arrested, too. We spent the night in separate cells. I was released unscathed, but poor little Kuba, who was so undersize he wore a high school badge on his sleeve as a joke, got beaten up. This incident cost us part of a day's shooting in addition to the full day we spent attending Munk's funeral in Warsaw.

The other bad news was something I couldn't share with the others. Whenever I tried to call Barbara at her Rome hotel, the Parioli, I failed to reach her. I had a funny feeling that the desk clerk was being deliberately evasive. The next thing I knew, someone sent me a clipping from an Italian movie magazine showing Barbara and Gillo Pontecorvo nightclubbing together. Although Barbara had never said a word about Pontecorvo, everything suddenly fell into place:

her frequent absences from Rome and the trip to Yugoslavia she'd casually mentioned in one of her letters. One night, having booked a call from a restaurant, I finally got through to her.

She sounded odd – more embarrassed than remorseful. 'Didn't you get my letter?' she asked. I said no. She said she'd sent me a long letter 'explaining things.' She paused, then added, 'It wasn't a nice letter.'

I pretended not to understand what she was driving at, but I knew. Her letter, when I did get it, confirmed all my worst fears. It also reinforced my view of Barbara as a sweet but rather weak and childish creature – too scared to come out with the truth when a lie was more hurtful still. She didn't mention Pontecorvo even then, simply said she needed 'time to think.' I tried to call her again, several times, but never got through.

My life was going adrift once more. I recall an evening spent alone on the houseboat, waves pounding the hull, clouds scudding across the moon, a gale lashing the trees on land, where the others were having a party. A sort of prayer took shape in my mind – a prayer for strength to finish the picture, for the sense of proportion that would keep me sane and prevent me from taking my personal troubles out on other people. Later that night I went ashore and made an effort to seem as lighthearted as the rest of the party. There was no one I could talk to about Barbara; I was too proud to share the news of my rejection, even with Frykowski or Kostenko.

Autumn had come by the time we finished shooting, and we drove back south from Mazury along forest roads carpeted with red and gold fallen leaves. Lipman, the cameraman, was chauffeuring Kuba Goldberg and me in the prop Peugeot. Sometime after nightfall we came to a bend. For one heart-stopping moment, I realized that Lipman had taken it too fast. We were skidding on a layer of damp leaves and heading straight for the woods. I just had time to shield my head with my arms before we crashed.

A strange sight met my eyes when I came to a few minutes

later. I crawled out from a fetal position under the dashboard to find that there was a tree growing out of the Peugeot's hood. The headlights, though still on, had developed a squint. I was bleeding from the nose and ears but was otherwise unmarked. Lipman and Goldberg were merely shaken.

After a long wait for help I was taken to a hospital in the nearest town. A young intern examined me and diagnosed a fracture at the base of the skull. I was put to bed and told not to move. Feeling better next morning, I got up and went to the washroom. But the walls slid upward, the floor tilted, and I lost consciousness for several days. My parents came to see me in the hospital, and Wanda stayed behind. She rented a room nearby and brought me home-cooked meals every day. I was touched but also embarrassed.

Against doctor's orders, I discharged myself after two weeks. There were still some yacht interiors to be shot in Warsaw, and I was impatient to get back. Shooting in controlled conditions seemed incredibly easy, and we wrapped it up in only two days.

Now, like a cuckoo slipping an egg into another bird's nest, I had the undeveloped negative of *Mammals* processed along with the last scenes of *Knife in the Water*. Thanks to Komeda, who wrote the music, and Bossak's clout, one of the 'short' production companies underwrote the remaining production costs. Because Frykowski wasn't an official member of the film community, his name was excluded from *Mammals* credits. I felt wretched about it, and Frykowski was bitterly disappointed. This typical bureaucratic nastiness arose, we knew, because his father was one of Lodz's few surviving 'private sector' entrepreneurs.

The postproduction work on *Knife* had to be done in Wroclaw, so I was on the move again. Laskowski threw a farewell party at his home. There I met an attractive young fashion model named Renata. 'Don't waste your time on her,' Laskowski whispered, 'she's all gong and no dinner.' I immediately took that remark as a challenge. I guided Renata out onto the balcony. We looked at the city lights and talked for what seemed like hours. I could sense her interest, which elated me. My elation must have been contagious, for soon we were climbing the fire escape to the roof, where we made love in the teeth of an autumn gale.

None of *Knife in the Water*'s original sound was usable, so we had to recreate the sound track from scratch. Only Niemczyk postsynchronized his own voice. Not being happy with the other two, I myself supplied the hitchhiker's voice and had Jolanta dubbed by an experienced actress – who thought the film was awful. Renata, whom I'd been dating since our rooftop encounter, came to visit me in Wroclaw. She loved the film when I showed her part of it. This not only sent my stock up with her but made me feel better because it suggested that young people, at least, would grasp what the picture was about.

Now came the last hurdle, the dreaded *kolaudacja* at which ministry and party officials formally viewed the finished picture and then discussed it. Rumor had it that the chairman of these discussions, Jerzy Lewinski, always ran to the toilet as soon as a film had been shown. This enabled him to gauge his fellow consultants' mood on his return before committing himself. Sure enough, when the lights went up, Lewinski headed for ths men's room. He came back to find the reaction generally favorable. The party's senior representative was alone in pressing for a definite ending to the film. 'Either have them go home or go to the police,' he insisted, 'one of the two.' The idea that an audience should be left to draw its own conclusions about the outcome of a story was anathema to him: an ending had to be either 'positive' or 'negative' – preferably the former. Bossak suggested removing two shots from the closing scene to minimize its ambiguity. This set the official mind at rest.

The press showing was a disaster. After the *Ekran* article the critics were determined to pan my film. Who could possibly credit the existence of a Polish sports reporter who owned both a Peugeot and a yacht? The members of Poland's *nomenklatura* were starting to get rich quickly at this period, and *Knife* was, among other things, an attack on privilege.

Whether motivated by spite or political zeal, most critics vociferously demanded to know what the film was about. My 'cosmopolitan' background was grist to their mill. 'All Polanski has is an international driving license and no film school diploma,' wrote one reviewer. *Polityka* printed an appreciative and literate review, but the prevailing tone was exemplified by *Youth Flag*, the official Young Communist magazine. 'Nothing touches us particularly,' it stated. 'The director has nothing of interest to say about contemporary man, and we don't identify with any of his characters.' Another reviewer echoed these sentiments by describing *Knife* as 'a story no one needs.'

Even Gomulka, the party's first secretary and Poland's effective ruler, got in on the act, calling its characters 'neither typical of nor relevant to' Polish society as a whole. After that, it would have taken a brave man indeed to say something nice about it. Bossak was more than brave; he was quixotic. In reply to a reporter he said, 'I am concerned with the opinion of three categories of people: filmmakers, artists, and filmgoers. As I see it, Comrade Gomulka falls into none of these categories. I am, therefore, only moderately interested in his views.'

The adverse publicity was such that Kamera abandoned all thought of giving the film a gala premiere and released it without publicity at a number of small movie houses. I didn't even stay for the opening. After this sort of official reception I knew I wouldn't be making another film in Poland for a long time to come. Saying good-bye to my father and Wanda in Krakow, I set off for France in the car that was all that remained of my marriage.

Spring was late that year, and the Sudeten Mountains still bore traces of old snow, pitted and icy, left over from the winter's blizzards. The bleak weather matched my mood. As I drove, I drew up a personal balance sheet. It seemed to be all liabilities and no assets. My film had flopped and my wife had left me. I'd lost one of my most cherished friends and narrowly escaped death in a car crash. No prospects or place

179

of my own awaited me in Paris – no money either, since my director's fee from Kamera had been paid me in unconvertible Polish zlotys. I was leaving one limbo for another.

FIFTEEN

Once I was across the West German border, my spirits revived. I decided to make a detour via Munich and look up Ignac Taub, who'd taken advantage of his involvement in a Polish -West German coproduction to settle there permanently. He now lived in a modern apartment house in a respectable quarter of Munich.

Taub looked plump and prosperous in a snappy tweed suit, the effect still spoiled by his ever-trailing shoelaces. He invited over another exile – Marek Hlasko, who had also recently defected to the West.

All three of us sat and talked, downing large quantities of vodka, first in Taub's apartment, then in one of those sleazy nightclubs that were Hlasko's second home. My two friends tried as best they could to exude confidence about their respective careers. But beneath it all I could sense they were out of their depth: Taub, for all his film experience, was now peddling transistor radios, and Marek Hlasko was trying to write in a foreign language.

As we got drunker, the conversation became earthier, and more and more hostesses appeared at our table, ordering drinks galore. I don't know what finally happened to the others, but I found myself alone with a very sexy girl who seemed to be passionately in love with me. Taub had lent me some cash, fortunately, because my companion had an unquenchable thirst for champagne. While I was settling the bill, she vanished. I never saw her again.

As much as I enjoyed Taub and Hlasko's company, I had to

admit they were obviously in no position to further my professional career.

I drove on to Paris, where Katelbach offered me temporary quarters at his home, a shabby little doll's house up in Menilmontant. It was a tight squeeze – I had to step over his brood of children to get to the minuscule bedroom for which he charged me a nominal rent – but at least I wasn't lonely.

Cybulski, who was just about to open in a Warsaw stage production of *Two for the Seesaw*, had wangled three days' absence to attend the Cannes Film Festival, where a picture of his was being shown. He'd recently signed a French film contract and was feeling flush, so he persuaded me to chauffeur him on a lightning trip to the south of France. Having nothing better to do, I jumped at the idea.

We hardly slept at all during our forty-eight hours in Cannes. Like all compulsive night owls, Cybukshi always knew of a place that stayed open later than the rest. Most of our drinking was done at the Chunga Bar. There were plenty of girls around, and Cybulski, an inveterate bird watcher, kept gripping my arm and hissing, 'Look at them! Who's getting it all? Someone must be fucking them, but who?'

It was the same when we moved on to St-Tropez for the last night of our jaunt, except that there we got lucky. After fruitlessly prospecting in various discos, we staggered off at dawn to a bakery for some croissants. There we met two spirited girls and bore them off to our hotel.

Naturally this was the morning when Cybulski – probably for the first time in his life – decided to rise early. He had to – he was due to play in Warsaw that night. Nice Airport was strikebound, he'd discovered, so we had to make a quick dash to Marseilles instead; otherwise he'd miss his Paris connection.

Utterly exhausted, I told him to drive. He said he didn't know how.

I reminded him that he'd driven a truck in *End of the Night*.

'That was movie driving,' he said. Reluctantly he climbed behind the wheel. 'Which is the brake?' he asked. I drove.

182

He kept looking at his watch. 'They'll be giving the audience their money back in six hours' time,' he said. 'Of course, I could always choose freedom.'

Barbara reappeared on the horizon when I returned to Paris. Predictably her liaison with Gillo Pontecorvo hadn't lasted long. She'd since made a picture in Japan and lost her heart again, this time to her German leading man, Karl-Heinz Boehm. When Pontecorvo came to Paris some months later and cried on my shoulder, I was able to tell him in all sincerity that I just knew how he felt.

Our reunion was like something out of a bad Italian movie. We sat in the Mercedes till dawn, talking in circles. She was eager to cut the proceedings short; Boehm, she said, would be waiting for her and worrying himself sick. Though loath to let her go, even at this late stage, I accepted the fact that a divorce was inevitable.

I found a lawyer through Lola Mouloudji and arranged to meet Barbara outside his office, opposite the Parc Monceau, which was in full bloom. I waited for her on the sidewalk – so broke that even going to a café would have been an extravagance. She didn't show up, and after pacing up and down for an hour, I rang Boehm's apartment. Barbara answered the phone. I was dumbfounded. How could she be so inconsiderate? Had she forgotten?

Her reply was quite dispassionate. 'I thought it would be best if we didn't see each other again.'

Then a strange thing happened. It was as if some invisible bond had snapped. I felt weightless – free as a bird. This was Paris, I told myself. I had talent, friends, and a lifetime ahead of me. I left the phone booth and sauntered down the street, whistling a tune, at peace with myself and the world. Even the trees in the Parc Monceau looked lusher than before.

I started hustling for film work, learning the hard way how films in the West got made – or, rather, how most of them didn't. For a start, I got in touch with Pierre Roustang, who was less affable now that Barbara had left me. He invited me to a cocktail party, but when I turned up, he snubbed me. I hardly knew anyone there and wondered why he'd bothered to ask me in the first place. I retired to the kitchen, where I got talking to another guest, who had noticed Roustang's behavior and made light of it. He was a little Frenchman with close-cropped hair and a scarred forehead. The more we talked, the more I took to him.

When our paths first crossed that night, Gérard Brach had just emerged from the throes of a messy divorce. His scar was the result of a blow from a stiletto heel, administered by his wife in an elevator. Earlier he'd spent five years in a sanitarium, recovering from TB. Gérard was so strapped for cash that when he'd originally taken a job as Roustang's messenger boy, he slept on a cot in the office, rent free. There was one major drawback, however: the building was kept securely locked from Friday night till Monday morning, and Roustang wouldn't give him a key. Rather than roam the streets, Gérard spent his weekends locked up inside. He whiled away the time by munching bread dunked in vinegar, the only diet he could afford, and dialing phone numbers at random, talking for hours when he made contact with women who were as lonely as he was.

After that party, Gérard Brach and I were inseparable. Each of us was as broke as the other, but a little money went a long way in St-Germain. Wine and movie seats were cheap, and we got a lot of conversational mileage out of beers sipped slowly in the Café de Flore or Les Deux Magots.

Soon after I met Gérard, I called Ignac Taub. He said I was wasting my time in Paris and told me to get to Munich as fast as I could. 'Do we have a deal for you!' were his alluring words. He wouldn't say more, except that he promised I'd be directing a major war film.

When I reached Taub's smoke-filled apartment, a conference was in session. Taub was there, along with Marek Hlasko and another Pole, whom I vaguely remembered as a pillar of the Warsaw Writers' Club, though he'd never published anything. Robert Azderball was his name, and he spoke six languages atrociously, his own included.

Taub announced that he'd lined up a major German-Yugoslav coproduction deal. The picture was to be based on a novel by some famous Yugoslav writer, a noted World War II partisan, and Marek would be handling the adaptation. Azderball, who was incoherent with excitement, kept butting in to make sure I understood the great things that lay in store for all of us.

It all sounded mildly promising, but I was wary enough to ask a question or two. Where was the preproduction money coming from? How much did the author want for the film rights? I knew Taub was always on the verge of bankruptcy.

'Don't be such a wet blanket,' Taub told me. 'We've got a solid backer.' Azderball grinned sheepishly, and Taub went on. 'She's a lady called Rifka Shapiro. Pots of money. Azderball's banging her; they're getting married. We're all having dinner at her place tonight.'

Rifka Shapiro, who owned a garment factory, lived with her mother in a luxury apartment crammed with expensive yet tasteless furniture. She turned out to be a short, dumpy, inexpressibly ugly Jewish girl with bow legs. It was quite impossible to guess her age. Every inch the proud, proprietorial fiancé, Azderball kept overpraising all aspects of the meal. 'Some herring, that, eh?' he enthused. 'And how about this borscht! Just wait till you try Rifka's meatballs – they're heaven!' All the while he was winking at us behind her back.

Rifka's mother ate nothing, just sat there. Her conversational contributions were limited – she was deaf and spoke only German and Yiddish – but straight to the point.

'Rifka,' she said, 'you like a movie, buy a ticket. Buy every seat in the house – it'd be cheaper.'

'Mama,' said Azderball, 'you stay out of this.' Under his breath, he added, 'Or we'll send you to an old folks' home.'

Marek and I exchanged glances. He was reveling in the whole setup. It was perfect copy for use in one of his short stories.

Back at Taub's apartment, we reviewed the situation.

Rifka was smart – far smarter than Azderball. What if she had second thoughts and failed to come through with the finance?

'In that case,' Marek said with glee, 'Azderball will simply have to marry her for love.'

We decided, the four of us Poles plus Rifka, to drive to Belgrade and discuss matters with officials of the state-owned Yugoslav film company, our prospective partners. Marek owned a slick BMW sports convertible, a divorce present from his German actress wife. Rifka showed up in a black Mercedes sedan. Unlike her furniture, it had clearly seen better years.

The author whose book we proposed to buy was waiting for us at a restaurant somewhere along the Adriatic coast. Taub and Azderball greeted him effusively but didn't introduce the rest of us. For some reason they decided we should sit at a separate table, so we did, watching them go to work on the poor author. 'What's his name anyway?' I asked Rifka.

'Zdenko something,' she said.

Marek said he looked like an asshole and christened him 'Zdenko Dupowic,' *dupa* meaning 'asshole' in Polish. At some stage during lunch the author rose and went outside to inspect the Mercedes with Taub, who was all smiles and animated gestures. He kicked the tires, tested the suspension, and sat behind the wheel, looking dubious. By this time it was obvious that the Mercedes formed part of the deal. Meanwhile, Marek had started flirting with Rifka. Never a devotee of moderation, he also found time to devour two enormous steaks in short order. Then, growing bored, he announced his intention of driving on ahead with Rifka. We arranged to meet up at one of those vast gas stations-cum-restaurants that are the only notable feature of the Belgrade Highway.

Lunch over, Taub and Azderball shook hands with the author and saw him off. 'We've got a deal,' Taub told me, beaming. 'It's all lined up on a car-plus-cash basis. We'll drop the Mercedes here on the way back.'

By the time we got to the rendezvous I'd fixed with Marek,

the Mercedes had developed a grave internal complaint. It was knocking like crazy and reeking of hot oil. Marek hadn't arrived yet. He drove up more than an hour later, accompanied by a rather flushed-looking Rifka. I took him into a corner.

'You screwed her!' I said. 'How could you?'

'Azderball won't mind.'

I told him it was not his morals I was questioning, but his sense of aesthetics.

Marek drew himself up. 'It's all in a good cause,' he said with as much dignity as he could muster.

The Mercedes, needless to say, refused to start. A mechanic diagnosed a blown gasket, carried out a general inspection of the engine, and expressed doubts whether the car was worth repairing at all. There went the author's fee.

Taub and Marek raced on ahead to Belgrade in the BMW to meet our Yugoslav associates, promising to send a car for the rest of us. That left me marooned with Azderball and Rifka. When evening came, fed up with them and the whole situation, I hitched a ride in a truck.

The Yugoslav driver and his partner were perfect hosts. They not only made me comfortable in the bunk at the rear of their cab but insisted on treating me to slivovitz at every roadside café on the outskirts of Belgrade – their regular homecoming ritual. When we finally squealed to a halt outside the Hotel Metropole at 6:00 A.M., they poured me into the lobby under the disapproving gaze of the hotel staff. I spent the rest of the day throwing up. Taub was careful not to introduce me to any Yugoslav production people till the next day.

We went through the motions of discussing our joint project, even driving out into the country to inspect possible locations. Then we all went home.

I never heard another word about our project, Rifka Shapiro, or Zdenko Dupovic.

I became more than ever convinced that my future, if any, lay in Paris. This was the crest of the new wave phenomenon.

Films were being made very cheaply, and in most cases very badly, by inexperienced young amateurs. Many of them flopped, but those that succeeded shattered the notion of what made a hit. The French film industry was in turmoil because there was no longer any surefire success formula. Producers took wild gambles, afraid that if they passed up some completely unknown director or turned down some flimsy, unintelligible screenplay, they might miss out on something big. Intellectual snobbery also played a part. Loath to be branded as philistines, critics lauded ill-made 'highbrow' pictures that were not only slow-moving but pretentious and boring.

I myself would never be part of the new wave crowd, nor did I want to be. I was too much a professional – and a perfectionist. Though I found François Truffaut's *Four Hundred Blows* charming, and Jean-Luc Godard's *Breathless* appealing, the other films, apart from Claude Chabrol's early ones, dismayed me by their amateurism and appalling technique. Sitting through them was, for me, an almost unbearable form of torture.

Roustang, who was alive to this trend and always on the lookout for new projects, commissioned me to write a screenplay. His idea was thoroughly predictable. 'Why not write the story of a Polish girl who comes to Paris and falls in love with a Frenchman?' he said one day. 'I'm thinking of a low-budget project along the lines of *Hiroshima Mon Amour*.'

I wrote a treatment and gave it to Gérard Brach to read. He didn't think much of it, and I didn't blame him. 'Okay,' I said, 'how about kicking it around together?' We did but got nowhere. In the end I suggested we forget about Roustang's story and write something to please ourselves – something we'd both enjoy seeing on the screen.

We found we had a great community of ideas, Gérard and I: the same kind of humor; the same sense of the absurd. Although I knew much more about film technique and film writing than he did, he learned fast. He was very flexible, too, and never minded scrapping something and starting again from scratch.

I'd often debated the mainsprings of musical composition. How, for instance, did a composer devise a melody? There was no single answer, I discovered, and the same applied to scriptwriting. Gérard and I began with isolated scenes and situations, ignorant of where they would lead. Gradually, by trial and error, by talking our way around a scene, we would develop a thematic fragment into a fully structured story line. Sometimes, in the course of this process, we would jettison the idea that had sparked it off in the first place. Such was the genesis of *Cul-de-Sac*, the original title of which was *Riri* – the French equivalent of 'Dicky.'

We started out with the notion of a household, cut off by water from the outside world, terrorized by a gangster on the run. The character of Dicky, the loudmouth misfit, was closely modeled on my friend Andrzej Katelbach.

To be perfectly frank, had I been asked at this stage what the theme was, I wouldn't have been able to answer. There was no theme, only the expression of our state of mind. Both Gérard and I had recently been let down by women, and the character of Teresa was born out of a slight need for revenge. It never occurred to me then that the film might be shot anywhere but in France, so Gérard and I drove to Brittany to look for a suitably isolated spot. We needed to find a causeway covered by the sea at high tide.

Finally, we showed the screenplay, now rechristened *If Katelbach Comes*, to Roustang. He was unenthusiastic – not surprisingly, since it bore no resemblance to his original idea about a Polish girl in Paris. At best, he said, it might make a short. Where screenplays were concerned, Roustang subscribed to a basic rule. 'In every picture,' he used to say in his breathless, hyphenated way, 'there have to be ten shock sequences – ten. Where are they? I don't see them.' He also urged me, when writing for the screen, to curb my 'Middle European' sense of humor.

Gérard, who'd cherished high hopes of our joint venture, was very depressed by this rejection. I was slightly less so, being long inured to such setbacks. Even though I was landing no director's assignments, the two of us were steadily learning more about the art of scriptwriting. There were no shortcuts, we found. We would read dialogue aloud to each other, testing every stress and intonation, pruning every superfluous word. Though Roustang dropped out of the running, in his office building, at 163 Rue du Faubourg St-Honoré, was another film outfit called Alpha Productions, a subsidiary of the West German distribution company known as Atlas-Films. The French-based boss of Alpha Productions drew up a contract. They took an eighteen-month option on *If Katelbach Comes*. I signed away my world rights for a $2,000 scriptwriter's fee and a director's fee of $8,000, these sums to be payable as advances against the 2 percent net profit, worldwide, that would accrue to me if the film were made. It was tantamount to working for peanuts, but I didn't care. As it happened, I never even got the peanuts. The deal fell through.

If Katelbach Comes was only one of several projects to occupy us at this period. Roustang kept us afloat with re-writing assignments from time to time, and I also turned out two TV scripts for Bertelsmann, the German publishing house, which at the time maintained a TV drama department. They earned me a small advance but were never made.

Then I received an invitation to the 1962 Venice Film Festival, where *Knife in the Water* had been officially entered. Largely at the insistence of his wife, who raved about my film, an old French producer named Pierre Braunberger bought it from Film Polski's representative for a modest $10,000. Though thrilled by this development, I left Venice before the awards were announced because I couldn't stand the suspense. I learned on returning to Paris that I'd won the Critics' Prize.

The long-awaited breakthrough seemed to have come at last; I could hardly believe my luck. The distributor Sammy Siritzky, who hadn't forgotten our lunch with Lax at the golf club in Cannes, liked the picture a lot and agreed to make his circuit available. I was in his office on the eve of *Knife*'s release, glowing with expectation, when he dealt me a hammerblow. 'My poor boy,' he said sadly, 'don't get too excited – your picture's bound to be a commercial flop. Braunberger hasn't spent a sou on promoting it. He doesn't appreciate the value of publicity.' Aghast, I said I'd go straight around and see him, but Siritzky shook his head. 'It's too late now. Always remember, a film is like a match – you can only light it once.'

Gérard and I went to one of the movie houses where *Knife* was showing. It was almost empty. The sparse audience cat-called and laughed in the wrong places. I was astonished to see that Braunberger hadn't even bothered to post an allusion to the Venice award on the marquee. He argued that such a highbrow label would only have turned people off. The trouble was, he hadn't turned them on in the first place.

To exorcise his guilt over the handling of *Knife in the Water*, Pierre Braunberger fobbed us off with a vague promise to finance a short. Gérard and I didn't waste a minute. We came up with a sexually explicit parody of *Snow White*. We started spending days in the corridors of Braun-berger's cluttered Champs-Elysées office, where the parquet floors were worn thin by an endless procession of would-be filmmakers of whom Claude Lelouch was the leader.

When we actually got to see him, Braunberger said yes to everything, including our Prince Charming – a Mongoloid news vendor on the St-Germain-des-Prés – and our choice of musical accompaniment – a homosexual yodeling choir. The project was finally scrapped when Braunberger balked at the expense of hiring a troupe of midget wrestlers to play the Seven Dwarfs.

Some small measure of consolation came my way when Film Polski entered *Mammals* for the Tours Film Festival and it won first prize. Tours – for shorts only – carried considerable prestige with critics, intellectuals, and discriminating filmgoers; with most producers, it counted for little. The prize itself, a bronze statuette by Max Ernst, was the first object of value I'd ever owned. I'd gone to Tours with Anatole Dauman, a producer of new wave and avant-garde films whom I'd been trying to interest in *Cul-de-Sac*. Anatole was an inveterate giver of snobbish dinner parties. I sometimes went to them for a free meal. He was genuinely impressed by *Mammals* but even more impressed by my dog, Jules. No producer wanted to hire a Polish director whose only feature film had sold a mere 15,000 tickets in Paris.

Gérard and I did land another writing assignment when an aspiring producer named Jean-Pierre Kalfon commissioned us to adapt a book called *Aimez-vous les Femmes*, a chilling little comedy about a Parisian secret society dedicated to the consumption of female flesh. Our screenplay was amusing, and there was a chance of my directing the picture. Unfortunately Kalfon and his partners thought it safer to use someone with new wave associations. Although our names appeared in the credits, we wished they hadn't. We needn't have worried, though; the film sank without a trace.

Even after the Venice and Tours awards no producer in Paris took us seriously. Gérard and I were hopeless at self-promotion. I still looked like a high school student and spoke French with a strong Polish accent. I was terrible at making small talk and had none of the social graces the French set great store by. Little Gérard, whose conversational approach was just as direct, cut an even less physically commanding figure. All in all, we failed to inspire confidence. In retrospect, I know it was Roustang who did most to help us weather these turbulent times. He was alone in suspecting that I showed some undefined promise and he didn't want to miss out on it. With the softly-softly technique of a Chinese moneylender, he kept advancing me small sums at irregular intervals, never flatly refusing a needed loan, never pressing for immediate repayment.

Our chronic poverty proved a handicap in our principal leisure-time activity: chasing girls. Roustang had acquired a luxurious apartment on the Rue Jacob because he felt that a Left Bank pad would make him seem hippier, more in tune with the times. On weekends he let us have the run of the place, so we used to take girls back there. Gérard pretended he owned the place, but once our playmates had spotted Roustang's voluminous suits and oversize shoes in the closets, they usually recognized us for the squatters we were.

192

On weekdays Gérard was banished to a vacant maid's room above the Rue Jacob apartment, hardly bigger than the bed it contained. Where living expenses were concerned, we pooled our meager resources. Stretching every franc as far as it would go, we haunted the local cafés, accompanied by Jules, like two ill-assorted parents with a child forever trailing at their heels. Although our fees and Roustang's loans and handouts kept Jules in dog biscuits, we were permanently broke and continued to patronize the cheapest bistros and cafeterias.

Across the courtyard from me, in an apartment two floors below, lived a tall, good-looking girl who often walked around naked without closing her shutters or drawing her curtains. Gérard, who was particularly intrigued by her, consulted the *Annuaire par Rues*, the Paris telephone directory that listed subscribers under their addresses. He called all the likely numbers in the building, one after the other. The girl was in full view of our window, so he was able to dial and watch her at the same time. As soon as she lifted the receiver, he went into his spiel: he'd dialed her number at random; he was lonely and needed someone sympathetic to talk to. Instead of hanging up on him, she listened intently.

After the conversation had gone on for some time, she came out with a rather odd remark. 'There's something you should know about me,' she said. 'One side of my face is scarred. I've been badly burned.'

'There's something you should know about me, too,' Gérard replied.

'You're short,' she said, just like that.

They arranged to meet at a café near the Jardin du Luxembourg. Gérard deliberately got there a few minutes early and sat waiting at the counter. When the girl appeared, his nerve failed him. She looked so tall at close quarters he didn't dare come down off his stool and identify himself. He just sat there, feeling more and more like a heel, until she finally gave up and left. This sad and offbeat little episode inspired us to start on a screenplay which we called *The Girl Opposite*.

One of our favorite pastimes was surveying the hooker scene at Les Halles. It was still an extraordinary free spectacle – pure, never-ending street theater. Whether as participants or observers, we found its rituals fascinating. The bold invitations, the uniquely French terms of endearment – 'my little cabbage,' 'my big rabbit' – the promises of wild, erotic bliss, of perversions, thrills, and romantic illusions – all these were in stark contrast with the sordid reality: the rickety stairways, the rented towels, the old crones who had to be tipped, the girls' cryptic, telegraphic remarks as they passed each other on the stairs, the smell of cheap talcum powder, and the incredibly swift, perfunctory nature of the sex act once a sucker had been hooked. 'Want me to undress, *chéri*?' was the usual preliminary question; then if the answer was yes, an exorbitant price was named.

Sometimes, simply to hold on to my self-respect, I said 'No, you don't have to.' Whatever else happened, the girls made a point of inspecting every client and rinsing his dick in the washbasin. Gérard was so short he had to stand on tiptoe – the ultimate humiliation.

The lure of Les Halles was far more theatrical than erotic. Strolling indecisively along the narrow streets, we used to watch the girls for hours, until, as almost always happened, our first choices had gone upstairs with someone else. Sordid or not, Les Halles was fun, and we came to know several of the resident hookers quite well.

I got to know a very different kind of girl in St-Germain-des-Prés. Nicole Hilartain worked for Air India, modeled occasionally, wanted to be an actress, and had the cool good looks of a young Louise Brooks. She was having an affair with a Polish architect I knew vaguely, but one day, while the three of us were sitting in Café Deux Magots, she started playing footsy with me under the table. It was all very French and titillating, though I felt a bit guilty about my friend. We soon became lovers though Nicole continued her affair with the architect. She didn't share my embarrassment at this turn of events, which the architect never guessed at. I felt painfully awkward when the three of us were together, whereas

Nicole seemed to delight in our triangular relationship.

One of Roustang's more ingenious ideas was a gimmick that enabled him to produce a full-length feature film for only a fraction of its total cost. The film would be composed of several self-contained sketches, and he would negotiate with production companies in half a dozen countries, assigning them national distribution rights to the completed film in exchange for a sketch to be included in it. That way, he himself secured the rights for France and the rest of the world. He now commissioned Gérard and me to write a sketch for his latest venture, *Les Plus Belles Escroqueries du Monde* (*The Most Beautiful Swindles*), which I was to direct in Amsterdam.

On a winter's day so bitterly cold we almost got frostbite en route Gérard and I climbed into my drafty old TR3 – which had replaced Barbara's Mercedes – and set off for Holland. After more than a year of unrelieved, hand-to-mouth subsistence, the Hotel Schiller on Rembrandt Square seemed like paradise. On full expenses while writing the script, we ate ravenously and gained a ridiculous amount of weight within days.

Snow-covered Amsterdam looked magical, and we both fell in love with the place. I wanted our sketch to be as much a portrait of the city as the story of a con game. Gérard and I were well accustomed to working together by now, and I think it showed. The script was sparse; much of the film required no dialogue at all. It told how a beautiful, slightly dotty French girl pretended to fall for a gullible Dutch businessman and stole a diamond necklace by means of a neat and simple stratagem – hence the title, *River of Diamonds*.

Roustang and his Dutch coproducer liked our script. After several weeks of suspense came the amazing news that we were actually going to make a film of it.

My first act was to hire Jerzy Lipman as my cameraman and import him from Poland. Nicole, whom I cast as the thief, played her with just the right mixture of poise, insolence, and amoral unconcern. I was happy to have her all to myself at last and realized I was quite in love with her.

I persuaded our Dutch coproducer to bring Christopher Komeda over from Poland to write the music. He would not only be the best but the cheapest, I argued. Komeda came with his wife; it was their first trip abroad together.

We lived well, enjoyed ourselves, and made a nice little film, but when shooting was over and we headed for home, we were broke as usual. By the time *River of Diamonds* was in the can, Roustang had called for payment on all his various loans, and that swallowed up my entire $5,000 fee.

Before leaving Amsterdam, with our last guilders Gérard and I bought some cigars at the station – Gérard a decent box for his brother, I a larger, flashier one. I wanted something to show for several months' hard labor.

We got out in Paris at the Gare du Nord, shabby suitcases in one hand, cigars in the other. Just as we were leaving the platform, a stern-faced figure barred our path. 'Anything to declare?' We stared at him as if he were crazy, but the plain-clothes customs officer simply repeated his question.

'No,' we said innocently, 'nothing to declare.' At this we were marched away to an office where an inspector sat ensconced behind a desk. Our cigars were plunked down in front of him like courtroom exhibits, and our captor announced that we'd failed to declare dutiable goods.

'Surely we're allowed to bring in one box of cigars apiece?' I protested.

'Only if you declare them,' ruled the inspector.

I started flinging my arms around. Gérard tearfully pleaded that he'd only bought the cigars as a gift for his brother. Close to tears myself, I turned abusive. 'Well,' the inspector said to his minion, 'what shall we do with them?' It sounded like a toss-up between life imprisonment and summary execution. Timid Gérard merely had his cigars confiscated; I, because of my belligerence, lost mine and was fined 100 francs into the bargain. The gods, I felt, were ganging up on me once more.

SIXTEEN

Nicole resumed her double life with me and the architect after returning from her film assignment in Amsterdam. Although she swore she loved us both with equal intensity, and may well have, the setup became too much for me. I pressed her to choose between us, but she couldn't make up her mind. Fond of her as I was, I cut the knot. Her Gallic poise deserted her for once, and our final farewell was a tearful one.

When May came, Gérard and I responded gladly to the siren song of Cannes. We went there determined to make friends and influence people – remind them of our existence, build up connections, bend the ear of some amenable producer. We also went, of course, to see as many new films as possible. I now found another cinematic masterpiece to share *Citizen Kane*'s pedestal. In part because it dealt with the problems and pressures of a film director, Fellini's – smote me like a revelation. It was all I'd ever dreamed of seeing on the screen, emotionally as well as visually.

Between orgies of filmgoing, we hung around and prospected in the places that mattered. As usual, the terrace of the Carlton Hotel was a prime rendezvous for all who wished to see and be seen. A youngish American was particularly conspicuous there; he always seemed to be surrounded by a bevy of lovely girls. Tall and dark with slightly projecting teeth, he had a relaxed, feet-on-the desk American manner. He introduced himself as Victor Lownes, a partner of Hugh Hefner's in the Playboy organization, and he bought me a drink on the spot. If ever I came to London, where he was launching Playboy's European operation, I was to look him up without fail.

Everyone, including the critics, agreed that our *River of Diamonds* sketch was a little gem. Unfortunately the other directors' contributions were so slipshod that *Les Plus Belles Escroqueries* flopped all over Europe. At Cannes, however, Roustang contrived to unload it on a wealthy U.S. exhibitor, Walter Reade of Walter Reade Theaters, for quite a substantial sum – a coup that inspired him to take a two-page spread in one of the festival magazines to say, 'Thank you, Walter Reade!' Flushed with success, he now came up with another brainstorm designed to capture Reade's interest. Entitled *Chercher la Femme*, this latest in his series of multinational projects was to describe the adventures of an American visiting various European countries in search of the perfect bride. Impressed by my work on *Les Plus Belles Escroqueries*, Roustang commissioned me to write the screen play with Gérard; he even put me on a monthly salary. His fellow producer, Serge de Dietrich, who was helping back the project, eventually bought him out. We finished our script and waited for Dietrich to complete the financing. He never did, but at least I had something to show for *Chercher la Femme*. Taking advantage of my unaccustomed, if short-lived, status as a man with a regular income, I spent the bulk of Roustang's salary on a racy little Mini Cooper.

Though single once more, now that I'd broken with Nicole, I was hardly carefree. Brief interludes of lush, expense-account living on location and at film festivals continued to alternate with far longer spells of dire poverty. It was feast or famine, and now, after Cannes, we were starving.

A brief taste of the good life came my way on August 1, 1963, a couple of weeks before my thirtieth birthday, when I flew to Canada for the Montreal Film Festival. I was put up at the Hotel Windsor, all expenses paid, in company with such luminaries as Jean-Luc Godard, Francesco Rosi, and Lindsay Anderson.

No sooner had I returned to Paris than I was off again, this time to New York, where *Knife in the Water* was being shown at the city's first-ever film festival. Archer King, an executive of Kanawa Films, the small independent film company that had bought it for U.S. distribution, wrote and urged me to be present. My fare and living expenses were met by the festival authorities.

When my Air France plane touched down at Idlewild, Archer King was there to meet me in person. An ebullient, fast-talking New York Jew, he showed up at the airport with his PR girl, Eleonor Silverman, a plump and energetic blonde. Together they bore me off to the brand-new Hilton on the grandly named Avenue of the Americas.

I was boarded and lodged like minor royalty but given no spending money at all. And of course, I had practically none of my own. This gave rise to some awkward little problems. For instance, a bottle of shampoo leaked all over my suitcase and ruined my one and only suit. Archer King graciously arranged for it to be cleaned and pressed in time for my appearance at Lincoln Center, the scene of the festival.

My first impressions of the United States were strangely mixed. Although some of them matched my preconceived notions about the American way of life, others were significantly different. Like most Poles, I nursed a stereotyped image of Americans: gentle black GIs giving chewing gum to children; plump and pampered WASPs living high off the hog in immensely tall buildings. Some of my illusions were dispelled at once by the reality of New York. The Avenue of the Americas boasted skyscrapers like the Hilton and the Time-Life Building, but it also contained some pretty run-down establishments: seedy little bars, novelty shops, and discount stores in varying stages of decay. The streets were potholed, filthy, and narrower than I'd imagined. All this struck me as surprising but oddly familiar and reassuring.

It was the people who surprised me most of all. Social intercourse in Poland is a stiff and gradual process. French formality is even worse, and I'd experienced little else for over two years. I now found myself overwhelmed with hospitality by total strangers who called me by my first name, welcomed me to their homes, and behaved as if we were the oldest of friends. One of them was Walter Reade. Walter invited me to his home, wined and dined me, and generally gave 'the boy from behind the Iron Curtain' a good time. I couldn't fathom why an influential exhibitor should bother with a Polish nobody, but he seemed to like showing me around. Jerry Schatzberg, then a free-lance photographer, also became a friend, and did his best to show me New York's night life. My childhood friend Richard Horowitz was now living in New York, likewise working as a photographer and a graphic artist with an advertising agency. He took me to a couple of parties in Greenwich Village, intent on introducing me to New York's postbeatnik society, but I spent most of my days at Lincoln Center. There I got friendly with a pretty dark-haired usherette.

I discovered that even Americans could be snobbish. Archer King passed on an invitation to dine at the home of his Kanawa Films partner, a wealthy WASP. I suggested bringing my usherette girlfriend along. He said it wouldn't be a good idea, so I didn't show up either.

I was interviewed quite a lot in New York during the festival, but my English was deplorable – so deplorable that when asked to introduce the festival showing of my film, I had to resort to a little gimmick. I was called to the stage and ushered in front of the microphone. In Polish I said, 'I'm no good at making speeches; that's why I make pictures. I suggest we start the film right away.' There were some titters from the uncomprehending audience. I paused, then repeated the sentence in French. This drew a smattering of applause. After another pause I said it again in very carefully rehearsed English. Even before they'd seen a foot of the film, the audience was on my side. I was to find out that in many ways New York audiences are the most responsive in the world.

After the showing I was besieged by questioners and well-wishers. Among them was a very intense, bespectacled young woman who gave me my first inkling of the importance attached to Freud in America. 'I found some of your symbolism fascinating,' she told me in laborious French.

'The knife represents the penis, of course!' Slightly taken aback, I made some noncommittal reply. Although I'd read Freud's introduction to psychoanalysis when it first appeared in Polish during the thaw, I hadn't realized how seriously he was taken on the other side of the Atlantic.

The culmination of my first New York visit came when a still from *Knife in the Water* appeared on the cover of the September 20, 1963, issue of *Time* ('Cinema as an International Art'). Eleonor Silverman was faintly disappointed by my lukewarm response to this major piece of free publicity. I knew, of course, that *Time* was an important magazine, but my main impression had been of its traditional covers – those old-fashioned portraits of public figures that the *Time* editors then favored. Running a black-and-white still from an Eastern European movie was a daring innovation which I was unable to appreciate.

Back in Paris when the festival ended, I had the customary feeling that something would come of my film's latest showing. Its only concrete and immediate result was a resolution on my part to learn English. I invested in a set of Linguaphone records and put in some conscientious work.

Professionally, however, I found it no easier to get things moving. Gérard and I were both in love with our script for *If Katelbach Comes*, as *Cul-de Sac* was still called, but its birth as a film was proving singularly difficult; it attracted a lot of predatory interest, notably from one Sy Stewart, a professional charmer and glib talker whose real name, I learned, was Blackie Ziegel. Stewart was hell-bent on producing a picture of mine – any picture, even *If Katelbach Comes*. If armed with an option on my script and services, said Stewart, he would raise the necessary finances in no time; of course, he himself could pay me nothing for the present. On the strength of this categorical assurance, I accompanied him to his lawyer's office. There I found that, in addition to granting him a free option, I was expected to sign a contract stating that he had, in fact, paid me a substantial sum for it – Stewart's device for hooking a prospective distributor. The terms of the contract were so unorthodox that his own lawyer outraged him by begging me not to sign it.

Stewart actually managed to raise some up front money but gambled it away at a London casino. By this time my innocence had worn thin. I went to the Paris office of the William Morris Agency and signed up with Giovanella Zannoni, one of their local representatives. The very act of acquiring an agent gave me a warm but deceptive glow of expectation.

My next interested party identified himself on the phone as Sam Waynberg, a producer living in Berlin but born in Poland. I was wary, since he'd gotten my number from Sy Stewart, but agreed to send him the *Katelbach* script for inspection. Soon after, Waynberg sent me a letter with a question no one had ever asked me before: Did I need money? Of course I did – and immediately received a perfectly good check for $2,000 in payment for a three-month option on the script.

In January 1964 came another junket, this time to Munich for a Polish Film Week. Here I was contacted at my hotel by another link in the Stewart-Waynberg chain reaction, Gene Gutowski, a London-based Pole with a U.S. passport. Gutowski was a handsome, well-groomed man-about-town with a refined taste in clothes and wine. His producer's track record was unimpressive – one minor German coproduction and a U.S. TV series – but his plans for us were extremely ambitious. He proposed to form some kind of long-term producer-director tie-up but insisted that London was the only place to get it off the ground. When he invited me over to stay with him and sent me a ticket, I went. His home turned out to be an elegantly furnished Eaton Place apartment filled with bronze busts of his wife, Judy. I discovered that, aside from being a bon vivant, Gene was a genuinely talented sculptor.

London was then an active filmmaking center, and all the majors maintained large offices there. Gene began making the rounds with me in tow. He aimed high – our first visits were to the London headquarters of United Artists, 20th

Century-Fox, and Columbia – but we got nowhere. Although I found that my name meant far more in London than in Paris, partly because of the excellent reviews and modest commercial success achieved there by *Knife in the Water*, no one wanted *Katelbach* to come – not even the London office of William Morris. I had expected my powerful and prestigious new agency to produce a pot of gold for me. The closest I came was a summons from the legendary Abe Lastfogel, chairman of the William Morris Agency. I went to his suite at the Dorchester. He sat, his legs dangling, a tiny, avuncular figure, with a beautiful basket of fruit at his side. He was very encouraging and full of interest – and gave me an apple.

I got something better from the Academy of Motion Picture Arts and Sciences. *Knife in the Water* was nominated for an Oscar in the best foreign film category for 1963, and I was invited to attend the Academy Awards.

I flew into L.A. first class and was met by a huge limousine sporting a Polish flag on the fender. I was then whisked away to the Beverly Hills Hotel like some visiting representative of a foreign power. It was like entering a safe new world. The hotel was set down in the middle of a lawn with palm trees, more like a secluded, luxurious spa. To walk across the outdoor red carpet and enter the vast lobby, with its weird wallpaper pattern of green vegetation, was to become part of a spacious, tranquil world. The impression was strengthened by the vaguely Spanish, rambling, low-story wings on either side. You felt so safe, so rich, so much a part of the film elite. Why couldn't everyone live like that! I was no naïve that I was amazed when the hotel switchboard operators, from the moment of my checking in, started calling me by my name.

I wasn't left to my own devices in the few days preceding the Academy Awards. I was delighted to receive a call from Bronislau Kaper, who offered to pick me up by car and give me a meal at his home. One of Hollywood's best-known composers, he was an institution in L.A. and a legend back home – living proof that a talented Pole could make it in America. Kaper, who had a graceful old house on Bedford

Drive and drove a glossy black Cadillac, initiated me into the esoteric Hollywood jargon and conventions he loved to mock. Despite the difference in our ages, he proved an entertaining companion and became a valued friend. I distinguished myself, when he came to collect me, by slipping on the hotel driveway and tearing my jacket and trousers. Every time I crossed the Atlantic I seemed destined to ruin my only suit.

Another treat in store for me was a guided tour of Disneyland in the company of some of my fellow Oscar nominees, including Fellini and his actress wife, Giulietta Masina. For all of us it was like discovering the America of our childhood dreams. Ever since I'd started salvaging *Snow White* trims from Krakow trash cans, Disney characters had occupied a special place in my affections.

I could communicate reasonably well in English now, and this added to the enjoyment of my stay. Being a client of the William Morris Agency helped after all. Although it never landed me a single professional assignment, one of its agents invited me to drinks at the Polo Lounge, then arranged for a blind date, who turned out to be Carol Lynley. I was on top of the world. Beautiful, baby-faced Carol, who had a terrific sense of humor, remained a close friend of mine for years to come. She must have taken to me right away because she invited me home. So if William Morris never achieved anything else, it did at least get me laid.

There was more to the States than New York, I discovered. Here in L.A. there were no skyscrapers; it was countrified living with all the desirable advantages of a city. Everything was neat and clean; I once saw a Japanese gardener trimming grass with scissors so it didn't encroach on the curb. I was also impressed by the detailed work that went into organizing the Oscar ceremony – in marked contrast with the slapdash confusion of the Cannes festivals. Here nothing was left to chance. We all were advised on what to wear – 'solid black or dead white dresses are bad photographically' – and how to comport ourselves – 'do not stop to accept congratulations on the way to the stage.'

I had arrived in L.A. without the least expectation of walking off with an award, but so much was written about *Knife in the Water* before the presentations, and the film people I met were so enthusiastic, that I started daydreaming. Mine, after all, was one of only five films selected out of dozens. One the other hand, it was competing against the superb piece of work that had so impressed me at Cannes: *8½*. In my heart of hearts I felt that *8½* was the obvious choice for the foreign film award.

The evening of April 13 found me seated in the center block of the Santa Monica Civic Auditorium next to Fellini and Giulietta, who was tearful with nervous tension. Though pretty keyed up myself, I managed to keep my composure. The suspense, as always on such occasions, was unbearable: the presenters seemed unable to tear open the sealed envelopes or decipher their contents. When *8½* got the Oscar, Giulietta burst into floods of tears, Fellini bounded onto the stage, and I applauded as loudly as anyone. I felt a trace of disappointment, deep down, but also a kind of elation. Losing to such a winner was no disgrace.

Once the Oscar ceremony was over, I moved out of my suite and into the cheapest room the Beverly Hills had to offer. Thrown back on my own resources, I fired off a desperate cable to Gene Gutowski, who sent me $400.

Before leaving the States, I made one last attempt to get something going there. During a stopover in New York I met with two of Darryl Zanuck's assistants at 20th Century-Fox, Joe Lebworth and John Shepritch, who expressed interest in my work.

'We have a great idea,' they told me. 'How would you like to remake *Knife in the Water* over here, in color, with three top U.S. stars?' The trio of principals they had in mind were Liz Taylor, Richard Burton, and Warren Beatty.

I said I thought it a ridiculous scheme. Why not hire me to make an entirely new movie? Because *Knife* was such a good story, they replied. I tried to convince them that since I'd had sufficient imagination for *Knife*, there was more where that came from. I failed. 'Will you sell us the rights?' they asked.

'You can have them for nothing,' I said loftily, and flew back to Paris.

On the London front, meanwhile, Gene Gutowski was progressively lowering his sights. He had hopes that our *Katelbach* script might appeal to Anglo-Amalgamated, an independent production company, but it didn't. Then he drew up a list of less prestigious outfits. His letter to the London head of Hammer Films struck an involuntarily despairing note. 'The only thing I beg you, having now tied up with Roman Polanski, is a quick yes or no. He has become my financial responsibility, and it's essential that he make a film immediately.' Hammer complied with his request: its response was quick but negative. Finally, Gene told me he'd found some London film people who were itching to embark on a project with me. I suspect he'd been keeping them up his sleeve all the time, but only as a last resort.

'The Compton Group' rejoiced in a high-sounding name, an elaborate letterhead, and a board of directors that included the Earl of Kimberley. Everything seemed to suggest that it was a major entertainment and communications conglomerate. Actually it owed its existence and main revenue to a small, seedy Soho establishment called the Compton Cinema Club, which showed what currently passed in London for porno movies. It was a 'club' because that was the only way around the British censorship laws. What the Compton Cinema Club showed – and what the Compton Group occasionally made – were timid soft-porn films. Most of its programs comprised U.S. or Scandinavian imports with lurid titles.

The Compton Group had been making so much money out of this operation that it was anxious to change its image, so its interests coincided with Gene's and mine. Thanks to this combination of circumstances, two more figures on the fringe of the film industry entered my orbit: Tony Tenser and Michael Klinger, who owned the Compton Group. I flew over to London for exploratory talks with them.

Michael Klinger's father, a Polish Jew, had been a presser in a tailor's sweatshop in London's East End. Thickset and bald, with heavy horn-rims, an ever-smoldering King Edward cigar, and an inexhaustible fund of Jewish jokes, Klinger spoke only a few words of Polish but was fluent in 'Jewish,' his term for Yiddish. He had been variously employed, in the course of a checkered career, as a sausage salesman, a bouncer, and a nightclub manager.

Tony Tenser, another East End Jew, had adopted a completely different persona. A tall man with a clipped gray mustache, he held himself ramrod straight and could have passed, except when betrayed by certain rare vocal inflexions, for a retired colonel.

Despite their eagerness to make a film with Gene and me, however, neither Klinger nor Tenser would consider *If Katelbach Comes*. What they wanted was a horror movie. Back in Paris, Gérard and I started work. We completed the script for *Repulsion* in seventeen days.

SEVENTEEN

Gérard Brach and I wrote *Repulsion* with one overriding aim in mind: to ensure that Klinger and Tenser financed it. To hook them, the screenplay had to be unmistakably horrific; they were uninterested in any other kind of film. Anything too sophisticated would have scared them off, so the plot of *Repulsion* – a homicidal schizophrenic running amok in her sister's deserted London apartment – included blood-curdling scenes that verged on horror film clichés. Any originality we achieved would have to come through in our telling of the story, which we wanted to make as realistic and psychologically credible as we could.

Having a good idea of the kind of fear we wished to convey, we sought inspiration from situations familiar to us. Most people, at one time or another, have experienced an irrational dread of some sinister unseen presence in their home. An unremembered rearrangement of furniture, a creaking floor-board, a picture falling off the wall – anything can trigger this sensation.

Our central character, Carol, the manicurist, was based on a girl Gérard and I had known in St-Germain-des-Prés. Apart from her beauty, the most striking thing about her, on first acquaintance, was her air of sweet innocence and demure serenity. It was only when she started living with a friend of ours that another facet of her personality emerged. He told us strange stories about her – how she was simultaneously attracted to and repelled by sex as well as prone to sudden, unpredictable bouts of violence. This tied in with our secon-

208

dary but no less important theme: the lack of awareness of those who live with the mentally disturbed, familiarity having blunted their perception of the abnormal.

The Compton Group's response to our screenplay was favorable. Michael Klinger flew over to Paris to clinch the deal, suffering from hay fever and swallowing antihistamines like jellybeans. All that jolted him out of his torpor was the hair-raising way I threaded my brand-new souped-up Mini Cooper through the Paris traffic. I knew he was serious about making *Repulsion* when he told me that one of the clauses in my contract would prohibit me from bringing it over to London. He drove a hard bargain: for writing, directing, and producing, Gérard, Gene Gutowski, and I were to share $5,000 and a percentage of the net profits. It was a grotesquely low figure, but I'd have accepted even less for a chance of directing my first feature film in the West.

Now that *Repulsion* looked as if it were going to happen, I felt bound to lay the facts before Sam Waynberg, whose *Katelbach* option had some weeks to run. He wasn't at all put out. We'd still make *Katelbach*, he said confidently. In the meantime, *Repulsion* would serve as a welcome potboiler. What was more, he wanted to coproduce it if he could raise the money. Failing that, he hoped to buy the German distribution rights.

The only sad thing was that I had to part with Jules; I couldn't submit him to the six-month British quarantine requirement. Anatole Dauman's passion for Jules came in handy; that's where I left him. After boarding Jules out, I flew to London, where Gene found me an apartment a few doors down from his own home in Eaton Place. It was the most luxurious pad I'd ever occupied: three well-furnished rooms in a typical Georgian house with a colonnaded portico, half a dozen steps leading down to the sidewalk, and a façade thick with glossy white paint. Klinger not only paid my living expenses but provided me with a car – a staid, sluggish brown Vauxhall sedan. I discovered that he'd had it doctored by the rental garage so it wouldn't do more than fifty miles per hour, but I got my own back by surreptitiously enrolling at the Brands Hatch Racing Stables and starting Formula Three driving lessons.

I brought Gérard Brach over to keep me company – my instinct was that of the immigrant worker bringing over his family as soon as he could afford to do so – and meanwhile, work was proceeding on an English adaptation of our French screenplay. David Stone, a promising young British writer, turned out an excellent version, working in consultation with me and Gérard. Because our plot posed censorship problems, Klinger advised me to submit the screenplay in advance to John Trevelyan, secretary of the British Board of Film Censors. This proved to be a wise move. Trevelyan, who had liked *Knife in the Water*, read *Repulsion*, knew what to expect, and was prejudiced in its favor before a single frame was shot.

My choice of a cameraman led to some good-natured wrangling with Klinger. As I saw it, the only person who could do justice to our black-and-white picture was Gil Taylor, whose photography on *Dr Strangelove* had deeply impressed me. I also saw his wonderful work on the Beatles film *A Hard Day's Night*; Richard Lester, the director, was mixing it at Twickenham Studios, where *Repulsion* was to be made. Klinger protested that Gil Taylor was one of the most expensive cameramen in the business, but I held out for Taylor and got him.

Atmospherically *Repulsion* would stand or fall by the apartment where most of the action took place. Together with my art director, Seamus Flannery, I built a model of it on my livingroom floor, making drawings whenever my English failed me during our detailed discussions. My aim was to show Carol's hallucinations through the eye of the camera, augmenting their impact by using wide-angle lenses of progressively increasing scope. But in itself, that wasn't sufficient for my purpose. I also wanted to alter the actual dimensions of the apartment – to expand the rooms and passages and push back the walls so that audiences could experience the full effect of Carol's distorted vision. Accordingly we designed the walls of the set so they could be moved

210

outward and elongated by the insertion of extra panels. When 'stretched' in this way, for example, the narrow passage leading to the bathroom assumed nightmarish proportions.

I had a few problems where casting was concerned. With the aid of *Spotlight*, the voluminous and invaluable British stage and screen directory, I picked out Ian Hendry, John Fraser, and Patrick Wymark. Hendry and Fraser, who were much in demand, agreed to do the film for far less than they could have commanded. *Knife in the Water*'s critical acclaim made them curious to discover what it would be like to work with an exotic new talent.

I had a somewhat harder ride when it came to hiring Catherine Deneuve, my female lead. I auditioned a number of girls, including Francesca Annis – Compton's choice, because she'd already played in a Compton film and wouldn't have cost them much. Though sold on Deneuve, Klinger called her a needless extravagance. He capitulated only when I dug my heels in. In fact, her exceptional beauty and talent made a great contribution to the film as a whole.

Sam Waynberg, till now just a voice on the phone, appeared in the flesh to hammer out his deal with Compton. The boss of Planet Films GmbH turned out to be blue-eyed and florid-complexioned, with fair hair receding at the temples. He habitually played the fast-talking, know-all-the-angles film tycoon, and his first encounter with Michael Klinger was shrouded in cigar smoke. They quickly developed a love-hate relationship, sweetened by Waynberg's unexpected delivery of some up front money for *Repulsion*, in return for which he secured the German distribution rights. As essentially kind and likable man, he proved a welcome buffer between me and Compton.

I acquired another ally in Bob Sterne, my Klinger-appointed production manager. A big, burly South African with a heart of gold, he was forever torn between his loyalty to Compton and his fast-growing enthusiasm for my way of doing things.

I was now getting to know, and was falling in love with, the London of the 'swinging sixties.' I soon found that, whereas neither my shorts nor *Knife in the Water* had lifted me out of the rut of obscurity in Paris, London responded to youthful talent; I had gained a reputation there quite fast. This, after all, was the era when Cockney photographers and an obscure Merseyside pop group became celebrities overnight.

One young member of my new crowd was Douglas Hayward, then unknown but soon to become renowned as London's leading showbiz tailor. Gene Gutowski brought him along to my place and had me measured for a navy blue blazer and some gray flannels that would help me blend with my Eaton Place surroundings. Gene also fixed me up with my first London date, Viviane Ventura, a strikingly beautiful Colombian girl, who introduced me to the Ad Lib Club, one of swinging London's focal points. Situated high up in a building off Leicester Square, the club had huge windows, a spectacular view of the West End, and a doorman to park members' cars. It was a microcosm of the new London – reflection of its easygoing, friendly atmosphere, its cultural vitality and sexual revolution. The Shake was still in vogue, and the Ad Lib's black chef would periodically erupt from his kitchen onto the crowded floor, mingling with the dancers and wielding a frying pan like a tambourine. Legend had it that Brian Morris, who ran the club, never paid him – just let him out to dance once in a while.

Membership in the Ad Lib Club, whose habitués included the Beatles and the Rolling Stones, brought me into contact with a wide range of colorful characters, but few were more colorful than Victor Lownes, the Playboy executive who'd once bought me a drink at Cannes. I took him up on his invitation to get in touch and was promptly invited to a party at his big rented house in Montpelier Square.

Victor seemed to embody all the qualities commonly ascribed to Americans. He was tough, fast-talking, energetic, self-assertive, outspoken, and – by European standards – brash. He worked as hard as I did during the day, supervising the construction of the Playboy Club on Park

Lane, but he played even harder at night. Victor was a celebrated host. His drawing room doubled as a study-cum-office, and it was hard to spot the transition between his working day and the parties he threw most nights of the week – parties attended by nearly every visiting star in the American showbiz community. Victor gloried in his affluence and connections; to him, entertaining and having fun were all part of the job. He courted celebrities, less for snobbish reasons than because – as he used to say – they had to be more interesting than nonentities or they wouldn't have gotten where they were. Some people called him an exhibitionist; I preferred to think of him as a man without hang-ups and hypocrisy. Something in my own makeup meshed with his, and our friendship blossomed quickly. We spent many evenings together, playing chess or eating out at the Chelsea and Soho restaurants, mostly Italian, that were currently multiplying like amoebic forms of life. The Trattoria Terrazza, our first hangout, was followed into existence by Alvaro's, the Arethusa Club, then Mario and Franco's on Romilly Street.

Victor's parties were a source of, or set the seal on, several lasting friendships. I was originally introduced to Warren Beatty by John Shepritch, one of the 20th Century-Fox executives who'd proposed to cast him in an Americanized version of *Knife in the Water*. Dick Sylbert, a designer whose work I'd admired ever since seeing *Baby Doll*, I dreamed of using as soon as I landed a picture with a budget big enough to afford him. Both were seen at Victor's whenever they came to London.

Another personal connection had its origins nearer home. Across the way from me in Eaton Place stood a house visited daily by a succession of pretty girls. Gene and I noticed this phenomenon and decided to investigate. We ascertained that they were calling on a Dr Anthony Greenburg. We had him tagged at first as a gynecologist, but he turned out to be a plain GP. He was also a slimming expert; hence the flock of beautiful women. A little, chain-smoking teddy bear of a man with thick horn-rimmed glasses, a shock of auburn hair, and a high-pitched giggle, Anthony became our own doctor and, ultimately, a close friend. We introduced him around and invited him to parties, and it wasn't long before he joined the inner circle of our growing London set. So did a tall, good-looking young Canadian who gate-crashed my own first party with a luscious girl on each arm and a tiny puppy nestling in his jacket. Though only on the fringe of London showbiz, Iain Quarrier was very much at the center of the London scene, and I profited a lot from his social know-how – his almost uncanny knowledge of who, where, and what was 'in' at any given moment.

Looking back, I find it strange that those first few months in London should have brought me into contact with so many people who were to play an important part in my life. While Gérard and I were still putting the finishing touches to *Repulsion* with David Stone, I received a call from someone who said we'd met in Paris. I didn't remember, but I asked him around for a drink anyway. His name was Simon Hessera, and his considerable ambitions ran the gamut from scriptwriting to direction and production. He showed us a screenplay of his and asked our opinion. Its futility was exceeded only by its author's personal charm. Simon proved to be delightful company – a mimic and raconteur of un-rivaled skill – and his one-man cabaret made a welcome addition to our social scene.

Unlike Simon Hessera, who was permanently broke and thoroughly un-English – he was a French Moroccan Jew – Andy Braunsberg lived in a gracious Regent's Park house and made an ultra-British impression despite his German Jewish origins. Tall and slim, with dark brown hair and a slightly feline way of walking, he had been through the public school mill and bore its unmistakable impress. When we first met at a party in his garden, Andy was in the process of 'eating dinners' at the Middle Temple – i.e., studying law, with a view to becoming a barrister. I soon discovered, however, that his real interest in life was show business in general and films in particular. He cherished vague hopes of entering the production and distribution field.

214

On the eve of shooting, Bob Sterne produced a thin, gangling young man in a brown velvet jacket and a bright pink tie. He'd just come down from Oxford and was very keen to 'break into' filmmaking. I was so taken with his obvious enthusiasm – and his unlikely-sounding name, Hercules Belville – that I hired him on the spot, though his lack of a union card meant that he could be employed only as a runner.

Our first day's shooting left me amazed and rather perturbed by Gil Taylor's way of doing things. He mostly used reflected light, bounced off the ceiling or walls, and never consulted a light meter. As the rushes were to show, however, he possessed such an unerring eye that his exposures were invariably perfect. A big, statuesque man with the air of a country squire, Gil had camerawork experience dating back to the 1930's. He'd taken part in hazardous wartime raids on Germany with the Pathfinders, the flying eyes of the RAF Bomber Command, and was deaf in one ear as a result. We differed on only one point. Gil disliked using a wide-angle lens for close-up of Catherine Deneuve, a device I needed in order to convey Carol's mental disintegration. 'I hate doing this to a beautiful woman,' he used to mutter.

In the same way, Tom Smith, my makeup man, couldn't understand my insistence on filming Catherine without any makeup on her face. My reason for using almost none – just a discreet accentuation of the eyes – was that I wanted to catch the smallest nuances in her mood and knew that these would be veiled by conventional screen makeup. At this period most film stars performed beneath a cosmetic crust so thick it would have served for a Kabuki production.

Being still unversed in the ways of film unions, I didn't know that if extra shooting time was required, the subject had to be raised in the morning and discussed by all concerned. Late one afternoon, when we were way over schedule, the crew worked an hour's overtime without a murmur. It was the overflowing bathtub scene, and to have stopped halfway through would have been disastrous. Although the crew would have been well within their rights to do so, no one 'pulled the lights.' From everyone's sub-sequent astonishment, I gathered that this had been a unique and historic occasion.

Because I had no special effects team and handled the effects myself, they took longer to set up than expected. The simplest hallucinations were the hardest to stage. The sudden appearance of cracks in the walls proved to be our biggest headache. For each and every take, they had to be replastered and repainted so that they could be made to open up again at the touch of a lever. One little prop – the sprout-ing potato that marks the passage of time as Carol's mind slowly gives way – was borrowed straight from my child-hood. It sprang from my recollection of the bean my grand-mother had grown in her kitchen just before the war.

Working with Catherine Deneuve was like dancing a tango with a superlatively skillful partner. She knew exactly what I required of her on the set and got right inside the skin of her part – so much so that by the time shooting ended she herself had become withdrawn and a little crazy. Despite her supreme professionalism, Catherine did have one hang-up: she wouldn't appear nude, or even seminude, and at first insisted on wearing something under her diaphanous night-gown. I objected to panties, so she held out for a body stocking. When it came to it, however, she did her takes in the nightgown only.

Ian Hendry liked a drink or two at lunchtime, a habit which never impaired his acting but wrought perceptible changes in his face when we resumed shooting in the after-noon. He also became exhausted during the final scenes, which required him to carry Catherine, who was far from fat but no lightweight, and got a little annoyed at the number of takes I made him do.

Neither the cast nor the crew presented any major problems despite my still inadequate command of English. The main trouble, which reared its head almost as soon as shooting began, lay elsewhere. I'd already encountered it, to some extent, when making *Two Men and a Wardrobe* and *Knife in the Water*, but this time it was aggravated by my unfamiliar surroundings. Klinger and Tenser made two discoveries that preyed on their nerves: the film had been unrealistically budgeted on the low side, and I was taking longer to complete it than they had expected. The problem was a complex one inasmuch as they wanted to change their Compton Group image by making a quality film on the cheap. In addition, neither man was a truly professional producer. Money they knew about, but not the technical aspects of filmmaking. I found it difficult and sometimes impossible to explain to them what I was after and why certain things took time. In order to justify the making of *Repulsion* to myself, I had to give it a significance that would set it head and shoulders above the average horror movie. This meant that I had to make the picture on my own terms. The only way I could upgrade it was by injecting the kind of quality that was time-consuming and, thus, more expensive than Compton had bargained for.

Because my going over budget and over schedule in *Repulsion* bred an enduring myth to the effect that I was a wayward and irresponsible director, my so-called extravagances are worth a closer look.

One of my immediate problems with Klinger and Tenser was to sell them on the rhythm of the early part of the film. The first fifteen minutes of *Repulsion* were purposely conceived as a buildup to that sickening split second when Carol has her first real hallucination – when she suddenly glimpses, reflected in the mirror on the wardrobe door as it swings shut, a menacing male figure in the corner of her room. This shock effect, which had filmgoers jumping out of their seats, required a deliberately low-key approach. Klinger wanted me to shorten the preliminary scenes illustrating Carol's drab day-to-day existence, but I put my foot down. The audience must be lulled into a state of near boredom, I told him, then zapped.

Tenser and Klinger were puzzled by what they saw on their periodic visits to the set. When Carol discovers the cutthroat razor belonging to her sister's lover, for example, I found that it didn't stand out clearly enough. Since it played a crucial part in the story – Carol later uses it to murder the landlord – it needed highlighting in an unmistakable way. I eventually got the desired effect by affixing a strip of silver foil to the handle. This meant that the razor shot alone took several hours to complete. Klinger didn't understand why. I argued that an ill-lit shot at this stage would have robbed the scene of its meaning.

There were more complaints of time-wasting over the scene where Carol kills Colin, her suitor. This was complicated, being shot partly on the landing and partly through the peephole in the front door, which had to be made oversize for the camera's benefit. I wanted it done from the victim's viewpoint. When Carol hits him on the back of the head with the candlestick, all one sees is the peephole lurch, followed by a quick pan down the door as the camera conveys the dying man's last few visual impressions. The drops of blood that spatter the door had to be in proportion to the magnified peephole. Props man Alf Pegley, a young Londoner with a ripe sense of humor, used a bicycle pump filled with my 'secret formula' for blood – cochineal and Nescafé. This took time, numerous rehearsals, and repeated takes, all of which Klinger thought unnecessary.

Yet another scene requiring a lot of preparation was the one in which Carol, completely demented by now, sees hands pawing her as they reach out from the hallway walls. I wanted twenty hands; Klinger, ten at most. He suggested I economize by shooting each wall in turn, which would have been impossible as well as artistically inept. His reasoning was simple: behind each pair of hands was an extra, and extras cost money. But I got my way. Gérard Brach's hands are in that scene, as are those of Hercules Belville. His long, bony, elegant fingers looked peculiarly sinister.

Klinger and Tenser, who felt I was indulging in needless refinements, urged me to cut down on takes and shoot faster. As a result, *Repulsion* became an artistic compromise that never achieved the full quality I sought. In retrospect, the special effects strike me as sloppy, and the sets could have been more finished. Of all my films, *Repulsion* is the shoddiest – technically well below the standard I try to achieve.

Bob Sterne was so committed to the film by now that he sometimes resorted to risky shortcuts. When delays held up the staging of the road accident – which Carol fails to notice while roaming the streets in a trancelike state – Bob decided to take a chance and stage it without waiting for police permission. Although we managed to complete the scene, some vigilant Londoners called the cops. Sterne was summonsed and had to go to court, where he drew a hefty fine.

Crisis meetings, lectures, and recriminations became more and more frequent as shooting proceeded. They wore me down to such an extent that I told Gene Gutowski I was ready to quit. As someone whose worldly possessions could be packed in a single suitcase, what did I have to lose?

The incessant complaints that I was wasting money culminated in a blazing row at the studio. It was then that Gil Taylor and Ted Sturgis, my assistant director, came to the rescue and urged Klinger to stop breathing down my neck. Even if we did go over budget, they told him, the finished product would be worth every penny. Grudgingly Klinger agreed to let me do things my way.

I showed up on set the next morning red-eyed from lack of sleep. It was a crucial day – we'd reached the continuous take in which Carol murders the landlord – and I went through it in a kind of daze. Thanks to meticulous planning, Catherine Deneuve's acting skill, and a certain amount of luck, we shot eight minutes of effective screen time – an impressive amount for one day. The pressures on me lessened after that, mainly because the rushes indicated that for all its shortcomings, *Repulsion* was going to be quite a picture. It may have been unrealistically budgeted at £45,000, but it came in cheaply even at the £95,000 it ultimately cost.

Despite all the friction and tension, I was thoroughly enjoying my time in London. Most nights found me at the Ad Lib, where I discovered that English girls were more straightforward and less calculating than any I'd known. If they wanted to go to bed with you, they did so; if not, they made this clear from the outset. My relationships were happier and more lighthearted than they'd ever been – more affectionate, too. For the first time in my life I began to feel truly at ease with the opposite sex. It dawned on me that in lovemaking, as in acting, sport, or music, being relaxed is the key to a good performance. I must have been rather an inadequate lover till then – too uptight, too fearful of being rebuffed.

My liking for English girls extended to everything English – to cabbies, grocers, salesclerks, barmen. Not that I realized it, the heyday of swinging London coincided with the last few golden years of what is now a vanished age. The traditions of an older, more trustful London still lingered on. Restaurants, garages, tailors, even laundries rendered monthly accounts, and overdrafts were respectable. I could tell my credit was good, socially as well as financially, when French girls who'd snubbed me in Paris called me up and asked to be taken out.

One day my old flame Gesa showed up at the studio. Now a reporter for *Brigitte*, a West German fashion magazine, she was no longer the sweet young ingenue I remembered but still very attractive. Recalling our Paris idyll with nostalgic tenderness, I assumed that we'd pick up the torch again. I was disappointed and annoyed when, after dinner at the Ad Lib, she asked me to drop her off at her hotel. I did so but had been home only a few minutes when the doorbell rang. Peering through the curtains, I saw Gesa outside. She stood there for quite some time, ringing at intervals, before finally giving up. Later she sent me a note regretting our obstinacy – hers in not coming back with me and mine in refusing to answer the door, 'for I could see your curtains dance,' she wrote.

I was more than compensated for my pigheadedness when Jill St John came to London to make a film. Taking advantage of a brief meeting in L.A., I called and asked her out to dinner at a cozy restaurant on the south coast. The manager refused to admit any woman wearing slacks, even a curvaceous redhead like Jill, so we drove all the way back to London and got stinking drunk on vodka at a Polish restaurant in South Kensington. Breakfast at her apartment the next morning was a remorseful business, but the preceding night was a glorious introduction to a lighthearted affair.

One of my worst moments during the making of *Repulsion* came when shooting was over and I viewed the rough cut for the first time. This is the approximately edited film, more or less complete but without music and sound effects, lacking bits of dialogue, unevenly printed. It tends to leave a director wondering what on earth he's come up with after weeks and months of effort. The rough cut has lost the excitement of the daily rushes without acquiring the atmosphere of the finished picture; everything's there, but nothing's quite right. Now I can steel myself to face rough cuts in the knowledge that they're always depressing to watch; then I was still inexperienced enough to think my depression justified.

There was only one person around on whom I could rely for a completely objective verdict. Bronislau Kaper was over in London, working on the music for *Lord Jim*. Without a word to anyone, I showed him the film as it stood. He pronounced it 'very powerful' but had one major reservation. There were three murders, not two, in the original version. The jealous wife of the character played by Ian Hendry shows up at the apartment, convinced that her husband is there. Because she sees Colin's body in the bathtub, Carol kills her, too. Kaper sagely remarked that this murder was too rational to fit the psychological pattern, so I cut it out.

The film had yet to be mixed. One of the most grueling aspects of filmmaking, this process demands extreme patience, and my patience was taxed to the limit by the equipment then in use at Twickenham. French studios already employed the 'rock and roll' system, which enabled the various sound tracks being mixed to be run back and forth in synch. If anything went wrong at Twickenham, one was forced to stop, rewind them all, and start again from scratch.

Stephen Dalby, the sound supervisor at the mixing studio, wasn't accustomed to my meticulous ways. He failed to see why the process couldn't be rushed, as it was with the average

B feature. In *Repulsion*, sound plays a key role. When Carol starts hallucinating, her senses become steadily more acute; she hears everything amplified – faucets dripping, nuns playing catch in a convent garden. Luckily Dalby's assistant, Gerry Humphreys, shared my enthusiasm and didn't allow me to become discouraged by Dalby's undisguised irritation. After mixing *Repulsion*, I had it projected at Klinger's Compton Cinema. The sound still wasn't right even then, and I knew I'd have to go through the whole laborious business again. I did.

What made this doubly disappointing was that Gene had arranged an end-of-assignment skiing vacation – my first in years – and I couldn't wait to get away. Half expecting him to postpone his departure for the week it would take me to finish the picture, I was rather hurt when he set off on schedule with Judy, his wife, and left me behind. After another hectic week in the dubbing theater, I managed to get the sound track right. Then I joined Gene and Judy at the Austrian resort of Sankt Anton. They were taking lessons from a ski instructor, Hans Möllinger, a former member of the Austrian national team. Being badly out of practice, I followed their example. It wasn't long before Hans and I took off on our own, not only skiing but *après* skiing, too. Every girl's idea of a handsome ski instructor, Hans was amusing company, shrewd and enterprising as anyone of sound peasant stock could be.

In a fit of extravagance we all took off by car, Hans included, for St Moritz. The action in this far more fashionable winter sports center was intense; in fact, the lobby of the Palace Hotel was such a popular rendezvous for gorgeous women that Andreas Badrutt, the proprietor, had taken to charging an entrance fee. Hans and I made the most of our brief stay in the Engadine, on and off the slopes. Gene, always a cautious soul, declined to come out skiing on our last day there because he feared some eleventh-hour injury. We returned to find him with his arm in plaster: while walking to the post office to mail some postcards, he'd slipped and broken a bone.

We returned to London and prepared to clear our final hurdle, the British Board of Film Censors. *Repulsion* couldn't escape an X rating – that we'd expected – but Trevelyan was also empowered to cut whole scenes out of a picture. He attended the screening with Dr Steven Blake, a psychiatrist whom he always employed as a consultant on any film concerned with sex or violence. Trevelyan told me how impressed he'd been. To my delight, he proposed to leave everything just as it was. He didn't even ask me to tone down the sound of Carol's sister's noisy lovemaking in the room next door to hers – a daringly explicit touch for 1964.

Dr Blake inquired how Gérard and I had researched the theme, how we came to know so much about schizophrenia. Carol, he said, was a clinically accurate study of a homicidal schizophrenic. It embarrassed me to have to admit that we'd simply used our imaginations.

The other private screenings we held drew good responses. Klinger and Tenser stopped nagging me, though Tenser's feathers were still ruffled. 'It's like ordering a Mini Cooper,' he complained, 'and winding up with a Rolls.'

I shrugged. 'So what's wrong with that?'

To get us some coverage, Victor Lownes suggested a nude *Repulsion* layout of Catherine Deneuve in *Playboy*, using additional photographs to supplement the sparse material in the movie itself. Catherine refused when I called her in Paris, but there are few women, film stars included, who can resist an appeal to personal vanity. Assuring her that one of my Cockney photographer friends, David Bailey, would handle the assignment with artistic discretion, I asked her at least to see David if I got him to fly over. She not only saw him and did the layout, she married him.

Repulsion opened in London, where it earned excellent reviews and did brisk business. More good reviews greeted the picture when it opened all over Europe, though some critics ran true to form by pronouncing it inferior to *Knife in the Water*. Then Columbia bought it, too, and Klinger realized that he had a minor world hit on his hands – all for a £95,000 outlay.

Gene Gutowski and Sam Waynberg, who'd more than earned his associate producer's credit for *Repulsion*, felt that the time was ripe to sell Klinger on *Cul-de-Sac*, as *If Katelbach Comes* had finally and irrevocably been retitled. Sam Waynberg was particularly anxious to get the project off the ground. His rabbi grandfather, he said, used to quote the barber who lathered his customers in double-quick time, before they could have second thoughts. Even now, however, Compton were nervous about taking another gamble on me.

It was the 1965 Berlin Film Festival that helped Klinger make up his mind. *Repulsion* carried off the Silver Bear Award and pulled in big audiences. Overwhelmed that the Compton Group had actually garnered an international prize, Klinger pounced on the Silver Bear statuette and never surrendered it to me. That and Sam Waynberg's fast talk did the trick at last. After a session with Klinger in Berlin, Sam came to me with the news that he'd badgered him into financing *Cul-de-Sac*.

As Sam put it, 'He's all lathered up – let's get shaving.'

Portrait as a child.

Above With my father and Wanda; *below* Clowning in Gdansk with Kostenko and Kuba Goldberg.

Left With my first wife, Barbara
above Directing Deneuve.

Rosemary (Mia) runs to Guy (John Cassavetes); Howard Koch, Jr. in the background.

Sharon.

Our wedding. *Beginning second from left:* Jean Gutowski (Best Man),
Barbara Parkins. Between Sharon and me: my father and Victor Lownes.

With co-author of the screenplay,
Ken Tynan *(right)*.

The Witches.

One of our defective catapults.

With Jack Nicholson.

In Paris, after my trouble in Los Angeles. I released this photo hoping to get the *paparazzi* off my back.

Nastassia Kinski.

Directing Nastassia as Tess.

As Mozart in the Warsaw production.

Returning to the Lodz film school.

My father and Wanda.

EIGHTEEN

Making *Repulsion* had been a means to an end: *Cul-de-Sac*. Now, three years after writing it, Gérard and I had a deal at last. Michael Klinger and Tony Tenser approved a £120,000 budget with the proviso that we secure a completion bond. This meant we had to go to the expense of taking out insurance with a company that would guarantee to finish the picture if it ran over schedule and budget. Film Finances, a leading British concern, agreed to underwrite *Cul-de-Sac* for a hefty premium. As before, Gene was our producer, and Sam Waynberg put up some money in return for the German distribution rights. I got a more appropriate director's fee of £10,000.

Compton still had an itch to do things cheaply, however. For some weeks Klinger toyed with the notion of a Yugoslav coproduction deal. The prospect of another Rifka Shapiro 'special' appalled me. Every Yugoslav coproduction I'd ever sat through had been a commercial and artistic flop, I argued. Besides, what about our characters stranded in a house cut off by the sea? Wasn't Klinger aware that the Mediterranean had no tide to speak of?

We flew to Yugoslavia just the same, talked to some government officials, scouted every yard of beach at a number of unsuitable Adriatic locations, and even made a trip to the Kossovo region in the far south. 'Don't stray too far down the coast,' our interpreter warned us. 'The Albanians are trigger-happy.'

With Klinger finally convinced, I embarked on a haphazard survey of the British coastline in a frail single-engine

Beagle. Flying conditions were atrocious, with sick-making turbulence and massive fogbanks that rendered the whole operation futile. I decided on a more rational approach and consulted the Royal Geographical Society. Its staff couldn't have been more helpful; they came up with some photographs of a location they thought might suit our requirements: Holy Island, a speck of land three miles from the Northumbrian coast and linked to the mainland by a causeway exposed at low tide only. It seemed to be just what Gérard and I had envisioned from the first.

The old firm – Bob Sterne, Gil Taylor, and I – took off on a reconnaissance trip. Gene was otherwise engaged. To my surprise and annoyance, I'd discovered that he was setting up a West End musical, *Passionflower Hotel*, on the side. Since the company we'd formed to handle our joint professional future on a profit-sharing basis, Cadre Films, had come into being at his insistence, I was doubly aggravated by his concentration on an outside interest.

Holy Island turned out to be an ideal location. Cut off by sea from the mainland for hours at a time and surrounded by vast expanses of hard, shelving sand at low tide, it even had a castle that could serve as our main set. Gene was delighted when I called him with the good news. If I liked the location so much, he said, I should settle for it right away; there was no need for him to come up north. Gene's negligent attitude enraged Klinger and opened a rift between them. Gene was, after all, supposed to be producing the picture.

I'd gone up in the world since *Repulsion*, so I now rated a casting director, Maude Spector, whose assistance proved invaluable. When writing *Cul-de-Sac*, Gérard and I had loosely based our two male principals on Pierre Roustang and Andrzej Katelbach. Guided by sketches I drew for her of the physical types I required, Maude Spector swiftly and efficiently lined up Donald Pleasence to play George, the craven, effeminate husband. Though different in build, he bore a striking resemblance to Roustang. The role of Dicky, the loudmouthed gangster, was harder to fill. What we really needed was a Wallace Beery type. If ever a U.S. company were to finance the picture, we used to fantasize, we'd hire Rod Steiger or Jackie Gleason. British actors in that mold were few and far between. Then, one day, Gene phoned and told me to turn on my TV set because there was a man taking part in a chat show who might appeal to me. A burly, gravel-voiced American actor named Lionel Stander was holding forth so volubly that no one else could get a word in. He looked and sounded just right, so I contacted him at once. Stander had quit the U.S.A. for political reasons and was carving out a new career in London. A snappy dresser and a big spender, he lived there with a young American Indian girl and their child, and was itching to land a major film assignment. I hired him on the spot.

For the minor roles Maude Spector helped me find a supporting cast of excellent British character actors. I also signed Iain Quarrier for the small part of Teresa's lover. All he had to do, I told him, was look British and learn to walk on his hands. Iain, who had acting ambitions, was tickled pink.

That left me with a not unfamiliar problem: my female lead. Attracted to the idea of using a complete unknown, I seriously considered hiring Charlotte Rampling – though her very special looks weren't matched by her acting experience – but lost out to the Boulting Brothers, who put her under a multifilm contract. Then I screen-tested a large number of aspiring young actresses and photographic models. None of them had the requisite acting ability, though Jacqueline Bisset's outstanding beauty made me think twice. I decided to hire her, but only for a tiny walk-on part. Dropping the idea of using a nonprofessional, I settled for Alexandra Stewart, a Canadian actress with a lot of new wave experience in France. She seemed to fill the bill, so I started rehearsals with her and the two men, only to find that she looked too wholesome and healthy to play the offbeat, slightly kooky role of Teresa. Alexandra, who realized she wasn't right for the part without being told, was big enough to admit it and spare me what would otherwise have been an awkward situation. I was growing desperate, with shooting only a few days away, when I heard that Françoise Dorléac, Catherine

Deneuve's sister, was in London.

Accompanied by Gene and Stander, I went to see her at the Connaught Hotel. Stander showed up in a pink linen suit, his gray silk cravat held in place by a black pearl tiepin. Stander's angry bluster – 'This is a cravat, you silly little man! Cravats existed before ties were invented!' failed to shake the Connaught's immutable ties-only rule. An assistant manager refused to let him past the lobby, so we talked to Françoise there. Although I hadn't wanted a French girl to play Teresa, the script could easily be adapted. I hired her without a test, and we were ready to roll.

Holy Island, also known as Lindisfarne, was a strange place reputed to be haunted by innumerable ghosts. Its tiny, inbred community of under 300 inhabitants – sheep farmers and fishermen, poachers and wreckers – resented outsiders descending on them for longer than a day or two. The island had a small mead brewery and no fewer than six pubs, which remained open at all hours of the day and night. There wasn't a single resident policeman to enforce the British licensing laws that required pubs to close in the afternoon and turn their customers out at 11:00 p.m. On one occasion, so the story ran, two constables from the mainland had come to carry out a spot check. It was a bitterly cold winter, and none of the islanders would give them shelter. Cut off by the tide, they were forced to spend the night in the open. One of them died of exposure as a result. Somehow, the glee with which the locals recounted this tale seemed psychologically consistent with their principal sport, which was to kill as many sitting ducks as possible with a single shot from a homemade cannon loaded with rusty nails.

Our cast and crew stretched the island's accommodation to the limit. I demanded and got a trailer, which I parked in a secluded spot near the cemetery, while the others were distributed around the various pubs and guesthouses. Ours was an uneasy amalgam of personalities from the first, and I found it better not to mingle too closely with the cast after hours. Luckily for me, I had at least three congenial companions.

One was Jackie Bisset, whose nature was as lovely as her looks. She was thrilled to be on location and quite undaunted by the island's discomforts. The others were Jack MacGowran and his delightful wife, Gloria. Jack had only a minor part as Dicky's wounded sidekick, but he stayed on the island from start to finish. The weather was so unpredictable – 'Never seen anything like it in twenty years!' said the locals – that we took forever to film his scenes. Jack was not only a fine actor but also a true professional and real trouper who would remain half-immersed in icy water for hours without complaint. It was on Holy Island that Gérard and I resolved to build our next screenplay around him.

We started shooting in August, one of the island's few so-called reliable months, but the light altered drastically every few minutes. Sudden storms and fast-changing cloud patterns played havoc with our daily schedules. The weather was a repeat of what it had been during *Knife in the Water*, forcing us to interrupt scenes, to start on new ones or revert to half-completed ones that would now match the light. An added drawback was that Holy Island, one of Britain's earliest monastic foundations, happened to be a tourist attraction, so the castle was unavailable to us on weekends. Whenever prevented from shooting by an influx of visitors, we sought what entertainment we could. Having brought my Mini Cooper to the island in defiance of Klinger's veto, I amused myself by practicing 360-degree spins on the sand flats at low tide. Our pub sessions were enlivened by Alastair McIntyre, my film editor, who could put on a hilarious Scottish vocal act. Last but not least, there was Jackie Bisset's consoling presence. We were spending more and more time together, mostly out of doors because my trailer seemed to hold some curious attraction for earwigs.

It is never long, during the making of any film, before the off-set atmosphere begins to reflect that of the story itself. Not all the tensions of *Cul-de-Sac* could be shed when the assistant director called, 'It's a wrap!' at the end of the day. Gérard and I had written a black comedy about three characters condemned to close proximity under isolated conditions – a study in neurosis with the thriller conventions turned upside down. Unfortunately our trio of principals soon started playing their parts for real.

Donald Pleasence, our most experienced actor, had the central role yet seemed to want to upstage everyone else. He hogged the camera in a variety of ingenious ways. Not always an easy man to deal with or be with despite his outstanding talent, Pleasence looked down on the rest of the cast and was subtly mean to them. He presented me with a *fait accompli* by arbitrarily shaving his head prior to shooting. Although this lent his performance an extra twist, I was annoyed that he hadn't consulted me first.

Lionel Stander's trouble was an inordinate resemblance to his screen persona, Dicky. In real life, as in *Cul-de-Sac*, he was a loudmouth, a bully, and a compulsive talker who had to be the center of attention at all times. He amused us at first, and we listened sympathetically to his accounts of clashes with McCarthy investigators and persecution at the hands of the Hollywood right-wingers who had compelled him to seek work in Britain. He had ordered twenty pounds of genuine pastrami from the Stage Delicatessen in New York, and we began by eating his pastrami, laughing at his jokes, and providing him with the court he needed. Then, as the same old stories received their umpteenth airing, we tired of pastrami, Stander, and the sound of his raucous laugh.

Françoise Dorléac was difficult in her own way. She arrived on Holy Island with twenty valises and a snapping, yapping, almost hairless chihuahua. She had smuggled it into Britain in her handbag, contravening the quarantine regulations. She suffered agonies during her periods, which rendered her incapable of working for days at a time. Bored and miserable, she disliked both Stander and Pleasence on sight. Françoise was too quintessentially French to join in the pub crawling that was our only form of after-hours relaxation. She regarded the Holy Islanders as barbarians and took violent exception to the conduct of the cockerel that was especially imported for the film along with a harem of hens.

She kept swinging at it with a broom whenever it pecked or copulated with them.

Holy Island claustrophobia took its toll on everyone. We were far too exposed to each other's company, and complaints of all kinds – about rooms, food, and the conduct of some of the crew – flew thick and fast. Tweed salmon is supposed to be the best in the world, but the pub cooks stewed it till the flesh turned to gray mush, whereas the skin, by some mysterious process, became even tougher. The islanders' staple dish was boiled mutton, and the crew conveyed their opinion of it in a ritual that steadily lost its entertainment value as the weeks went by: whenever they had boiled mutton for lunch, they returned to the set bleating like sheep. Even ultra-British Gil Taylor succumbed to the general mood of irritation. One night, convinced that Iain Quarrier was picking on him, he punched him hard in the face. As he put it, 'Iain gets a bit boring after dark.' Iain had become a bit boring during the day, too. Although I'd given him weeks in which to practice walking on his hands, his performance on the day amounted to two or three faltering steps. On a mundane level, the colony of earwigs in my trailer was multiplying fast. I would return, exhausted after a day's shooting, to find my bed crawling with the shiny, wiggly bugs. I did my best to fight them with massive doses of DDT.

My immediate problem, however, was Lionel Stander. Lazy at heart, he tackled his role with an almost manic enthusiasm that proved to be regrettably short-lived. Whenever I picked him up on his delivery or gestures, he would enumerate the reasons underlying his decision to speak or move in a certain way. He construed all my suggestions as an affront, assuming them to be motivated by hostility toward him as a person or disdain for him as an actor. I had to waste long minutes reassuring him that there was neither animosity nor a conflict of personalities involved, merely a wish to get things right. He would then proceed to overpraise me, telling me that he'd never been so ably directed in his life.

All these digressions swallowed up precious time. It became clear to me that unless we got some bright, windless spells, we would quickly fall behind schedule. When Stander's enthusiasm waned, as it very soon did, we slowed down even more.

Quite how Stander hurt his knee – whether he really did stumble and wrench it, as he claimed – is something known only to him. No one on the set could recall any such incident, but one day, to our dismay, he started limping – theatrically – and using a stick. The crew, who had gradually come to dislike him, pointed out that he didn't always limp the same way. 'Which knee is it today, Lionel?' became a stock salutation. Klinger believes to this day that Stander had only one aim in mind: to spin out the shooting for as long as possible because his contract entitled him to extra daily fees if we overran a certain date.

Tensions boiled over in the scene where Dicky removes his belt and thrashes Teresa for giving him a hotfoot. During rehearsals Stander started thrashing away in earnest. 'It's only a rehearsal!' I kept shouting. Stander countered by complaining that François squirmed too much.

We had to do several takes. After chasing Françoise and pinning her down on the castle cobblestones, Stander was supposed to administer the beating while seated astride her. When the moment came, he hit her with the buckle end of the belt, genuinely hurting her. Françoise fought back fiercely, knees grazed and bleeding, and not all her convulsive struggles were acting. Then, in the middle of this highly realistic take, Stander stopped and looked up. 'You stupid cunt,' he said, 'you hurt my knee.'

Knowing that the crew were ready to kick his teeth in, I called a halt. Stander limped off. François was sobbing by now. 'What can I do?' I said to her in French. 'The man's crazy.' Realizing that he'd gone too far, Stander apologized. Somehow we finished the scene without further incident.

Soon afterward Françoise announced that she'd lost a filling. Since she trusted only French dentists, she insisted on taking two days off. We rearranged our shooting schedules with the utmost difficulty, and she flew over to Paris. Unbeknown to any of us, she took her chihuahua with her. All went well until she returned to Heathrow, where a customs officer searched her handbag and got bitten for his pains. Françoise was detained. Gene was in London for his musical, luckily, but it took all his fixer's finesse to sort things out; breaking the British quarantine regulations was a serious offense. The chihuahua was flown back to Paris, making Françoise more miserable than ever. She eventually found solace in the arms of Roy Ford, Gil Taylor's assistant cameraman, and became much more relaxed.

Between the weather and Stander's knee, we were falling as badly behind schedule as I'd feared. Klinger and Tenser came to the island, bent on cutting out scenes and revising their familiar complaints about too many takes. Admittedly, they did have problems. Being responsible for the completion guarantee, Film Finances were getting jittery. I offered to put my percentage of *Repulsion*'s profits on the line, and even part of my director's fee. Sam Waynberg tried vainly to dissuade me; but I did, in fact, pledge my *Repulsion* earnings, and it was several years before I could draw any part of them.

Then another health problem arose. This time it was Lionel Stander's heart. He started complaining of chest pains, so we whisked him off to a Newcastle hospital for tests. They proved negative. Under questioning, however, Stander admitted to a previous history of cardiac trouble, which he'd failed to disclose when completing his insurance questionnaire for the film. The insurance company blew its corporate top and threatened to pull out. If anything happened to Stander on location, said the underwriters, they'd disclaim liability.

They finally relented, but only if he restricted his working hours to six per day. We immediately held a summit conference attended by all involved in the film's financing. It looked as if we'd have to cut our losses and stop shooting. Even our absentee producer, Gene Gutowski, turned up. Because he neglected to consult the tide tables, however, he and his small son remained marooned for hours on the tarpaulin top of a truck submerged by the incoming North Sea. A boat tried to rescue them but failed, so they had to wait till the tide receded. This incident, which filled Klinger with grim satisfaction, left Gene a nervous wreck. The truck was a write-off, but for once the expense could hardly be blamed on me.

Gérard Brach saved the day. Infiltrating the Stander camp, he spread the story that I was so bowled over by the quality of Stander's acting that I'd decided to star him in my next film, *Chercher la Femme*. But, said Gérard, owing to the actor's heart trouble and his temperamental behavior on the set, I was conducting an agonizing reappraisal of the whole idea.

It worked like a charm. Miraculously Stander's knee and chest pains vanished. No longer afflicted by palpitations, he worked whatever hours we wanted him to work. Throughout our last couple of weeks on Holy Island his behavior was impeccable.

My next visitor was Jill St John. We'd finished shooting Jackie Bisset's scenes, fortunately, so she'd already left. The only problem was, Jill was less of a sport about the earwigs. My losing battle with them – they actually seemed to thrive on DDT – came to an end when Sam Waynberg visited my trailer on the day of Jill's arrival. He was so appalled by the horror-film extent of their invasion that he rented the mead brewery manager's house for me and insisted I move there right away. The earwigs had won.

What remained to be shot, at the time of this major financial crisis, was one long and complicated scene in which a tipsy Donald Pleasence begins by telling Stander about his marital problems. During his incoherent ramblings, a plane flies overhead. Stander mistakes this for a rescue bid by the mysterious Katelbach. When his theory proves unfounded, he fires at the plane in a fury. The noise of the shots brings Françoise Dorléac out of the sea.

I wanted to stage this scene in a single shot at the 'magic hour' before dusk, bringing the plane into the frame without a cut. Long takes are always preferable when filming emotional scenes because they enable actors to stay right inside their roles.

The atmosphere on the set was so tense, and everyone so edgy, that even Gil Taylor deserted me, insisting it couldn't be done. He invoked RAF know-how and said that getting airplanes to appear on cue was difficult to the point of impossibility.

Undaunted, I rehearsed the cast and crew all day. I'd had a little soundproof booth built on the beach, just behind the camera, for the radio operator who directed the plane's movements. His headset and microphone enabled him to talk to the pilot and listen to the actors on the ground at the same time. I asked him to use his discretion when cuing in his airborne partner, and his judgment proved unerring.

There had already been several delays. Françoise, who hadn't objected to nudity in a bedroom scene with Pleasence, was reluctant to appear nude on the beach. I convinced her that she'd be filmed at long range. Then she decided the water was too cold. I explained that all she had to do was drop her bathrobe and run into the distant shallows. As soon as the camera panned off her, following the two men, she could come back onto the beach. Toward the end of the scene she had to reenter the shot, wet and donning her robe as though she'd been swimming.

We were halfway through the third take, with Pleasence and Stander doing their stuff beautifully, when Gene, who was standing behind me, whispered, 'Françoise has fainted!' Pleasence and Stander carried on with their dialogue.

'Well, get her to unfaint!' I hissed back. My one and only concern was that she should reappear in the shot on cue. When she failed to make it, I had to cut. It came hard because this had been the best take so far.

We watched as a small procession made its way up the beach, carrying an inanimate Françoise. Everyone was exaggeratedly solicitous about her. Already quick to complain whenever they got a chance, the whole crew seized upon this incident as if it were the last straw. Françoise had apparently fainted because of the cold, and they did their best to make me feel like a monster. Pleasence, on behalf of them all, lodged a formal protest. There was even talk of a strike, though Françoise herself was right as rain the next day and bore me no grudge.

We shot seven minutes and forty seven seconds of screen time that day in that one shot, and although Klinger made us pack up and leave Holy Island before the film had been completed to my satisfaction, that was basically it. After reshooting some scenes at Shepperton Studios, we were through. The strain on my nerves had been considerable, though. I felt absolutely drained. I spent several days holed up in a room at the London Hilton, seeing no one, taking no calls, just staring into space for most of the time. I didn't even feel like seeing Jackie Bisset.

Not even the prospect of acquiring a new home had any immediate effect on my morale. Gérard had spotted a For Sale sign outside a charming little house at 95 West Eaton Place Mews, just off Eaton Square. It was a recently converted mews house, two stories joined by a spiral staircase. My bank balance was almost zero, but my prospects were good. Thanks to some merchant banker friends of Gene Gutowski's, I obtained a low-interest loan and bought the lease.

Pulling myself together, I emerged from my hideaway. There was *Cul-de-Sac* to be edited and furniture to be bought for the new house. Gene's wife, Judy, took me and Gérard to the London Bedding Center to choose a bed.

The salesman, a distinguished-looking gentleman who could have passed for a retired ambassador, took obvious pride in his merchandise. 'Guaranteed for twenty years,' he said of one bed. 'And that,' he went on, pointing to another, 'is guaranteed for life.' I couldn't conceive of anything more macabre than buying a bed with a view to dying in it. He asked exactly what I had in mind, king-size or queen-size. Being unfamiliar with these regal terms, I was duly impressed.

I went up to one of the largest beds on display and tested the springs. Judy, a careful spender, always reprimanding me for my extravagance, pronounced it far too big for me.

236

'Is Madam a large person?' the salesman inquired discreetly.

Judy seized Gérard and drew him down onto one of the smaller beds, where they simulated sleep. The salesman said, 'Yes, indeed, sir, that bed is quite adequate for two persons of average build.'

'Sure,' I said, 'but how about three?'

He looked puzzled. 'You mean the baby, sir?'

I bought one of the largest beds in the store.

Shortly after it had been delivered, Victor Lownes threw a party. Some dancers from Gene's musical came, and one of them, a pretty, baby-faced blonde, took a shine to me.

LSD, still legal at this period, was the rage in London. Victor, who'd tried some, asked me if I'd like to have, as he put it, 'an experience.' I was very down on drugs, principally because I hated the supine apathy they induced in certain of my friends, but I'd heard a lot about LSD and was in the mood for anything.

'Okay,' I said, 'but go easy on the stuff.'

He said he'd give me only five drops. For all that meant to me, he could have said fifty. My blond dancer decided to take some, too. Before long, we were necking in a corner, and I asked her to come home with me. The new house was bare of furniture, but at least I had my monumental bed.

As we were leaving, Victor said, 'Sure you can drive?'

'Of course,' I replied, feeling perfectly normal at this stage.

'You'd better stay,' he advised, but I had other things on my mind. His parting words were 'Roman, remember, whatever happens, it won't last.'

We climbed into my Mini Cooper and drove off. Everything was fine till we passed Harrods. Then the wooden steering wheel changed shape. It felt different, too. Suddenly I realized that my surroundings were unfamiliar to me. Get a grip on yourself, I thought. You're taking this great chick home. There's Harrods, and there's a church. A church? What church? I had no idea where I was, so I stopped the car.

'I'm lost,' I said.

The girl sat back, relaxed and smiling. 'So why not have a little rest?' she said. There was something odd about the way she looked, but I couldn't pin it down.

With superhuman effort, I found my way home at last. As soon as we got inside, we started necking again. It felt good. The girl said, 'Those stairs – aren't they fantastic? Isn't that green marvelous?'

The only stairs I could see were red.

There was nothing to sit on, so we went upstairs to the bed. The lack of curtains bothered me; the light hurt my eyes. I draped a blanket over the window.

The girl sat close beside me. I began talking to her, but I soon became aware that she wasn't listening. She was motionless and completely withdrawn.

'That really was a hell of a thing they did,' I said, 'giving us that stuff.'

'Who?' she said, then: 'Who's they?' LSD must induce some form of paranoia, I thought; I was blaming others for something I'd done quite voluntarily. I also decided the effects were wearing off.

'No,' she said quietly, 'I think they're getting worse.'

Determined to remain in command of the situation, I came up with a brilliant solution. 'The thing to do,' I said, 'is to try to throw up.'

By now she was passively repeating the tail end of everything I said. 'Throw up,' she muttered. We'd ceased to be a mutually attracted couple and become total strangers.

I went into the bathroom and switched on the light. Everything exploded. I stared at myself in the mirror. My hair was a mixture of fluorescent green and pink; my face kept changing shape. 'Whatever happens,' I repeated, over and over, 'it won't last.'

I lifted the toilet seat and tried to vomit, but I couldn't. I looked down and spat, and my spittle made concentric, rainbow-colored ripples of incredible beauty. They drifted out toward the extremities of the bowl.

I started to fill a water glass from the faucet. 'I'm putting my fingers around the glass,' I told myself. 'Now I'm picking it up. Why am I doing this? To get a drink of water.' It was as though all my movements had to be broken down in the brain, like the components of a jump-cut sequence.

I carried the glass of water into the bedroom. The girl was lying on her back, half-undressed, staring at the ceiling. We held each other quite platonically. 'Here,' I said, 'this'll cheer you up. Whatever you're feeling, it won't last.'

I switched on a transistor radio and saw – actually *saw* – the music issuing from it. A black female voice was singing the blues. 'Look at that voice,' I said. 'Can you see it, too?' There was no answer.

Although the night was one of alternating horror and depression, I also had moments of extraordinary lucidity. My brain was an ultrasophisticated computer capable of any intellectual feat. I could almost see it function, but it sometimes felt as if it were all jammed up – as if someone had rammed a screwdriver into the works. How can I play with my head this way? I thought. I must fight back – try to be rational.

There were fleeting moments of ecstasy, too. We never made love, but I touched the girl's stockings and couldn't get over how fabulously soft and fine they felt – like cobwebs or clinging gossamer. 'How beautiful you are,' I said – and she was. She looked like a princess in a children's story book.

'What?' she snapped harshly. 'What did you say?' – and suddenly she underwent a transformation. Hers was now a Lotte Lenya face, extravagantly daubed with mascara and black lipstick. To my horror, her eyes and mouth became three spinning swastikas. I made a mental note of all these things; my brain was crystal clear and alert enough to convey that my hallucinations stemmed from a kind of cerebral short circuit.

As the night wore on, it seemed to me that I was experiencing everything it normally takes a lifetime to experience – every possible state and emotion from love, sex, and war to

239

death itself. Then, in the middle of it all, a bright idea occurred to me: this was an ideal time to psychoanalyze myself.

I tried. I touched my thumb with one of the fingers on my other hand. 'First comes love,' I said aloud. A square took shape above my thumb, filled with the signs of the tarot and zodiac, and hung in midair.

I raised my index finger. 'Then comes sex.' A rectangle appeared.

The third finger symbolized work or a job. Another rectangle.

While this was going on, the girl and I drifted steadily apart. She became more and more withdrawn, barely conscious of my presence. I was talking to myself and seeing things; she was engrossed in her own private nightmare. Both of us suffered bouts of anguish and sorrow, weeping but not coming together in our pain. We wept in isolation, without holding each other.

Later, still lying on the bed, I seemed to see everything through a fisheye lens.

I went to the bathroom for the twentieth time. Looking at myself in the mirror, I almost screamed: My eyes had no irises, just empty black holes.

This made me panic, but it also brought me to my senses. As soon as I could walk, I told myself, I'd go to Gene Gutowski's and get help.

It must have been five in the morning when I rang his bell. Characteristically Gene rose to the occasion. He gave me a glass of milk – I could feel three rims when I put it to my lips, not one – and sent Judy around to my place to fetch the girl. We wound up in bed together after all – Gene's bed – and Tony Greenburgh came and gave us massive Valium injections. It was late afternoon when we woke, feeling groggy but otherwise little the worse for wear. The girl went off to the theater – how she performed I'll never know – and I went home. We never met again. Neither of us wanted to remember what the other had witnessed.

240

I told Iain Quarrier about my trip.

'Great, eh?' he said.

'No,' I said, 'it was horrible.'

While still hallucinating, I'd grasped a peculiar fact: there was nothing in my nightmarish visions about Holy Island, nothing about *Cul-de-Sac* and its attendant tribulations. My depression had gone. In some strange way, the acid had cured it.

NINETEEN

For all my problems with the Compton Group, filmmaking in the mid-1960's was relatively quick and easy by the standards of today. Now the average feature film takes two years to complete, from start to finish, and the legal and financial problems are far more complex. While editing *Cul-de-Sac*, I was promoting *Repulsion*; while promoting *Cul-de-Sac*, I was preparing *The Fearless Vampire Killers*. That made me a film-a-year director. Michael Klinger and Tony Tenser may not have been Warner Brothers, but they were certainly fast.

I was now introduced to the phenomenon of the promotional tour. *Repulsion* opened in Stockholm, Paris, Munich, and, finally, New York and Los Angeles. I was on hand most of the time. The Vienna opening was important to Sam Waynberg, so I made a point of attending it. In return, he did his best to make it worth my while.

Once the press conference and premiere were over, Sam bore me off to a nightclub called the Moulin Rouge, an erstwhile theater with red plush boxes and lots of gilded stucco. Patrons wined and dined in the stalls. They could also cavort on the stage, which doubled as a dance floor during intermissions between striptease acts and spot numbers performed by jugglers and acrobats.

This being Vienna, our party would hardly have been complete without a third man. A tall, aging playboy with graying sideburns, he was a Polish friend of Sam's from way back and owned a chain of laundries. At a signal from the Laundry King, as I nicknamed him, a gaggle of hostesses and strippers converged on our table. My spirits sank. All I could think of were those predatory females who'd proved so elusive during my night out in Munich with Marek Hlasko and Ignac Taub. I was all for moving on, but Sam kept plying me with champagne and telling me to be patient. I did my best to relax, and then the Laundry King announced that the time had come for us 'to answer the inexorable call of nature.'

Pretty stewed by this time, we climbed the stairs to the dress circle. I noticed as we did so that some performing poodles were going through their paces on the stage. In my maudlin state, I was filled with nostalgia for Jules and Paris.

But that wasn't all I noticed as we went upstairs. Each of us had acquired a female partner. My own companion ushered me into a box, where she improvised a couch out of three or four red plush stools. Then she sat me down, unzipped my fly, and, without more ado, started fellating me. In the midst of this unexpected proceeding, the curtains behind me were swept aside. Stricken with embarrassment, I simultaneously zipped myself up and rolled over into a fetal crouch. 'Don't worry, *Liebling*,' I was told, 'it's only the waiter.' After opening a bottle of champagne, the man withdrew.

My companion now removed her clothes, with the exception of her high-heeled shoes, black fishnet stockings, and garters, which made her look like a Kokoschka drawing. While she was undressing me, I glanced over the parapet. A remarkably dexterous conjurer was hard at work below. With similar dexterity, the girl produced a condom from nowhere and fitted me with it. Then, having sluiced herself with champagne, she straddled me and engaged in some vigorous fornication. She later tossed the used rubber into the champagne bucket.

I preserve a hazy recollection of Sam, stark naked, pursuing an equally naked girl from box to box. When we were done, my own girl and I got dressed and sat on our stools, chatting demurely and sipping champagne. We surveyed the stalls, now empty. The last patrons had left, the stage curtains were drawn, and chairs were being upended on tables. Stationing themselves just below us, the orchestra struck up a Viennese waltz and gazed soulfully in our direction. With a nonchalant air, the Laundry King produced a big wad of 100-schilling bills and tossed them down. Like autumn leaves, they fluttered toward the musicians, who discreetly retrieved them without missing a note.

Not every promotional tour culminated in such a spectacular finale.

My U.S. *Repulsion* tour was memorable chiefly because it enabled me to see a lot of Jill St John, who not only met me at Los Angeles airport but let me drive us home to Bel Air in her Ferrari. Jill lived in a cozy stone house of her own design, with expanses of thick white carpet and a bathroom as filled with plants as the patio that led off it.

I'd never stayed in a Hollywood home before, always in hotels, and I appreciated its luxury and tranquillity. Only one little incident gave me pause for thought. I noticed a toy revolver lying on Jill's bedside table. At least, I thought it was a toy. When I started playing with it, she told me it was loaded. Being unused to girls who kept loaded handguns in their bedrooms, I was taken aback. Jill explained, as if it were the most natural thing in the world, that she needed it, that it made her feel secure. I hadn't associated Hollywood with crime, except the screen variety. People seldom locked their doors there, and it had always struck me as the safest, most law-abiding community imaginable.

The editing of *Cul-de-Sac* was still incomplete, so I couldn't take a long vacation, but I did need to get away. I met Victor Lownes, Andy Braunsberg, Tony Greenburgh, Gene Gutowski, and Hans Möllinger in Sankt Anton, Austria. Klinger was angry with Gene and me for, as he put it, deserting our posts, but we had a good time in spite of him.

It was Sankt Anton that started me thinking seriously about my next project. I'd often talked of writing a vampire spoof with Gérard. Whenever we went to horror movies in Paris, audiences were reduced to laughter. Why not make a film they could laugh with, rather than at?

Skiing down the serenely impressive Arlberg Valley, I

realized what the setting for a picture of this type should be: not a tatty rural location situated conveniently near a film studio – the rule with most Hammer productions – but swaths of frosted pine trees, massive snowdrifts, and majestic mountain peaks. I still had no detailed idea of the form the plot would take, but I knew I wanted it set in a brilliant white landscape like this. As with Mazury and *Knife in the Water*, the setting imposed itself before the story line crystallized.

We wouldn't be making our next film with the Compton Group. We knew our relationship with Klinger and Tenser was damaged beyond repair. Its deterioration had been slow but steady. Although Gene may have spent more time in London than on Holy Island during *Cul-de-Sac*, he was forever on the receiving end of vituperative letters from Klinger, some justified, others not. Because of our skiing vacation, Klinger withheld our fees for five weeks, resuming payment only when Gene threatened to sue.

More financial bickering followed when *Cul-de-Sac* opened in London and continental Europe. The Compton Group's accountants failed to produce contractual statements for months on end, and even when they did, their handiwork showed signs of creative bookkeeping. What else could have explained the fact that our share in *Repulsion*'s sales amounted to £425 for Sri Lanka and £500 for Burma, whereas France earned us only £364 and 15 shillings?

The atmosphere wasn't improved when Klinger started dredging up trivialities from the past, quibbling about minor expenses incurred while *Repulsion* was being made, like Catherine Deneuve's £40 hairdresser's bill from Vidal Sassoon. This he pronounced exorbitant and refused to pay. There was nothing for us to do but to look around for another source of finance.

With the great British filmmaking boom at its height, independent Hollywood producers were visiting London in droves during the mid-sixties. Among them was Ben Kadish, who knew Gene Gutowski and had met me in L.A. Kadish was an associate of Marty Ransohoff and John Calley, who ran a production company called Filmways. It was evident that Kadish meant to put down roots in London. He had moved there lock, stock, and barrel, complete with his family and a basset hound which he had quarantined for the regulation six months. When Filmways expressed interest in our vampire spoof idea, we started making plans.

Filmways, which was in a very different league from the Compton Group, had a multipicture distribution deal with MGM. Although I'd never heard of Marty Ransohoff before, he possessed considerable filmmaking experience, having turned out hundreds of TV commercials before becoming the independent producer of *The Beverly Hillbillies* and such feature films as *The Americanization of Emily* and *The Sandpiper*. A smooth, persuasive talker with a slight lisp and sparse strands of hair combed carefully across a balding pate, he cultivated the laidback look – chinos and sweat shirts – and racy language of the unorthodox, new-style Hollywood independent. Producers and executives from the old school couldn't be expected to understand artists like me, he announced. With him, things would be different; he himself was an artist.

Halfway through our talks, Ransohoff saw *Cul-de-Sac* and promptly bought it for U.S. distribution, claiming that he adored it. Inside almost every producer lurks a frustrated film editor, but Ransohoff, as I found to my dismay, was more than a would-be editor; he was a compulsive butcher of other people's work. 'Let him finish the picture,' he used to tell his associates; 'then I'll do my number.' It was hardly surprising that no directors lasted long with Filmways, even when – like Norman Jewison, J Lee Thompson, and Arthur Hiller – they had multiple-film contracts.

Jill St John was wary of Ransohoff from the first. Bright as well as beautiful, she observed him closely through her long lashes when the three of us had dinner together during one of my exploratory trips to L.A. 'I think he's a phony,' she told me. 'I don't trust him.' All well and good, but how could I fail to trust a man who'd just demonstrated his enthusiasm for *Cul-de-Sac* by buying the U.S. distribution rights? I trusted him so much, in fact, that I agreed to give him the final cut of *The Fearless Vampire Killers* for the Western Hemisphere.

Meanwhile, Gérard and I were polishing off our *Vampire* script. Our basic aim was to parody the genre in every way possible while making a picture that would, at the same time, be witty, elegant, and visually pleasing. The script was a joy to write; Gérard and I spent much of the time in fits of laughter. The role of Professor Abronsius was conceived from the start as a vehicle for Jack MacGowran, whom we'd vowed to use ever since Holy Island, picturing him as a snow-dusted Albert Einstein. Iain Quarrier was a natural for the vampire count's homosexual son and heir. I myself proposed to play Alfred, Abronsius's assistant, and had ear-marked Jill St John for the part of Sarah, the innkeeper's succulent daughter.

But Filmways had other ideas. A name kept cropping up whenever the project was discussed: Charontais, or was it Charontait? That's how I mentally spelled it at first, French fashion, and that's how little I knew about her. I eventually discovered that Filmways had under a multifilm contract an actress named Sharon Tate. She was currently costarring with David Niven and Deborah Kerr in *Thirteen*, later retitled *Eye of the Devil* because its distributors were afraid that an unlucky number would jinx the box-office receipts. Everyone said she was very beautiful – a girl to watch.

When Marty Ransohoff visited London with his partner, John Calley, Filmways threw a party at the Dorchester to celebrate his arrival. It was there I was introduced to Sharon Tate. We shook hands, made polite conversation, and ex-changed phone numbers before going our separate ways. I remember thinking her an exceptionally good-looking girl, but London was full of good-looking girls. More to the point, she was very much the all-American beauty – not what I had in mind for *Vampire Killers*. I was, however, sufficiently impressed at least to call her when Filmways stressed how eager they were to use an actress already under contract.

Sharon was living just around the corner from me, in an

Eaton Place apartment rented for her by Filmways. It was hung with paintings by David Hockney, who had only just begun to make his mark, and she shared it with her woman voice coach and a Yorkshire terrier puppy called Guinness. We arranged to have dinner together, and that was when my view of her changed.

Sharon was more than just stunning to look at. She wasn't naïve or stupid or a cliché starlet. Her background was conventionally middle-class but not without unusual features. Her father, an intelligence officer in the U.S. Army, had been stationed in Europe, and she spoke Italian fluently. She'd won several beauty contests as a teenager and had always hankered after a career in films despite her father's fear that Hollywood might make her easy meat for predatory males, if not turn her into a high-class hooker. In the end she simply hitched her way there and started making the rounds of the film and TV studios. After landing a few minor parts, she was spotted and signed by Marty Ransohoff – her first real break. She soon got to know a lot of people on the fringes of show business – the kind that thought it smart to cultivate the drug scene. I said I couldn't stand the types that lolled around at London parties, dazed and glassy-eyed from the effects of grass. Sharon said she smoked when the atmosphere and company were right; then it was a good sensation. I described my disastrous LSD trip. She said she'd taken LSD several times, and it wasn't necessarily scary. With some misgivings, we talked ourselves into taking a mild trip.

I drove her back to the mews house, making a brief stop at Iain Quarriers's place to pick up some acid. Iain gave me a cube of sugar with a one-person dose on it – 'Great stuff, believe me!' – and I split it between us.

My house was half-furnished by now, with curtains over the windows and the latest in stereo gear installed in the drawing room. Wide-awake with LSD, we listened to music and talked for hours, but the hours seemed to speed by. Sharon told me a lot more about herself, beginning with her sense of guilt at having come back with me at all. She was still involved with Jay Sebring, Hollywood's star hairdresser, and had lived with him for a while. In other respects, her sexual experiences had been relatively few and not always pleasant. Someone had raped her at the age of seventeen, but I believed her when she said it hadn't left her emotionally scarred. All that conflicted with the serenity in her beautiful face was a childish, incongrous habit of now and then nibbling at her nails. I teased her about it, telling her that it not only looked unsightly but betrayed a fundamental lack of self-assurance.

I suppose it was inevitable that we should go to bed together, but we didn't do so till dawn was breaking. Not at all scary this time, the acid lent our lovemaking a touch of unreality. Afterward we talked some more until I had to leave for Heathrow to catch a plane to Sweden, where I was scheduled to address a group of students at Lund University.

Thoughts of Sharon preoccupied me throughout the flight. What had impressed me most about her, quite apart from her exceptional beauty, was the sort of radiance that springs from a kind and gentle nature; she had obvious hang-ups yet seemed completely liberated. I'd never met anyone like her before.

We made a date when I called her a few days later, but she broke it. We made another, but she broke that, too. I called her again. She'd love to have dinner with me, she said, but she couldn't desert her dialogue coach. Why not, she didn't say. I thought she was playing games. 'Okay, Sharon,' I said quietly, 'why don't you go fuck yourself?' She told me later that this brush-off was the first thing that really whetted her interest in me.

We did meet again, with increasing frequency, but not to make love. Perhaps because of her continuing involvement with Sebring, we reverted to a more formal relationship. Ransohoff and Kadish were becoming more and more insistent on my giving her a part in *Vampire Killers*. Kadish raised the subject over drinks at Victor Lownes's place while Sharon herself was present. I made no secret of my quite objective belief that Jill St John was a natural for the part. I liked Sharon, I said, but personal considerations couldn't be allowed to obtrude. She simply didn't look Jewish enough. Though I didn't realize it at the time, Sharon was very hurt by my forthright views on the subject. Kadish urged me to test her all the same, so I agreed. Although Sharon's sun-kissed, milk-fed southern looks hardly fitted the role of a Jewish innkeeper's daughter, I wanted to accommodate my producer if possible.

She came to the studio, and I concealed her ash blond hair beneath a red wig, which altered her appearance considerably. She suddenly looked the part. Then we did some tests in costume – MacGowran, Sharon, and I.

Ransohoff wanted me to concentrate on directing and drop the idea of playing Alfred, but John Calley saw the tests and liked them. That I fitted the character couldn't be denied. I was short, youthful-looking, and strong enough for a physically demanding role. I was also in my element in snow.

Before Sharon could be hired, we had to square the British actors' union. My own employment presented no problem now that I was a permanent resident in the United Kingdom and a member of both Equity and ACTT; but Sharon was American, and the film was technically a British production. After much debate Equity agreed that full American financing rendered Sharon's participation acceptable.

Gene Gutowski took Hans Möllinger off to help him look for suitable Alpine locations. They sent back reports of a sensational Austrian castle deep in snow – just what we were looking for. I went to see the place for myself and found it ideal. Then, on the eve of the crew's departure from London, came a panic-stricken call from Gene: thanks to a freak change in the weather, all the snow had melted.

Frantically we set about reorganizing our plans. Gene and Hans scoured Europe for other possible locations and came up with an imperfect alternative, Val Gardena, a snowy plateau high in the Dolomites near an Italian ski resort called Ortisei. There was no castle at Ortisei, so all the castle sets would have to be studio-built – a far more expensive proposition. Their design and construction began at once on MGM's lot, the most modern in Europe. Only a few days later than originally scheduled, the crew and cast of *Vampire Killers* descended on Ortisei.

Filming in snow possesses a charm of its own, but it also poses problems. We arrived at the height of the winter season, and vacationers resented the way we monopolized the ski lifts and cable cars. Rooms were in short supply, so we had to be dispersed in a dozen widely scattered hotels. Simply assembling the crew and cast at a prearranged spot on the plateau turned out to be diabolically difficult. In defiance of a clause in my contract forbidding me to do any such thing, for fear I might injure myself, I got around fast on skis. The rest of the crew, who weren't as mobile, had to haul heavy generators and camera equipment through the snow, sometimes for long distances, before a day's shooting could start. This was a laborious, grueling, punishing business.

Roy Stevens, my assistant director, was largely instrumental in saving the day. Having worked on such epics as *Doctor Zhivago* and *Lawrence of Arabia*, he was inured to logistical problems. Roy rented half a dozen snow scooters and procured snowcats as transportation for the crew. Above all, he contrived to keep everyone laughing when scooters overturned, trucks got stuck in the snow, or the crew lost their way and spent hours getting to the right place, only to find it blanketed by fog.

Our first month's outdoor filming became a series of ingenious improvisations, mainly because the last-minute switch from one location to another had left us so little time to revise our shooting schedules. The fact that we were filming in Italy entailed the employment of a certain number of Italian technicians, and that, in turn, bred some international friction. Gene Gutowski rightly suspected the Italians of robbing us blind. By and large, however, and despite British complaints about the local beer, our motley team got on well in its claustrophobic mountain retreat. There was none of the overt hostility that had afflicted the making of *Cul-de-Sac*.

One of my minor problems was Terry Downes. I'd hired this young former world champion middleweight boxer

251

because his face and physique were perfect for Kukol, Count von Krollock's hunchbacked servant. Terry was one of the gentlest men imaginable, despite his looks, and his part required no previous acting experience. He did, however, develop a couple of quirks when drunk. One was to perform a weird striptease act, the other to vent his hatred of Germans. Ortisei's commonest language is German, which makes it popular with German and Austrian tourists. Terry showed up there accompanied by two bodyguards, bookmaker pals of his with scarred faces and cauliflower ears. He celebrated his first night on location by picking a fight with some German guests in the hotel bar. He and his 'mob' not only made mincemeat of them but wrecked the joint as well, whereupon the Italian police threatened to deport us en masse. We asked Terry's chums to leave and made sure that from then on, he was never left unsupervised in the evenings. All that remained was a communications problem. Coupled with one of the thickest Cockney accents I'd ever heard, Terry's slurred and punchy enunciation made him almost unintelligible.

Hans Möllinger acted as stunt man for all the really dangerous scenes. Our trickiest moment came during the sequence in which Kukol tries to prevent Abronsius, Alfred, and the inn-keeper's daughter from fleeing the vampire count's castle. Hans, doubling for Terry Downes, had to grab a coffin and hurtle down the snow-covered slopes to cut them off at a pass. We made several takes with Hans using a coffin mounted on runners – the three of us galloping along in our horse-drawn sleigh, Hans overhauling it on his bizarre toboggan. The first time he was a little early. I altered the timing slightly to bring him in closer. On the fourth take I overdid it: Hans shot across our front, shaving the shaft of the sleigh with his head and only narrowly missing the horses' hooves. That, needless to say, was the take I used. Roy Stevens and I played stunt men, too. I ignored Filmways's instructions and did all my own skiing as Alfred. Because Alfie Bass, our innkeeper, wasn't up to it, I dressed

252

Roy in Alfie's costume and had him scale the wall of the inn to get to the chambermaid's bedroom.

It was at Ortisei that my relationship with Sharon progressed beyond the casual stage. We hadn't made love since that one first night in London, and there were butterflies in my stomach when she joined us on location. We dined together soon after shooting had begun. Then I walked her back to her hotel. When I asked, rather haltingly, if she wanted me to come upstairs with her, she gave me one of her uniquely dazzling smiles and said yes. That marked the real beginning of our love affair.

We returned to London and the man-made snows on the MGM lot. Although Sharon stayed on at her rented Eaton Place apartment, we spent more and more time together. Not surprisingly her acting in the film began to suffer as our emotional involvement deepened. It was a question of trying too hard. She told me later that the more she came to know me as a lover, the more ill at ease she felt on the set. Though devoid of the natural performer's self-confidence, she burned to do well – to prove to herself that she could accomplish something in her own right. Giving her the necessary reassurance wasn't easy. *Vampire Killers* was behind schedule, but my tendency on such occasions is to become more exacting rather than less. I started doing more and more takes with Sharon – on one occasion as many as seventy.

Other factors conspired to delay us as well. Under close examination, almost every shot in *Vampire Killers* reveals some kind of special but time-consuming effect such as snow, dust, or cobwebs. Douglas Slocombe, my cameraman, was lavish with lighting and rather on the slow side.

Above all else, the British film unions made life difficult; they became increasingly militant and restrictive. They had the upper hand, now that so many film companies were working in Britain, and had started to put the screws on directors and producers alike. Gone were the days when my crew would work beyond the 5:20 P.M. deadline without

253

advance notice, as it had on *Repulsion*. Everyone involved in the making of *Vampire Killers* worked strictly to rule. This became a nightmare toward the end of shooting because initial delays at Ortisei had prolonged our schedule. MGM had prior commitments, so we were obliged to move to Elstree Studios. Then, when we ran out of time at Elstree, we had to transfer to Pinewood. The last thing we shot at Elstree was a ballroom scene, and it was imperative that we complete it in five days. The elaborate makeup of some sixty vampires took hours to apply, so we could shoot only from midday on. With admirable foresight, Gene had come to an agreement with the crew providing for two hours' overtime a day. Unhappily two of the studio personnel, a gaffer and a grip, were engaged in a long-standing dispute with the Elstree management over an extra sixpence on their hourly overtime rate – 'Nuffink personal, guvnor,' as one of them put it. This meant that the rest of the crew couldn't work the two hours' overtime after all. The irony of the situation was that because of Gene's agreement, we were obliged to pay them for the overtime whether they worked it or not. Such were the ways in which Britain's film unions ensured the early demise of the British film industry.

Anatole Dauman visited during a trip to England. He brought me best regards from my dog, Jules, and expressed his wonder at the opulence of the sets and the size of my budget. 'You've really made it over here' was his verdict.

'Have we?' I asked Gérard Brach when Anatole had gone. In view of all my problems, I wasn't so sure.

Sharon moved in with me while we were still shooting at Elstree. It was a gradual process – one that matched the increasing amount of time we spent together. Little by little her clothes began to accumulate in my bedroom closet. Then she suggested making it semipermanent. 'Don't worry,' she told me, 'I won't swallow you up like some ladies do.' Knowing my fear of possessive women, she made it clear in all sorts of ways that she understood my life-style and had no intention of cramping it. I'd never received such an assurance from anyone else.

She moved in shortly after Easter, when shooting was suspended for a few days. I'd planned to take her to St-Tropez, but my Polish passport made last-minute foreign travel difficult, so we decided instead on a trip to Eastbourne, the English south coast resort. It was a horrific experience. We spent one night on narrow twin beds in an old-fashioned Charles Addams-like hotel where ties had to be worn in the dining room and the lounge was full of geriatric cases playing bingo. 'I don't think I can stand this,' I said. 'Let's go back to London.' We spent the rest of the brief vacation at my place, listening to records, talking, and making love. I discovered yet another side of Sharon: she was a homebody – a superb cook and a dedicated housewife.

She began to make a tremendous difference in my life. We took to spending more evenings at home and entertaining more people, some of them Hollywood friends like Warren Beatty, Dick Sylbert and Yul Brynner, others 'locals' like Victor Lownes, Andy Braunsberg, Simon Hessera, Larry Harvey, and Michael Sarne, who had just finished directing his first feature, *Joanna*.

Jay Sebring, Sharon's former boyfriend, also showed up in London. I hadn't wanted to meet him, but she insisted on the three of us having lunch together. We met at Alvaro's, just around the corner. I felt dreadfully awkward, but he wasn't at all as I expected. Rather taciturn, he kept regarding me quizzically as if to say: is he good enough for her? It was Sebring who put me at my ease by conveying that he accepted the loss of Sharon without rancor. He was gently amusing over lunch, self-deprecating but never abjectly so. We developed an immediate rapport, almost as if we'd known each other for years, and he quickly became a regular member of our circle.

The vast majority of my friends, especially Gene Gutowski, who claimed to have been the matchmaker, were delighted that Sharon had moved in with me. The only person who advertised his disapproval was Marty Ransohoff. He himself may have had designs on Sharon, though that possibility didn't occur to me till later. I only recall his display of annoyance at our obvious happiness. 'Sharon's become more sure of herself lately,' I told him after we'd been living together for a couple of months. 'She's shaken off some of her hang-ups.'

Ransohoff glowered. 'Yes,' he retorted, 'she's shaken off some, and she's acquiring others.'

Sharon displayed no hang-ups when Filmways wanted her to appear nude in a *Vampire Killers* layout for *Playboy*, as Catherine Deneuve had done in the case of *Repulsion*, especially when it was suggested that I handle the photography myself. Personally I wasn't too enthusiastic about the idea, but there was no doubting its publicity value.

Sharon's nude bathtub scene in *Vampire Killers*, from which a still was selected for the layout, formed the subject of one of the numerous Filmways memos that were now coming my way. Ben Kadish wrote: 'I would be less than candid if I were to overlook the fact that there appears to be an imperceptible mustache on Sharon Tate in this scene. You will probably want to reshoot it.'

I wrote back: 'You will be even more alarmed to know that she is also growing a pair of balls.'

The nude scene also evoked a series of injunctions against overstepping the bounds of propriety. The following MGM memo, forwarded to me after their executives had read the script, illustrates the extent of the prudery then afflicting the film industry and the extraordinary changes that have taken place since:

Page 5 – Please avoid any overemphasis on the girl's cleavage.

Page 7 – Please avoid any overexposure of the girl throughout this bathing sequence.

Page 14 – Alfred's intimate caressing of the girl would be unacceptable as described in scene 101.

Page 17 – It would be important to avoid excessive gruesomeness throughout this production. Specifically, we ask that you eliminate the 'bloodstained mouth.'

Page 21 – The double meaning dialogue on this page should be toned down. Specifically, we ask that you eliminate the expression ' . . . have a quick one?'

Pages 22-4 – The attack on the girl will have to be done with restraint since she is in the midst of her bath. Please avoid undue nudity. Also, the 'biting' and 'gulping' could not be approved as described at the bottom of page 23.

Page 30 – We cannot approve the line 'I'll stick it somewhere up you . . . '

Page 59 – We cannot approve the expletive 'Jesus!' Also, on this page we ask that you avoid using the word 'whore' twice.

Page 63 – We caution you against nudity in connection with this bathing scene.

Pages 75-6 – It is quite obvious that Herbert is to be characterized as a homosexual. We do not object to this fact, but do ask that you avoid any physical advances on his part toward Alfred. This would refer to any embracing or fondling, while his attack as a vampire would not prove objectionable.

And so on and so forth . . .

I was growing rather wary of MGM. I was also growing suspicious of Ransohoff, particularly when I found that Sharon's agent was his agent, too, and had helped renegotiate her contract downward. Ransohoff summoned her to Los Angeles to play opposite Tony Curtis in a comedy – *Don't Make Waves* – at a paltry $750 a week.

From L.A. she sent me funny, affectionate letters in her spindly handwriting. 'Roman,' she wrote in one of the first I received, 'you should see my fingernails, they're growing up a storm. I can't believe it – you just wait – I'll be able to scratch your back with long sexy nails.' She also described the house she'd rented from a friend: 'I know you'll enjoy it so much. It's a love house and a space house – a very strange feeling of being on the moon.'

She was right. As soon as I'd completed the rough cut of *Vampire Killers*, I took it to L.A. to show Ransohoff and Calley. The week I spent there with Sharon was as fantastic as the house itself – a sort of honeymoon. Enforced separation had made us hungry for each other. I have never made love more often, or with greater emotional intensity, than I did with Sharon during those few days together. We were so wrapped up in each other that when Marek Hlasko phoned from somewhere in town, I made an excuse not to see him. I felt that Marek, with his propensity for physical violence, his incessant drinking, and his love of all-night binges, would somehow break the spell.

Professionally my week in L.A. was less agreeable. I was considerably shaken, on showing the rough cut to Ransohoff, to be told that he didn't like it one bit. My morale was somewhat restored when I showed it to Bronislau Kaper, who said he found it a wonderfully funny film.

It was a wrench leaving Sharon, but I had to get back to London, where Komeda was waiting with a score all ready for mixing once the editing had been completed. We were badly over budget – I'd spent more time on the picture than anyone had bargained for – but I still believed it all had been worthwhile.

Meanwhile, Sharon wasn't enjoying *Don't Make Waves* too much. Already tense, the atmosphere on the set was marred by tragedy when a young stunt man drowned after parachuting into the Pacific. Sharon said she couldn't sleep without me. 'I really enjoy every second I'm with you,' she wrote. 'I always feel so happy. Really, I don't know how to write it but I just love everything you are about. I know it sounds mushy but I simply love you.'

We spoke a great deal on the phone, so her letters contained little in the way of news. She regretted this. 'I always end up telling you everything I want to have as a surprise or tell you in my letters before they get to you,' she wrote. One item of news she reserved for a letter was her introduction by a girlfriend to the latest fad, a vibrator: 'I got one and boy it really feels strange. You should get one, it's really funny.

258

Mine won't plug in on English current but I must try it on you. And it's also good for stiff necks!'

Sharon completed *Don't Make Waves* and returned to London. No sooner was she back than I had to visit the States again. I took the completed film, fully mixed with Komeda's wonderful music, to show to some MGM executives in New York. The company was in the throes of a complicated proxy fight when I got there, and the energies of its top executives were directed elsewhere. Everyone was on the phone or in conference with legal advisers. No one had time to see my film.

When I finally managed to arrange a screening, it was attended by one little old vice-president with a strong Russian accent. He was on the phone eight or ten times during the film and absent for at least ten minutes. Clearly preoccupied with higher things, he said nothing throughout. My own reaction was to wonder what sort of people I was dealing with. Here was a project they'd spent more than $2 million on. I'd had to fight tooth and nail for Panavision, for adequate time, for the right kinds of sets and locations, and now they couldn't be bothered to view the finished product. Not that I knew it then, the whole atmosphere was symptomatic of the situation that arises when a major studio invests heavily in a picture and then loses interest in it. Hollywood is like that: a spoiled brat that screams for possession of a toy and then tosses it out of the baby buggy.

Eager to know when *Vampire Killers* would be released, I called Marty Ransohoff in Hollywood. The essence of his message was 'Wait and see.' The picture was too long as it stood, he said; some work would have to be done on it. In other words, Ransohoff had yet to do his number.

With nothing to show for a year's work but an unwanted movie, and no other projects in sight, I felt thoroughly depressed. Richard Horowitz suggested I join him for a few days' skiing in Vermont to clear my head. Sharon wasn't pleased, to say the least, when I phoned to tell her I'd be back a little later than planned. Before we set off, I took a call from Bob Evans, Paramount's newly appointed vice-president in charge of production. He said he knew how keen I was on skiing and added, 'We have a skiing picture for you.' He wanted me to come straight to Hollywood and read a script called *Downhill Racers*. I'd said I'd sooner put in some skiing first, then come to Hollywood.

When I got there, Bob listened patiently to my tales of woe about *Vampire Killers*. My first experience of working with a U.S. company had been an unmitigated disappointment, I told him. Besides, I now had Cadre Films and my partner, Gene Gutowski, to consider.

Bob said the Cadre situation could be handled and made no attempt to defend MGM. Then he said, 'Before you read anything else, I'd like you to look at this.' He pushed a stack of printer's galleys across the desk. '*Downhill Racers* was just a pretext to get you here. Read those galleys right away.'

Back in my Beverly Hills hotel room, I wrestled with the long swatch of yellowish paper. The title was *Rosemary's Baby*. My reaction to the first few pages was 'Hey, what is this, some kind of soap opera?'

But I read the rest of the book at that sitting. By the time I was through my eyes were popping out of my head. When Bob Evans called the next morning and asked my opinion of the book, I gave it a rave review.

'I thought so. Want to do it?' he asked.

'Yes,' I said. 'I want to do it.'

TWENTY

I was beginning to learn Hollywood's golden rule. You had to strike while the iron was hot or the moguls grew bored and lost interest. *Rosemary's Baby* got off to a model start in this respect: a quick yes from me, a prompt agreement from Paramount for me to write the script, and preproduction work soon thereafter. Gene Gutowski flew to L.A. to help hammer out the details. One novelty of the situation was that I needed a lawyer for the first time in my life. Gene arranged for our affairs to be handled by Wally Wolf, a junior partner in an up-and-coming law firm specializing in show business deals. Another novelty was that my director's and scriptwriter's fees came close to Hollywood's going rate. Although our agreement with Paramount assigned Gene no producer's role in the current project, we concluded provisional deals for two more pictures, one of them *Downhill Racers*. If they were made, we would handle them as a team.

The producer on *Rosemary's Baby* was Bill Castle, a redfaced giant of a man with a thatch of close-cropped white hair and a cigar permanently clamped between his teeth. Castle was a veteran director and producer of cheap horror movies who had rushed out and bought the film rights of *Rosemary's Baby* with his own money, then resold them at a tidy profit to Paramount, with which he had an exclusive contract. He'd wanted to direct the picture himself, but Bob Evans had put his foot down, insisting that it was a director's film and Bill wasn't quite up to it.

I flew back to London and started on the script, for once without Gérard. I reread the book – the magic still held –

penciled out the irrelevant passages, and dictated a preliminary draft to Concepta, our Cadre Films secretary. Pacing the little study on the top floor of my mews house, I worked all day, day after day. The rate of progress seemed incredible.

The fact was, Ira Levin's novel followed a cinematic pattern. There were none of the gray areas or weak spots that authors tend to camouflage with purple prose or tricks of style when their story line falters. At the same time one aspect of *Rosemary's Baby* bothered me. The book was an outstandingly well-constructed thriller, and I admired it as such. Being an agnostic, however, I no more believed in Satan as evil incarnate than I believed in a personal god; the whole idea conflicted with my rational view of the world. For credibility's sake, I decided that there would have to be a loophole: the possibility that Rosemary's supernatural experiences were figments of her imagination. The entire story, as seen through her eyes, could have been a chain of only superficially sinister coincidences, a product of her feverish fancies. The machinations of her next-door neighbors, the witches' Sabbath at which the Devil possesses her in her husband's presence, even the final scene around the baby's cradle, had to have some rational explanation. That is why a thread of deliberate ambiguity runs throughout the film. The witches' Sabbath and Rosemary's possession by the Devil *could* have been a nightmare; Guy *might* have scratched her while making love; the series of accidents *could* have been merely coincidences.

Much of the narrative in the second part of the book concerns itself with Rosemary's gradual conviction that she is being manipulated by evil forces. I had to convey this to the audience through action and dialogue. I did this by inserting a long scene in which Rosemary, more and more alarmed at what is happening to her, tells Dr Hill of her suspicions. He listens, sympathetic at first, and then betrays her by summoning the infamous Dr Saperstein in his consulting room and abandoning her to him.

The solitude of my intensive work on the script was relieved by daily calls from Sharon, who was house hunting in L.A. Before long she told me she'd found a marvelous place – a bit expensive, she said, but could she go ahead and sign the lease?

I saw why she'd fallen in love with the house when I showed up with the finished but slightly overlong first draft under my arm. It was one of those old Santa Monica mansions on Ocean Front, just off the Pacific Coast Highway, with a walled, tree-shaded garden, an ornamental pond, and a swimming pool. It had cavernous closets, masses of Audubon and Victorian flower prints, an enormous curving staircase down which Gloria Swanson might have made an entrance at any moment, and a somwehat masculine master bedroom lined with acres of somber paneling. The place had reputedly been built for Cary Grant, and the fact that it now belonged to Brian Aherne lent it an additional cachet. Like many of the Hollywood houses I came to know so well, it closely remembled a Hollywood film set of the thirties. This was no coincidence; when old-time stars and directors had had homes built, they had commissioned their art directors to design them. Although my per diem was substantial, the rent was a wild extravagance. I didn't really need such a large house, nor was it really my style. I'd have much preferred something more modern, but at least this caricature of a Hollywood mansion was good for a laugh among friends. Besides, Sharon's delight in it was all that mattered with me.

Taking my script to Paramount's secretarial pool, which was situated at the top of the writers' building, I asked the elderly woman supervisor whether anything could be done to make it look shorter – like using more single-space typing. A faraway look came into her eyes. 'The last person who asked me that,' she said, 'was Mr Von Sternberg.'

The secretarial pool was only one of Paramount's wide range of facilities. It maintained numerous departments manned by technicians versed in every aspect of filmmaking, and many Paramount staffers had spent their whole working lives on the premises. One such veteran was the secretary assigned to me for the duration of the film, Thelma Roberts, whose memories went back before the dawn of the talkie era.

A smart, tough-talking lady with dyed red hair, she gave an impression of primness and chilly efficiency, but this was deceptive. Thelma's icebound exterior masked a warm, generous nature. She fussed over me like a mother hen, showing me the ins and outs of the mazelike Paramount bureaucracy, shielding me from the importunities of actors and agents alike.

The Paramount commissary gave an inkling of Hollywood's pecking order. It comprised a separate dining room for VIPs and producers, directors and stars, and a vast, hangarlike cafeteria for the common herd, usually thronged with extras in every conceivable kind of costume. They ate beneath a gigantic blowup of Victor Mature playing Samson. The menu cover, inscribed 'See the Ten Commandments, Keep the Ten Commandments,' was signed by Cecil B. De Mille. It was characteristic of Paramount that employees were told to see the movie first.

One of my first steps when I recruited the team for *Rosemary's Baby* was to hire Dick Sylbert. Not only was he a personal friend and the best production designer in the business, but I could at last afford to employ him. I was doubly delighted because the real star of the picture would be the New York apartment where Rosemary and Guy go to live. Built on the Paramount lot, this set required much more than a conventional design job.

My prime concern was to re-create the specific mood and atmosphere of the year in which the action took place – 1965, or only two years earlier. Anthea Sylbert, Dick's sister-in-law, who designed the costumes, captured the contemporary look to a T. I decided to include glimpses on TV of Pope Paul VI's New York visit, which was fresh enough in people's minds to ring the right bell, together with a shot of the 'God Is Dead' issue of *Time* magazine. I also put in another highly topical allusion. 'Don't tell me you *paid* for this?' says Guy when Rosemary comes home with her hair bobbed. 'It's Vidal Sassoon,' she retorts, 'and it's very in.'

My casting procedure was unorthodox. As in *Cul-de-Sac*, I

began by making sketches of suitable faces for some of the characters. These were worked up into detailed portraits by a Paramount artist, and Hoyt Bowers, who headed the casting department still maintained by Paramount in those spacious days, set about matching them. This was how we came to hire such old-timers as Ralph Bellamy, Sidney Blackmer, Elisha Cook, and Patsy Kelly, none of whom I'd seen on the screen for years. Ruth Gordon I knew from more recent movies. She was the one member of the cast who differed markedly from Ira Levin's description of her character in the novel. Levin had made her big and jolly. In the film, Ruth proved extraordinarily effective as a small, birdlike, quintessential New Yorker.

Where Rosemary herself was concerned, Paramount fixed me up with a whole series of auditions with every available prospect in Hollywood, known and unknown. Charles Bluhdorn, president of Gulf & Western, the company that had just acquired Paramount, had revived the obsolete practice of putting young talent under long-term contract, and I interviewed every filly in his stable without result. I'd hoped that someone at Paramount might put Sharon's name forward; but nobody did, and I felt it would be out of line for me to do so.

It was Bob Evans who first mentioned Mia Farrow. All I knew about her was that she was married to Frank Sinatra, so I sat through some *Peyton Place* TV episodes to see how she came across. We then met and discussed the role at a nightclub called The Daisy. Although Mia didn't fit Levin's description or my own mental image of Rosemary – a robust, healthy, all-American girl – her acting ability was such that I hired her without a screen test.

That left the part of Guy, the young actor on the make. Laurence Harvey badly wanted to do it, but I needed someone who could play a clean-cut young American with the kind of looks favored by makers of TV commercials, plus enough fire and temperament to put him in the big time. I persuaded Warren Beatty to read the script. He procrastinated, as usual, and finally rejected the role as not important enough. Warren's parting shot was 'Hey, can I play Rosemary?'

I then thought of Peter Beard, the photographer, who'd been in *Hallelujah the Hills*. Peter had the requisite good looks but was rightly doubtful of his competence as an actor. I also auditioned a few real-life TV commercial actors, none of whom was good enough.

Among my many tryouts was a complete unknown who'd played in some eminently forgettable horror films. His name was Jack Nicholson. I never seriously considered him for the part – rightly so, in my opinion. For all his exceptional talent, Jack's faintly rakish and sinister appearance disqualified him for the role of an upstanding, clean-cut, conventionally handsome young actor.

Robert Redford had been my number one candidate for all sorts of reasons: his good loods; his talent; the credibility he would have brought to the part. Unfortunately, Paramount and Redford were in the midst of a feud. He had signed to star in a western called *Blue* but walked out on it, sensing disaster. Paramount's management was furious with him. I naïvely thought that if Redford could be persuaded to work on *Rosemary's Baby*, it would square things with the studio. Besides, I had another card up my sleeve. Knowing that Redford was a keen skier, I intended to broach the idea of a follow-up in *Downhill Racer* – I had already changed the title; it was more interesting to focus on *one* racer than on the entire team. When I consulted Bob Evans, he advised me to approach Redford directly.

We met at Oblaths, the favorite Paramount hangout. Redford was attracted to *Rosemary's Baby* but thoroughly sold on *Downhill Racer*. While we were waiting for our food, a Paramount lawyer came up to our table, asked Redford to step outside, and served papers on him for breach of contract. Redford returned, pale and shaking with anger. 'Did you tell anyone we were meeting here?' he demanded. Only Bob Evans, I said innocently. Evans, equally innocently, had told Bernie Donnenfeld, Paramount's other vice-president in charge of administration – who had promptly dispatched the lawyers. The whole affair was an example of corporate bungling – Paramount's legal department had a life of its own – but that was the end of Robert Redford as Guy.

With Redford and Beatty ruled out, we lowered our sights. John Cassavetes, whom I'd met in London and regarded as a 'cerebral' actor, struck me as an acceptable compromise. Evans expressed doubts when I recommended him for the part, saying that he was too much of a 'heavy' and that he was also known to be trouble on the set. I disregarded this and felt he'd make a workmanlike job of it.

We started rehearsing as if for a play, on an empty stage with no decor or props of any kind, just a contour of the set taped on the floor. I began badgering the studio to buy me a videotape deck; they were just coming onto the market. When they balked at the expense, I agreed to buy the deck back at a discount when we were through. I wanted to record scenes, then play them back to Cassavetes and Mia for analysis and discussion. Both, at this stage, were highly enthusiastic about the film and my directing methods.

When the first day's shooting finally came, I experienced a strange letdown. I felt none of the expected thrill as my rented Mustang convertible swept through the famous Cecil B. De Mille Gate – which I remembered from seeing *Sunset Boulevard* at film school – and skirted the mock eighteenth-century block that concealed the Paramount headquarters. I had sixty technicians at my beck and call and bore responsibility for a huge budget – at least by my previous standards – but all I could think of was the sleepless night I'd spent in Krakow, years before, on the eve of making my very first short, *The Bicycle*. Nothing would ever match the thrill of that first time; the reality would never measure up to the dream.

However thorough the groundwork that goes into a film, shooting it is always very different from preparing it. Cassavetes had been cooperative, extremely friendly at our preliminary rehearsals. As soon as shooting began, however, he started living up to his reputation as a difficult subject,

267

questioning every aspect of my direction and constantly arguing about delivery. I quickly discovered that he had no gift for characterization, could play only himself, and was lost if he had to act without his beloved sneakers. He also objected to the nude scene in which Guy and Rosemary make love on the bare floor of their newly acquired apartment, protesting that he wasn't 'in the skin flick business.' Mia was equally reluctant to do this scene, but for a different and more understandable reason: she felt apprehensive about Sinatra's reactions.

I enjoyed a marvelous rapport with Mia. Despite her fey, Californian ways, she turned out to be as professional as her pedigree – second-generation Hollywood, daughter of Maureen O'Sullivan and the director John Farrow. Mia threw herself into the part of Rosemary with complete dedication. She knew it might establish her as a star, but she also loved the script for its own sake and wanted the picture to be as good as she could help make it.

The only problems I had with Mia were not connected with my direction. Before long, even in the early stages of shooting, *Rosemary's Baby* began to attract a lot of publicity. It seemed that Sinatra didn't like his wife receiving so much attention as a performer in her own right. There was also the question of completing the picture in time to mesh with Sinatra's own schedule. He was due to start shooting *The Detective* as soon as our fifty-day schedule was up and wanted Mia in his picture by Thanksgiving. When it became clear that we wouldn't be through until after Christmas, he angrily demanded that she simply walk off the set. She refused to do so, and her failure to obey him made him madder still. He knew we were shooting slowly, with numerous takes – a process he scorned because he never did more than one or at most two takes of anything. He started putting pressure on Bob Evans, and there were heated exchanges on the phone. Later he took his revenge in an unforeseen way.

I couldn't quite fathom the Mia-Sinatra relationship. Sharon and I dined with them a couple of times. Good host and good company though he was, Sinatra never disguised that his was a man's world. What he liked best was man talk at the bar of his Beverly Hills home. Mia, on the other hand, was a sensitive flower child, a sucker for every conceivable cause from ecology to the rights of American Indians, and a committed opponent of the Vietnam War, which Sinatra supported. They didn't appear to have a single thing in common, yet it was apparent to all who saw them together that this was no marriage of convenience and that Mia was deeply in love with her husband.

When I suggested that Vidal Sassoon himself should come to Hollywood to cut Mia's hair, Bill Castle decided to hype the occasion into a spectacular 'photo opportunity' for the Hollywood press. Bleachers were set up on a sound stage, and there, in front of photographers and TV crews, Vidal Sassoon removed Mia's locks. Throughout this proceeding, like the true hippie she was, Mia kept up a verbal assault on the press for troubling to cover such an insignificant function instead of applying their investigative energies to the plight of deprived and underprivileged American Indians.

By the end of the first week's shooting I was one week behind schedule. The Paramount management promptly recommended throwing me off the picture, but Bob Evans, who was fascinated by the rushes, backed me to the hilt; if I went, he told headquarters, he would go, too.

Charlie Bluhdorn was new enough in the top job to feel that a studio boss should know every single thing about every project in progress. While we were on location in New York, he learned that I was using a Yellow Checker cab for the cemetery scene. To my annoyance, props produced a red one instead, so I told them to go away and come back with the real thing. Charlie seized on this incident as an example of the 'crazy Polack's' maniacal perfectionism. It became a ritual joke: 'Zat grazy Polack didn't like ze color of ze cab.' I told him he shouldn't even know about such trivia, much less worry about them. He said he knew all that went on at Gulf & Western.

My devotion to authentic detail was growing with every

picture I made. I also wanted to adopt the same subjective approach to the theme as I had tried to achieve in *Repulsion*. This time my material resources were infinitely greater, and I was determined to make full use of them. Much of the film is seen through Rosemary's eyes. In trying to convey this subjective immediacy, I often staged long, complicated scenes using short focal lenses that called for extreme precision in the placing of both camera and actors. A common expedient is to use longer focals, which enable the camera to shoot a scene from farther away. This is far less time-consuming but also far less visually effective and convincing. Ideally the lens should be at the same distance from the subject as the eye of the notional observer.

I was heavily influenced at this time by a book that has exerted a lasting effect on my approach to filmmaking. This brilliant and illuminating work, Professor R L Gregory's *Eye and Brain; The Psychology of Seeing*, lent scientific confirmation to many of the ideas I'd instinctively believed in since my filmschool days – for instance, on the subject of perspective, size constancy, and optical illusions.

One of Gregory's contentions is that our perceptions are shaped by the sum of our visual experiences. We see far less than we think we see because of past impressions already stored in our minds. This goes some way toward explaining what happened when the movie was finally released. Many people emerged from theaters convinced that they'd seen the baby, cloven hooves and all. In fact, all they'd really seen, for a split second, was a subliminal superimposition of the cat-like eyes that glare down at Rosemary during her nightmare in the early part of the film.

I soon discovered that conditions at Paramount weren't so very different from those I'd encountered in London with Compton and in Poland with Film Polski. Whether under capitalism or communism, with a big budget or a small one, the powers that be react the same way when a director falls behind his schedule. Studio executives conferred, agonized, wrote memos to Bill Castle, and started to harass me. Though pleased with the rushes, they simply wanted me to deliver within my fifty-day shooting schedule. When I wouldn't – in the interest of quality – the hassles began.

Most of the pressure originated at Paramount's New York headquarters, for which *Rosemary's Baby* was just a minor picture being handled by some Polish director making his U.S. debut. The heat from New York was relayed to me by Bernie Donnenfeld. Barely a day passed without my being called off the set and into some meeting at which I was berated for my unconventional methods.

On the Paramount lot one day Otto Preminger asked me why I was looking so glum. When I summarized my problems, he made light of them. After all, why should I care? I told him there was talk of replacing me.

'Ridiculous!' he retorted in his Teutonic baritone. 'Are they happy with the rushes?'

More than happy, I said; they were delighted.

Very slowly, as though addressing a moronic child, he said, 'Roman, remember this: You can go over budget as much as you like, provided the rushes are good. They only replace a director when the dailies are lousy.'

Shortly afterward, at one of our many heated crisis sessions, Bernie Donnenfeld returned to the attack. Why didn't I try to cut down on takes, at least for an experimental period?

'Look,' I said, 'I've had it up to here. You want me to shoot fast? No problem. I'll shoot twenty pages of script a day from now on and bring in the picture by the end of the week. I hope you'll like it.'

Agitated glances scurried around the table. 'Bernie,' Bob Evans said at length, 'we're jerking off.' He turned to me. 'Roman, just go back on the set and do it your way. I'll take responsibility.' Knowing the pressure he was under, I was grateful. There were no more major hassles after that, and I completed the picture about four weeks behind schedule. When everything was in the can, we'd gone some $400,000 over a $1.9 million budget – a trifle compared to what the film ultimately earned.

271

There was one moment, three-quarters of the way through shooting, when I seriously thought the picture would never be completed. We were in the middle of the party scene. Very pregnant by now and suffering from mysterious abdominal pains, Rosemary decides to regain contact with the world outside the stifling confines of her apartment by throwing a party for some friends from the old days. We were just ready to roll when Sinatra's lawyer, Mickey Rudin, turned up. He said he had some important papers for Mia, so I called a break.

Like all the principals, Mia had a mobile dressing room of her own – one of the roofless trailers that enable stars to enjoy some privacy without leaving the sound stage – and they withdrew there. After a few minutes alone with her, Rudin emerged and left without saying a word. When it was time to resume shooting, no Mia. All eyes turned toward her dressing room, a pink one on which she'd painted some flowers and butterflies. I knocked on the door. No response. When there was no answer to my second knock, I just went in. There she was, sobbing her heart out like a two-year-old. At first she was completely inarticulate. Then she managed, haltingly, to tell me that Rudin had come to inform her that Sinatra was starting divorce proceedings. What hurt her most was that Sinatra hadn't deigned to tell her himself, simply sent one of his flunkies – a callous move that didn't endear him to me. Everyone on the set of *Rosemary's Baby* knew that he and Mia were at odds, and not just over the schedule for his next picture, but sending Rudin was like firing a servant. She simply couldn't understand her husband's contemptuous, calculated act of cruelty, and it shattered her.

I realized, as I tried to comfort her, that she genuinely loved Sinatra and was destroyed by what had happened. There was little I could do. I went to inform Bob Evans, who was utterly thrown by this latest development and feared it might kill the whole project. Then I went back to Mia. 'Would you like to go home?' I asked.

'No,' she said, 'I'll be all right. Just give me another minute or two.'

And shooting resumed as if nothing had happened. Mia managed to get through the rest of the day and the rest of the film, but her deep depression persisted.

MGM was now ready to release *The Vampire Killers* so I asked for a screening of the version cut by Marty Ransohoff. I immediately realized that I'd made a huge mistake giving him the final U.S. and Canada cut, though the enormity of that error didn't hit me until much later. Ransohoff, after trying to change the title to *Pardon Me, But Your Teeth Are in My Neck*, redubbed all the actors' voices to make them more American-sounding. He fiddled with Komeda's music and cut twenty minutes from the film rendering it incomprehensible. To compensate, he then added a ridiculous cartoon prologue which attempted to explain all about vampires.

Watching this, I felt the way a mother must feel when she finds out she's given birth to a deformed child. The man had completely butchered my work. I tried to take my name off the credits, ashamed to be connected to a film I now considered terrible, but my contract with MGM wouldn't allow it.

I gave an interview to *Variety*, saying all this. Ransohoff immediately called me and said, 'You better shut your trap. If you want to fight us, we've got enough money to bury you.'

I didn't shut up; I gave other interviews. Meanwhile, the film sank without a trace. It was only years later, as my version was released around the world, that it became successful as something of a cult film.

Despite all my problems, Sharon and I were having fun becoming part of the Hollywood scene. It was always party time in Beverly Hills and Bel Air, and we could have gone out every night of the week. As a popular young couple rising in the film world, we were showered with hospitality by Hollywood residents ranging from the old-established, like Danny Kaye, Otto Preminger, and Ruth Gordon and Garson Kanin, to the younger and more hip, like Mike Nichols or John and Michelle Phillips of the Mamas and the Papas.

Sharon's closest girlfriend, Wendy Wagner, lived with Robert Mitchum's son Jimmy. Both were regular visitors, and both smoked a lot of grass. In fact, Jimmy's skill at joint rolling was such that I jokingly offered to hire him as a demonstrator in an instructional film. Sharon and I deliberately mixed these representatives of the old and new Hollywood at our parties, and they got on surprisingly well.

Gene and Judy Gutowski had moved from London and were semipermanent houseguests. Brian Morris, whose London Ad Lib Club had burned down, felt convinced that Hollywood could use a proper disco, and was attempting to duplicate the Ad Lib formula in L.A. Simon Hessera, still hanging on financially by his eyebrows, was likewise trying to get something together in Hollywood, as was his brother, Henri Sera, who fancied his chances as a singer.

Never having had a swimming pool before, I was always urging guests to sample it. One of them, Wally Wolf, my newly acquired lawyer, borrowed a pair of briefs and plunged in. It took him only four prodigious butterfly strokes to swim from end to end, swamping half the garden in the process. My jaw dropped – I'd never seen anyone move through water so fast.

'Did you ever compete?'

'I was on the Olympic team,' he modestly admitted.

'Where?'

'Oh, London and Helsinki. I made the water-polo team in Melbourne and Rome.'

I glanced at Gene Gutowski. 'You sure this guy knows his law?' I muttered. All the lawyers of my acquaintance were bald, bespectacled, and sedentary.

Our rented Santa Monica mansion was spacious enough to accommodate plenty of houseguests in addition to Gene and Judy. Among our first visitors were two Polish expatriates, the poet Czeslaw Milosz and his wife. Then, rather to my trepidation, Sharon's parents paid us a visit. Any qualms I may have felt about this first meeting with them were soon dispelled by their warm and friendly acceptance of my relationship with their daughter. They brought us a present: a

Yorkshire terrier puppy, sired by Guinness, which I promptly christened Dr Saperstein, after the sinister character in *Rosemary's Baby*.

Later on, my father and Wanda flew out to spend a couple of months with us. Though proud of Sharon, the house, and my new life-style, I was secretly relieved when they returned to Krakow. My father felt I was living too extravagantly, that, as he put it, the bubble could burst overnight. My greatest disappointment was that he and Wanda seemed to get so little enjoyment out of America. They criticized the food, the climate, the distances, and the way our circle used the house as their own. My father was obsessed with the idea that people were ripping me off and taking advantage of me. He was right, up to a point, but he failed to appreciate my own attitude: though well aware that some of my friends were parasites, I happened to enjoy their company. Where Wanda was concerned, Sharon scored a major success by introducing her to grass. One night, while staring at the fire in a slightly stoned condition, Wanda was heard to remark, 'Look, it's like little horses jumping all over.'

'Horses jumping!' my father huffed, and stalked out of the room.

It was during this period that Gene Gutowski's marriage to Judy began to fall apart. One source of discord was that Judy had had an affair with a colorful Broadway character, Hilly Elkins, and Gene found out about it. They were staying with us at the time, so the atmosphere in the house was electric. We got used to their flare-ups, which were followed by long, passionate reconciliations, but I wished they'd either make it up for good or separate. One day, while Tony Curtis and I were sitting in the living room, the sound of yet another furious battle shattered our peace.

Tony looked uneasy. 'Maybe you'd better go after them.'

'Happens all the time,' I told him casually.

'Maybe,' he said, 'but this time Gene's going upstairs with Judy right behind him.'

'So?'

275

'So she's holding a damn big kitchen knife behind her back.'

I managed to separate them, but the next day Gene went out and bought an automatic.

The trouble was that like all warring couples, Gene and Judy made a point of involving their friends, notably Sharon and me, who served as ammunition in their running battle with each other. They could also be malicious.

On one occasion, when Sharon and Judy both were out of town for the weekend, I bedded a sexy young model who'd been giving me the come-on for weeks. I'd thought I could rely on Gene's discretion until Czeslaw Milosz overheard a venomous little aside from Judy to Sharon. According to him, Judy said sweetly, 'It must be nice, living the way you and Roman do – I mean, allowing each other such complete freedom. Like when you and I went off to Big Sur and Roman screwed that girl and you didn't mind in the least!' Sharon never mentioned this to me, but Milosz did. 'If I were you,' he said, 'I'd get them out of here. They're trying to turn Sharon against you.'

If they were, they certainly didn't succeed. Our life together was a sheer delight. Sharon introduced me to the America she knew: not only junk food, drive-ins, and popcorn at the movies but the California coast, Big Sur, and Topanga Canyon. Some friends of hers lived in Topanga, and we used to spend whole afternoons there. In their garden, which overlooked a cliff, they had a crude swing – a tire on the end of a long rope – and I shall never forget the thrill of soaring higher and higher through the branches, over the cliff, glimpsing the extraordinary view, hearing the wind whistle around us.

An equally thrilling but deplorable incident occurred during one of our weekends in Palm Springs. It was before Mia and Sinatra split up, and we were staying at Sinatra's luxurious ranch-style compound, with its separate guest bungalows and elaborately equipped game room. Steve McQueen, who lived in a smaller house nearby, insisted on taking us for a spin in one of his dune buggies, an open

Land-Rover fitted with outsizé airplane wheels. He tossed a couple of mattresses into the back for Mia and Sharon while I got in beside him. Then he proceeded to race across the desert in the total darkness, through clumps of scrub, over wild bumps, into the occasional sickening void. It was like flying blind through a sandstorm. I could hear what sounded like girlish giggles but later found out were squeals of genuine alarm. Steve McQueen was an old friend of both girls, so I didn't say anything, but the sight of Sharon's bruises afterward convinced me that he was an asshole.

With shooting completed, a long-standing problem came to a head. Bill Castle clung loyally to an old editor who was not up to the creative cutting required by *Rosemary's Baby*. Having shelved this difficulty for as long as possible, I was in despair. It was Dick Sylbert who talked Bill into hiring Sam O'Steen. Just in the process of finishing *The Graduate*, Sam spent several days with me, viewing every bit of footage we'd shot. With a skill and imagination that took my breath away, he condensed the picture, first to four hours and then to its final running time of two hours and sixteen minutes.

It proved surprisingly easy to persuade Bob Evans and Bill Castle to hire Komeda to write the music, and one of my happiest interludes in Hollywood began when he arrived and came to stay with us.

He was bemused by L.A., by the traffic and sheer size of it. He was also delighted to have shed a nagging, possessive wife, and he soon fell hard for an Israeli actress. On one of his Hollywood excursions – I'd lent him a Yamaha motorbike which I kept as a sort of toy – he was stopped by a police car for going too slowly. When he explained in fractured English that he was scared to go any faster, the patrolmen escorted him home to make sure he didn't come to any harm – a friendly gesture so wildly at odds with Polish police practice that it bowled him over.

Komeda composed two possible lullabies for *Rosemary's Baby*, both so good that we wavered a lot before choosing the one we eventually used as a leitmotif. Though probably less commercial than the other, it suited the context better. It had

277

to be hummed softly, hauntingly, at the start of the film, and instead of using a professional singer, I asked Mia to record it for the sake of vocal continuity – an important factor. To my surprise and delight, she proved able to hum quite well, and there's no mistaking the owner of the voice that accompanies the opening credits. Not for the first time, a film of mine had derived an added dimension from Komeda's wonderfully imaginative music.

For Charlie Bluhdorn's benefit, Bob Evans held a private screening of *Rosemary's Baby* in the luxurious projection room at his home. Bob sat on my right; Charlie lolled on my left. I couldn't understand why the air conditioning had been turned up full blast until Bob whispered that Charlie had just flown in from New York and needed to be kept awake. His bright idea didn't work – Charlie kept dozing off – but Bob wasn't worried. By that time he sensed that Paramount had a hit.

Putting the finishing touches to *Rosemary's Baby* entailed a trip to London for some last-minute dubbing of Mia, who'd already started work on a film there. It occurred to me that I'd be in London for Victor Lownes's birthday. Sharon and I conferred with Gene Gutowski. What could we give a man like Victor?

'He's got everything except a golden prick,' said Gene.

'Right,' I said, 'that's what we'll give him.'

Sharon, who knew a Hollywood jeweler named Marvin Himes, called him right away.

'Marvin,' she said, 'do you have a golden cock?' He thought she meant a cockerel. 'No,' she said, 'I mean a penis.'

'To hang on a chain?'

'Life-size,' she said.

Marvin's response was absolutely deadpan. 'If you supply the model, we'll make you one.'

Sharon, Gene, and I conferred again. 'You're a sculptor,' I told Gene. 'You do it.'

The unfortunate Gene toiled all night. Armed with his

masterpiece, Sharon and I presented ourselves at Marvin Himes's shop the next morning.

Marvin summoned his staff. 'Boys,' he said casually, 'I want this in gold by tomorrow. I take it, Roman, you want it hollow?'

As hollow as possible, I told him. Even with gold at an absurdly low price, it was still an expensive joke.

The clay model was deposited, erect, on Marvin's coffee table. He and his craftsmen sat around it with mugs of coffee in their hands, discussing their latest assignment as if it were all in a day's work. They measured it with calipers, made notes, decided to cast it in sections.

'How do you want it finished?' Marvin asked. 'Glossy? Hammered?' When I hesitated, he said, 'I suggest we give the head a high polish and hammer the testicles.'

'Anything you say, Marvin.'

He asked about the inscription.

' "To Victor Lownes," ' I said, ' "First Prize." '

I was leaving the next day. On the way to the airport we stopped to pick up our trophy. It wasn't ready. The engraver had been delayed by a flat tire and was still working on it. Hell, I thought, I've planned this ridiculously expensive present, and now it's all for nothing. Leaving Sharon at the shop, I drove on to the airport alone.

I only just made the plane. Sam O'Steen, who was accompanying me to London, watched me stagger in and slump down beside him, panting. 'Nice of you to drop in,' Sam said. He wanted to know what happened.

'I'll tell you later. I need a drink first.' I was too annoyed to make a joke out of it.

The passenger door of the airplane was secured, and we prepared to taxi off. Suddenly there was a commotion, and the door opened again. Drawing on her gentle charm and irresistible powers of persuasion, Sharon had sweet-talked the ground staff into delivering a small object wrapped in chamois. They'd contacted the captain just in time.

The stewardess came to my seat, bearing Victor's only partly concealed birthday present. There was a prim expression on her face. 'This is yours, I believe,' she said, deliberately averting her eyes.

I showed the present to Sam and explained whom it was for.

'How are you going to get this thing through customs?' he said.

I hadn't thought of that.

'You'll just have to stuff it down your pants,' he said.

Which I did. Negotiating Heathrow Airport customs hall was an uncomfortable experience. Incapable of bluffing my way through at the best of times and convinced that my face betrayed signs of panic, I felt sure some official would start asking questions. In fact, all that aroused official interest was our can of film.

'We have to do this postsynch job,' Sam began.

'You *what*?'

It was four hours before they allowed us to leave with the can, and even then Paramount's London office had to send some people to get it cleared. Throughout this time Victor's Golden Prick Award continued to nestle inside my jeans.

The film was released with an elaborate advertising campaign built around the line 'Pray for Rosemary's Baby!' – a slogan so obtrusive that some people must have mistaken it for the title.

Long lines immediately formed outside every movie house showing it. Bill Castle couldn't resist touring Westwood Village and feasting his producer's eyes on the crowd that wound its way around the block. He used to stand and stare and add up the receipts in his head. The film's runaway success was a shock from which he never fully recovered.

It was such a success that Bill felt guilty. At a mutual friend's wedding reception he bore down on me with a glass of champagne in his huge fist. 'Ro,' he said euphorically, 'I'm giving you some points on the picture, and I want Paramount to match me.' It was the last I heard of this plan to cut me in on the profits. Although *Rosemary's Baby* helped stave off some of Paramount's growing financial problems, I never did make anything out of it except my initial fees. Bob Evans showed his appreciation in the only way open to him: he moved me into the biggest, most luxurious office on the Paramount lot.

But the Brian Aherne house is what I remember most vividly whenever I think back on this, my first spell in Hollywood: friends dropping in, Sharon cooking for us all, and me playing records from Aherne's vintage collection on an old-fashioned phonograph of his, which I'd managed to repair. To this day I can never hear one number – 'Baby, It's Cold Outside' – without recalling the radiance of those California evenings, the peace and well-being I felt, the joy of living with Sharon, and the satisfaction that sprang from doing what I most wanted to do in the film capital of the world.

TWENTY-ONE

For the first time ever, I didn't have to hustle for a living. The overnight success of *Rosemary's Baby* turned me into something of a Hollywood golden boy, deluged with scripts and propositions from studios all over town. Paramount wanted me on its lot, and Bob Evans was eager to exploit my new status as a 'hot' young director by putting me to work again fast.

Although I owed a certain loyalty to the Paramount people, my feelings toward them were mixed. While I was still in the throes of *Rosemary's Baby*, and long before it dawned on them that they had a commercial hit, they had gone cold on our other two Cadre-Paramount projects. They not only rejected the synopsis of a western spoof commissioned from Gérard Brach but started making things difficult for *Downhill Racer*. I put a lot of work into it, developing a script with Jimmy Salter, and experimented with camera equipment and harnesses that could be used on skis. Gene and Hans Möllinger went off to scout locations at the European ski resorts where major championships were held. In the end Paramount and I agreed to differ: they wanted the picture made in the States; I wanted it all shot in the far more photogenic Alpine resorts. The project was dropped, but not for long. Some months later *Variety* announced that Paramount would be making *Downhill Racer* after all, but with another director. The star: Robert Redford. Hollywood feuds were short-lived, it seemed.

The piles of scripts I was being asked to consider were all of a kind – horror stories, exclusively concerned with madness and the occult – and they didn't interest me in the least. They merely confirmed the impression I'd gained when 20th Century-Fox wanted me to remake *Knife in the Water* immediately after its release: that studio executives were former lawyers and agents with little artistc imagination. Their credo was that once an idea had worked, it could be made to work again and again – and then again. Similarly, once a director had succeeded in a particular genre, he was as much a prisoner of his image as any typecast actor.

I became conscious of something else, too, this time about myself. On the one hand, I wanted to pursue a glamorous Hollywood career – it was possible to become extremely wealthy – and on the other, I knew I'd find it hard to direct a film I hadn't written or at least coauthored. Despite my desire to succeed, I had to do it on my terms. I just didn't fit the conventional Hollywood mold.

Although my newfound recognition elated me, I felt something of the postnatal lethargy that had afflicted me after *Cul-de-Sac*. Not only was I unattracted by the work being offered me, but I yearned to relax, read, travel. I needed to recharge my batteries generally. Wally Wolf urged me to employ the right kind of agent, one who could help mold my future. I was disenchanted with agents, not having used one since letting my wholly unproductive William Morris contract lapse after *Cul-de-Sac*, but Wally said he knew the ideal outfit for a director who preferred to write his own screenplays. Predominantly a literary firm, the Ziegler Ross Agency had access to some of the best new material before it was published. It also had a partner, Bill Tennant, who was eager to take me on. Tennant turned out to be a handsome young go-getter who hurled himself into the fray on my behalf and became, for the next few years at least, a good and valued friend. For the moment his sage advice was not to rush into anything. As he put it, 'There's nothing wrong with doing nothing.'

In Sharon's company, I discovered that doing nothing could be very agreeable. The months that followed the completion of *Rosemary's Baby* were a halcyon period in my life.

After extending the lease on his house several times, Brian Aherne reclaimed it for his own use. Accompanied by a hard-core group of cronies – Christopher Komeda, Simon Hessera, and Brian Morris – we moved to the Sunset Marquis, one of those peculiarly American establishments that are half hotel, half apartment house, superficially flashy but relatively cheap. Our stay there was a brief one. Sharon, who was less enamored of the place than the rest of us, disliked what she termed its 'early Jewish' decor and hankered after something with more character.

She got her way when we made a move to the Chateau Marmont, just off Sunset Boulevard, Sharon's favorite hangout in her early Hollywood days. This absurd Victorian building, with its green turrets and balconies, was run by an almost invisible staff and had reputedly been owned long ago by Greta Garbo. For Americans, to whom anything a few decades old seems romantic, it held a special appeal. Sharon loved its rundown appearance and old-world atmosphere, not to mention the crazy layout of its shabby rooms; she felt at home among the actors, musicians, and writers that constituted its regular population. You could sense, simply by walking down its corridors, that the place had had its quota of real-life dramas, of slashed wrists and overdoses, just as you could almost get stoned from sniffing the haze that seeped through the various keyholes. Our quarters at the Chateau Marmont were a fourth-floor apartment with a kitchenette. Here we evolved a daily routine that began when Morris and Hessera showed up in their bathrobes for Sharon to cook us a communal breakfast.

Hessera had just left a firm that made TV commercials, so he was doing what he did best – living as well as he could manage while keeping his friends entertained. Brian Morris was still engaged in trying to start up a night spot. We each chipped in $7,000 for shares in Bumbles, as it became known, but this was only a drop in the bucket. Brian developed a perfectionism worthy of Erich von Stroheim. Victor Lownes – another shareholder – flew over to check on his progress. A down-to-earth businessman and experienced club manager, he was horrified and came away with the impression that Brian was crazy. He was probably right; Brian even insisted on having china that matched the motif on the ceilings. Bumbles ultimately established itself as one of Hollywood's 'in' spots, but without Brian Morris.

Komeda, much in demand after *Rosemary's Baby*, had debated whether or not to return to Poland. Knowing how unhappily married he was, I'd talked him out of it. 'You've unloaded your wife,' I told him. 'That's an achievement in itself.' He couldn't have gone home at once in any case because he was writing the music for *The Riot*, a prison movie produced by Bill Castle.

Sharon and I began commuting to London and Paris – now that we could afford it – for business as well as pleasure. Doing nothing was fine, but Cadre Films was only being kept afloat by my earnings from *Rosemary's Baby*, and Gene Gutowski was anxious to get something off the ground. Together with an Italian writer, Ennio de Concini, I started developing a script based on the life of Paganini. Andy Braunsberg, who'd been pressing to join our Cadre team, had meanwhile produced a film of his own, *Wonderwall*, with a script by Gérard Brach and a cast including Jack MacGowran, Iain Quarrier and Jane Birkin. He now introduced me to a British screenwriter, Ivan Moffatt, who had an idea for another project which Andy wanted to coproduce. Concurrently with the Paganini script, Moffatt and I started work on *The Donner Party*. This was the true and tragic story of some nineteenth-century settlers who, after being harassed by Indians on their long westward trek, meet their doom in the snows of the Sierra Nevada. The enterprise on which they embarked with such high hopes ended in starvation and cannibalism.

I was at last able to spend more time with my friends. A recent addition to our crowd was Peter Sellers, whom I'd met with Britt Ekland in an Italian restaurant near the Paramount studio while filming *Rosemary's Baby*. My first impression of him was of a sad, shy man who hid his essential melancholy

285

behind a fixed smile that revealed his rather prominent teeth. At our first meeting Peter certainly wasn't as amusing as I'd expected. He'd recently suffered two heart attacks, his marriage was shaky, and his manner conveyed profound depression. In our company, which included Jay Sebring, the scriptwriter Jimmy Poe, Peter Lawford, Warren Beatty, and, of course, Simon Hessera and Brian Morris, he underwent a gradual transformation. It was through us that he met Mia Farrow – a true soulmate if ever there was one. Like her, Peter was heavily into the whole range of crackpot folklore that flourished in the 1960's, from UFOs through astrology to extrasensory perception. They both liked dressing up as rich hippies, complete with beads, chunky costume jewelry, and Indian cotton caftans.

Lovable though he was in many ways, Peter's idiosyncrasies could be a drag. Just as, on the set, he would walk off if anyone appeared wearing purple, an 'unlucky' color, so he would walk out of restaurants if he picked up 'bad vibes.' To my embarrassment, this often happened at the Luau. I grew to dread the moment when, after ordering, Peter would whisper, 'Ro, I can't stand it . . . bad vibes in here . . . let's go somewhere else.'

In a good mood, however, Peter could be even funnier among friends than he was on the screen. During our many long evenings together, he and I and Simon Hessera used to improvise comedy acts, parodying Italian movies, grand opera, bullfights, and so on. It was Simon's French accent that inspired Inspector Clouseau's famous 'Do you have a rheum?'

I didn't realize it at first, but there was another, more violent side to Peter. Planning a communal Christmas vacation in Cortina, I flew to London with Sharon and took Peter to dinner at a Chinese restaurant so he could meet some of the people who'd be joining us in the mountains. Seated across the table from him was Tony Greenburgh. Their discussion – about the nature of a doctor's *moral* obligation toward a patient bent on destroying himself with cigarettes or alcohol – turned into a heated argument. Tony matter-of-factly stated that there was no way a doctor could stop such patients, nor could he be held responsible for their plight. Tony didn't realize just how sensitive a subject he was dealing with, for Peter, despite his heart condition, was not only drinking and smoking to excess but experimenting freely with drugs of all kinds.

The two voices rose in pitch and volume, bringing general conversation to a halt. Most of those present assumed that Peter was indulging in one of his gags, even when he sprang to his feet and strode around to Tony's side of the table. 'You're wrong, Doctor,' he shouted hysterically, 'you're wrong, you're *fucking wrong*!' So saying, he grabbed Tony by the throat and started squeezing. Judy Gutowski, still under the impression that Peter was playacting, giggled and told him not to be so silly. The rest of us sat there, transfixed. Like me, they could see it wasn't an act. Tony was choking and turning purple as Peter genuinely tried to strangle him. I jumped up and pried Peter's fingers loose, then gently persuaded him to sit down. He buried his face in his hands and began to sob. Although we tried to repair the damage, pretending that nothing had happened, the evening was in ruins. Some vacation *this* is going to be! I told myself.

Komeda, who should have been with us that night, was too ill to leave L.A. One day shortly before we were all due to leave for Europe – he was crazy about skiing and couldn't wait to get away – he showed up at Paramount looking awful, with two black eyes and a bump the size of an egg on his forehead. He'd fallen and hurt himself quite badly while roaming the Hollywood hills after a late-night binge with Marek Hlasko. True to his he-man image, Hlasko had picked him up, using a fireman's lift. Then, being even drunker than Komeda, he'd stumbled and dropped him, injuring him some more. After that, although Komeda's doctor assured him there was nothing seriously wrong, he started complaining to me of chronic headaches and an inability to concentrate. On the eve of our departure his girlfriend, Elena, phoned to say she was worried about him. Would I come over? Komeda looked worse than ever when I got there. He

287

said he had the flu – there was an epidemic of it in L.A. at the time – and felt too ill to travel. Instead of flying over to London with us the next day, he would join us later.

We assembled at Cortina just before Christmas, still without Komeda. Peter Sellers, now in one of his most endearingly manic moods, insisted on showering us all with expensive presents. He distributed them in a makeshift Santa Claus costume: Sharon's fox fur coat, a red ski cap on his head, and a white ski cap as a beard. Typically enough, he was so depressed again by Boxing Day that he left early. It was a portent of far worse things to come. A few days into the new year, Bill Tennant called. He said Komeda was very sick indeed.

'I know,' I said.

'He's in the hospital.'

'With flu?'

'It wasn't flu; it was a clot on the brain. They had to operate.'

It appeared that, on the basis of encephalogram readings, a brain injury had been diagnosed.

We raced to the hospital as soon as we got back to L.A. Komeda had tubes up his nose and another tube in his throat, where they'd given him a tracheotomy. His head was shrouded in bandages. His eyes were open but unseeing. He was comatose – unconscious. Emaciated, with sunken cheeks, he had a strangely childish, petulant expression on his face.

I spoke to him in Polish, very slowly. 'Krzystof,' I said, 'if you can hear me, squeeze my hand.' He squeezed. I left my hand in his, but his fingers continued to tighten spasmodically, for no discernible reason. I never discovered whether the first pressure had been intentional or involuntary.

Sharon was distraught over what had happened to Komeda; it was her first real brush with tragedy. We visited him daily, but he got no better. I had such faith in scientific progress and American medical expertise that I was positive he would pull through. He didn't. He came out of his coma once to scrawl a few disjointed words in Polish and once to beat time faintly on the counterpane when I played him some music on a tape recorder, but he never fully regained consciousness. He died shortly after being flown back to Poland by his wife. My only consolation was that since coming to Hollywood, Komeda had been uninterruptedly happy.

Sharon, who was busier than I at this period, was cast for a part in *Valley of the Dolls*. Although it was an important break, she didn't think much of either the book or the movie. She dismissed it as an exploitation picture and felt she wasn't doing anything artistically worthwhile.

'You're the better half,' she once told me ruefully, speaking about us as a couple, hating the fact that the industry saw her only as a pretty face.

This certainly didn't apply to Mark Robson, her director in *Valley of the Dolls*, whom I bumped into on Sunset Strip while the film was in production. 'That's a great girl you're living with,' he said. 'Few actresses have her kind of vulnerability. She's got a great future.'

Valley of the Dolls was followed by a part in *The Wrecking Crew*, which starred Dean Martin. After working all day on the set, Sharon would return to our latest rented home, Patty Duke's house on Summit Ridge Drive, and insist on cooking for me and the whole gang. Her repertoire included Virginia ham, upsidedown cake, and all the great southern dishes she'd learned from her mother.

All our friends adored Sharon. It wasn't just her looks that captivated them, though her beauty was breathtaking and her miniskirts emphasized her marvelous legs. She was among the first to flaunt these symbols of the sexual freedom of the sixties. Miniskirts were erotic yet innocent, romantic and charming and somehow vulnerable, so different from the forbidding, aggressive look of the seventies. When Sharon appeared in one, the whole street would turn and stare: men with admiration; women with envy; elderly matrons with vitriolic disapproval; old gentlemen with nostalgic appreciation.

There was far more to Sharon than a lovely face and a sexy

figure. What enchanted me about her as much as anything was her immutable good nature, her natural high spirits, her love of people and animals – of life itself. Overdemonstrative, oversolicitous women had always made me uneasy, but Sharon struck the perfect balance between affection and concern. Though more a spectator than a participant in our gags and shenanigans, she had a great sense of humor. She was also a born housewife. Aside from cooking like a dream, she used to cut my hair – a skill acquired from Jay Sebring. She liked to pack my bag whenever I had to take a trip. She always knew exactly what to put in – so much so that I can never pack or unpack, even today, without thinking of her.

She once asked me to define my ideal woman.

'You're it,' I told her.

She laughed. 'Come on!'

'Seriously,' I said.

'What would you like me to be that I'm not?'

'Nothing,' I said with complete sincerity. 'I wouldn't want you different in any way.'

The Wrecking Crew, in which Sharon was cast as a kung fu expert, brought a new figure into my life. The studio had hired an instructor to give her lessons, and she was keen for me to meet him. 'The two of you would get along like a house on fire,' she said, and promptly invited him to dinner. That was how I first met Bruce Lee.

Despite his many friends in the Hollywood film community, Bruce had so far failed to realize his acting and filmmaking ambitions. The studios' interest in him was confined to his status as Hollywood's leading martial arts instructor and consultant. He could teach any form of armed or unarmed combat, but his preference went to jitkundo, which he defined as 'scientific streetfighting.' He despised karate and considered it a waste of time. Although he was the gentlest of men, he felt that any such skill should have some practical purpose.

Bruce was almost inhumanly methodical in his pursuit of excellence, and the physical discipline to which he subjected himself combined a ballet dancer's punishing routine with a conjurer's hours of relentless practice. A great showoff, he never missed an opportunity to demonstrate his art. Before long we rigged up a training area on Patty Duke's driveway, and he was giving me lessons in – among other things – the celebrated Bruce Lee side kick. He was always urging me to go ahead and attack him while off guard. 'I'll be ready for you,' he assured me. 'You won't hurt me, but you may learn something.'

For all his india rubber physique, Bruce had a minor disability: he was shortsighted and had to wear glasses or contact lenses. After one of our workouts, while he was tying a shoelace with one foot propped on the fender of his car and his glasses halfway down his nose, I took him at his word and aimed a side kick at him. Without even glancing up, he flicked out a hand and caught my foot. 'Try again sometime,' he said, and suggested I study the footwork of Dr Saperstein, our Yorkshire terrier.

It was around this time that Mia and Peter Sellers started their romance, and the four of us saw a lot of each other. We spent one weekend at Joshua Tree, a spectacular stretch of desert near Palm Springs. Because of its reputation for UFO sightings, it was much in vogue. After smoking some grass one evening, Mia and Peter wandered off into the desert, hand in hand. I picked up a stick and tiptoed after them.

They were deeply engrossed in a mystical dialogue about the stars, the infinite, and the likelihood of extraterrestrial life. I decided to enrich their experience and threw my stick high in the air so it landed at their feet – a real-life manifestation of the inexplicable.

'Did you hear that?' I heard Peter whisper in awe.

'What was it?' Mia whispered back.

'I don't know, but it was fantastic. *Fantastic!*'

At this point they found the stick that testified to the presence of the supernatural in a treeless, uninhabited desert.

'We've got to tell Roman and Sharon,' Peter said. 'They'll never believe this.'

I scurried on ahead through the darkness, back to the motel where we were staying, and got there just in time to fill Sharon in. When they arrived, panting, at our door, we both expressed suitable wonder.

For some time now I'd realised that Sharon was something permanent in my life. The thought of marrying and raising a family scared me, not because it might encroach on my freedom – Sharon, I knew, would never let that happen – but because personal ties made me feel vulnerable. This fear was a hangover from my childhood, from the insecurity I'd experienced at the age of five or six, when my family began to disintegrate. The only way of not getting hurt, I'd always felt, was to avoid committing myself deeply in the first place. There was implicit insecurity in any relationship – the awareness that any emotional attachment carried the risk of heartache. Even keeping a pet dog was an invitation to sorrow because of its shorter lifespan; one day you had to part from it.

Against this was the fact that Sharon made no secret of her strong desire to have a child. Although she never mentioned marriage, and despite her liberated California life-style, I knew that her Catholic upbringing made marriage important to her.

I proposed off the cuff, over dinner in a restaurant. The date we settled on – January 20, 1968 – fell a few days before her twenty-fifth birthday.

We decided to get married in London; that was my real home and the place where most of our friends lived. It wasn't simple to arrange – I had to prove the validity of my divorce from Barbara Lass, and the Polish documents were a long time coming – but we fixed it in the end.

The night before the wedding Victor Lownes insisted on throwing a stag party in what he termed the good old British tradition. Sharon wasn't too happy about being left out. As for me, I didn't know what to expect. To my surprise, Victor seemed to have organized a pretty formal affair. A group of good-looking male guests – including Terence Stamp and Michael Caine – sat around in his drawing room, nary a girl in

292

sight, until some of the guests got fidgety and left. Even I was growing bored by the time Victor's well-laid plans matured. The doorbell rang, and his house was invaded by an over-whelming stream of beautiful women. Before long there were couples all over the place, including the sauna, in various states of undress. Some of the guests had a memorable night, and Victor's reputation as a wild party giver was further enhanced.

The wedding ceremony at the Chelsea Registry Office in the King's Road turned into a media event, with photo-graphers outnumbering the guests. Much to my delight, my father and Wanda came over from Krakow for the occasion. Gene Gutowski was my best man and Barbara Parkins the bridesmaid.

Sharon wore a cream-colored taffeta minidress, and I sported an olive green Edwardian jacket – a tribute to some hard selling by Jack Vernon, a Hollywood boutique owner. We were a grotesque sight. Looking at our wedding pictures now, I'm struck by the oddness of everyone's clothes at this, the zenith of the 'rich hippie' era.

There were several parties afterward. The biggest of them, at the Playboy Club, was attended by what seemed like the whole of London and half of Hollywood. Candice Bergen, Joan Collins, Leslie Caron, John Mills, Laurence Harvey, Anthony Newley, Warren Beatty, James Fox, and Mike Sarne also showed up later at a shindig given for us by Tony Greenburgh. Halfway through the festivities Sharon and I bowed out. We couldn't take any more parties or cham-pagne, so we headed for West Eaton Place Mews and holed up in our house, which was littered with gifts, flowers, and congratulatory telegrams.

There was a revival – almost a continuation – of the wedding jamboree when *Rosemary's Baby* opened in Paris shortly afterward. With Peter Sellers and Mia and a crowd of other friends, we took over L'Hôtel, the Left Bank hotel that had just opened in St-Germain-des-Prés. We were a strange-looking bunch. Sharon, who'd broken her ankle getting out of bed, was limping around in a plaster cast, and I'd acquired a lipful of stitches from some Spaniards on the Avenue Wagram. One of them had goosed Sharon while we were on our way to a movie, I'd lashed out at him, and his pals had rallied to his defense. As for Peter and Mia, they were in the heyday of their Indian period, all beads and chains and billowing muslin. Mia, with her inveterate hatred of press photographers, pointedly made faces at them whenever they followed us around.

Still a regular companion of ours, Peter continued to oscillate between his manic and depressive moods. He and I devised a silly game. Miming a village idiot, he would get behind the wheel of his latest Rolls Corniche – he changed cars with extravagant frequency – and pretend he was driving for the very first time. I played the instructor. 'Press the right-hand pedal,' I'd say, 'gently – no, too hard, keep it like that. Now turn the wheel to the left – the *left* – that's enough. *No*, too much. Now straighten out, now the other pedal . . . harder. Now remove your foot – both feet. Now turn the wheel to the right till I say stop. . . .'

Peter never tired of this charade. One night in London, at the Arethusa Club, he made me sample some 'honey' he'd brought back from Rome. I nearly passed out, it was so heavily laced with hash. Later he tried to humor me by playing our village idiot game in his girl-laden Rolls, but the hash proved too much for me. Feeling faint, I made him stop and got out. He tottered after me.

'What's the matter, Ro?'

'I'm ODing on that honey of yours,' I said. 'Where are we anyway?'

He peered around in search of a street sign. We were somewhere near Sloane Square.

'I don't mean the street,' I said. 'I mean the *city*.'

Invited to be a juror at the 1968 Cannes Film Festival, I drove Sharon down to St-Tropez in my red Ferrari, which had been shipped over from L.A. We spent a few quiet days at the Hôtel de la Figuière before plunging into what I knew would be an exhausting circus. Although my jury membership entitled us to a suite at the coveted Carlton, I asked Robert Favre Lebret, who'd directed the festival ever since the war, to put us up at the Martinez for old times' sake.

There were plenty of friends in evidence at Cannes, notably Gérard Brach and Claude Berri, who'd given up acting for production and made his first film. With them came Claude's brother-in-law, Jean-Pierre Rassam, an ebullient young Franco-Lebanese with a massive beak of a nose and plump little fluttering hands. Jean-Pierre, who believed that Gérard had the makings of a director, was determined to produce him.

Neither Sharon nor I sensed the imminence of the 'revolution' that almost toppled the Fifth Republic. My first inkling that the events of May 1968 were about to impinge on the Cannes Film Festival came when François Truffaut roused me from a deep late-morning sleep and urged me to join him in the Palais du Festival's Jean Cocteau theater. My presence was essential, he said. He and his friends were discussing how to engineer the reinstatement of Henri Langlois, director of the Paris Cinémathèque, who had recently been dismissed by André Malraux, De Gaulle's minister of culture. It was a protest meeting against his dismissal that had sparked off the May disturbances.

I arrived to find the meeting in full swing. The room was thronged with journalists and hangers-on of the kind that seem to spend their entire lives trailing from festival to festival. Several filmmakers – Godard, Truffaut, Louis Malle – were also present, and it didn't take me long to grasp the real purpose of the meeting: not the reinstatement of Langlois but the disruption of the festival itself. 'No more festival of stars!' cried one of the more vociferous orators. 'What we need is a festival of dialogue!' I had a sudden flashback to Lodz and a certain meeting in the football stadium, with its feverish and futile rhetoric.

I was invited to speak. Organize a symposium by all means, I said, but don't forget what happened at this year's gala opening. The inaugural film had been a revival of *Gone with the Wind*, and when Clark Gable made his first appearance on the stairs of Tara, the festival audience went wild with applause. Had his ghost appeared on the Croisette, pandemonium would have ensued. Show business couldn't dispense with stars.

This wasn't what my listeners had expected. A voice from the stalls – Claude Makovski's – shouted, 'You're being unconstructive, reactionary! The festival's over – finished. We've seen to that!'

'Claude,' I replied from the stage, 'who do you represent here? You aren't a critic; you aren't a producer; you aren't a director; you aren't showing a film here; you aren't even a guest.'

Makovski was, in fact, the manager of a small Left Bank movie theater who'd once claimed he wanted to produce a film of mine back in the old days in France. He also happened to be the lover of Nelly Kaplan, who was no longer Abel Gance's assistant and had just directed her first short, called *Picasso*.

I realized that I was disappointing Truffaut and his allies. Because I'd responded to his phone call, they assumed I must be on their side. The meeting broke up in clamorous confusion. Together with Malle, the only other jury member present, I was asked to sound out the others. Did they wish the festival to proceed, or would they yield to the left-wingers' demands and resign in sympathy with the May 'revolution'?

My own views were clear. I thought it utterly absurd to disrupt the festival on the ground that it was an elitist, capitalist symbol. I knew, for example, that Claude Berri and Jean-Pierre Rassam, with their very limited resources, had been largely responsible for bringing the Czech film *The Firemen's Ball* to Cannes, and I realized how much this meant to its director, Milos Forman. I recalled my own years in Poland and the intense excitement whenever a Polish film was accepted for Cannes. I knew what it meant to a small country to take part – the hopes; the prestige; the two short weeks of glamour and freedom.

For once I found myself on the same side as the USSR. The Soviet member of the jury, the poet Vsevolod Rozhdest-vensky, considered the notion of canceling the festival so outrageous that he had declined even to attend our emergency session. Monica Vitti, another member of the jury, shared my sentiments. 'I was invited here,' she purred in her sexy Italian voice. 'It would be discourteous to accept and then bow out.'

But there were waverers, too. The British director Terence Young reminded us that he lived and worked with French technicians and their unions, so out of solidarity with them he proposed to resign. Louis Malle had already resigned. As for our president, the writer André Chamson, I don't recall his precise reaction to the crisis, but I think he was pretty ineffectual.

The festival authorities tried to keep going. They put on an afternoon screening of Carlos Saura's *Peppermint Frappé*, but Saura, a revolutionary hard-liner, wanted it withdrawn from competition. The general audience they claimed to represent – *les masses* – knew little or nothing of these efforts to stop the festival in its tracks. They sat there, firmly intent on seeing a movie. Saura and his companion, Geraldine Chaplin, tried to halt the proceedings by clambering onto the apron and holding the curtains shut. They opened anyway, with Saura and Chaplin dangling from them. When the force of gravity asserted itself and the militant couple fell to the stage, members of the audience leaped up, and fighting broke out between them and the activists. Figures began tumbling into the potted begonias and geraniums below. The film ran for a few minutes, flickering over the grappling bodies, giving the whole thing a phastasmagorical air – an involuntary homage to Federico Fellini. Then the lights went up, and projection ceased to a chorus of whistles, boos, and catcalls. Jean-Pierre Rassam emerged from the fray with a bloody nose.

Cannes now succumbed to the same heady fervor that gripped Paris. There were meetings, processions, demonstrations, rallies, and shouts of 'Our comrades, the students from Nice, have arrived!' By this time the general strike was spreading throughout France. Train and plane services were grinding to a halt, gas stations running dry. Exhibitors began to pack up and go home, and the festival ended in complete disarray. At least one comfort-loving revolutionary, the French director Claude Lelouch, transferred his yacht to the safety of the Italian Riviera. Sam Spiegel, like the hero of some updated *Exodus*, took a crowd of gilded refugees aboard his own palatial yacht, the *Malanais*. The staff of the Martinez, who mistakenly believed me to be one of those responsible for the festival's demise and their own considerable loss of earnings, turned sulky and snubbed me. The masses didn't seem to appreciate the intellectuals' efforts on their behalf.

There was no point in staying in festivalless Cannes and no way of getting to Paris. With a small party of friends, I decided to sit it out in Rome. Sharon and I drove the few miles to the Italian border in my Ferrari, which still had California plates and just enough gas for the trip. Mike Sarne followed close behind in his Rolls convertible, accompanied by Frank Simon, a young American director whose documentary about a gay pageant, *The Queen*, had been the toast of Cannes.

The only problem was, my Polish passport contained no Italian visa. I decided to bluff my way through. Sharon flashed her U.S. passport, and I claimed to have lost mine. Sarne, whose powers of persuasion were remarkable, talked the frontier guards into admitting us. Thereafter our little band of refugees proceeded to have a week's unscheduled fun in Rome.

Sharon and I returned to London, then left for Los Angeles once more. Sharon's film career was progressing far better than mine. A funereal atmosphere reigned at Paramount. Expensive failures like *Darling Lili*, *Paint Your Wagon*, and *The Molly MaGuires* had lost a fortune. Bluhdorn responded by stripping Paramount of its salable assets. He dismantled the studio, fired many of the skilled technicians who'd spent their whole lives on the lot, and transferred Paramount's headquarters to a small building in

Beverly Hills. When I visited the studio at the height of this upheaval, people were wandering around like lost souls, talking agitatedly or staring gloomily into space. I was reminded of the fateful day in Krakow when the authorities declared all Polish currency worthless.

For want of anything better to do, I began writing *A Day at the Beach*, a screenplay based on a short story by the Dutch writer Heere Heresma and conceived as a low-budget picture within the scope of Cadre Films. It concerned an alcoholic who takes his small daughter on a day trip to a seaside town – an outing that ends in a prolonged binge and, ultimately, in disaster. This was to be Simon Hessera's first directorial attempt and Paramount were dragging their feet over financing it. Charlie Bluhdorn and Bob Evans were in London on business, so Gene Gutowski decided to make a final pitch. I flew over for a working lunch with them at Gene's apartment. Peter Sellers, who had agreed to play an unpaid cameo part, was also invited as, of course, was Simon. Between them, Peter and Simon so mesmerized Bluhdorn with their clowning that he'd have signed anything. Paramount had some funds in Denmark it wanted to invest, so Simon flew to Copenhagen to line things up for shooting there.

At this juncture Sharon became pregnant. It was an accidental pregnancy since she'd been using an IUD. Our L.A. doctor pronounced it a near miracle and put it down to Sharon's animal vitality. He asked me what we intended. I told him we would keep it, of course; we'd wanted a child in any case. He thoroughly approved, commenting that it certainly looked like a gift from God.

If the truth be told, I was rather thrown by the news. A child seemed such a luxury, such an important event, that I felt it deserved the same careful planning as a film. I wanted the circumstances to be just right – a bigger house and adequate time for preparation. What was more, Sharon had contracted to make a picture with Vittorio Gassman in Rome and London, and I knew that her pregnancy would be obvious by the time shooting ended. I urged her to tell the director, Nicolas Gessner, but she wouldn't. 'Everything's

299

going to be fine,' she said soothingly.

Terry Melcher, the young record impresario, was splitting up with Candice Bergen, so their rented house off Benedict Canyon was on the market. Sharon, who had always liked it, contacted the owner, Rudi Altobelli, and we signed the lease on February 12, 1969.

It was an attractive place in many ways – a country house with a flower-filled garden enclosed by a post and rail fence. The interior was all white walls and exposed beams, and the furniture included a rocking chair, comfortable sofas, and a short grand piano. Most important of all, there was plenty of room for the baby, not to mention the British nanny Sharon had set her heart on.

Set back from a narrow, winding road called Cielo Drive, the house itself could not be seen from Benedict Canyon. Candice Bergen had rigged up some Christmas lights along the fence, and we left them there, switching them on whenever guests were expected so as to guide them to their destination.

The one drawback, from my point of view, was a certain lack of privacy. There was a smaller house on the grounds occupied by the caretaker, a young man named William Garretson. We didn't need a caretaker, and I asked Sharon if she was sure she wanted someone living on the premises; but she seemed unconcerned. 'He's a nice young man – very discreet,' she said. 'No, it doesn't bother me.'

Almost as soon as we moved in, Sharon had to leave for Rome to start filming. I flew with her as far as London, where I remained for business reasons. I wasn't too happy about the way things were going, with either Cadre Films or my own career. *Brigadier Gérard*, which Gene Gutowski had produced in Rome with Jerzy Skolimowski directing, had been such a disaster that no major distributor would release it. Simon Hessera's *A Day at the Beach* showed signs of going down the same drain. I saw the rushes almost daily, and the male lead, Mark Burns, simply wasn't right for the part. By now, however, it was too late to change.

I felt I'd been idle long enough. The batteries were re-

300

charged and I was eager to make another picture. Sandy Whitelaw, United Artists's vice-president in charge of production, sent me the galleys of a book he thought would make a fine movie, Robert Merle's *The Day of the Dolphin*. I had reservations about the book and some qualms about leaving Paramount. On the other hand, I had no formal contract with them, and they had had no real qualms about giving *Downhill Racer* to another director.

Still undecided, I joined Andy Braunsberg aboard a plane for Brazil. We both were going to the Rio Film Festival, I as a guest, Andy to show *Wonderwall*. While our plane droned south through the night, I gave Andy an earful of my problems. With Cadre Films going nowhere fast, I felt it was time to wind up my partnership with Gene Gutowski. My worries would be fewer as a straightforward director. On the other hand, there weren't any properties around that really interested me, not even *The Day of the Dolphin*. To pass the time, I told Andy the story, The more I outlined the plot, the more enthusiastic Andy became. Whether or not it had something to do with the magnificent sunrise flaring on our left, Andy's euphoria infected me. 'The hell with it,' I said. 'I'll do the picture.' Andy capped my lightning decision with one of his own by asking to come in as associate producer.

The Brazilian authorities were very security-conscious. They took away your passport at every opportunity: on arrival, checking into your hotel, making an airline booking. There was also a hectic carnival atmosphere – the festival was more a pretext to have fun than a movie showcase – and disorganization reigned supreme. When I booked a flight out of Rio, my passport was taken once more and promptly lost. This was disastrous because I'd resolved to catch a glimpse of Sharon by returning to London via Rome. Pulling a few strings, I got myself smuggled aboard a plane, but when I landed in Rome, my troubles began in earnest. Without a passport, I was a nonperson. The Italian authorities confined me in a cell-like office for hours, not even allowing me out to say hello to Sharon, who happened to be shooting a scene at the airport itself. After innumerable phone calls and arguments I was permitted only to board a plane for London.

It was a relief to be back in a civilized country. The British immigration officers were far more understanding, though it took me a long time to obtain another passport and even longer to replace my various visas. I decided I'd had enough of this nonsense and proposed to apply for British citizenship – I felt far more at home in England than anywhere else – but was advised that having been born in Paris, I would find French citizenship an easier proposition.

I settled down to some solid work on *The Day of the Dolphin* in my mews house. Dick Sylbert was again to be my designer. As usual in the case of a major new Hollywood project, no one quibbled about research and preproduction costs. Anything I needed, I got, and I was working with renewed relish. I had a wife I loved and a child on the way. I was still young enough to experience the strange, spine-tingling realization that happiness is here and now, not just around the corner or entombed in some golden memory of long ago. Professionally as well as personally, London, in the early summer of 1969, was radiant with promise.

As if to remind me that every horizon, however radiant, conceals a cloud or two, I received an anguished call from Wojtek Frykowski in L.A. We had asked him and his girl-friend, Abigail Folger, to look after the Cielo Drive house in our absence. After getting out of Poland, Wojtek had led a checkered existence in Paris and New York, where he'd been introduced to Abigail by Jerzy Kosinki. The two of them came out west, Wojtek in the hope of breaking into movies. Still the tough, macho charmer, he lacked the talent to succeed. I was determined to find him a job on *Dolphin*– something that would exploit his aquatic skills – but Wojtek was as accident-prone as ever. His latest phone call proved this yet again: while parking the car, he'd managed to run over Dr Saperstein.

The dog had been a member of our family, almost like a child. I was miserable – appalled at the prospect of breaking

302

the news to Sharon. I consulted Victor Lownes. 'First,' he said, 'buy another dog.'

I already had one surprise present on order for her – a white vintage Rolls Silver Dawn – but I knew it wouldn't make up for the loss of her dog. I phoned Sharon in Rome and told her that Dr Saperstein needed some female company. Then I bought a Yorkshire terrier puppy, which we christened Prudence. Later, when Sharon joined me in London, I broke the news that Dr Saperstein had 'disappeared.' It sounded plausible enough – Saperstein regularly took off like a randy little tomcat and returned, looking shamefaced, after a couple of days on the prowl. Sharon never did get to know what really happened.

She was very pregnant by this time and lovelier to look at than ever. Gessner had only just managed to pilot her through her film in time with the aid of an ingenious wardrobe and some skillful camerawork. Although her beauty moved me as deeply as it always had, I encountered a problem which I found impossible to broach point-blank. Now that she was so noticeably, exuberantly pregnant, the love and tenderness I felt for her went hand in hand with a total inability to make love to her.

We'd made love almost every night since starting to live together. In some very feminine way, Sharon regarded this as proof of my continuing affection; as long as we made love, she felt, nothing could go seriously wrong with our relationship. Now that we'd ceased to do so, she was afraid that my feelings toward her might be changing, that my lack of desire might become ingrained. For my part, I longed for the time when her body would return to normal; I failed to understand how men could have sex with their wives till the very last moment. Sharon eventually found a theory that reconciled her to the situation. 'It's a subconscious fear of harming the baby,' she said. 'Lots of men feel the same way.'

The baby had become the focal point of her life. She read every available book on childbirth and baby care and went on a marathon buying spree for baby clothes. Quite unabashed by her appearance, she didn't object to being photographed; in fact, she reveled in it. Our conversations revolved around the unborn child. I wanted a girl, but she was convinced it would be a boy and debated what name to give him. She asked if there was anyone I'd particularly admired as a boy. Only half-joking, I told her that my hero between the ages of twelve and fifteen had been the founder of the Boy Scouts, Robert Baden-Powell. She doubted if it would be fair to saddle our child with a name like Baden Polanski.

It had always been taken for granted that Sharon would have the baby in America. No airline would fly her across the Atlantic – she was in her eighth month by now – so I booked her a stateroom on the *QE2*. In due course, forwarding agents came to remove several massive trunks filled with things for her and the baby, and we paid farewell visits to our favorite London haunts. We spent our last evening together at Harry Saltzman's newly opened restaurant overlooking the Thames. Sharon had never looked more beautiful. The last picture I have of her, taken only a few days before she sailed, is a little Polaroid test for a photoportrait due to appear on the cover of *Queen* magazine. Another legacy from her is the book she left behind in our bedroom: Thomas Hardy's *Tess of the d'Urbervilles*. She'd just finished reading it and said it would make a wonderful movie.

My Ferrari had already been shipped back to the States, so I borrowed Simon Hessera's Alfa Romeo convertible and drove her to Southampton in time to have lunch on board. Never having set foot in a big ocean liner before, we explored it like excited children, Sharon with tiny Prudence nestling in the crook of her arm.

Something about this parting made it different from other, more casual leave-takings, and both of us had tears in our eyes. 'Okay, go now,' Sharon said abruptly. We walked down the companionway to the main exit. She hugged me tightly, pressing her belly against me in a way she'd never done before, as if to remind me of the baby. As I held and kissed her, a grotesque thought flashed through my mind: you'll never see her again. If nothing had happened, I might have no recollection of this premonition; as it is, the memory remains indelible. While walking off the ship and back to the car, I told myself to snap out of it, forget I'd ever had such a morbid feeling, call Victor Lownes, have a ball, see some girls.

I noticed on the way back to London that Sharon had left her bag in the car – a cheap canvas army surplus shoulder bag. To my delight, I found that it was possible to call the *QE2* at sea between certain hours. I got through to Sharon, and the more we talked, the more absurd my premonition seemed. There was nothing important in the bag, she said, then went on to tell me that Prudence enjoyed the motion of the ship; it kept her favorite toy, a squash ball, rolling all the time. 'It's a pity you didn't come, too,' she added. 'There are movies and a gym; you'd have loved it.'

That night I went to Victor Lownes's place and wished I hadn't. Simon Hessera and I sat chatting with some girls we didn't know while Victor banged some chick in his bedroom. Conversation languished. One of Victor's horrible Pekingese had diarrhea on the drawing-room carpet. That did it. I went upstairs and knocked on Victor's door. He was getting dressed. The girl, whom I'd never seen before, was still in bed.

'Victor,' I said, 'I thought we were going to have a party. All that's happened so far is your dog's crapped on the carpet.'

He followed me downstairs, fuming.

'Why didn't you clean it up?'

I couldn't believe my ears. 'You mean you expect us to clean up your dog shit?'

'You sit here,' he snarled, 'all of you, doing nothing, drinking my booze –'

'Shove your booze,' I said. 'I don't expect my guests to clean house when they visit me.' Simon and I left. The girls stayed.

I didn't go out much after that. The new script was proving harder to finish than I'd expected. Unlike *Rosemary's Baby*, *The Day of the Dolphin* had a number of structural flaws.

Remedying them for the screen was a major problem. So was figuring out how to make the dolphins talk. In the book they articulated like human beings, but in a mixture of squeaks and grunts. I knew that audiences would laugh themselves sick at any attempt to reproduce such sounds in a movie. Just to complicate matters still further, I realized when the script was almost finished that I would have to dispense with one of the book's main characters. Once I finally made the necessary and time-consuming adjustments, I still found myself tinkering with the ending and one last sequence that simply wouldn't resolve itself. In an attempt to speed things up, Andy Braunsberg suggested enlisting the help of Michael Braun, an American writer based in London.

I postponed my departure for Los Angeles again and again. Sharon and I talked on the phone every day, sometimes more than once. She was growing impatient. On August 8, a Friday, we had a longer talk than usual. She told me about a stray kitten she'd found in the garden – how she was feeding it with an eyedropper and trying to tame it. The kitten was a lot of fun, she said, but she sounded edgy. California was in the grip of a terrible heat wave, which must have been especially hard on a woman in her condition. Aside from that, the baby was due in two or three weeks' time, and she didn't want any houseguests around when it arrived. Fond as she was of Wojtek and Abigail, she wanted them out of the house, but she didn't know how to make this clear without hurting their feelings. I also suspected, though she didn't say so, that she was planning an elaborate party for me on my birthday.

It dawned on me, as we talked, that I was getting nowhere with the ending, even with Michael Braun's help, and that the sequence I'd been working on could probably be cut altogether. 'That's it,' I said, 'I'm coming. I'll finish the script over there. I'll leave tomorrow.'

I couldn't hop a plane the next day, a Saturday, because I needed a U.S. visa and the consulate was closed, but I made up my mind to do so the following Monday or Tuesday, as soon as the visa was granted.

That Saturday I had some good news: a letter from the U.S. immigration authorities confirmed that Marie Lee, the English nanny Sharon had selected, 'because of her kind eyes' – after placing an ad in *The Times* and interviewing dozens of candidates – would be given a U.S. work permit.

I lunched with Tony Greenburgh and Simon Hessera. Conversation was rather subdued. We had just learned of the sudden death of a friend of ours, Danielle, Dick Sylbert's ex-girlfriend. She was a beautiful French girl in her early twenties, and the news had come as a shock. 'Makes you wonder who'll be next,' I remember saying.

I went home to see what Michael Braun had come up with in my absence. Later, when Andy Braunsberg joined us, we discussed what he and Michael would have to do in London after my departure and started mapping out a timetable.

Gene Gutowski, who felt it was stupid of Victor and me to perpetuate our recent quarrel, arranged a reconciliation dinner for us at a Kensington restaurant.

It was around 7:00 p.m. London time when the call came through from Los Angeles.

TWENTY-TWO

Although it was Winny Chapman, our cleaning lady, who raised the alarm after finding the bodies at 8:00 a.m. on Saturday, August 9, 1969, the chain of events leading to the phone call was set in motion by Sandy Tennant, Bill's wife. She and Sharon, who were close friends, spoke on the phone or saw each other every day. When Sandy called our Cielo Drive number and got no reply, it worried her. She knew that someone should be home because Sharon had had no plans to go out. Having heard reports of a fire in the hills north of Los Angeles, she was afraid that something might have happened.

Jay Sebring's business associate, John Madden, had also become apprehensive by this time. He phoned Sebring's home and was told that his bed hadn't been slept in. Next, he phoned Sharon's mother, who had also tried Sharon's number and got no reply. Mrs Tate fueled Sandy's fears by calling her on the off chance that she'd heard something. Sandy then called Bill, who was playing tennis. He cut his game short at once and set off for Cielo Drive, knowing nothing.

By the time Bill got there reporters and photographers were milling around a couple of hundred yards from the house; the police had set up a roadblock and cordoned off the drive. The press had been alerted by their routine monitoring of police shortwave transmissions. All they knew was that there had been a multiple murder in one of the houses on Cielo Drive.

It was Bill who first identified Sharon, Wojtek, Jay, and

308

Gibby Folger. Until then the police hadn't known who they were. Immediately afterward Bill was sick over the garden fence. Then he elbowed his way through the press and dashed to the nearest phone. His call came through just as I was leaving the house for my rendezvous with Victor Lownes. I recognized his voice at once and asked how he was.

'Bad.' His voice sounded remote, muffled. That was odd because the transatlantic connection was usually so good it made callers sound as if they were right next door. He said, 'There's been a disaster at the house.'

I thought he might be referring to some domestic crisis of his own. His marriage was under a certain amount of strain at the time.

'Whose house?' I asked.

'Yours,' he said. 'Sharon's dead. Wojtek's dead, too, and Gibby and Jay. They're all dead.'

I heard myself say, 'No, no, no.' Andy and Michael were looking at me curiously. I couldn't take in what Bill was saying.

'What happened?' I asked.

My mind seized on the notion of a landslide. If they'd been buried, some of them might still be rescued. Please let Sharon be alive, I thought.

Then he said, 'Roman, they were murdered.' He started to say something else in a choking voice, but I put the receiver down on the desk. Andy picked it up and took over.

I began walking around and around in small circles, my hands clenched tightly behind my back. I could hear Andy calling Gene Gutowski. 'Come over here right away,' he said. A moment later he shouted, 'Just get over here!'

I don't remember much else. According to Gene, I kept moaning, 'No, no!' and punching the walls, then banging my head against them so hard he was afraid I'd injure myself. He put his arms around me and held me tight. 'Did she know how much I loved her?' I asked him in Polish, over and over again. 'Did she? Did she?'

Tony Greenburgh was out for dinner and couldn't be reached, so another doctor came and shot me full of some

309

sedative. I have a recollection of Warren Beatty and Victor Lownes arriving, as well as Dick Sylbert, Simon Hessera, and, finally, Tony. I also remember the continual ringing of the phone and Victor shouting, 'Get off the line!' Just before I passed out, I heard him talking briskly and efficiently to the duty officer at the U.S. Embassy. Then he called the ambassador at his home, woke him up, and persuaded him to authorize the issuing of an emergency visa.

I was still under the effects of the tranquilizer the next morning. Victor took charge and arranged for a Pan Am car to drive me through the staff entrance at Heathrow, straight onto the runway. Gene, Victor, and Warren accompanied me on the flight. Very groggy, I slept most of the way there. At Los Angeles airport an immigration officer boarded the plane to stamp my passport. I was ushered off first and spirited out through a back way. Gene and Victor stayed behind to face the press.

I was driven to Paramount Studio and installed in a suite that had recently been Julie Andrews's dressing room, where I slept and slept. Partly because a Paramount doctor kept me sedated, partly because I was still in a state of shock, I had no clear idea of what was going on during the three days that followed. I was only barely aware of my immediate and extensive questioning by the police. This was when the rumors started.

Various friends took turns keeping me company – Warren, Gene, Wally Wolf, Dick Sylbert, and Bob Evans. I called Paris and tried to speak to Gérard Brach but broke down. And all the time I had the feeling that Sharon wasn't dead, that I was in the middle of a bad dream, that she'd suddenly come walking in.

The murders had spread ripples of irrational terror throughout the Hollywood community. Despite their fears, all the stars came to the funeral. It was like some ghastly movie premiere. The only absentee was Steve McQueen, one of Sharon's oldest friends. I never forgave him for that.

Her funeral was unreal: I had to keep reminding myself where I was. I sat next to Sharon's mother, hugging her and crying. The priest delivered a very moving address, but while he spoke, the same thought recurred again and again: inside that coffin is Sharon's body. However hard I tried to concentrate, all I could think of was the scar on Sharon's left knee. It was a little white scar – the result of a cartilage operation after a skiing accident. Throughout the service all I did was visualize the scar I would never see again.

Danny Bowser was the first detective on the case to interview me. It was right after the funeral, and his visit compelled me to pull myself together. I still felt numb; the only thing that kept me going was my need to find out what had happened. I accompanied Bowser to LAPD headquarters, where the officer in charge of the case, Lieutenant Bob Helder, joined us for a long, exhaustive discussion. This was only the first of several such exploratory sessions aimed at discovering who might have been responsible for the killings.

Danny Bowser wasn't, strictly speaking, on the investigative side of the case. A tall, tough, good-looking man with graying hair and one glass eye – a memento of a shoot-out – he belonged to the Special Investigation Section. One of his responsibilities was to keep in touch with me. I got to know him well enough to admire him as both a detective and an individual. For all his toughness, he was a very gentle guy with a great sense of humor.

I hadn't even looked at a paper since August 9. It was Victor Lownes, always a voracious reader of newspapers and magazines, who first drew my attention to the stories currently in the press. 'All kinds of crazy things are being written about Sharon,' he fumed.

As soon as the murders were discovered, the media took their cue from Hollywood gossip and started churning out allusions to orgies, drug parties, and black magic. Not only the bitchiest but also the most insecure community in the world, Hollywood was striving to find an explanation that would put the blame fairly and squarely on the victims and thus reduce the threat to Hollywood as a whole. Sharon and those who died with her, the argument ran, were responsible for their own deaths because they had engaged in sinister practices and ran with the wrong crowd. Nothing of the kind could ever happen to ordinary, decent, God-fearing people. The fact that a perfectly ordinary couple, the La Biancas, had been killed in similar circumstances the following day was conveniently overlooked.

There was a corollary to the 'they brought it on themselves' thesis; these were the films you made, so this was the life you led – and the death you died. Headlined 'Why Sharon Had to Die,' one article that appeared in the wake of the murders summed up the attitude of Hollywood and the media in general. It stated that we had brought the appalling tragedy on ourselves by pursuing a kinky, dissolute, drug-oriented life-style.

'A fascinating whodunit' was *Newsweek*'s description of the tragedy. It wrote:

> Almost as enchanting as the mystery was the glimpse the murders yielded into the surprising Hollywood sub-culture in which the cast of characters played. All week long the Hollywood gossip about the case was of drugs, mysticism and offbeat sex – and, for once, there may be more truth than fantasy in the flashy talk of the town.
>
> The theme of the melodrama was drugs. Some suspect that the group was amusing itself with some sort of black magic rites as well as drugs that night, and they mention a native Jamaican hip to voodoo who had recently been brought into Frykowski's drug operation. Some such parlor rites might account for the hood found over Sebring's head and the rope binding him to Tate. Indeed, a group of friends speculates that the murders resulted from a ritual mock execution that got out of hand in the glare of hallucinogens.

Time adopted a similar tone: 'It was a scene as grisly as anything depicted in Polanski's film explorations of the dark and melancholy corners of the human character.' *Time*, too, alleged that the murders had ritual overtones and claimed: 'A hood covered Sebring's head.' Later it recorded equally fanciful details: 'Sebring was wearing only the torn remnants of a pair of boxer shorts. One of Miss Tate's breasts had been cut off . . . there was an X cut on her stomach. . . . Sebring had been sexually mutilated, and his body also bore X marks.'

Like *Newsweek*, *Time* made much of 'theories on sex, drugs and witchcraft cults . . . fed by the fact that Sharon and Polanski circulated in one of the film world's more offbeat crowds.' According to *Time*, we 'habitually picked up odd and unsavory people indiscriminately, and invited them home to parties.' The smear-by-innuendo technique was abundantly used: 'How much of a role drugs played in their world is hard to discern. . . . Polanski is noted for his macabre movies. . . . There also appeared to be a dark side to the other victims.' Frykowski was 'a hanger-on with sinister connections to which even the tolerant Polanski objected.' Abigail Folger was an 'aimless heiress.' Summarizing, *Time* opined that 'the most likely theory' was that 'the slayings were related to narcotics.'

The police investigators knew the true facts. Sebring had been fully clothed when he died. He had not been sexually mutilated, nor was there any hood over his head, just a cloth one of the policemen had used to cover his face because his wounds were so appalling. Sharon was not nude either, and her breast had not been cut off. Last but not least, the killings were not drug-related.

A year had to pass before the truth emerged at the trial and five years before a full and reasonably accurate account of what happened was presented in *Helter Skelter*, a book by Vincent Bugliosi, the L.A. district attorney. Even so, the harm done during the days immediately after the murders has never been put right. To this day there must be large numbers of people who remember only what they were fed by the media.

More nauseating still were those who made capital out of the murders, boasting of their intimacy with Sharon and me and relaying their hypocritical hindsight to readers around

313

the world in syndicated articles. Typical of this numerous breed was the Hollywood gossip columnist Joe Hyams, husband of Elke Sommer, who had starred with Sharon in *Wrecking Crew*.

In previous months Hyams had desperately tried to worm his way into our circle. When Sharon and I finally yielded to his repeated overtures and accepted a dinner invitation, the Hyamses' sycophancy and overeagerness to 'make it' with the 'right' Hollywood people were so blatant that I made a mental note never to be trapped again by them or anyone like them. It was Hyams who wrote 'Why Sharon Had to Die' and he who first spread the rumor that we'd been in the habit of picking up strangers on the Strip and bringing them home for orgies.

I had no idea that Hyams was cooking up this series of despicable falsehoods. He called me shortly after the murders, claiming that he had some useful information to impart. I was so eager for information from any source, however tenuous, that I heard him out. I decided later that he'd simply been milking me for copy. He wrote as if he'd been an intimate friend of ours. One of his articles was headlined 'The Last Time I Saw Sharon.' It didn't mention that the last time had also been the first and only time. Hyams had asked Sharon on this occasion if she would be averse to having sex on the screen. 'If it's tastefully done, it could be beautiful,' he quoted her as saying. 'I wouldn't mind one bit. In fact, I'd enjoy shocking the hell out of some of those Midwestern audiences.' He ended his piece thus: 'She shocked them all right.'

Sex, drugs, arcane rites – that, the media obviously felt, was what the public wanted, so that's what they gave them. The truth, as one of the girl killers testified before a grand jury, was less colorful. When she and her accomplices burst into the house after cutting the telephone wires, they found Sharon, eight months pregnant, chatting with Jay Sebring. Wojtek Frykowski was asleep on the living-room couch, and Abigail Folger was reading a book in her bedroom. Their fifth victim, Steven Parent, had been getting into his car after

314

visiting William Garretson, the caretaker.

Hollywood society being so eager to self-dramatize and impress, scores of people later claimed to have been invited to the house that night. Some of them may simply have gotten their dates wrong. Sharon was planning a big party for August 18 – my birthday – and had already issued some invitations, but no one was expected that night, not even Jerzy Kosinski, who later said that had it not been for a piece of luggage going astray at an airport, he would also have been among the victims.

Drugs, which formed the chief topic of conversation in Hollywood after the killings, were wrongly seen as their cause. I told the police we all smoked pot – I hardly knew anyone in Hollywood who didn't – but by local standards we were almost abstainers. Sharon had stopped smoking altogether the day she learned she was pregnant. I smoked moderately, Jay, Gibby, and Wojtek quite heavily. I was also aware that Wojtek and Gibby experimented with mescalin, and that Jay was a secret coke user. While searching the house, detectives found a roach in an ashtray in Sharon's bedroom, almost certainly smoked by one of the others, a pinch of marijuana in a sitting-room cabinet, and another ounce in Gibby's bedroom. They also found a minute quantity of cocaine in Jay Sebring's Porsche in the yard outside.

The press painted an astonishingly inaccurate picture of Wojtek Frykowski, describing him as 'a major drug purveyor.' In many ways, Wojtek was one of the squarest people I've ever known. I enjoyed his company and felt a sense of loyalty to the old friend who'd enabled me to make *Mammals* and later fallen on hard times. I didn't begrudge Wojtek his taste for the good life. Certain visitors to our Cielo Drive house objected to his everlasting presence, called him a lounge lizard, and criticized him for sunning himself beside the pool with a glass of wine always at hand. But it was my house, Wojtek was my friend, I didn't mind his drinking my wine, and there was nothing evil or underhanded about him.

The myth of Wojtek the big-time drug dealer stemmed largely from a report that he'd had dealings with known pushers. Sometime in April, Sharon and I had given a big party. Gate-crashers turned up, as they often did at Hollywood parties. Three of them became obstreperous and were ejected with Wojtek's help. One of the trio, who knew him, swore to get even. All three turned out to be small-time pushers, and it was this incident that gave rise to the drug connections theory. The whereabouts of all three men were carefully checked, but all had cast-iron alibis for the night of the murders.

Abigail Folger, Wojtek's girlfriend, was a wealthy coffee heiress who had been introduced to him by Kosinski. She was also a dedicated social worker who left the house early each morning to teach at a downtown center for under-privileged black children and returned, worn-out, in the evenings.

It was inevitable, I suppose, that the press should fasten on Jay Sebring. The fact that he had spent a lot of time at our house was seen as proof of an unhealthy relationship between the three of us. The truth was that despite his material success and veneer of playboy self-assurance, Jay was fundamentally a gentle, lonely person who looked on us as his only real family – the only people he felt truly secure with.

No account of the killings was complete without an allusion to Jay's sex life. The press discovered, by interviewing his former girlfriends, that he had dabbled in mild bondage and fake whippings. This was quite enough to turn him into a cross between Gilles de Rais and the Marquis de Sade. It seems to be a fact of life that any conduct even slightly at variance with the norm becomes doubly reprehensible if the person concerned dies a violent death. So poor Jay, who wouldn't have hurt a fly and whose sexual habits had been no more bizarre than those popularized by *The Joy of Sex*, was posthumously branded as a weirdo. I could find no resemblance between the press portraits of Jay Sebring and the Jay Sebring I'd known.

Finally, there was the videotape of Sharon and me making love, found by a detective on the little mezzanine over the living room. One writer later claimed that the police had unearthed a whole collection of pornographic movies and stills involving famous Hollywood stars. Although I was never questioned about the tape, I should no doubt be accused of concealing a significant aspect of our life-style if I failed to mention its existence.

The videotape recorder was the one I'd bought from Paramount after having used it to tape rehearsals of *Rosemary's Baby*. It was a rare toy in the late 1960's, and we played with it a good deal. One night I suggested switching it on and making love. 'Fine,' said Sharon, 'what characters shall we play?' The whole thing was frivolous rather than lewd and exhibitionistic. Gene's only comment when I told him what we'd done was 'Why, do you want to check your technique or something?' At the back of my mind was the idea that it would be hilarious to play the tape years later, when we were old. It wasn't to be.

The black magic allegations were utterly fantastic; there never was a 'Jamaican hip to voodoo' among our acquaintances. The gossip about witchcraft originated when a reporter discovered that there had been a Ouija board in the house. Unlike the press and the gossipmongers, the police gave no credence whatsoever to tales of stray pickups, orgies, drug excesses, and black magic. Bob Helder and Danny Bowser behaved with cool professionalism, but I could sense their sympathy. I admired the way they set about the investigation, and we formed a friendship that stood the test of time.

There is, I think, at least one error in Bugliosi's otherwise admirably accurate account. *Helter Skelter* takes the LAPD to task for failing to follow up a lead that might have exposed the Manson 'family' earlier – a lead based on similarities between the deaths at Cielo Drive and that of Gary Hinman, a music teacher murdered ten days earlier, also by Manson's followers. Bob Helder was well aware of this, however. He told me, very soon after we first met, of a possible lead involving a bunch of hippies living in the Chatsworth area under a commune leader, 'a crazy guy who calls himself Jesus Christ.' I distinctly recall my lukewarm response to this information. 'That's just your antihippie bias,' I said.

I had no idea, of course, how close Helder had been to stumbling across the Manson trial, but I did, instinctively, feel that the usual murder motives weren't applicable. 'If you're looking for a motive,' I told one of the officers, 'I'd look for something that doesn't fit the routine pattern – something much more farout.'

Though anxious to help, I knew that first I would have to dispel any suspicion that I might have been implicated in the killings. During our long sessions together Helder and Bowser urged me not to overlook any clue, even if it related to my closest friends. It was logical for them to treat everyone, me included, as a potential suspect, so I told Bowser I wanted to undergo a polygraph test. 'Christ, Roman, you must be a mind reader,' he said. 'Chief Houghton asked me to see if there was some way of getting you to take one, and I just didn't know how to bring it up.'

We went straight to the LAPD and the first person we bumped into was Chief Houghton. Bowser told him that I'd volunteered to take the polygraph test and Houghton, looking surprised, muttered, 'Mmm, that might be a good idea.'

'What is this?' I demanded. 'Bowser told me you were desperate for me to take the test and now you act like you couldn't care less!'

The Chief flushed and looked embarrassed. 'Don't believe everything this guy tells you,' was his only rejoinder.

'I'll tell you one thing,' I said to Houghton. 'He's a better actor than you are.'

I did then take the test, which was a big relief.

The police still favored the theory of personal revenge, though I couldn't think of anyone with a reason to get even with any of us. Bowser and Helder said I must assume that whoever was responsible concealed a deeply disturbed personality beneath a normal exterior. I was told to treat my closest friends as potential suspects, without, of course, arousing their suspicions. I insisted on offering a $25,000 reward for information leading to any arrest and conviction. The LAPD was of two minds about the usefulness of this, but I was adamant.

Moving out of my quarters at Paramount, I stayed for a while with Michael Sarne, busy directing *Myra Breckinridge*, at his beach house in Malibu Colony. His neighbors got up a petition requesting him to move me out. 'The presence in your house of Mr Polanski endangers our lives,' it said. Michael told them to stuff it.

My urge to visit Cielo Drive grew stronger as the days went by. It sprang from a mixture of motives. For one thing, I wondered if the police might have overlooked some clue to the killers; for another, I was drawn to the house by a strange nostalgia – an illusory feeling that something of Sharon might still be lingering there.

Tommy Thompson, a *Life* reporter with whom I'd been friendly when he was heading *Life*'s London bureau, got in touch with me at this stage. He said he wanted to set the record straight because, having known Sharon and me in London, he realized how false and malicious the current stories were. Thompson persuaded me to take him along – eight days after the murders – when I finally brought myself to visit Cielo Drive. Bowser took us there. The police had sealed off the house, preventing any curiosity seekers from intruding. A photographer, whose presence Thompson hadn't prepared me for, fell into line behind us. A clairvoyant named Peter Hurkos also appeared with his agent and tried to talk his way in. Bowser told him that if he was good at what he was doing, he would have foreseen that Bowser would be there to keep him out. Maybe I was still a little dazed; maybe I felt that any stone was worth turning. I gave Hurkos permission to come in with us. He insisted on taking Polaroid pictures of the interior of the house – he needed them, he said, for his work – then promptly sold them to the press, together with a lot of fanciful drivel. The piece in *Life* was accurate enough in its way, but it didn't put an end to the

319

more scurrilous press allegations; in fact it gave rise to a rumor that *Life* had paid me $5,000 to pose for a photograph on the porch.

I kept on asking Bob Helder how I could help him narrow the field. The police had already begun checking the alibis of all our friends and acquaintances. Like them, I was inclined to believe that the killer or killers belonged to our circle. Helder thought it likely that friends and acquaintances, if they did have something to hide, would be less guarded with me than with the police and might let a clue slip in the course of conversation. There was one lead worth pursuing, he said. Detectives had found a pair of horn-rims at the scene of the crime. Much later this information was made public and circulated to opticians throughout the United States. At this stage, however, no one knew of the discovery apart from the investigators themselves. So, if I could find out whether someone I knew wore glasses that matched the prescription of the pair found at Cielo Drive, we might be on to something.

After I'd spent some days at Malibu Colony, Dick Sylbert allayed the fears of Mike Sarne's neighbors by inviting me to stay at his own, more secluded beach house on Old Malibu Road. It was built on stilts, and there was something infinitely soothing about the sound of waves washing around and beneath me – something suggestive of a port in a storm. As for Dick himself, he was the soul of kindness, mothering me, getting me up in the mornings, making my breakfast, trying to take my mind off things. I didn't let on, though, not even to him, that I was conducting my private investigation.

The first unwitting object of my attentions was Bruce Lee, whom I met most days for a workout at the Paramount gym. One morning he mentioned, quite casually, that he'd lost his glasses. I said I'd never liked his old pair anyway and took him to an optician's, where I selected some new frames for him as a gift. As I hoped and suspected, his prescription bore no resemblance to the lenses found at the scene of the crime.

I bought a Vigor lens-measuring device – a gadget the size and shape of a pocket watch. This I carried at all times and surreptitiously used to check the glasses of friends and acquaintances, but without result.

Cars, too, came within my range of possible clues. Whoever carried out the killings had arrived and left by car and must have left traces of blood in the vehicle. Although it would almost certainly have been cleaned, detection was still possible.

Testing for bloodstains proved tricky. The police gave me the requisite chemicals in two glass vials. I had to dip a Q-tip in one solution and swab the part of the car I was checking, using a different Q-tip for each area checked. The Q-tips then had to be dipped in the second vial, and they would turn blue if there was any trace of blood on them.

Danny Bowser took me to S.A.C. Electronics, a workshop in the Valley that supplied the LAPD with various listening devices. Here I bought a pin mike, a transmitter, an easily concealed miniature tape recorder, and bugs to be left in people's homes.

Although it would be easy enough to dismiss all my detective work as a form of temporary derangement, this was before there were any clues leading to the Manson 'family.' At times the atmosphere of suspicion verged on paranoia. I remember Victor Lownes, in a state of high excitement, telling me that Jerzy Kosinski had just the right 'profile' to be the killer because of something he'd written in one of his books.

Another likely target was someone much closer to me, John Phillips of the Mamas and the Papas. We'd seen a lot of John and Michelle while I was making *Rosemary's Baby*. Since then they'd separated, and Michelle had taken her baby off to London with her. John had snatched the baby and brought it back to the States. At the time of the murders Michelle was living with the French actor Christian Marquand. John's outward calm, I knew, concealed a capacity for deep, burning anger. It so happened that I'd had a one-night stand with Michelle while Sharon was filming in Rome. Now it was essential for me to know if she'd ever told him. I went to see her, duly wired up; we talked a lot about

John's violence and the intensity of his rages. Yes, Michelle said, she'd told him. Could the knowledge really have provoked such a bout of murderous fury?

By this time the police had run checks on everyone we knew. I'd supplied them with a list. Although John Phillips had been dining at a Japanese restaurant with Michael Sarne and a party of friends at the time of the murders, there was just the kind of gap in his alibi that might have enabled him, after the meal, to get to Cielo Drive.

I slipped into John's garage late one night and carefully examined one of his cars, an E-Type Jaguar, for bloodstains. The tests proved negative. The only object of interest I found was a machete in the trunk, but it didn't remotely fit the police description of the weapon they were looking for.

As I sneaked out of the garage again, a patrol car slowed and pulled up beside me. Not unnaturally the patrolmen thought I was a would-be car thief. I told them I'd left something in John's car and hadn't wanted to disturb him so late at night. Luckily my name was so much in the news that after checking my ID, they believed my story and let me go.

John gave me a second opportunity to check on him. We'd arranged to meet at a recording studio, and when he arrived in his other car – a vintage Rolls convertible – a police car pulled up behind him. He'd been booked for nonpayment of fines for traffic violations. Although it was a relatively trivial offense, the police insisted on taking him down to the station. He tossed me the keys of the Rolls. 'Take care of the Jolly Green Giant, will you, Roman?' he said. I knew what he meant. John never went anywhere without a green carpetbag containing assorted pills and dope.

I parked the Rolls and removed the bag. Inside was John's Gucci diary. Flicking through it, I noted that all the entries, from first past to last, were printed in block capitals. What chilled me was that the lettering bore a distinct resemblance to the word 'PIG' that had been scrawled in blood on the door at Cielo Drive. I quickly photocopied some sample pages and sent them, together with photographs of the 'PIG' inscription, to a handwriting expert in New York. He submitted a long-winded report full of jargon, in which he neither confirmed a match nor entirely ruled it out. For this he charged more than $2,000.

I paid up. By this time I was inured to getting bills from all quarters. Paramount charged me rent for my three nights in Julie Andrews's dressing room, and Rudi Altobelli, our Cielo Drive landlord, sent me a massive bill for damage sustained by his carpets and upholstery; the bloodstains had absolutely ruined them, he complained. At this stage money seemed quite as trivial and unimportant to me as material possessions. I now proceeded to give away anything that reminded me of my years with Sharon: her white Rolls to Sandy Tennant; my Ferrari, which she'd loved driving, to her father, Paul Tate. Paul, meanwhile, was busy conducting an undercover investigation of his own. Convinced that drugs were at the root of what had happened, he grew a beard and haunted the seedier parts of the Strip disguised as a hippie.

Inevitably all kinds of sick, crazy people came up with so-called inside information about the case and tried to contact me. I managed to fend off most of them, but some were so persistent, and so plausible, that I sat through several sessions with a variety of certifiable lunatics. One, in particular, stands out in my memory. An unemployed actor, he claimed on the phone to know 'everything' but refused to breathe a word unless I saw him in person. I consulted Danny Bowser. Though skeptical, he agreed to listen in on the conversation. We set up a meeting in my office on the Paramount lot. Danny hung around long enough to see the man arrive. Then, while my secretary stalled him in the waiting room, Danny darted into my office through a side door and hid in a closet.

My visitor was a rather foppish middle-aged man. 'Are you alone?' he asked nervously.

'You can see I am,' I lied. He lunged for the closet door, but I headed him off. 'If you've something to tell me, let's hear it. If not, get out.'

He plunged into an incoherent tale about Odessa, the secret Nazi organization which, he claimed, was active in

California. Its agents had killed Sharon and now intended to kill me. He himself, he assured me, had several narrow escapes.

What made the man's story still harder to follow was his habit of switching abruptly from Odessa to himself and his professional problems, seeking my advice on parts, agents, studios. In the midst of his disjointed ravings about a Nazi murder squad at large, he surveyed his reflection in the desk top, then looked up and said, 'Think it would help if I grew a mustache?'

After he'd gone, Danny Bowser emerged, sweating and cursing, from the airless closet. 'Flabby faggot in a pearl gray suit,' he growled into his walkie-talkie, 'five-eight, one-eighty pounds, toupee. Check his license plates, that's all.' And to me: 'Sorry, Roman, just another kook.'

Everyone advised me to bury myself in my work, but I couldn't. I was listless and prone to fits of weeping at unforeseen moments – driving along the freeway; sitting in airplanes; watching a sunset. With police investigations and my own amateur efforts stalled, I resumed work on *The Day of the Dolphin*, but my heart wasn't in it. I traveled with Dick Sylbert to Miami, St Thomas, and Mexico to look at possible locations, but all I could think about was what had happened on August 9.

I started having sex again quite soon – perhaps a month after Sharon's death. I wasn't looking for women who resembled her; the act was merely a release, proof of my continued existence. I gathered from what I overheard that I was now 'the notorious' Roman Polanski. Some of the dirt had stuck: I'd been mixed up in unspeakable goings-on, sinister excesses that had somehow caused my wife's death.

I paid a brief visit to London but, still obsessed with the case and unable to do anything but brood, returned to Los Angeles. By this time *The Day of the Dolphin* was in the hands of United Artists, which was cooling on the project. As scripted, it was expected to cost $5 million. UA had hoped to do it for $4 million. Although I could have cut one or two expensive scenes without hurting the film, I didn't say anything. My behavior may have been illogical, but it was dictated by my mood. Unable to work, I didn't care when UA finally bowed out.

My friends did their best to entertain and amuse me. Warren Beatty, in particular, kept up a stream of improbable stories, mostly relating to his hyperactive sex life and containing details I'm sure were invented just to make me laugh. Meanwhile, Lieutenant Bob Helder and I continued to meet from time to time in secluded, unfashionable restaurants. He treated me with unfailing kindness and candor, more like a colleague than a potential witness.

Then, one day, he asked me to meet him in yet another out-of-the-way eating place. His first words were 'Roman, we're onto something big.' He went on to describe a conversation that had taken place, on November 2, between Susan Atkins, a member of the Manson 'family,' and another prison inmate. This was the first real lead – the one that eventually unraveled the mystery – and it came about largely in consequence of my reward. The other prisoner had read about it and decided to risk telling the police what she'd heard. She wound up sharing the $25,000 with the boy who later found one of the murder weapons – a revolver – near Benedict Canyon.

From then on Helder gave me almost daily progress reports. He briefed Paul Tate as well, but always separately. Strangely enough, as soon as I learned the truth about the murders, my obsession vanished. I theorized it didn't matter who'd done the killing; the gory details were interesting only to those for whom it was just another lurid murder story. To me, whether Sharon died from being stabbed or in a car accident made no ultimate difference. She was gone – that was the only thing that mattered. There was no remedy for death.

What hurt me most, when the media started playing up Manson and his 'family,' was their complete lack of remorse for slandering Sharon's memory and spreading such a pack of lies about us all. Once Manson was arrested, they behaved as if they'd known all along of his gang's involvement in the massacre.

My own feeling was that the murders might not have been as motiveless as they seemed. Manson's rage was that of the spurned performer – one who seeks revenge on others for his own lack of talent and recognition. Bitterness and frustration were his probable motives for sending a raiding party to what he still thought of as Terry Melcher's house; to get his own back on someone who had declined to cut a record of his mediocre compositions. The random murder of the La Biancas – an ordinary couple with no show business affiliations – so soon afterward was probably an attempt to confuse the issue.

Strangely, from the moment the killers were apprehended, I felt no further desire for revenge. I might well have, but I didn't. Far stronger was the guilt I still feel at not having been in the house on August 9. To this day I believe that had I been there when the gang of three women and one man climbed over the fence and broke in, Frykowski and I might have tackled them and, between us, driven them off. Frykowski's multiple wounds showed that he must have put up a fierce struggle on his own.

The thing that amazed me about the Manson 'family' was the extent to which it had been dominated and exploited by a single individual. Prior to the murders, I'd never thought of hippies as potentially dangerous. On the contrary, I'd found them an attractive social phenomenon – one that had influenced us all and affected our outlook on life. I'd also seen their movement as one more proof of American affluence. What other society in the world could have supported such a sizable fringe of people who, though wholly unproductive, contrived to live relatively well?

Clearly I'd underestimated the dangers latent in the hippie life-style, for which Sharon and I both had felt a certain admiration, seeing only its absence of cant, its freedom from hang-ups and hypocrisy. 'I want a hippie wife,' I remember telling Sharon on one occasion. I had not expected that she would lose her life because of this obscene perversion of hippie values.

Sharon's death is the only watershed in my life that really matters. Before she died, I sailed a boundless, untroubled sea of expectations and optimism. Afterward, whenever conscious of enjoying myself, I felt guilty. A psychiatrist I met shortly after her death warned me that it would take me 'four years of mourning' to overcome this feeling. It has taken far longer than that.

There used to be a tremendous fire within me – an unquenchable confidence that I could master anything if I really set my mind to it. This confidence was badly undermined by the killings and their aftermath. I not only developed a closer physical resemblance to my father after Sharon's death but began to take on some of his traits: his ingrained pessimism, his eternal dissatisfaction with life, his profoundly Judaic sense of guilt, and his conviction that every joyous experience has its price.

There have been other consequences, too. I doubt if I shall ever again be able to live on a permanent basis with any woman, no matter how beautiful, bright, easygoing, good-natured, or attuned to my moods. My attempts to do so have always failed, not least because I start drawing comparisons with Sharon.

There are little things, like packing a suitcase or getting my hair cut, or dialing the 213 code for California or the 396 code for Rome, that invariably steer my thoughts back to Sharon. Even after so many years I find myself unable to watch a spectacular sunset, or visit a lovely old house, or experience visual pleasure of any kind without instinctively telling myself how she would have loved it all.

In these ways I shall remain faithful to her till the day I die.

TWENTY-THREE

Once the killers had been identified, there was nothing to keep me in Hollywood. I knew that my own inner survival depended on banishing the past few years from my thoughts until I was strong enough to cope with the memory of them.

I flew off to Paris to see Gérard Brach and other old friends of my pre-Hollywood period. Although it was a comfort to be with them, my stay in France was made hideous by the press photographers who hounded me at every turn. Now that the Manson gang had been rounded up, I had naïvely expected this kind of harassment to cease. I had even imagined that the media, which had turned me into a monster overnight, printing so many lies about us and implicitly blaming me for Sharon's death, would acknowledge their error and, if not set the record straight, at least leave me in peace.

I couldn't have been more mistaken. Only those who have been besieged by *paparazzi* can understand why their victims sometimes lose patience and lash out when subjected to some peculiarly brazen invasion of privacy by this ruthless and aggressive breed. One night in Paris, after Gérard, Jean-Pierre Rassam, and I had been pursued inside a restaurant, flash-gunned throughout our meal, and trailed halfway home, I turned on our persecutor in a quiet street and snatched his camera away. The other two held him while I extracted the film and searched his pockets for the other roll he'd taken. Just as I realized he was holding it clenched in his fist, he popped it into his mouth. I tried to pry his jaws open – Jean-Pierre even tickled him in the ribs – but in vain. His fortitude was worthy of a better cause.

More in need of seclusion than ever, I welcomed it when Victor Lownes invited me to spend Christmas 1969 with him at Gstaad in the Swiss Alps, where he'd rented a chalet. As always, Victor did things in style, flying over his butler, two spectacular Maltese twins who later appeared in a *Playboy* centerfold, and a party of assorted friends.

Although Victor was determined to give me a good time, the atmosphere in the chalet didn't help. He was having problems of his own – his 'steady' ex-Bunny, Connie Kresky, was growing tired of his persistent philandering – and Victor, a hospitable but domineering bull in a china shop, couldn't really cope with me in my present state. I believe he thought there was no sense of loss that girls, booze, and parties couldn't dispel. Victor meant well – he'd been genuinely fond of Sharon and proved a tower of strength during the weeks immediately after her death – but I needed the sort of careful handling he couldn't provide. I must have been an exasperating houseguest, moody, irritable, and prone to uncontrollable fits of grief that sent me off into solitary crying spells, usually in the middle of one of Victor's carefully orchestrated festivities. Two weeks in his chalet were as much as I could take. I needed to be alone. Andy Braunsberg, who'd flown over to Gstaad to join the party, found another chalet to rent outside Gstaad, a comfortable old wooden house full of peasant furniture. I moved in and resolved to ski until sheer exhaustion and physical punishment drove away my nightmares and bouts of self-reproach.

Little by little I began to emerge from my shell. Gstaad in winter is a watering hole for the international jet set. There were also some film luminaries around – people like Curt Jurgens, David Niven, and Julie Andrews – but I didn't spend much time with them. The leisured, casual superrich I got to know were very different from the frenzied first-generation Hollywood tycoons of my acquaintance. Peter Notz, a Swiss industrialist with a wide range of social contacts, took me under his wing and introduced me to this

329

rarefied circle. He also introduced me to the exclusive Eagle Club at the summit of the Wasserngrat, hoping to make me a member, but the manager, an elderly French aristocrat, objected.

'Wasn't he the one involved in that crime in Los Angeles?' he asked.

'But he was a *victim*,' Notz protested. 'They killed his wife!'

'All the same, it wouldn't be good for the club.'

I was blackballed.

Notz was as much a member of the jet set as any careful Swiss businessman could be. By a happy coincidence, his chalet was situated close to the Montesano, a finishing school for young ladies. Notz, a bachelor, seemed to know all the prettiest inmates, and two or three American girls were always hanging around his house, listening to records, playing the guitar. For all his Swiss reserve, Notz had a trinity of ruling passions: flying, skiing, and girls.

One couldn't spend long in Gstaad without becoming aware that it was the finishing school capital of the world. Hundreds of fresh-faced, nubile young girls of all nationalities populated the Montesano School, Le Mesnil, Le Rosay, and La Videmanette. They haunted Gstaad's cafés and hotel lobbies during the week and were permitted a Cinderella's outing till midnight on Saturdays. Their increasingly emancipated behavior began to alarm the school authorities as the American sexual revolution sent ripples washing against these Swiss bastions of propriety and decorum.

It was now that Kathy, Madeleine, Sylvia, and others whose names I forget played a fleeting but therapeutic role in my life. They were all between sixteen and nineteen years old, schoolgirls no longer but not yet worldly-wise women with professional or marital ambitions. At this stage their dearest wish was to escape, however briefly, from the straitjacket atmosphere of boarding school routine.

They took to visiting my chalet, not necessarily to make love – though some of them did – but to listen to rock music

330

and sit around the fire and talk. What drew them into my orbit was the lure of forbidden fruit – of staying out late when the should have been tucked up in a dormitory.

The risks they ran were considerable. At a prearranged time I would turn up in my car and wait near the school. The silence was uncanny. Even when it wasn't actually snowing, everything would be muffled in a thick white blanket. There was a fairy-tale quality about those nights, with the occasional car illuminating the ghostly landscape as it passed, its tires crunching softly through the snow.

Whoever had made a date with me would attend evening roll call and wait till lights out before putting on boots and ski clothes. With a nightgown on top, just in case something went wrong and she was caught, my date would clamber over the dark wooden balcony and drop silently into the snow – a dimly seen, ethereal figure in white. Then came a dash to the car and a quick, crisp getaway.

Sometimes, while waiting at the wheel with the engine idling for warmth's sake, I would wonder what the hell I was doing there.

What *was* I doing there? What did we talk about, those girls and I? Music, books, school, skiing, friends, parents. What did we have in common? That's a question I've often been asked. I've never tried to analyze such friendships closely. I can only say that like so many girls of their age, they had untapped reserves of intelligence and imagination. They weren't using their bodies to further their careers; they weren't on the lookout for parts; they didn't want to hear about distribution rights or film finance – not even about the Manson murders. And they were more beautiful, in a natural, coltish way, than they would ever be again.

Generally speaking, what applied to them has applied to most of the friends I've made and kept since Sharon's death. Fewer and fewer of them are in show business; more and more of them are quite unconnected with the film industry. Showbiz people tend to talk shop to the exclusion of everything else, but my architect friends don't harp on their structural disasters any more than my doctor friends discuss their patients' terminal diseases or my businessmen friends their narrow escapes from bankruptcy.

The first hint that I was pulling myself together came when I read *Papillon* and thought at once what a wonderful film it would make. Its main appeal for me lay in Papillon's toughness and resilience, his will to survive, his unquenchable zest for living, and his yearning for freedom. The author of this amazing autobiographical account of an escape from Devil's Island, the Frenchman Henri Charrière, was living in Caracas, still technically an escaped convict. I called him. He expressed interest but told me that the film rights were owned by his French publisher, Robert Laffont. I was delighted to hear that Walter Reade was pursuing the project.

Done the right way, *Papillon* would be a spectacular and expensive film. I already had a star in mind for the name part: Warren Beatty had just the right combination of good looks, toughness, and charm. Like Papillon, he could con anyone into anything. I sounded him out, got a fairly enthusiastic response, then tackled the subject of finance.

Walter Reade, who was anxious for me to direct the picture, spent his winters at St Moritz, so I went there for a preliminary discussion. Peter Notz flew me to the Engadine in his plane and amused himself on the ski slopes while Walter and I talked.

The Walter Reade I knew was a tall, handsome, courtly New Yorker with a passion for skiing and the good things of life. I hadn't realized that he was also a cautious, almost penny-pinching businessman. As an exhibitor making his first venture into production, he arbitrarily decreed a budget of not more than $3.5 million. I was familiar enough by now with budgeting to know that given the nature of the book, this was a wholly unrealistic figure. For the moment I let it ride.

The weather on the return flight to Gstaad was foul. Sitting beside Peter Notz in the cockpit as we wove our way through cloud-capped mountains, I speculated on what might happen if he had a coronary or even a sudden attack of stomach cramps. Obsessed by this notion, I resolved to take flying lessons at the first opportunity.

Budget apart, the project was beginning to take shape. Henri Charrière was given an amnesty by the French government, largely because of his book's success, and returned to Europe. I invited him and his wife to stay with me at Gstaad. Curiously reminiscent of *Cul-de-Sac*'s Dicky in appearance, Charrière was a big man with an endearing blend of charm and unsophistication, and we hit it off extremely well. As for my prospective star, of whom Charrière had never even heard, Warren Beatty flew over to Paris, where I joined him at the Hilton with the freshly typed English translation of *Papillon* under my arm. I was eager for him to read it as soon as possible.

All our good resolutions were knocked on the head when Simon Hessera, who happened to be in Paris, joined us for dinner the first night. Seduced by his entertaining company, we embarked on a whirlwind round of parties, discos, and girls. The second day was a repetition of the first. So was the third. And the fourth. By this time, Simon had dropped out and moved to another hotel. Knowing Warren, I grew uneasy. 'Okay,' I said, 'that's it.'

He grinned. 'You're absolutely right, we've had our fun.' But over dinner that evening, after a couple of glasses of wine, he said innocently, 'Let's just see what Simon's up to.' The result: we dragged him out of bed and painted the town for the fifth consecutive night. I was so frazzled for lack of sleep I couldn't take any more. We'd been in Paris almost a week, and Warren still hadn't read a page of the book.

'Shit,' I told him, 'I've had enough.'

I flew to London for a day or two. The phone in my mews house rang before I was awake the next morning. It was Warren. 'I'm not going to appear bare-ass,' he said. 'It's a hang-up I have. What did you say the budget was?' It was his way of letting me know he'd stayed up all night reading the typescript.

I rejoined him in Paris and fixed a meeting with Robert Laffont and Henri Charrière on the first floor of the Café de Flore – the gay floor. Warren had loved the book, as I'd known he would, and wanted to do it.

That left only one hurdle to be cleared: money. I went back to Walter and tried to make him see reason, but it was no use. To everyone's regret, the project folded. Charrière started work on another book and Warren returned to the States. Andy Braunsberg, who had been hoping to coproduce the picture, sought solace with me on the slopes of Gstaad.

The first of our guests at Gstaad was Bruce Lee. Regular skiing had put me in very good shape, which impressed him, and we resumed my martial arts lessons. In return, I tried to teach him to ski but failed miserably. Despite the coordination and reflexes that made him such an effective fighter, Bruce simply couldn't master this unfamiliar sport. His disastrous showing on the slopes did not, however, prevent him from making a great hit with my jet set acquaintances. The men were impressed by his feats of strength and agility, and women by his charm and Oriental good looks.

My chalet started filling up. Sam Waynberg injected his own special brand of warmth and good humor, and Bill and Sandy Tennant arrived with a suitcase full of scripts and publishers' proofs.

I couldn't spend the rest of my life skiing, if only because I was running out of money. The effect of the Manson killings had been to redouble my inflex of ghoulish scripts, all of which I turned down. After Sharon's death few subjects seemed worthy of effort. Besides, I knew that my next film would come under scrutiny less for its quality than for its subject matter. An adventure story like *Papillon* would be acceptable; a comedy, a horror film, or a thriller was out of the question.

Ever since my young days in Krakow, I had wanted to make a film of one of Shakespeare's plays. This, I felt, might be the time. The major tragedies had already been admirably adapted for the screen, but *Macbeth* was an exception. Orson Welles and Kurosawa both had tried with varying degrees of success – or, as I believed, of failure. One day on the ski slopes I said to Andy Braunsberg, 'Why don't I do *Macbeth*?' He loved the idea. We packed up at once and left for London.

Bill Tennant was less than overjoyed when I called him with news of my latest brainchild. His actual words were 'What are you doing to me?' Deciding to go it alone, I flew over to New York and lined up what I thought was an excellent deal with Allied Artists. Although nothing was put on paper, their obvious enthusiasm was heartening.

Unfortunately I'd reckoned without my agent's lovingly proprietorial care. Eager to prove his worth by securing me the best contract possible, Bill insisted that we could get a far better deal elsewhere. He proceeded to negotiate with Universal, only to have them back out. Now, because I'd bowed to his advice, I had no deal at all. I was less disappointed than furious with myself for reneging on an oral agreement with Allied and behaving in exactly the Hollywood manner I despised in others.

Undaunted, I returned to London and sounded out Kenneth Tynan, whom I'd known since my early days in England, on the subject of collaborating on a *Macbeth* screenplay. A leading drama critic and literary director of Britain's National Theatre, Tynan had once invited me to direct an avant-garde play that failed to pass the censor. He was very interested in films as well, and we had often discussed the possibility of working together. His response to my suggestion was prompt and enthusiastic. With no prior financial commitment from any producer, just a small personal loan from Victor Lownes to cover development and production costs, we set to work.

Closeted in the mews house, I found myself reveling in work for the first time since Sharon's death. Each morning saw me champing at the bit for Tynan to arrive and our daily stint to begin. His eccentric taste in clothes, especially his off-white suits and broad pink ties, never failed to astound me. I was even more impressed by his encyclopedic knowledge of Shakespeare and uncanny knack of extemporizing Shakespearean blank verse to fit any occasion.

Tynan and I agreed on almost every point. We realized that this exceptionally long play couldn't be turned into a film without extensive cuts and that many scenes would have to be kaleidoscoped into a visual whole.

We were also determined to cut across long-established theatrical clichés. In the film Macbeth and his wife are young and good-looking – not, as in most stage productions, middle-aged and doom-laden. This was intentional. As Tynan put it, 'They don't know they're involved in a tragedy; they think they're on the verge of a triumph predicted by the witches.' In his view their tragedy was that in trying to fulfill the witches' prophecy, they uncovered a dark side of their own natures, the existence of which they'd never suspected.

I didn't feel bound by Elizabethan theatrical convention. Shakespeare, for example, had limited himself to three witches onstage, but on the screen a whole coven seemed to make more dramatic sense in the scene where Macbeth seeks their prophetic advice. The important thing was to construct a spectacular and coherent framework that would underpin and amplify the text, lending it even more resonance.

We both agreed that Lady Macbeth should be nude in the sleepwalking scene. It would render her more vulnerable and human. Quite apart from that, everyone slept naked in her day. The wearing of nightclothes was a social and theatrical convention, not least because women's parts in Shakespeare's time were played by young boys.

My treatment of another scene was based on a childhood experience. This is the moment in Act IV when the murderers dispatched by Macbeth burst in on Lady Macduff and her small son. I suddenly recalled how the SS officer had searched our room in the ghetto, swishing his riding crop to and fro, toying with my teddy bear, nonchalantly emptying out the hatbox full of forbidden bread. The behavior of Macbeth's henchmen was inspired by that recollection.

There were some stage conventions that had no meaning-

336

ful place in a film. In Shakespeare's day it would have been inconceivable to act out the murder of a monarch. This is why Duncan's assassination occurs offstage. Tynan and I felt it essential to show this central incident and discussed at length how best to stage it.

It was a very hot day when we came to tackle this scene, and we were both working stripped to the waist. Impersonating Macbeth, I made Tynan stretch out on a bed in the den of the mews house, crept up with a paper knife, and started stabbing him. He grabbed my wrist and wrestled the makeshift dagger out of my hand. We'd repeated the scene a number of times, with variations, when Tynan caught sight of some people watching us from the balcony of the house across the street. A group of middle-aged Belgravia residents were gazing at us, transfixed, sherry glasses frozen in midair. I waved, inviting them to join us. At this they hurriedly turned away and broke into animated conversation among themselves, pretending not to have seen us – let alone watched us – in the first place. They doubtless assumed that our antics were all part of the swinging London scene.

If *Macbeth* has always been surrounded by a host of theatrical superstitions, film producers tend to wince at the very sound of Shakespeare's name. With our screenplay completed, Andy and I found ourselves in possession of an apparently unsalable commodity. There was only one possible source of finance I hadn't yet tried to tap.

The Playboy empire boom had hit its all-time high. Playboy casinos were flourishing, Playboy hotels were springing up all over the States, and the gambling revenue from London's Playboy Club had made Victor Lownes, and his organization, very rich indeed. I showed our *Macbeth* script to Victor, who was highly impressed by what he called its 'luminously accessible' treatment of a theme whose full implications had always escaped him. 'I'm going to show it to our film people,' he said, 'with a strong personal recommendation.' In the face of some opposition from Playboy's new film division, Playboy Productions, he pushed the project

337

through. The deal was clinched at Marbella by Hugh Hefner himself. He flew there in his black *Bunny* DC-9, with a retinue of girls and courtiers, played a lot of backgammon, and gave the go-ahead. Playboy Productions advanced $1.5 million, and Columbia, which decided to distribute the picture, added another million.

This development coincided with the opening of the Manson trial, which put me back in the headlines again. The *Daily Telegraph* alleged that I had declined to appear as a witness because the prosecution wouldn't pay my fare. This time I sued for libel and won. I never was invited to testify because there was no evidence I could have contributed. Reading about the court proceedings was bad enough; observing them at first hand would have been unendurable.

On the strength of our Playboy deal, Andy and I formed a company called Caliban Films. We took over Cadre Films's offices and acquired a secondhand Rolls-Royce Phantom Six as a company car. It was so vast that whenever I drove it, I felt I should be standing up. We engaged a chauffeur with impeccable manners called Armand de Saint Herpin – a Britisher despite his aristocratic-sounding French name. I enlisted yet another Britisher with a French name, Hercules Belville, who had worked with me on *Repulsion* and *Cul-de-Sac*. He was the same tireless worker and even more infatuated with filmmaking, but he still didn't have the necessary union cards, so I could only make him assistant to the producer.

The production cycle has a rhythm I ignore at my peril, though it sometimes proves my undoing. I like to start shooting as soon as possible after a screenplay has been written. The faster the preproduction, the better. To me, it's essential that the freshness of the concept be captured on film at the earliest possible moment. In the case of *Macbeth* I was anxious to make a start that same fall, while Playboy Productions's interest was still at its height. Apart from that, I needed the kind of brooding, gray, autumnal skies so typical of the British Isles. This left us with absurdly little time in which to work out our production schedule, and *Macbeth*, with its medieval scenery, its elaborate costumes, its horses, battles, and action sequences, promised to be an immensely complicated film to make. Just how complicated, I was to find out the hard way.

Where casting was concerned, I left my options open – as usual – till the eleventh hour. My Macbeth, John Finch, was hired only a few days before shooting was due to begin, after I had met him by chance on a plane from Paris. For Lady Macbeth, I toyed with numerous possibilities. Tuesday Weld might have gotten the part if she hadn't declined to do the nude sleepwalking scene. I also considered an extremely promising young actress named Vickie Tennant, but her boyfriend said no. I signed Francesca Annis when shooting was already in progress, after seeing her in *The Heretic*. She had come a long way since her Compton Group days and was now an accomplished stage actress.

It was Timothy Burrill, my new production manager, himself a Welshman, who suggested Wales as a suitable location far closer to London than Scotland. Our choice was vindicated by the beauty of the countryside and the great, empty stretches of beach near Portmeirion, where our huge crew was put up. Portmeirion, built to resemble an Italian Renaissance city in stucco miniature, provided us with a comfortable and convenient base of operations. Clough Williams-Ellis, the creator of this ultra-British architectural folly, gave us a warm welcome and made us feel thoroughly at home – which was more than the weather did.

Portmeirion was almost flooded that fall. It was another case of 'Never seen anything like it in twenty years!' At first we welcomed the leaden skies and sinister, bizarre-shaped clouds, but it wasn't long before we were enveloped in an icy, almost incessant downpour, unable to shoot except during brief intermissions. The rain came at us horizontally, lashing our faces, seeping into everything. Makeup ran, beards came unstuck, horses panicked. When the rain stopped, fog reduced visibility to a few yards. The locations we'd chosen for the witches' scenes became accessible only to four-wheel-drive vehicles capable of crossing the sea of rich, greasy mud in which we spent our days. The weather played havoc with our shooting schedule, which had to be drastically revised. There were times when I felt I was making an underwater epic.

I had a few human problems, too. The local farmers took us for all they could get. Complaining that our activities were reducing the frequency with which rams were supposed to hump their ewes, they demanded compensation; Timothy Burrill thrust hundreds of crisp pound notes into their hands. Then they claimed that we'd left a gate open and allowed some sheep to escape; that cost us another £200. Although we'd rented the land on which we were filming, one canny farmer held up the proceedings by stationing himself in the background, complete with sheep and Land-Rover; it took £300 to get him to budge. Finally, we were required to pay for damage allegedly done to the farmers' moorland, already deeply rutted by the wheels of their own trucks and tractors.

But these were minor inconveniences compared to the afflictions of our disaster-prone special effects team, which we nicknamed special *de*fects. One of the experts, whose job it was to operate an elaborate fog machine, was last seen fleeing from his contraption just before it exploded in a cloud of blue smoke. We had catapults that were supposed to send fireballs crashing into Dunsinane Castle. The designer of these gadgets had airily demonstrated their efficiency with a spoon and a sugar cube. That worked fine on a restaurant table, but when he actually wound up one of his outsize crossbows and unleashed it, the flaming missile fell limply at our feet. We devised a primitive mortar to propel the missiles farther – creating the impression that they came from the catapults; we could hide our cheating with clever editing – but they still fell way short. We improved the design, increased the explosive charge, and poured gasoline down the mortar barrel; this time the lethal fireball soared well over the castle and landed on the beach beyond, where it would have killed anyone crazy enough to be out in such weather.

It was amazing, for all that, how much shooting we

managed to get through in these conditions and how relatively inexpensive it was. Being unable to afford the army of extras required for a picture of this type, I had a lot of cheap dummies stamped out of plastic. These worked wonders in the background, but we couldn't dispense with people entirely. When we moved north, Burrill sent scouts to Newcastle to recruit volunteers from among the unemployed waiting outside the labor exchanges there. He hired 1,000 extras for less than $8 each a day, with a hot meal thrown in, to march on Dunsinane in the guise of Birnam Wood.

Film guarantors, as everyone in the industry knows, act as a deterrent – a form of blackmail directors hope will never be used. Firms specializing in film completion guarantees are aware of this; that is how they make their profits. Their real function is to help investors raise money in the first place. An independent production company has a far better chance of obtaining finance if it can show potential backers a completion guarantee contract – which, paradoxically, adds to the cost of the film it plans to make.

In the case of *Macbeth*, Playboy Productions had signed a contract with Film Finances, the company Michael Klinger had used for *Cul-de-Sac*. Now, Film Finances started breathing down my neck. Victor Lownes, torn between our friendship and loyalty to his employers, was powerless. He lacked the experience that would have told him whether or not our delays were avoidable and couldn't understand why some of our studio setups at Shepperton took so long. When he came to the conclusion that we were wasting Playboy's time and money, he lost his temper, and we had many shouting matches on the phone.

Under pressure, Playboy Productions fired Andy Braunsberg and replaced him with David Orton, a Film Finances supervisor who was to cut costs and carry out some drastic rescheduling. Another director, Peter Collinson, was also put on a retainer by Film Finances and started hanging around the Shepperton canteen. It was all very discreetly done; the guarantors' main fear was that the cast and crew might refuse to work with another director.

341

Playboy was naturally uninterested in a *Macbeth* by Peter Collinson. Hefner flew to London, retinue and all, and moved into the top-floor suite of the London Hilton. The issue was whether the rest of the picture should be turned over to the film completion people and a new director or whether Playboy Productions would ante up another half million dollars and allow me to complete it.

At a meeting in Hefner's suite attended by Lownes and representatives from Film Finances, I presented an account of what we'd done so far, what remained to be done, and why we were running late. Everyone, I said, was working as fast and as well as humanly possible. All I could do was carry on with the job. To show my good faith, I suggested that the remaining third of my fee be withheld. 'The only other thing I can give you,' I told the meeting, 'is a pint of my blood.' The first offer was gladly accepted.

Hefner was generous; he decided to absorb the unscheduled cost overruns. Film Finances were delighted. They kept their fee without having to meet the expense of completing the picture their way, which would have cost them something, though far less than the $500,000 advanced by Hefner. We all could relax again. Mistakenly I thought the famous *Macbeth* jinx had been beaten at last.

A Royal Command Performance had already been scheduled for December 1971, so I flung myself into the editing and postproduction work in an attempt to make up for lost time and meet the deadline. I was clear in my own mind that the key to *Macbeth*'s success was a spectacular opening in London, where the critics would be far more appreciative than their American counterparts of what I'd been striving to achieve. Then some Columbia brass flew over to see the rough cut. Their reaction was lukewarm. They doubted the public's ability to endure two hours and twenty minutes of Shakespearean drama, wanted to preview the film and examine the possibility of shortening it, disputed my assurance that all would be ready in time. Although they put out a smokescreen of the jargon habitually used by U.S. distributors eager to wash their hands of a picture they wish they'd never become associated with – phrases like 'We need to do it justice' and 'It needs careful handling' – the fact was, they couldn't get excited over a film in which they had such a small financial stake. To my deep dismay and disappointment, they canceled the London opening in favor of a New York premiere at Hefner's newly acquired Playboy Theater on West Fifty-seventh Street.

A January opening in New York is cinematic suicide – people tend to stay home after the Christmas frenzy. Quite apart from that, the American press made it clear that Playboy's sponsoring of *Macbeth* was a piece of unpardonable impudence. 'Francesca Annis comes across like a spot-crazy Playboy bunny,' wrote a critic in the New York *Daily Mirror*. 'At the screening I attended, the loudest audience reaction was the laughter that greeted "A Playboy Production" at the new Playboy Theater, where we would hope there are no staples in the middle of the screen.' An AP review, widely syndicated throughout the United States, stated that Macduff's son was 'filmed in prepubescent totality,' and columnists Earl Wilson and Frances Taylor actually misspelled the title –*MacBeth*.

My own motivation was heavily underscored. 'Polanski is most at home dealing with black magic,' said *Time*. 'His affection for the supernatural is so unrestrained that many of the movie's straight scenes have an almost cursory air.' *Newsweek* found my making of the picture 'a rationalization of a psychic compulsion.' My *Macbeth*, it said, was a 'work of art – in the grand manner of Buchenwald, Lidice, and, yes, the Manson murders.'

Macbeth contained only a small fraction of the gore that characterizes any Sam Peckinpah movie, but the violence was realistic. *Macbeth* is a violent play, and I've never believed in cop-outs. One committee that decided to award it an X rating complained of its violence, and a female member of the same committee found it intolerable that 'that nice little boy' should have been 'savagely murdered.' Most American critics assumed that I'd used the film for some cathartic purpose. In fact, I'd chosen to make *Macbeth* because I thought that Shakespeare, at least, would preserve my motives from suspicion. After the Manson murders it was clear that whatever kind of film I'd come out with next would have been treated the same way. If I'd made a comedy, the charge would have been one of callousness.

A film's commercial success depends on those crucial weekend box-office returns after its first release, and *Macbeth*'s were poor – the reviews had seen to that. The publicity, in execrable taste, might have been tailored for some schlock costume drama. Several movie houses displayed a still photograph from a rehearsal break – with extras wearing wristwatches and glasses. One of them was actually peeing against a boulder.

The acclaim *Macbeth* received later in the year from British critics suggested that adherence to our original plans might have launched the film on quite a different career. Frivolous and typically British headlines such as 'Macbrilliant' and 'Macbeth Is a Winner' concealed a far more literate and adventurous perception of filmed Shakespeare. Playboy's losses were never recouped, however. At $3.5 million the picture had been ludicrously cheap to make – I defy any filmmaker to put more on the screen for the same sum – but Victor Lownes, fiercely loyal to Hefner, was nonetheless upset by this, his master's first real failure. Matters weren't improved by an innocent but unfortunate remark of mine. Asked during an interview at the London Playboy Club why I'd joined forces with the Playboy organization, I replied, '*Pecunia non olet* – money doesn't smell.' Although I hadn't meant it maliciously, that was the end of my friendship with Victor Lownes. He felt I'd bitten the hand that fed me and worked himself up into a lather. Leaping to the conclusion that I'd feigned friendship merely to extract finance from Playboy, he started writing letters, some involuntarily funny, in the tone of a jilted lover. My 'golden prick' was returned with the following note: 'In view of recent developments, I no longer want to have this full-length, life-size portrait of you around the house. You'll have no difficulty in finding some 'friend' you can shove it up.'

I donated the thing to Release, a charity that looked after reformed drug addicts. Instead of having it melted down, however, someone in the organization provoked a lot of unwelcome publicity by deciding to auction it. Rumors spread that it was a cast of my own anatomy, which, wrote Victor in another of his tirades, was 'a delicate if highly erroneous implication you would doubtless relish perpetuating – reality being what it is.' I was so shaken by his persistent outbursts of written rage that I sent this latest letter to a graphologist for analysis. I have no record of his findings. I only knew that *Macbeth* not only reinforced the stereotyped and inaccurate belief that I was a spendthrift prima donna of a director, it cost me a close and valued friendship.

TWENTY-FOUR

I wanted to make another film at once, just to prove I still could. After all my problems with sets, wigs, costumes, special effects, and horrendous weather, it was understandable that my thoughts should have veered in the direction of stark simplicity – with the emphasis on stark. Tynan and I started work on an erotic screenplay – no clothes, no sets – but got nowhere and soon gave up.

With no script, no ideas, and almost no money left, Andy and I were only too pleased when Jean-Pierre Rassam, who had become the most active producer in France, invited us to Paris. Still in his twenties, Jean-Pierre always had half a dozen projects on the boil at once. Although he had nothing concrete to offer us, he was very attracted by the idea of a joint venture. We signed some kind of letter of intent, on the strength of which he agreed to keep us financially afloat while I developed a script with Gérard Brach.

My filmmaking ideal has always been to involve audiences so deeply in what they see that their visual experience approximates living reality. Anything that enhances this 'wraparound' effect – color, large screens, stereo sound – is an asset. A logical extension of the same idea is 3-D. Using Jean-Pierre's funds, I made a series of 3-D tests with the aim of applying the process to a really spectacular erotic film. Though quite impressive, they convinced me that further technical development was needed.

Lured by the ski slopes of Gstaad, I retired to my rented chalet with Gérard and embarked on the script of an erotic comedy. Jack Nicholson was now a frequent houseguest – I'd introduced him to the joys of skiing – and we often talked of working together. With this in mind, Gérard and I started writing a part for him. Provisionally entitled *The Magic Finger*, our story was built around the casting of a film. The central character was that of a powerful producer modeled partly on Sam Spiegel and partly on the French producer Léonide Moguy, who had evolved an original way of auditioning actresses. 'You're a good-looking girl and you move well,' he would say, 'but how do I know you've got talent? Screen tests are expensive.' Out would come his hand across the desk. 'Here, try sucking that.' And the candidate had to suck Moguy's little finger, first with hatred, then with revulsion, then with love, then with abject devotion.

Gérard and I initially saw our heroine as the innocent victim of a wicked producer and his sex-crazed sidekicks – a girl who undergoes a series of hair-raising experiences that almost culminate in her submission to a fate worse than death. The part we'd written for Jack Nicholson didn't attract him, but he said he'd look out for something else we could do together. Jean-Pierre Rassam, who didn't bother to read the script but liked the sound of the story, thought it might appeal to Carlo Ponti and offered it to him on a coproduction basis. The outcome was an invitation to us from Ponti to come to Rome for talks.

Ponti's offices were in a Roman palazzo on the Piazza Aracoeli, a maze of lofty rooms full of filing cabinets, antiques, and cans of film, with secretaries typing away in odd corners. Ponti himself spent the day at his monumental desk, talking into three phones at once. Creditors were always waiting in line to see him, clutching unpaid bills, some despondent, others philosophical. His practice seemed to be to pay out a little at a time – just enough to keep the wolves at bay.

It was too late by now for a winter film, so Ponti suggested we substitute the Italian Riviera for our original setting, a ski resort, and offered us a generous expense allowance while we rewrote the script. With Ponti's money, Andy Braunsberg rented us a handsome old house on the outskirts of Rome, the

347

Villa Mandorli. Here, in a parklike enclave shared with such exalted neighbors as ex-Queen Soraya and Franco Zeffirelli, our little team enjoyed a life-style normally denied to people with resources as slender as ours.

Our rewrite ended up as a completely new script entitled *What?*, which somehow reflected the absurdity and extravagance of the outgoing sixties. We discarded the character of the producer in favor of an eccentric millionaire modeled vaguely on Calouste Gulbenkian, the oil magnate known as Mr Five Percent. Our would-be actress became a hippie flower child closely resembling an American girl who'd spent some time at our chalet – the type whose worldly possessions fit into a shoulder bag and who goes through life equipped only with a comical, zany kind of innocence. This particular girl carried a bulky diary wherever she went, and Gérard was always trying to sneak a look at the contents. When he finally got hold of it, he beckoned me over in high excitement and pointed to a page. The entry read: 'Ate a boiled egg today.'

Almost of its own accord, our screenplay turned into a ribald, Rabelaisian account of the adventures of a fey, innocent girl, wholly unaware of the sort of company that surrounds her in a weird Riviera villa inhabited exclusively by phallocrats.

When the script was completed, the funds Jean-Pierre Rassam had hoped to invest in the project failed to materialize. Ponti, however, had set his heart on making a film with me, so he took it over completely. It wasn't until later that I grasped the full extent of his generosity toward me. In common with most European producers, Ponti seldom risked his own money on a venture. For *What?* he made an exception; the $1.2 million it cost were his.

Armed with Ponti's go-ahead and the loan of one of his villas near Naples as our principal set, we started preproduction work and casting. Marcello Mastroianni and Hugh Griffith were the only names in the cast. The others were amateurs and unknowns, mostly jet set acquaintances from Rome. I had my usual problem with the female lead. After vainly combing New York and Los Angeles, I found the perfect embodiment of our heroine practically on my own doorstep. Sydne Rome was a young American actress trying to carve out a career in Italy.

What? was the first picture I ever brought in ahead of schedule. The Italians made a habit of working up to twelve hours a day, but there were compensations. We stayed at the San Pietro di Positano, a superb hotel built into a cliff face overgrown with pink begonias. From there, by taking the elevator to the moorings at the foot of the cliff, I was able to water-ski to the set every sunrise in glorious Mediterranean weather.

Of *What?* itself, little need be said. The picture was a success in Italy, a modest success elsewhere in Europe, and a flop in America. By the time it was made, however, all of us had fallen hopelessly in love with Italy and Rome in particular. By common consent, we decided to put down roots there.

Ours was a close-knit little commune with high expectations: Andy Braunsberg would be our producer and set up the deals; Gérard Brach and I would turn out the screenplays; Hercules Belville, now a fixture, would stay on as my full-time assistant. And that's how it remained as one year slid into the next, and the next, and the next. Rome was to be our base for four whole years, and even though the experiment ultimately failed for a number of reasons, they were years that soothed me back into something like a normal existence. In Rome no one can brood for very long.

Ponti wanted to continue our association, so Andy began casting around for some projects. Inspired by my 3-D experiments, he planned a brace of Andy Warhol movies with Joe Dallessandro, *Flesh for Frankenstein* and *Blood for Dracula*. Once Warhol and company descended on the Villa Mandorli, it became too small. Andy found us a new house on the Via Appia Antica and turned over our former abode to the Warhol crowd. We weren't sorry to leave; they were a nice enough bunch, if somewhat camp, but their taste in friends was snobbishly confined to the ultrachic and aristocratic upper crust of Roman society.

The Via Appia Antica house was a delightful place. Set on spacious grounds containing a vineyard and a big swimming pool, it was screened from the ancient Roman road by a centuries-old wall and approached by way of a long gravel drive with a massive wrought-iron gate at one end. Rented for $3,000 a month from the Countess of Warwick, it had a huge drawing room, filled with priceless antiques, and half a dozen principal bedrooms. The house was so large that all of us – Gérard, Andy, Hercules, and I – could enjoy complete privacy. We employed a housekeeper named Olga, a fat old 'mamma' who probably robbed us blind but cooked unforgettable pasta. The rest of the staff comprised Giuseppe, Olga's son-in-law, who waited table; two gardeners; a live-in maid; and a cleaning woman. This gave us all the amenities of a hotel in a country house setting.

It was a blissful mode of existence in many ways, but money was needed to maintain it. Gérard and I kicked a number of ideas around without success, our efforts not assisted by the comings and goings of Andy's new associates or by a subtle change in Andy himself. Perhaps because he was disenchanted by our joint ventures – *The Day of the Dolphin* had come to nothing, and *Macbeth* and *What?* were anything but commercial triumphs – he seemed to be pouring all his enthusiasm into the Warhol projects. It was hard to work in an atmosphere fraught with unspoken resentment.

By rights, therefore, I should have leaped at the chance when Jack Nicholson phoned one day to tell me that there was a script I simply had to read and that directing it could be mine for the asking. I didn't, though. My months in Rome had convinced me that Europe was my true home – I loved the sheer antiquity and asymmetry that made it so different from modern, four-square America – and I had no desire to reopen old wounds by returning to L.A. I didn't swallow my reluctance until Bob Evans called to add his own plea that I should join him on the projected picture, which he himself was to produce while still remaining a Paramount vice-president – an unprecedented concession on the studio's part.

On my arrival in Hollywood, Bob Evans gave me a bulky script to read. Brimming with ideas, great dialogue, and masterful characterization, it suffered from an excessively convoluted plot that veered off in all directions. Called *Chinatown* despite its total absence of Oriental locations or characters, it simply couldn't have been filmed as it stood, though buried somewhere in its 180-plus pages was a marvelous movie. The story was in the best Chandler tradition, yet its private eye hero, J.J.Gittes, was no pale, down-at-the-heel imitation of Marlowe. Robert Towne, the scriptwriter, had conceived him as a glamorous, successful operator, a snappy dresser with a coolly insolent manner – a new, archetypal detective figure. Unfortunately the character of Gittes was overwhelmed by the intricate and almost incomprehensible plot. The screenplay required massive cuts, drastic simplification, and the pruning of several subsidiary characters, all of them beautifully drawn but contributing nothing to the action.

Bob Towne had worked on *Chinatown* for two years and rightly regarded it as the best thing he'd ever done, but I knew him well enough not to pull any punches. I told him what I thought of his script over lunch at Nate 'n Al's, the Beverly Hills delicatessen. He was naturally disappointed by my qualified enthusiasm. I may have been a little overcritical because of my low morale. I was in L.A., where every street corner reminded me of tragedy. I was also about to turn forty – a depressing moment in any man's life.

Towne agreed to draft a shorter, simpler version of his screenplay, and I gladly returned to Rome. The idea of working in Hollywood again did not appeal to me but it soon became obvious that someone had to earn some money to keep the commune going. Towne's revised script, when he finally completed it, was almost as long as before and even more difficult to follow. If *Chinatown* were ever to become a

351

movie, it would mean two months of really intensive collaboration, pulling the screenplay apart and putting it together again.

Although L.A. was the last place I wanted to be, I did want to do the movie. Not just for the money, which was good, and the profit percentage points, which I'd never been offered before, but because I was eager to try my hand at something entirely different – in this case, a potentially first-rate thriller showing how the history and boundaries of L.A. had been fashioned by human greed.

Before Bob Towne and I got down to work, I stayed at Dick Sylbert's huge, dark Art Deco apartment on Fountain Avenue. Dick adored the place, but it only deepened the depression I already felt. Beverly Hills had changed since the Manson murders, which had somehow set the seal on the hippie, flower child era. The relatively innocent use of psychedelics and grass was on the wane. Cocaine and Quaaludes were now the rage. Nearly all my friends were either dead or long gone, their houses shuttered and deserted. I'd even lost my agent. Bill Tennant had simply walked out of his office one day, not bothering to empty his desk drawers, and never come back; soon afterward he walked out on his wife as well. It was plain loneliness, coupled with the need for some activity outside my work, that reminded me of my vow to take flying lessons, and I started spending every spare moment at the Santa Monica airport.

I felt a little better when Jack Nicholson let me temporarily move in with him. Bob Evans, who knew I was still pining for Rome, put in a lot of time driving me around Hollywood and visiting houses for rent. He wanted me to have fun – to live in a fun house. We went to see a split-level bachelor's pad on Sierra Mar, with a waterfall, a swimming pool, and plenty of room for work and play. 'It's a sexy house,' Evans said. 'I want you to take it.' It belonged to George Montgomery and commanded a superb view of L.A. There's no more beautiful city in the world, provided it's seen by night and from a distance. I took the place and started work there with Towne.

Bob Towne is a craftsman of exceptional power and talent.

Every line of his screenplays testifies to his ear for dialogue and skill in conveying mood. He's also a very slow writer, delighting in any form of procrastination, turning up late, filling his pipe, checking his answering service, ministering to his dog. Throughout our collaboration on *Chinatown*, I might have been in partnership with a twosome – Towne and Hira, his gigantic sheepdog – and at times I got the impression they were ganging up on me.

After working eight hours a day for eight weeks, I felt we'd hammered out a marvelous shooting script – marvelous except in two respects: I was alone in wanting Gittes and Evelyn Mulwray to go to bed together, and Towne and I couldn't agree on an ending. Towne wanted the evil tycoon to die and his daughter, Evelyn, to live. He wanted a happy ending; all would turn out okay for her after a short spell in jail. I knew that if *Chinatown* was to be special, not just another thriller where the good guys triumph in the final reel, Evelyn had to die. Its dramatic impact would be lost unless audiences left their seats with a sense of outrage at the injustice of it all. The right ending was important for several reasons. *Chinatown* was a great title, but unless we set at least one scene in L.A.'s real-life Chinatown, we'd be cheating – pulling in the public under false pretenses.

We never surmounted these two major hurdles while working on the screenplay, and I wrote each of these two scenes the night before they were actually shot. To this day Towne feels my ending is wrong; I am equally convinced that his more conventional ending would have seriously weakened the picture.

While we were busy writing, Dick Sylbert and my assistant director, Howard Koch, Jr., were scouting locations; Anthea Sylbert was designing costumes. An immense amount of work went into reproducing the thirties style. Unlike Bob Evans, I saw *Chinatown* not as a 'retro' piece or conscious imitation of classic movies shot in black and white, but as a film about the thirties seen through the camera eye of the seventies. I wanted it to be evocative of the world and period of Dashiell Hammett and Raymond Chandler, but I

353

wanted the style of the period conveyed by a scrupulously accurate reconstruction of decor, costume, and idiom – not by a deliberate imitation, in 1973, of thirties film techniques.

Evans and I talked about this at great length. If we purposely imitated the look of, say, *The Maltese Falcon*, I argued, *Chinatown*'s main characteristic would be its resemblance to a good old Hollywood thriller. I wanted Panavision and color – the works – but I also wanted a cameraman who could identify with the period. Still flushed with the success of *The Godfather*, Evans was all for using Gordon Willis, but he wasn't available – and anyway, I had a different look in mind. Stanley Cortez, I felt, would be a good choice; he'd worked with Orson Welles on *The Magnificent Ambersons*, that splendid evocation of a vanished world.

There was never any doubt as to who would play Gittes. Jack Nicholson was an old friend of Towne's and had been associated with *Chinatown* from the outset. He'd discussed the central role with Towne long before anything went down on paper and had even hoped at one stage to produce the picture himself.

For father and daughter, I'd wanted John Huston and Faye Dunaway from the first. Everyone agreed on Huston, but Bob Evans favored Jane Fonda for the part of Evelyn. She turned it down, so Faye was hired despite Evans's reservations about her being a 'difficult' actress. I knew Faye well, or thought I did. Formerly Jerry Schatzberg's girlfriend, she'd stayed with us briefly in Rome the previous summer, during a romantic interlude with Andy Braunsberg. I felt I'd be able to cope with her.

The rest of the cast presented little difficulty. Small roles are easy to fill in a place like Hollywood. In almost all my films at least one cameo part is played by a complete non-professional. Some faces simply cry out to be put in a movie. In *Chinatown* the director of the old folks' home was Jack Vernon, the boutique owner who'd sold me the Edwardian jacket I wore at my wedding.

We started shooting one exceptionally hot October day.

This was the orange grove scene in which Gittes is set upon by a bunch of dispossessed farmers and badly beaten up. It was imperative to start with this scene because we'd booked the orange grove early on, complete with oranges, and the owner was desperate to harvest his crop before it rotted on the trees.

Looking at the first few days' rushes, I couldn't fathom what was going on and thought I must be losing my grip. Everything was coming out in shades of ocher and tomato ketchup. I went down to the lab to investigate, convinced that something was seriously wrong, either there or with Cortez's exposures. In fact, the fault was in the printing. Without telling me, Bob Evans had instructed the lab to print our dailies so they looked just like *The Godfather*.

Even when this had been corrected, our results still left a lot to be desired. Cortez was full of old-fashioned charm, but he hadn't worked for several years. Completely out of touch with mainstream developments in the technology of film-making, he began asking for equipment that was no longer in use. We watched his performance with growing dismay. He used an inordinate amount of light and was so excruciatingly slow that had we kept him on, we would never have completed the picture. Bob Evans passed the buck to me; it was my distasteful duty, on the tenth day of shooting, to tell Cortez that he was being replaced. John Alonzo took over, which helped speed things up. *Chinatown* is the only other film I have ever brought in ahead of schedule – six days ahead, to be exact.

·If Bob Evans had been right about Cortez, he was doubly right about Faye Dunaway. I'd rooted for her on the ground that her special brand of 'retro' beauty – the same sort of look I remembered in my mother – was essential to the film. Possibly because I'd given Faye an exaggerated idea of her makeup's contribution to the feel of the picture, she started spending more and more time on her face. Whenever we had to cut during the first few seconds of a take, she insisted on making up all over again. It got so I couldn't take it anymore.

355

Not only did she fuss over her appearance to an almost pathological degree, but she had a thing about Blistex. She applied the stuff to her lips so regularly that the crew celebrated her last day's shooting by presenting her with a special Blistex Award – a jumbo-sized four-foot tube built by the art department.

Makeup wasn't my only problem with Faye. The hesitations and pauses that characterized her delivery were born of necessity, not art. They were her way of trying to remember what she had to say next, for she seldom knew her lines and was always pestering me to rewrite them. Things reached the stage where simply to save time, I agreed to all her suggestions on principle. Almost invariably she'd end by saying, 'You know, maybe it was better the way it was' – and we'd revert to the original script.

Faye's insecurity was such that every time I dropped some insignificant line of hers in the interests of polishing a sequence, she took it as an affront and accused me of mutilating her part. The whole thing came to a head during the scene in which she and Jack Nicholson meet in a restaurant after he's had his nose slashed. The camera was over her shoulder, and one strand of her hair was catching the light. It was one of those freak situations where, if nothing were done, the audience's attention would be focused on a single illuminated hair.

'Cut,' I said, and summoned Faye's hairdresser. In total silence, with the lights still burning, she did her best to flatten the rebellious hair. It popped up again and again. No amount of lacquer seemed to do the trick. Faye, being the only person on the set unable to see what was wrong, couldn't understand what all the fuss was about. At last, hoping she might not even notice, I took the hair and plucked it out.

Howard Koch yelled, 'Lunch break, everybody!' in an attempt to defuse an explosive situation. It didn't work.

Faye, who can swear like a teamster truck driver, was having a fit. 'I don't believe it!' she screeched. 'I just don't believe it! That motherfucker pulled my hair out!' Her hysterics were earsplitting, obscene, and only in their early

356

stages. After lunch she let it be known that she wasn't going back on the set.

That one little hair provoked the kind of crisis directors dread and producers and agents secretly revel in. Before it started, Bob Evans reminded me that he hadn't wanted 'that meshuga' in the first place. I was stuck with 'the dreaded Dunaway,' as she was unofficially known, and would have to take the consequences.

The meeting opened with Freddy Fields, Faye's agent, looking uncomfortable and Faye herself still mad as hell. Fields started enumerating her many grievances against me. I'd been cast in the now familiar role of monster. 'I was wrong to do it,' I said, 'but that doesn't alter the fact that she's nuts and a menace.'

This sent Faye into such a paroxysm of foulmouthed abuse that neither Evans nor Fields knew where to look. I was delighted. That's the way she is, I gestured behind her back, grinning slyly. Freddy Fields diplomatically saved the day with much soothing talk about the need for the show to go on. Faye had shot her wad. The psychodrama had done her good, and anyway, she'd exhausted her vocabulary. We resumed the over-the-shoulder shot as if nothing had happened.

Jack Nicholson proved the complete opposite of Faye in every respect. Jack's on the wild side. He loves going out nights, never gets to bed before the small hours, listens to music and smokes grass. Early-morning calls are even more agonizing for him than they are for me; but he comes on the set knowing his lines and everyone else's, and he's such an exceptionally fine actor that the worst piece of Hollywood dialogue sounds crisp when he delivers it. We'd looked forward to working together for years, and we enjoyed every minute.

Even with Jack, though, I did have one blistering row. We'd reached the scene where Gittes is kept waiting in the office of Mulwray's successor and discovers some clues in the framed photographs on the wall – no big acting deal from Jack's point of view. A basketball freak, he was far more interested in a televised game between the Lakers and the New York Knicks than in any developments on the set that day.

My main concern was lighting. I wanted to convey the feeling of late afternoon, with strips of light from a venetian blind illuminating the wall while Jack went from photograph to photograph. As Jack put it, he was simply a nose in the shot. The lighting problems were complex, and it was getting late – well into the crew's overtime. I wanted to get things right, but I also wanted to finish the shot that day. Jack kept running back to his mobile dressing room to watch the Knicks and Lakers. The game ran into overtime as well, and he was never there when I needed him.

'I told you we wouldn't finish this fucking scene,' he said when dragged onto the set for the umpteenth time.

I said, 'Okay, it's a wrap' – not really meaning it, confident that Jack, the ultimate professional, would insist on my finishing off. This time, however, he showed that he could be a bastard, too.

'Okay,' he said, 'it's a wrap.' With that he jerked the venetian blind down and walked off to his dressing room.

I was furious. It would take hours to set everything up again. Grabbing a heavy mop, I charged into his dressing room and tried to smash the TV set. The trailer was so small, I couldn't get a good swing at it. The set went dead, but the spectacular implosion I'd hoped for didn't occur. I clouted it again, smashing it beyond hope of repair. 'Know what you are?' I yelled as I swung at it. 'You're a fucking asshole!' Then I took what was left of the set and hurled it out of his dressing room. I saw Howard Koch wince. Later I learned it was his TV.

Jack's response was dramatic in its irrational fury. He stripped off his clothes under the apprehensive gaze of all present and left the stage. Too mad to do anything but quit, too, I headed for the parking lot.

Jack, who found he needed some clothes after all, got dressed and left the studio without a word to anyone. Quite by chance, we drew up alongside each other at a red light on

Marathon Street. I could read his lips through the window of his beat-up VW. 'Fucking Polack,' he was saying.

Suddenly struck by the comedy of the situation, I grinned at him. He grinned back, and we both started laughing. This being a Friday evening, there would be no more shooting till the following Monday. We both knew that word of our row would have reached Bob Evans within minutes and that he must be worrying himself sick over this latest crisis. 'Let's not tell anyone,' Jack said gleefully. 'Keep 'em guessing.'

He redeemed himself on many occasions, especially when we came to shoot *Chinatown*'s most dangerous sequence. This was the reservoir scene in which Gittes gets swept away by a torrent of water when the sluices are suddenly opened. I wanted to do this in a single shot, with Jack's face clearly visible and coming into close-up as he hit the wire mesh barrier across the channel, so there was no possibility of using his stunt man, Alan Gibbs.

Jack, whom I'd taught to ski, always felt I took risks on the slopes. He was apprehensive of the shot because he thought that since I appeared to have no sense of danger on skis, I had no understanding of physical fear in others. In the movie business, he reminded me, even the best-planned special effects could go wrong. Being well aware of this, we saved the dam scene to the very end – in case something happened.

Jack was already dressed, with a wet suit under his clothes, when he said he wanted Alan Gibbs to test the impact of a body on the fence. Knowing that it would take four hours to prepare the set again after a full rehearsal, I sweet-talked Jack into doing the take without one. Like a true pro, he agreed. I was high up in a crane with the camera, just before the water started gushing, when Jack waved a finger at me. I thought he meant 'Up yours!' Finally, he shouted, 'One!' I caught on at last. It was an eloquent plea for just one take, and that's all it took. Jack hit the reinforced wire fence so hard that his shoes left a dent in the mesh.

Jack was not just a good sport and a talented actor. When the time came for my own little cameo appearance as the punk who slashes his nose, I got him to direct me. In the original script Jack's nose got slashed at a later stage and healed with the miraculous rapidity found only in the movies. Because Jack was the kind of actor who wouldn't moan at having to do most of his scenes with a bandage over his face or stitches bristling from one nostril, I decided to retain the wound for realism's sake.

The actual nose-slashing posed problems of its own. Logan Frazee, our special effects man, had originally suggested building a fake nostril, but I rejected the idea. I wanted to base the trick on illusion, not artifice. What we needed, I told Frazee, was a knife with a hinged tip. The retaining spring would have to be weak enough to give under the slightest pressure, making it look as if the blade were passing through the nostril. Distracted by a spurt of blood, audiences wouldn't notice the deception. Frazee built me just what I wanted: a hinge-tipped knife with a concealed tube down one side connected to a bulbful of blood which I squeezed as I slashed. Before every take Jack double-checked that I was holding the blade right side up.

The nose-slashing sequence still arouses boundless curiosity. Jack and I are both so sick of explaining how it was done that we sometimes say we did it for real. The effect was considered too gory by British and American TV networks, which edited it out. As usual, I conveyed more violence than was actually seen, for many of the preview reports, while enthusiastic about *Chinatown* as a whole, complained of too much gore. In fact, discounting Jack's nose and the brief death scene at the end, the picture has absolutely no bloodshed in it.

When shooting was over, everything – even Faye Dunaway's tantrums – proved worthwhile. Thanks to a postproduction team that included Sam O'Steen and many of those who had worked with me on *Rosemary's Baby*, editing proceeded swiftly and smoothly. The one person Bob Evans and I missed sorely was Christopher Komeda. For experimental purposes, I mixed one scene with some music by Philip Lambro, a young composer who had sent us a sample record.

360

Evans was so impressed that we hired him. Unfortunately Lambro's score turned out to be a disappointment. Bronislau Kaper, whom I took to see the preview in Santa Barbara, loved the picture as a whole but felt the music badly impaired it. I knew he was right but hadn't dared say so because of our deadline; release dates and theater bookings are normally sacrosanct and can't be changed. Bob Evans, for whom only the best was good enough, carried enough clout to break this rule. He insisted on rescoring and bullied the studio into a postponement. Jerry Goldsmith was hired to turn out a new score, which he did in record time.

I wasn't around for the musical remixing, so the final chapter of the *Chinatown* story reached me in the form of press clippings. An immediate critical and box-office success, the film picked up a clutch of Golden Globes and eleven Academy Award nominations and Bob Towne won a well-deserved Oscar for his screenplay, so the clippings made pleasant reading – all except one. Staring at me from the midst of the bunch was a Hollywood journalist's interview with Bob Evans. According to Evans, I'd hired 'a rinkydink friend' to write the music, so he'd had to step in and get Goldsmith to repair the damage. I was 'brilliant if channeled properly,' he was quoted as saying, but my problem lay in being surrounded by sycophants who flattered my ego. 'And then his films turn out badly,' Evans went on. 'It takes guts to be a producer, and I have guts.' Now, after *Chinatown*'s success, I'd acknowledged that he'd been right all along, and we were 'going to make another picture together soon.'

We never did team up again, and the excuse not to do so was always mine. It was the memory of that interview that made me say no. I'd considered Bob Evans more than a producer; he was a friend. Not for the first time, and certainly not for the last, a Hollywood experience had gone sour on me.

TWENTY-FIVE

It wasn't pique over Bob Evans's behavior or our differences over the score that prompted me to quit Hollywood before the final mixing of *Chinatown*. I had to leave for Italy to direct Alban Berg's *Lulu* at the Festival of Two Worlds in Spoleto.

Working in a theater again after more than twenty years was a tremendous thrill – the very smell of greasepaint made my heart beat faster – and the setting, which had a beauty all its own, enhanced my pleasure. A hill town with narrow medieval streets, Spoleto has a Roman amphitheater, Romanesque churches, and a couple of exquisite little eighteenth-century theaters. The festival is the highlight of its year, so my assignment was something of a challenge. Although I felt apprehensive, never having directed an opera before, I was surprised to find how much easier it seemed to realize my intentions on a stage than in front of a camera. A lot of the credit for this belonged to Christopher Keene, the American conductor, and our highly professional cast, most of whom were also from the States. I was greatly impressed by the exacting standards required of opera singers. Unlike film actors, they knew their parts perfectly before rehearsals began.

I was even entranced by the typically Italian pan-demonium that accompanied our preparations. Italians are wonderful show business workers – enthusiastic, responsive, and totally dedicated – but they thrive in an atmosphere of turmoil and chaos. Forty-eight hours before the premiere, half the costumes were missing, the scenery was a mess, and everyone was yelling at everyone else. The Italian belief in miracles seems justified, however, at least in Italy. The first night went off without a hitch, and the success of the production earned me numerous invitations to direct operas elsewhere.

But I couldn't make a living out of directing operas, and the success of *Chinatown* had brought me feelers from all over Hollywood. I returned to the Via Appia Antica, where Gérard and I began to develop one of the ideas we'd been toying with. Simply entitled *Pirates*, it was conceived from the outset as a grand, swashbuckling adventure-comedy – a genre I hadn't tackled before. After working so well with Jack Nicholson, I was determined to have him play the lead, a ferocious but endearing character named Captain Red, and wrote myself a fairly substantial part as The Frog, his long-suffering lieutenant. *Chinatown* had not only boosted my own prospects but made Jack a star.

As *Pirates* took shape on paper, the question of finance reared its head. I was all for going in with a Hollywood major – at least you could bank on getting your fees and didn't have to scratch around for resources – but Andy Braunsberg felt that an independent production, using European money and selling the rights country by country, would net us far more in the end. He lined up a deal with Goffredo Lombardo of Titanus Films, who advanced us some preproduction money. Jean-Pierre Rassam, who was still riding the crest of the wave and currently negotiating to buy Gaumont, France's biggest distribution company, also expressed interest in helping back the picture.

Like *Vampire Killers*, *Pirates* gave us a lot of laughs at the scriptwriting stage; that was just as well, because the atmosphere in the house was going from bad to worse. Andy had acquired a mentor from the ranks of the Roman aristocracy – an opium-smoking prince. Andy, too, started smoking but so discreetly and surreptitiously that it was a long time before we discovered the cause of his personality change. All we

363

detected at first was a tendency to procrastinate, a loss of interest in our joint affairs, and alternating spells of lethargy and irritability.

The situation wasn't improved when Andy became infatuated with Daisy, an attractive but unstable American girl, and introduced her into the household. Daisy, who'd had a serious affair with Christian Marquand, the French actor, and a less serious one with Ryan O'Neal, was patently unsuited to Andy. Their on-again, off-again relationship was punctuated by rows, fights, sulks, and reconciliations. When Daisy walked out, as she did more than once, Andy reacted with a mixture of anguish and relief. Almost as soon as she returned, they'd start fighting again. Daisy didn't seem to like anybody. She seldom exchanged a word with us and spent days brooding in her room until her next eruption of violence. She destroyed Andy's passport, his credit cards, his address book, his clothes, even attacked him with knives and bottles. Though far more spectacular, their rows reminded me of Gene and Judy's fights in Hollywood years before. They not only poisoned the atmosphere but had a debilitating effect on Andy, who was supposed to be running the *Pirates* project.

Under the same sort of influence, Jean-Pierre Rassam, too, began to show clear signs of physical and mental deterioration. For this I was partly, though innocently, responsible. One night in Paris we'd gone to a party at L'Alcazar, Jean-Marie Rivière's celebrated cabaret. My blind date, a girl named Babette, devoted most of dinner to telling me how films should be made. I was rather irritated, but she found a ready listener in Jean-Pierre. They not only left together but started living together.

The next thing I heard was that Babette had introduced Jean-Pierre to heroin. I was horrified. Too many friends and acquaintances from my early days in Paris and London had ruined their careers – even lost their lives – for me not to know what happened to people who got hooked on hard drugs. Whenever Jean-Pierre came to Rome, I lectured him, warned him, begged him to drop Babette and kick the habit.

He either flatly denied that he had a habit at all or laughed at my worries. Sadly I realized that he'd have to be written off as a prospective partner in our *Pirates* venture.

By now Gstaad had become a regular part of my year. The skiing was a major attraction, of course, but Gérard and I had always worked well there. That winter our continuing work on the *Pirates* screenplay wasn't helped when Andy came, too, bringing Daisy with him. She was still as volatile as ever, and their incessant rows cast a blight not only on our work but on what was meant to be a semivacation. I was almost relieved when a promotional tour for *Chinatown*'s benefit took me off to the Far East.

It was then, after I had rejoined Gérard in Rome to put the finishing touches to *Pirates*, that I contrived to lose our company Rolls and my own brand-new Dino Ferrari within a couple of weeks of each other.

Armand de Saint Herpin had been an excellent chauffeur and an almost overceremonious employee when Andy and I hired him in London prior to shooting *Macbeth*. The vintage Rolls we'd bought had served as my bedroom, office, and snack bar during those interminable drives to Shepperton Studios. In 1973, however, I was unwise enough to lend the Rolls and Armand to Jean-Pierre Rassam for the Cannes Festival.

Armand never recovered from that experience. Once having lived aboard Jean-Pierre's rented yacht and rubbed shoulders with the cosmopolitan, jet-setting movie crowd, he acquired delusions of grandeur. Thereafter he went around in a T-shirt, started calling me Roman, and told people he was in the film business. His gasoline bills in London were astronomical, even when I wasn't there, because he'd taken to moonlighting – hiring out himself and the Rolls for weddings and funerals. This came to light only after the car had been inexplicably involved in a serious collision when it should have been safely garaged.

Armand's fall from grace only reinforced my certainty that we and Caliban Films were accumulating too many overheads. I put the point to Andy. Why keep a company car in London when our future lay elsewhere? Why, for that matter, employ an absentee chauffeur? Andy suggested selling off what remained of the Rolls and getting Armand to drive the Ferrari out to Rome before firing him. I told Concepta, our London-based secretary, to load the car with as many of my personal effects as possible and send Armand over with it. We were enjoying one of our memorable late-night pasta dinners on the villa terrace when Olga's powerful contralto rang out.

'*Telefono!*'

At the other end of the line Armand's voice said, 'Roman, we're in trouble.'

'What do you mean, *we*?' I said clairvoyantly. 'You're the one who's in trouble.'

The Ferrari had been stolen from outside a freeway motel.

That was the end of Armand, though not, alas, of the Ferrari. My hopes of getting the insurance money were dashed, only a few days before payment was due, when the car turned up. Someone had picked it clean and beaten hell out of the engine, which never ran smoothly again. I wound up selling it for a song.

Pirates seemed to be maturing. With the aid of Lombardo's up front money, we booked a slot at Cinecittà Studios and started preproduction work. Our first step was to rehire Mara Blasetti, an excellent production manager who had worked with us on *What?*, and get her to budget the picture. Including the $1 million that was the least Jack Nicholson would ask for, she came up with a forecast of $8 million – well above what we'd expected. Lombardo, whose stake in the project was already nudging $300,000, said he couldn't possibly finance it on his own. I told him not to worry; after *Chinatown*, any distributor would jump at another Polanski-Nicholson venture.

My confidence was justified. We were wooed by all the Hollywood majors. Universal, 20th Century-Fox, Columbia, United Artists, Paramount – everyone wanted to make a picture with us, sight unseen. The competition was so intense that, paradoxically, I grew uneasy. If we weren't careful, I told Andy, we could find ourselves in the position of the guy who goes to a party swarming with beautiful, available women, flirts with them all, and winds up on his own. My vote, I said, went to Paramount.

Barry Diller, who had taken over Bob Evans's job, was visiting London. I flew there with a copy of our script, which still lacked an ending. He read it at once and said we had a deal. He wanted Paramount to provide all the finance and own the world rights, but loyalty to Lombardo made me insist that he shouldn't be eased out. Grudgingly Diller agreed that Lombardo should retain the non-U.S. territories in return for a proportional investment.

Back in Rome, we were joined for a few days by Dick Sylbert, now a Paramount vice-president. Going over the budget figures again, he arrived at a figure slightly higher than Blasetti's. Although Hollywood production costs would be higher still, Paramount decided on balance that they wanted *Pirates* made in the States. Andy, Hercules, and I prepared to move out. Gérard, always averse to traveling, especially by air, chose to remain in Europe. We said good-bye to the house on the Via Appia Antica. Now that the Red Brigades were flexing their muscles, it wasn't a bad time to leave. Rome had ceased to be the paradise it was when we first settled there.

Paramount wasn't the same either, now that most of the people I knew had left. The atmosphere was far more impersonal and bureaucratic. The executives flinched at *Pirates'* budget, since reassessed at a Hollywood figure of $14 million. They didn't want me to act as well as direct, and they grew tired of the way Jack Nicholson kept upping his fee. The fact that we had a deal didn't mean that negotiations were concluded. I had to sign promissory notes for every cent Paramount advanced to cover the costs of preproduction work. Now that it actually had us on its lot, it started dragging its feet.

367

It soon became clear that Barry Diller hadn't abandoned hope of Paramount's retaining the foreign rights. He asked Dino De Laurentiis, who was then tied in with Paramount, to sound out some European distributors. Quite unaware of our prior commitment to Lombardo, Dino called him and asked how much he would be prepared to pay for the Italian rights. Lombardo hit the roof. 'But it's *my* picture!' he protested. 'I'm into it for three hundred thousand already!'

That was the last straw. I called a meeting and announced that I no longer wanted the picture made by Paramount. To Diller's surprise and disbelief, I told him I was pulling out. It was a rare gesture of defiance by Hollywood standards, though honesty compels me to admit that I mightn't have made it if I hadn't still felt confident that another company would take *Pirates* over.

Sure enough, United Artists stepped into the breach. They had no studio of their own, so we moved out of Paramount and rented some offices at Burbank on the Warner Brothers lot. Here we continued putting together a unit, hiring technicians, designing boats and sets. Lombardo flew over to tie up the financial loose ends. Not only had he failed to raise any money, but he wanted UA to advance him his share of the budget. UA thought he was crazy.

I realized that marriage to UA was going to be even tougher than our engagement to Paramount. The lines between New York, Westwood, and Culver City hummed. Already demoralized by Daisy's sulks and flareups, poor Andy was deluged with quibbles and queries transmitted to him from Arthur Krim, UA's president, via Eric Pleskow, vice-president, and Mike Medavoy, a senior executive with special responsibility for the picture. They revised the overall budget, pressed for a shorter shooting schedule, and balked at Jack Nicholson's fee, which now stood at $1.5 million. In desperation Andy asked Jack to level with him. What exactly *did* he want? Jack's response was brutally succinct: 'I want *more*.' By advancing just enough money for preproduction but not enough to start shooting, UA kept us hamstrung. We bought a barge in San Pedro Harbor but couldn't afford to

368

hire the top-class specialists required for a picture of the kind
we planned to make. Meanwhile, I was signing enough pro-
missory notes to have papered the walls of our shabby
Burbank offices.

Arthur Krim was even more reluctant than Diller had been
to let me act as well as direct. I tried to hire Dustin Hoffman
for the part of The Frog, but he didn't want to play second
fiddle to Jack. Then UA gave the screw a final turn: I was
asked to become *Pirates'* completion guarantor myself – to
assume responsibility for every cent over budget but without
the guarantor's usual fat fee. To crown everything, Jack
Nicholson's agent demanded – in addition to a fee of $1.5
million – $50,000 for each day his client might have to spend
on the set after our original shooting schedule ended.

I called Bob Evans and asked him for some objective
advice. Lunching beside his pool that Sunday, I outlined the
latest developments. 'So if you do go over, you'll be paying
Jack fifty grand a day out of your own pocket, right? I didn't
know you had that kind of money,' he said, a bit sarcastically,
my mind was already made up, and he must have seen it.
'David,' he told his butler, 'bring Roman the phone.' More
in sorrow than in anger, I called Arthur Krim and told him I
was cutting my losses. One more day's delay, and I'd have
been down the drain for yet another week's preproduction
money.

My premonition had been correct. We'd gone to the party
and wound up on our own. After all our initial high hopes and
the enthusiasm shown by nearly every major Hollywood
studio, this latest experience left me thoroughly dis-
illusioned. Although some of the problems might have been
foreseen and forestalled by Andy, I couldn't lay all the blame
at his door. I'd sacrificed our original deal for Lombardo's
sake, as Barry Diller and a handful of Paramount executives
were aware, but all our subsequent troubles with the project
sprang from the rumor that it was Paramount that had gone
cold on it.

We had no choice but to postpone *Pirates* for a year and try
to set it up in Europe on a different basis. Timothy Burrill

had already begun tapping alternative sources of finance in London. At the same time, Claude Berri and the leading West German distributor, Horst Wentlandt, had pledged us some money in the event we could put the whole deal together.

Meantime, I couldn't remain idle. I hadn't made a film for two years and wanted to get my teeth into one right away. Knowing that Paramount had bought the rights to Roland Topor's novel *The Tenant* and that it was lying there for the asking, I went to Barry Diller and offered to do it. He said yes on the spot. Within days I was on my way to Paris with Andy and Hercules to set things up.

The Tenant was my fastest feature film ever – eight months from unadapted novel to first public screening – and I finished shooting it even before contracts were signed. I arrived in Paris with the book under my arm and made a simultaneous start on preproduction and the screenplay, the latter in collaboration with Gérard Brach.

It was hard work, but the mere fact of being back in Paris galvanized me. I fell in love with the city all over again, realized, once and for all, that it was my true home and the place I wanted to live from now on. I rented an apartment in the Avenue Montaigne, two minutes' walk from the Champs-Elysées, and applied for French citizenship on grounds of birth.

I had originally hoped that Jean-Pierre Rassam might coproduce *The Tenant*, but one look at him was enough to banish the idea. Drug dependence had reduced his weight by half, and his spacious apartment – also in the Avenue Montaigne – had become a squalid pad inhabited by a weird assortment of fellow junkies, one of them a doctor who later OD'd and had to be removed by ambulance with a hypo dangling from his arm. Jean-Pierre had lost all his business, all his money and hangers-on, but he hadn't yet been lucky enough to lose Babette.

Casting *The Tenant* presented little difficulty. The female lead went to Isabelle Adjani, who'd been in the running for

Pirates, and I myself played Trelkowski, the shy Polish-born office clerk whose creeping schizophrenia culminates in transvestism and suicide. When Paramount decided to increase the budget enough to bring in some American actors, I hired Shelley Winters, Melvyn Douglas and Jo Van Fleet.

We knew that a big slice of the budget would have to be spent on the elaborate composite set where most of the action takes place, a dingy old Parisian apartment house. Designed by Pierre Guffroy, a perfectionist who had worked on all of Buñuel's French films, it was realistic enough to live in and fully repaid the half million dollars it cost. Because we could build only two stories – the stage at Épinay Studios wouldn't have accommodated any more – we had to double the height of the façade with the aid of a huge mirror laid flat on the ground at its foot. The opening sequence, in which a remote-controlled crane-mounted camera explores the outside of the building and finally enters a doorway to film an interior, was one of the most intricate and satisfying shots I have ever attempted.

The Tenant brought me my first real contact with French technicians. Their professionalism was an eye-opener. My associate producer, Alain Sarde, took over most of the executive functions that should have been fulfilled by Andy, who spent the bulk of his time back in L.A., pampering Daisy. Didier Lavergne, the makeup artist, and Ludovic Paris, our hairdresser, were wonderful craftsmen. Since I was in drag for part of the film, they had to be. They also happened to be a remarkably good-looking pair – so much so that Shelley Winters couldn't get over it. 'Look at those two guys, and look at us,' she said, hooting with laughter. 'What's wrong with movies today? They're the ones who should be out in front of the camera, not us.'

Paris and Lavergne had to turn Isabelle Adjani into a real frump, which they did to perfection. Isabelle didn't object. She was a hard worker and displayed great powers of concentration; in fact, she sometimes tried a bit too hard, working herself up into a crying mood and running out of tears before

I was ready to shoot the relevant scene. From my own point of view *The Tenant* was a further education in the difficulties of simultaneously acting and directing. Once the camera starts rolling, you have to stop monitoring camera movements, forget about your fellow actors' delivery and positions, and lose yourself in your role.

Partly because of good word-of-mouth publicity and partly because it was the first feature film I'd made in France, *The Tenant* aroused a lot of media interest and earned itself an invitation to Cannes before shooting was completed. That presented us with an almost superhuman deadline, but our momentum was excellent. I was greatly assisted at the editing stage by Philippe Sarde, Alain's brother, whom I'd hired to write the score. Aside from being a brilliant film composer, Philippe had a discriminating eye and a vast store of technical knowledge.

All went well until the minister of culture requested a private screening. Though reluctant to show him the rough cut, I could hardly refuse. To my extreme annoyance, he turned up with a very good-looking young man in tow. The result of this breach of confidentiality was an article in *L'Express*, the French weekly, which tore the film to shreds. The minister's young protégé – a journalist – had taken advantage of the preview to scoop his competitors.

This vicious little piece proved a turning point. Even before the film reached Cannes, its reception was prejudiced. I'd gained an international reputation, but in France I'd always been a remote, almost mythical figure. Now that I'd made a picture there, I was flesh-and-blood, accessible and vulnerable – in other words, fair game. I became the victim of a phenomenon I'd observed elsewhere. Critics love to 'discover' new talents. Then, having praised them to the skies, they take an even greater delight in knocking them off the pedestals of their own creation.

I came in for this treatment when *The Tenant* was shown at Cannes in May 1976. All the interest the picture had generated prior to its first public screening was transmuted, almost overnight, into malice and spite. I was mobbed, but not in a pleasant way. Autograph hunters and *paparazzi* pursued me everywhere, jostling and crowding me until I felt like a caged animal being prodded with sticks by curious visitors to a zoo. A day or two of this harassment was more than enough. Gérard, who found Cannes even more claustrophobic than I did, Philippe Sarde, Hercules Belville, and I sought refuge in out-of-season St-Tropez.

When released, *The Tenant* drew some harsh reviews and wasn't a great success at the box office. One critic wrote that I'd 'taken over the part played by Catherine Deneuve in *Repulsion*, and one misses Deneuve.' Another claimed that my purpose in obtaining French citizenship had been to enter *The Tenant* for Cannes. That was absurd. For one thing, my papers didn't come through till two months later; for another, I could have directed a French entry even if I'd been Chinese.

The picture remains a flawed but interesting experiment, admired by some students of the cinema and regarded by others as a cult film. Its general reception in France was mixed. The public didn't take kindly to a frumpy Adjani, to the mixture of French and American actors, or to the story line itself. I was to blame in the last respect. With hindsight, I realize that Trelkowski's insanity doesn't build gradually enough – that his hallucinations are too startling and unexpected. The picture labors under an unacceptable change of mood halfway through. Even sophisticated filmgoers dislike a mixture of genres. A tragedy must remain a tragedy; a comedy that turns into drama almost always fails.

The Tenant's poor reception robbed me of my usual itch to get on with another movie as soon as possible. I was, in any case, committed to a theatrical assignment resulting from my visit to Spoleto in 1974. The Bavarian State Opera had engaged me to direct *Rigoletto* in Munich.

Preparations for the opera were in marked contrast with the free-and-easy turmoil of Spoleto. Everything was far better organized but far more formal, and the opera house staff conducted itself like a highly disciplined army. Artistically, too, far less scope was allowed for improvisation and innovation, and there were times when I regretted that my passion for the theater had brought me to Munich at all. On the other hand, opera is big in Germany. Newspapers charted our progress day by day, and public interest in the new production lent my work a sense of occasion that helped compensate for what I missed in the way of Italian charm. Although some purists were outraged that *Rigoletto* should have been entrusted to a mere film director, their snipings in the press didn't prevent opera fans from lining up all night before the box office opened for advance tickets.

Munich itself was an enjoyable place to be at this time of the year. The Oktoberfest was in full swing, and my arrival coincided with the city's annual *Modewoche*, or 'fashion week.' Models of all nationalities were all over the place, especially in my hotel, the Residence, where women seemed to outnumber men by at least ten to one.

One day a German gossip columnist invited me out on a double date with two girls he wanted me to meet. Both were young and, in different ways, strikingly beautiful. One of them was rather dowdily dressed. I asked her name. 'My friends call me Nasty,' she said. Her English was poor, my German nonexistent. Very late that night, after a long round of discos, the four of us ended up in my suite. Leaving Nasty with the journalist, I took the other girl, a stunning blonde, to bed. By the time I surfaced the journalist had gone. Nasty was half-asleep in an armchair in the sitting room. Taking her by the hand, I led her back into the bedroom.

We never repeated this threesome, though I saw a lot of both girls thereafter. I dated the blonde for several weeks, but it was Nasty who grew on me more and more. Her makeup and hairdo and clothes were all wrong. She was reserved and hard to fathom – a loner. One day, though, while sitting opposite her in a Munich beer garden and studying her face, I realized something: Nastassia Kinski's looks were unique in my experience. If there was such a thing as star quality, she had it.

Nastassia introduced me to her mother, who discussed her

374

career with me – she'd already appeared in a couple of undistinguished movies. Nastassia certainly had the looks needed for success on the screen, but the impression she gave in regard to most things, including her professional future, was one of cool indifference. She also didn't appreciate the importance of fluent English to an international film career. I pronounced it essential that she go to drama school, but first she must tackle her English problem. Now that I was based in Paris, I said she could have the run of my London house. Her mother's response to this suggestion took me aback. 'I couldn't let her go on her own,' she said; 'she's too young.' That was when I first learned Nastassia's age. She was only fifteen.

We made love more than once during my three months in Munich. Nastassia was a strange person. She preferred men to be aloof, hated them courting and running after her. She was poised and self-reliant, wryly humorous and quietly observant, quick to spot weakness in others, extraordinarily mature for her age. On the night we met I'd thought her a couple of years older than her friend, who was, in fact, seventeen.

While still in Munich, I started work on a slightly more frivolous assignment. *Vogue* of France had invited me to guest-edit its Christmas 1976 issue – an honor not to be spurned. Previous guest editors had included Hitchcock, Fellini, Marlene Dietrich and Salvador Dali.

The *Vogue* 'operation' was so French and so disorganized that it seemed a miracle to anyone visiting the editorial staff's cramped and cluttered Left Bank offices that any of their magazines got published at all. The *Vogue* name carried so much prestige that many models and photographers were happy to work for them for next to nothing. What accounted for their penny-pinching attitude was the immense cost of producing such glossy material, but their business methods didn't match the appearance of their magazines. Everything was improvised. There were no formal contracts, and my fee, I knew, would be nominal.

I began shuttling back and forth between Munich and

Paris on *Vogue*'s behalf. I had overall responsibility for text, pictures, and the issue's general appearance. I also had to produce an elaborate pictorial in an exotic setting – to show off some of the expensive baubles advertised in the magazine. I decided on a *Pirates* theme to be photographed in the Seychelles islands.

'Who's the girl going to be?' asked Robert Caillé, the editor.

'Someone you've never heard of,' I told him. 'Nastassia Kinski.'

Setting up the layout wasn't unlike planning a shooting script. On October 30, 1976, I flew off with Timothy Burrill, my production manager, and Ludovic Paris, doubling as hairdresser and male model. Nastassia had gone on ahead with the *Vogue* team and trunkfuls of clothes, jewelry, and perfume. Harry Benson, a former *Life* photographer, was in charge of pictures.

The Seychelles were the high point of my idyll with Nastassia. We started off on Mahé, then flew to a smaller island, Praslin, where we lived like extravagantly nurtured savages. Praslin is a miniature tropical paradise. Fish teem in the surrounding sea, and bats the size of flying foxes flit through palm trees that bear gigantic nuts shaped like ample female backsides – hence their local name, *cocofesses*, or coconut buttocks. Our quarters on this enchanted desert island were a little beach hotel run by a Frenchman. At the end of our working day he would set up some trestle tables on the sand, and there we would dine on grilled fish, fresh from the sea, and chilled champagne.

Although Nastassia and I didn't flaunt our relationship, it was impossible to conceal it. On Praslin we shared a mattress in a beach hut with only a couple of sheets to keep off the night breeze. Nastassia spent a lot of time on her own, swimming, idling in the shadows, strolling along the silver sands, or just gazing out to sea, but she became less reserved and more communicative as the days went by. I think our brief stay on Praslin was a memorable time in her life; I know it was in mine.

It was in the Seychelles that Harry Benson, a born comic who delivered his patter in an inimitable Scottish burr, came up with a bright idea. He proposed to photograph me buried up to my neck in sand with incoming waves breaking over my head – a form of capital punishment popular among pirate captains in days gone by. Even I shared the general view that this would make an excellent cover picture, so I climbed into my waterlogged pit at the 'magic hour' and was duly buried. Harry clicked away blithely as the waves pounded my protruding head. 'That's enough!' I sputtered.

'Just one more,' Harry kept on saying.

The tide was coming in fast. Our team, who had been standing by with spades, sprang into action as soon as Harry declared himself satisfied. They shoveled the sand away from my chest, my waist, my hips, then stood back. All I had to do was step out of my hole, but I couldn't. Each time a wave submerged me I felt free, but each time it receded the suction imprisoned my legs in a viselike embrace. What a ridiculous way to die, I thought.

Everyone assumed I was playacting. Then they started clawing the sand away, frantically. At last, by straining every muscle, I managed to extricate my legs and was hauled clear of the swirling water.

I hadn't set foot in Poland for fifteen years. Now, as Christmas 1976 approached, I felt an urge to spend it in Krakow with my father and Wanda. Although my naturalization papers had finally come through, I didn't want to flaunt my new French passport. Deciding to travel as a Pole, I even booked myself a seat with Lot, the Polish national airline.

Warsaw was fogbound that Christmas Eve, so my plane was diverted to Prague, where I found hundreds of Poles thronging the transit lounge. Not only bored but determined to reach my destination in time, I buttonholed a friendly Lot captain who helped me rent a car and extract a transit visa from the Czech airport police.

Prague gave me my first glimpse of the Eastern bloc since making *Knife in the Water*. Streets filled with shabbily dressed people, the characteristic stench of low-grade gasoline and cheap tobacco, the rudeness and indifference of the telephone operators at the seedy post office where I vainly tried to telephone my father – it all came back with a rush.

After a long drive over the Tatra Mountains I was delayed for nearly an hour at the border. The Czech frontier guards and customs officers shook me down like a suspected criminal, but the Poles on the far side were kindness itself. A woman customs officer waved me through, advising me to fill up at the first opportunity. Gas stations were few and far between, she said.

Krakow was another long drive away. I stopped a couple of times during the night in search of something to eat. The only place open in one small town was a nightclub, but the bouncer turned me away. He took it for granted I was drunk, like everyone else. By 4:00 a.m. lines of people could already be seen outside 'meat products' shops, patiently waiting in the snow for the doors to open.

After an emotional reunion with my father and Wanda, I set off on a nostalgic tour of Krakow. It made me feel like Rip Van Winkle. The city seemed entirely familiar – there wasn't a doorway, shopfront, or café that didn't evoke a flood of memories – yet utterly different. Its black, pockmarked façades were crumbling away, and whole streets had been condemned and cordoned off on grounds of public safety. My beloved Krakow was being destroyed by the Nova Huta steelworks and a nearby aluminum plant; their horrifying output of chemicals was eating into the very fabric of the city, ravaging the fine Renaissance architecture, pitting the cathedral's irreplaceable stained glass windows. It was all part of the Communist authorities' calculated attempt to industrialize and proletarianize an essentially 'bourgeois,' cosmopolitan seat of learning and culture – the only Polish city to have rejected them in the postwar referendum.

I noticed other changes as well. Young people seemed better dressed, better educated, and more polite than when I'd left Poland for the West. They were also surprisingly well informed about political and cultural developments in the outside world. A visit to a satirical cabaret directed by my old friend Piotr Skrzynecki – the one whose 'psychical aversion to firearms' had exempted him from military service – left me amazed by its audacious skits and frontal assaults on the regime, not to mention the way Piotr taunted the ever-present party censor in the audience. He even violated the most sacred taboo of all by hurling several veiled but wittily effective gibes at the Soviet Union.

I made the rounds of my other old friends. Billizanka was still active in the local theater; Renek Nowak was wheeling and dealing, as usual, between minor stage and screen assignments. Mietek Putek, whose parents had briefly harbored me before farming me out to the Buchalas at Wysoka, was now a police captain.

All couples develop certain eccentricities as they grow older, and my father and Wanda were no exception. The inefficient, insanely complicated Polish bureaucracy had accelerated this process. I found it both irritating and moving; for the first time I realized they were getting old.

Christmas over, I retired to Gstaad to work. Directing operas, editing fashion magazines, and making sentimental journeys were all very well; but my *Chinatown* bonanza was running out fast, and *The Tenant* hadn't done much to improve my financial position. Sue Mengers, my new agent, had secured me a deal with Columbia to adapt and direct Lawrence Sanders's thriller *The First Deadly Sin* for a combined fee of $600,000. I'd started reading the book while in Munich but deferred any serious work on it until *Rigoletto* and Christmas were behind me.

The First Deadly Sin proved harder to handle than I'd expected. It moved at a brisk pace but had weaknesses, in both plot and characterization, that were camouflaged in print but would have shown up clearly on the screen. The story concerns an outwardly respectable publishing executive who, under sinister influences, turns into a random killer and wields an ice ax on the streets of Manhattan. Much of the plot hinges on booking procedures – the killer is twice picked up for minor acts of violence but discharged – and on how the New York Police Department keeps its records. I needed to know how a New York precinct functioned, how suspects were booked, how detectives made arrests and sifted tens of thousands of items of evidence in homicide cases. Columbia agreed that I should spend some time observing veteran cops at close quarters.

I couldn't have gotten any closer if I'd tried.

TWENTY-SIX

It was the Christmas issue of *Vogue* that started it all.

I'd nearly drowned for nothing. The picture of me up to my neck in sand never appeared on the cover. At the last minute Robert Caillé thought it classier to go for a plain, glossy navy blue cover simply captioned 'Vogue by Roman Polanski.' To judge by the success of the issue, which sold like hot cakes and became a collector's item, he was right.

Gerald Azaria, editor of *Vogue Hommes*, another Condé Nast subsidiary, had been pestering me for an interview for some time. The idea didn't appeal to me – my press phobia still hadn't subsided – and I told him so quite frankly. During one of my frequent visits to *Vogue*'s editorial offices he said he was going to feature me anyway and use the rejected picture on the cover. I came up with a better idea. A recent *Vogue Hommes* issue had devoted several pages to photographs of adolescent girls by David Hamilton. They were in his usual romantic style, deliberately blurred and unfocused. I told Azaria I'd much rather do a similar series of my own, but not in the Hamilton manner. I proposed to show girls as they really were these days – sexy, pert, and thoroughly human. I was renewing my interest in still photography at the time, and *Zoom* and *Photo*, two French specialist magazines, were clamoring to publish some of my work.

Azaria jumped at the idea and begged me to act on it. Françoise Mohrt of *Vogue Beauté*, another glossy *Vogue* off-shoot, showed me a recent issue featuring pictures of an extraordinarily beautiful fourteen-year-old, Doushka, the daughter of Pascale Petit, a well-known French actress of the

381

fifties. She said that if I decided to go ahead with the project Doushka would make an excellent model. Azaria phoned me several times, both in Paris and after my return to Munich, to discuss the matter in greater detail. I told him I would cast my net wide, possibly selecting four or five girls of different nationalities: Swedish, French, American, German.

Just before I left for L.A. to continue work on *The First Deadly Sin*, I received a visit from Henri Sera, Simon Hessera's brother. Henri congratulated me on the Christmas issue of *Vogue*. When I mentioned my *Vogue Hommes* assignment, he said he knew exactly the kind of girl I had in mind. The younger sister of Tim,* his current date in L.A., Sandra,* was a fabulous-looking teenager who wanted to be a model and had already appeared in a TV commercial. He emphasized how photogenic she was.

Henri told me that the girls and their mother, Jane,* lived in the San Fernando Valley and gave me their phone number.

My first few days in L.A. were pretty hectic. I had a number of meetings with Columbia and my agent, Sue Mengers, and got the studio to line up my research trip to New York. I also met several times with Wally Wolf and another lawyer – an expert on immigration matters – to examine the possibility of my settling in the States for good. Sue and Wally had recently been pressing me to take this step, now that the Rome scene was over and most of my film offers were emanating from Hollywood. They advised me to stay on and finish the script in L.A., so I arranged for Hercules Belville to join me right away.

Among my visitors at the Beverly Wilshire Hotel was Ibrahim Moussa, an agent whom I'd known in Rome. Moussa, who had since moved to L.A., flipped at the pictures of Nastassia in *Vogue* and wanted to sign her up right away. He was undeterred when I told him she needed coaching in acting and English, so we agreed to share the cost of flying her and her mother to L.A. and paying their expenses while Nastassia took a crash course in English. I also

* Pseudonyms.

obtained her a scholarship at the Lee Strasberg Institute in return for a lecture I'd given there.

It was several days before I finally got around to calling the number Henri Sera had given me. Jane, Sandra's mother, answered the phone. She already knew I might want to photograph her daughter because Henri had spoken to Tim from Paris. She sounded enthusiastic; she'd meant to call me herself but hadn't known where to reach me. She suggested I drive out to the Valley the following day and gave me detailed instructions on how to get to her house. Actually, she said, Henri had introduced us on one occasion – at a Sunset Strip club called On the Rocks a few months previously. This rang a bell. I recalled bumping into Henri and a friend of his, out on a double date with Tim and another woman who acted like her sister but turned out to be her mother. Small world, I thought.

The next day, a Sunday, I drove out to Jane's home at the far end of the Valley – a longer drive than I'd expected. The house was small and nondescript, a typically suburban, middle-income California house with an ill-kept lawn, a pool, and a two-car garage.

Jane kissed me in the overly demonstrative way so many American women have. I surprised her by trying to kiss the other cheek and met air. I explained I was used to France, where everyone kissed twice as a matter of form.

She said I still used the same aftershave lotion.

It was Vétiver, I told her, wondering why and how she would remember a thing like that.

She showed me into the living room. A man was lounging in front of the TV set without really watching it. Over by the window stood a girl.

'This is Sandra,' Jane said. She told her to get a load of my aftershave. 'Isn't it great?'

The girl said, 'Hi.' She sniffed my cheek. 'It's all right.'

I gave her the once-over, trying not to make it obvious. After Henri Sera's rapturous description I was rather disappointed. Sandra was about my own height, slim and quite graceful, with an unexpectedly husky voice for her age – a good-looking girl, but nothing sensational.

'And this,' said Jane, 'is Bob.'

The man said hello. He didn't get up, just eyed me appraisingly. He was rugged and good-looking, though surprisingly pale for a Californian. Bob, I quickly gathered, was Jane's live-in lover. She told me he was on the editorial staff of a magazine called *Marijuana Monthly*.

Sandra, who'd disappeared while Bob was being introduced, made an entrance, then exited again. She did this a couple of times in the next half hour. Rather uncharitably Bob commented that she had an attention span of about five seconds. I felt it was simply a way of getting herself noticed.

I described the sort of layout I was planning – something quite different from David Hamilton's pastel, romanticized nymphets. 'You know Hamilton's pictures?' I asked. Jane said yes, but only, I suspected, because she didn't want to betray her ignorance. She said she hadn't known I was interested in magazines. I went to the car to fetch my Christmas issue of *Vogue* and showed it around. I was reluctant to talk too much about the *Vogue Hommes* assignment because I still wasn't sure that the girl would be worth photographing.

From Sandra's modeling prospects, conversation turned to Jane's own career and how tough it was to get a foothold in films. She asked if I knew a good agent. I gave her Ibrahim Moussa's number and said I'd have a word with him. She invited me to stay on and have dinner at The Yellow Fingers, a local restaurant, but I made an excuse. Before leaving, I said I'd call and arrange a photographic session. There was a repeat of the two-kiss ritual and the same momentary embarrassment when Jane withdrew her head too soon.

I did call, some days later, and fixed a time. When I arrived with my cameras, I found a circular hanger set up in the hallway and laden with all kinds of clothes for me to choose from. Bob, as before, was slumped in front of the living-room TV set. Jane and Sandra, who was wearing jeans and a patchwork blouse, hovered over me while I picked out various garments, including a long white Indian-style dress that belonged to Jane herself.

After loading the stuff into my rented Mercedes, Sandra and I drove up into the hills, which began just behind the house. If it hadn't been for the clothes and the cameras, we could easily have walked. We parked and made our way on foot up a narrow path through the scrub. It was steep, and we slithered around a lot, Sandra with the clothes draped over her arm, I toting the cameras.

It didn't take me long to realize that outside the house and away from Jane and Bob, Sandra was a different girl – lively, chattering incessantly. A typical California teenager, she punctuated her talk with the word 'like.' 'Like I hate having my mother around when I'm being photographed, because she says, like, do this, do that.' She told me she had a boyfriend with a black belt in karate.

Wanting her to relax, I went on chatting as I started taking close-ups of her. At this point I noticed a bruise or, rather, a love bite on her neck. I asked if it was the result of taking karate lessons from her boyfriend. She laughed. 'It was Chuck all right,' she said, 'but it wasn't karate.' I said I'd have to make sure I photographed her so the mark wasn't visible.

There were dirt roads crisscrossing the hill, and some boys were tearing around on motorbikes, making a tremendous noise. Sandra said she knew some of them.

I asked her to put something different on. She removed her blouse and picked up another. She wasn't wearing a bra but seemed entirely at ease – not in the least bit embarrassed. She had nice breasts.

I took pictures of her changing and topless. Then I asked her to unzip her jeans a couple of inches and hook a thumb in her waistband. She posed with professional aplomb. The motorcyclists had clustered around a pickup twenty or thirty yards away and were gawking. I thought she should put her blouse back on. 'They don't bother me,' she said. 'I don't care.' I insisted, feeling that her indifference to the boys was a pose – an attempt to appear worldly and sophisticated beyond her years.

We walked farther up the hill, and she posed topless again.

385

The sun was setting, so it wasn't long before the light ran out. I explained that doing a really professional job could take time – days even. As we retraced our steps, Sandra mentioned a recent *Playboy* cover she'd seen of a girl in a wet suit at sunset. 'Boy,' she said, 'they must have spent days getting that picture right.'

I'd shot two rolls of film in the time we'd been away from the house – under an hour. Stiff and a little tense at first, the girl had relaxed as the session proceeded. I guessed that her provocative poses and slightly glazed stare were her idea of a model's technique for enhancing her sex appeal.

Not far from the bottom of the hill we passed an elderly couple with a dog. Sandra started playing with the animal. She seemed to know the dog but not the couple. 'That's ours,' she said as we walked on. Then she told me it wasn't really.

'What do you mean?' I said. 'Either the dog's yours or it isn't.' She said it sometimes hung around the house.

Back home, Sandra retired to her room to change and hang up clothes while I sat talking to Bob and Jane in the living room. Bob began telling me about his magazine. It wasn't allowed on the newsstands, he said, but they were thinking of distributing it anyway, even if they got busted. He wanted me to set up an interview for him with Jack Nicholson because he knew Jack was an outspoken defender of soft drugs. I was noncommittal. Bob asked me to take some back issues of *Marijuana Monthly* to L.A. as a gift for Jack. He was gone for quite a while, gathering them up.

When he came back, he sounded off about publishing in general and, in particular, the lightning success of *Hustler*. Enviously, he showed me a couple of issues. Never having seen *Hustler* before, I was surprised that something so crudely explicit, with its almost clinical close-ups of male and female genitalia, should have scored such a commercial hit.

Sandra brought out the *Playboy* she'd mentioned on the hill and showed it to me. The picture she admired so much was a very elaborate, carefully contrived shot involving a sunset, reflections on the sea, and frozen spray. She was right

– it must have been extremely difficult to bring off. I obediently admired it, then left, promising to call and fix another session.

A few days later I flew to New York for my research on *The First Deadly Sin*. Columbia had booked me into the Plaza and arranged for me to spend some time with two New York policemen, Alan Goodman and Lou Perez. Instructors at the Police Academy, Alan and Lou were in the same mold as the fine bunch of cops I'd encountered after Sharon's death: honest, straightforward, and down-to-earth. They proved immensely helpful, taking me to a tough precinct to watch booking procedures, showing me the various forms employed, opening up precinct records, and generally giving me what I needed to make a realistic picture about New York police conducting a murder investigation. Alan and Lou, who knew my films, were good company. We talked for hours in various restaurants, including their favorite Chinese place in Greenwich Village. Wherever we went, I noticed that they instinctively chose a table where they could sit with their backs to the wall, facing the entrance.

I extended my stay in New York by a couple of days. I'd wanted to consult Lawrence Sanders about certain aspects of his book but found that he'd left by the time I got there, so was forced to talk with him on the phone instead. Bitten by the idea of doing some theater work in America, I also discussed with Joe Papp the possibility of directing an Isaac Babel play and saw a number of current Broadway shows.

Returning to L.A. on February 26, after an interval of ten days, I called Jane's number. I felt a little awkward on two counts. I knew from Ibrahim Moussa that Jane had gone to see him on my recommendation but that he'd declined to represent her. As for Bob, Jack had accepted his copies of *Marijuana Monthly* but was quite uninterested in granting him an interview. I was relieved when Sandra answered the phone. I apologized for my silence and explained what I'd been up to. We made another date for March 10.

I was late that afternoon. I'd had a lunchtime session with Wally Wolf and my accountant about the consequences of my applying for a green card – a resident immigration permit – and it must have been past 4:00 p.m. when I rang the doorbell.

Sandra opened the door, and we hurriedly began picking out some clothes with Jane. I told Sandra to be sure to bring along a pair of her tightest jeans. There was no hanger in the hallway this time. I also noticed something that had escaped me on my earlier visits, if it had been there at all. Heaped against the wall in the hallway were some cushions sprinkled with flower petals; perched on top was a large framed photograph of Maharaj Ji, the plump teenage guru who'd won such a following in the early seventies. Though curious, I refrained from asking about the family's involvement with him. There was another girl in the house, a very pretty brunette who kept flitting in and out of Sandra's room. No one bothered to introduce us.

Before we left, Sandra asked about the pictures I'd taken of her. I said I'd show them to her later. In the car she mentioned that her girlfriend was a model who'd done some TV commercials; her tone betrayed a mixture of envy and admiration. I told her we were on our way to Jackie Bisset's house, that her place would make an ideal setting for our pictures. Sandra didn't seem to care where we were going. She displayed the studied indifference typical of a teenager trying to be 'cool.'

While driving, I extracted a viewer from my camera case, together with the slides of our previous session, and invited Sandra to look at them. If there were any she didn't like or wanted me to destroy, I said, she had only to put them to one side. I made her fasten her seat belt before she started examining them; she did it reluctantly.

Casually flipping through the slides, she kept asking questions about the *Vogue Hommes* assignment: how many girls would I be seeing in all, and how many would eventually appear in the layout?

A long, rambling conversation ensued. Sandra told me her parents were divorced. Her dad lived back East, but she visited him once in a while. He drove a Ferrari – she knew all about cars. Then came a description of what went on at her school. She said there were, 'like,' two groups there. The 'good people' were the squares who did as they were told. Having started out as a square, she'd soon joined the 'bad people.' These, she said, were the fun crowd, who drank, popped pills, and defied authority. It wasn't easy to join the 'bad people.' – you had to be accepted. Sandra said she didn't go in much for grass – that was for older folks like her mother. Personally she preferred champagne. One Christmas, while staying with her dad, she'd gotten completely smashed on it. She'd also tried Quaaludes. She said that her sister, Tim, was a Quaaludes freak – she'd once been institutionalized for taking so many– and Sandra used to filch some from her now and then.

At some point she produced a wallet from her hip pocket and showed me a snapshot of Chuck, a slim, good-looking boy. He was a karate expert, she told me again. They'd met a few months back, and he'd asked her out for dinner. 'We went to bed together right away,' she added.

I asked how her mother related to Chuck.

It had been difficult at first, Sandra said, but now Jane was used to him. He'd spent the night once, sleeping on the living-room couch. When everyone was asleep, she tiptoed in and pounced on him, pretended to strangle him. Then they spent the rest of the night together. Still, she said, there was nothing she could do nights that she couldn't do in the afternoons.

I asked when she'd first started having sex.

'When I was eight.'

That shook me. I glanced at her to see if she'd meant it. She was quite serious.

'Who with?'

'Just a kid down the street,' she said. 'At that age you don't even know what's going on.' She spoke quite casually; it clearly held little significance for her.

The sun had almost dipped behind the trees by the time we reached Mulholland Drive. There was a lot of wind, which I liked, but the shadows were lengthening. I would have to make it snappy. Victor Drai, who lived with Jackie, was in the house with two men friends. I introduced Sandra and asked where she could change. Jackie, who'd been out shopping, arrived home, laden with parcels. She went into the kitchen and opened a bottle of white wine, but Sandra refused a glass. Jackie remained in the kitchen while Sandra and I went to take some shots beside the swimming pool. The light was perfect, but it wouldn't last long. Victor and his friends watched us from inside the house.

I kept asking Sandra if she was warm enough – the wind was getting stronger – but she said she was fine. Then the sun disappeared behind the ridge, and I called it a day. Sandra went in to change while I chatted with Victor and his two friends.

I realized I'd picked the wrong side of Mulholland Drive for that time of day. The light on the southwest side, where Jack Nicholson lived, would still be good. I dialed his number. The answering service connected me with Helena, a neighbor of his. Helena, Jack, and Marlon Brando all had houses inside the same compound and shared a common entrance, an electronically controlled gate at the end of a long drive.

I explained the situation to Helena. Could I use Jack's place while the light was still good? She said to come right over.

The gate to the compound was just across Mulholland. Helena answered the intercom and let me in, telling me to make sure the gate closed properly. There was a nut who hung around the place. He had gotten in once and tried to strangle Marlon Brando's secretary.

I parked the car outside Jack's house, Helena opened the door leading from the garage to the kitchen, and the three of us went inside. I introduced Sandra, who wandered off on a tour of the house with one of Jack's dogs frisking at her heels. I asked where Anjelica Huston, Jack's girlfriend was. Helena said she was out but wouldn't be long. Helena was working on a screenplay, too, and we discussed our respective problems. We both agreed that the worst part was writing the end.

Sandra reappeared and said she'd like something to drink – surprisingly, since she'd refused a glass of wine not long before. Opening the refrigerator, I saw stacks of beer and a bottle of champagne – Crystal, a good French brand. I asked Helena if Jack would mind my opening it. She said to go ahead, so I poured some for all of us. We clinked glasses and drank. Helena recalled how often I'd used to stay at the house and asked why I was such a stranger these days. 'Ah, well,' she said eventually, 'I must rush. That goddamned script.'

The cloud of steam from Jack's luxurious Jacuzzi had attracted Sandra's attention when she went exploring. It was at one end of his swimming pool, and Sandra thought it was 'real neat.' They had one at home, but nothing like this. She said she'd like to try it.

'Later,' I told her. 'Let's get on with the pictures.'

I began by photographing her against the bay window in the living room, with Franklin Canyon in the background below. When I asked her to remove her blouse, she did so without hesitation. I took some shots of her draped around a Tiffany lamp, holding her glass of champagne.

Then I asked her to change into something else. She chose a long, soft, hooded dress belonging to her sister. She stripped off her jeans while I knelt beside my camera case, changing lenses. I didn't want to stare at her while she was changing, but I was very aware of the flash of nakedness as she slipped the dress on. We weren't saying much now, and I could sense a certain erotic tension between us. We moved to the kitchen, where I photographed her sitting on the table, licking an ice cube, nibbling a piece of sugar.

I went to turn on the Jacuzzi. The whirlpool switches and the rheostats controlling the lights were in the bathroom. Sandra followed me in. It was getting darker, and I knew that even with the lights on there wouldn't be enough exposure, so I changed the lens to a 1.4.

Before photographing Sandra in the Jacuzzi, I decided to

call Jane. The session was taking longer than I'd expected. If Jane sounded annoyed and wanted the girl back right away, I would simply drive her home. If not, so much the better.

Sandra's manner on the phone to her mother was quite relaxed. She told her we were at Jack Nicholson's place. We'd taken a lot of pictures, and she was just about to try Jack's Jacuzzi. At this point I said hello to Jane and asked if she'd mind Sandra being late for dinner. I knew the traffic on Ventura Freeway would be heavy at this time of the evening. 'Dinner,' said Jane, 'is no big deal – just steaks.' She added that Henri was back from France and might drop in later.

Sandra undressed and got into the Jacuzzi while I went to get my camera. The water was up to her waist when I started photographing her. 'It sure is hot,' she said. I tested it with my hand. It certainly was, but she soon got used to the heat. She began moving around in the whirlpool, said it was nice, then sat down under the spray so water ran all over her head. I wished she hadn't – she didn't look too good with her hair wet.

She continued to move around as I snapped her, spontaneously adopting various poses. In some of them she held out her glass of champagne as though toasting me. It was getting so dark it made no sense to continue; the light meter wasn't showing any exposure. I went into the house to put the camera away, then came out and stood watching her. She said, 'Aren't you coming in?'

I said it was too hot; I'd rather have a swim. Fetching a towel from the bathroom, I stripped and plunged into the pool. I swam a couple of lengths before stopping at the Jacuzzi end. Sandra was looking at me oddly. She said she didn't feel good.

'What's wrong?' I asked.

She said her asthma was playing up.

'I didn't know you had asthma,' I said, and asked if she had anything with her – an inhaler or something. She said she'd stupidly left her medication at home.

'You shouldn't spend too long in all that steam,' I told her. 'Not if you're asthmatic. Come into the pool.'

She got out of the Jacuzzi and walked toward the pool, put one foot in and pronounced it too cold. She was wheezing quite audibly by now. She picked up my towel and said, 'I'd better rest awhile; otherwise I might pass out.' When I asked what I should do if she did, she made some flippant remark about mouth-to-mouth resuscitation. I left the pool and followed her into the house.

We went into a room on the ground floor. I'd slept there several times in the days when it had been a guestroom, but Jack now used it to house his enormous TV set. The windows were shuttered and the curtains drawn, so the place was almost in darkness.

We dried ourselves and each other. She said she was feeling better. Then, very gently, I began to kiss and caress her. After this had gone on for some time, I led her over to the couch.

There was no doubt about Sandra's experience and lack of inhibition. She spread herself and I entered her. She wasn't unresponsive. Yet, when I asked her softly if she was liking it, she resorted to her favorite expression: 'It's all right.'

While we were still making love, I heard a car in the driveway. It seemed to pass the house, so we carried on.

Suddenly, though, Sandra froze. The light on the phone had come on, which meant there was someone else in the house, making a call from another room. That stopped us both in our tracks, but it didn't suppress my desire for the girl. After whispered reassurances, Sandra gradually relaxed again. When it was all over, I opened the door a little and looked down the passage. 'Anjelica?' I called.

I heard her call back – 'Roman?' – and go on talking. From the sound of her voice, she was in the living room.

Sandra got dressed quickly and went to the living room to bundle up the rest of the clothes she'd brought. Obviously embarrassed by Anjelica's presence, she hurried out through the kitchen to the car. I followed, introducing her as best I could, gesturing and saying I'd be back. Sandra got into the car and sat there, she didn't want to go back inside. I felt I should. When Anjelica had finished her phone call, I explained that we'd been taking pictures and swimming. I didn't mention making love in the TV room, though that must have been pretty obvious. Nor did I need to tell her we'd opened a bottle of Jack's champagne – she had a glass of it in her hand.

I asked to use the phone and called the Beverly Wilshire to see if there were any messages for me. I also called Hercules Belville to fix up a working session for the following day. None of this took long; I was conscious of Sandra waiting in the car.

Anjelica asked why we were rushing off. I told her about Sandra's asthma attack and said I had to get her home. Anjelica was on the phone again by the time I left. We waved and smiled. 'Call you tomorrow,' I mouthed.

Sandra talked a lot during the drive home. She told me about her guitar lessons and her drama teacher. She was studying *A Midsummer Night's Dream* in school. I tried not to wince when she started spouting Shakespeare in a strong Valley accent, with no sense of rhythm. I got her to repeat the lines and did some coaching of my own. The subject of movies cropped up. None of Sandra's family had seen *Rocky*, so I suggested we all go see it the next week. My motives weren't particularly altruistic; it was one way to be sure I'd see her again.

We took about half an hour to get back. When we did, Sandra darted into the house ahead of me while I got the slides and viewer from the rear seat. Jane was in the hallway. I said I hadn't known that Sandra suffered from asthma. She said it wasn't serious. We joined Bob in the living room and started looking at the slides. I produced a half-smoked joint I'd found in an ashtray at Jack's place and passed it around.

Although the other two said little, I could sense a change in their attitude toward me. It clearly wasn't as friendly as it had been. I hadn't noticed anything when I came to pick Sandra up, but then, I wouldn't have had the time to take it in. Whatever underlay the couple's new coolness toward me, I thought, it couldn't be my photographs of Sandra. They seemed to like them.

I wasn't invited to stay to dinner. After kissing Jane and Sandra good-bye and shaking hands with Bob, I drove back to the Beverly Wilshire.

Later that evening I had a rather puzzling phone call from Henri Sera. He'd apparently spoken to Jane on the phone, and she was furious. She thought the photographs were 'horrible.' I couldn't understand it; she hadn't said any such thing a couple of hours ago. I asked Henri to come around and see them for himself.

He seemed a bit edgy when we met. I asked what the matter was, but he made no direct reply, just looked at the slides. He thought they were beautiful. If Jane and Bob didn't like them, I told him, I'd scrap the whole batch.

Still later that evening I had an appointment with Bob De Niro, who gave me a copy of *Magic* by William Goldman. He wanted to know if I'd be interested in making a film of it with him starring.

I spent the following day in my Beverly Wilshire suite, working on *The First Deadly Sin* with Hercules. A friend of Henri's named Jojo stopped by with a present of some Quaaludes. I put them in a prescription bottle of my own, though the label was for a different strength. That evening I had a theater date with some friends, including Frank Simon and Lisa Rome, Sydne's younger sister, to see Richard Dreyfuss in *The Tenth Man*.

We met, as arranged, in the hotel lobby. One member of the party asked me if I happened to have a Quaalude, so I went upstairs to get one. Hercules was still in my suite, packing up. I said good night again and rejoined the others.

We were about to leave the lobby through the front door when a man in a bowling shirt walked up to me and flashed a badge. 'Mr Polanski?' he said quietly. 'I'm from the Los Angeles Police Department. Can I talk to you? I have a warrant for your arrest.'

TWENTY-SEVEN

'We don't want to create a sensation,' said the man in the bowling shirt. 'Is there someplace we can talk?'

'Sure,' I said. I still had no inkling of what it was all about. Baffled, I turned to Frank Simon and handed him the theater tickets, saying something about meeting up later, 'if I can.'

The man wasn't alone, I saw. He had at least two or three other men with him; it was hard to pick them out in the crowded lobby. I asked him what I was being charged with. He replied in such a discreet undertone that all I caught was the word 'rape.'

'Rape?' I repeated, shocked and bewildered. Forgetting all I'd learned from my New York research, I asked if I could call my lawyer.

'Sorry, you haven't been booked yet. Let's go up to your room; we have a search warrant.' The words were uttered quite dispassionately, without a hint of animosity.

We walked over to the elevator. I still had the Quaalude clenched in my fist. I was just weighing the chances of dropping it down the crack between the elevator and the lobby floor when one of the escorting detectives murmured in my ear; he must have spotted it. 'Better let me have that,' he said, cupping his hand beneath mine. I let go of the pill, which he pocketed without another word.

Hercules was still in my sitting room. 'Herky,' I said, 'I've got a problem. These gentlemen have a warrant for my arrest.' It takes a lot to shake Herky's British composure, but I came close.

One of the men asked him if he would submit to a body

search. He nodded silently, was frisked, and then was asked to leave.

My suite received a thorough going-over. The cameras, slides, and undeveloped films were put on one side, the Quaaludes, too. Then, while we all sat around in a circle, the detective who had first accosted me recited the *Miranda* formula, reminding me of my rights.

I knew it by heart, thanks to my week with Goodman and Perez. I had a sense of déjà vu: it was like being on the inside of my own film. The atmosphere was surprisingly civilized and unemotional. One of the men, a deputy DA, gave me his card.

Sandra and Jane were mentioned. I didn't have to make a statement, but did I have any idea why a complaint might have been lodged?

Quite truthfully I said no. I was incredulous; I couldn't equate what had happened the day before with rape in any form. I said I'd met Jane and her daughter and described my visits to their home, as well as the photo sessions. Still not grasping the gravity of the charges or the extent of the trouble I was in, I felt that a thorough airing of the circumstances would exonerate me.

The DA announced that a search warrant had been taken out for Jack Nicholson's house, too. Would I accompany him there? I agreed.

In two cars, we drove up to the compound gate and rang and rang, but there was no response. To my companions' momentary alarm, I got out, scaled the fence, and opened the gate manually from the inside. It was an old late-night trick of mine. Many times, when staying at Jack's, I'd gotten in that way to avoid disturbing anyone.

We drove up to Jack's house. Anjelica opened a first-floor window and leaned out. 'Anjelica?' I called, surprised to see her. Subsequently I learned that she and Jack had just broken up and she wasn't actually supposed to be in the house over these past few days – that's why she hadn't answered the bell to let us in.

'I'm with the police,' I said. 'They have a search warrant.'

She came downstairs and let us in.

The cops started searching the house. One of them asked me where I had taken pictures of Sandra, so I showed him the pool and the Jacuzzi. Another went upstairs with Anjelica.

She came back down a few minutes later, white-faced. 'They've got it,' she said.

'It' was a pinch of cocaine in her purse. Some grass, too, had been found in a bedroom chest of drawers. I was asked if Sandra and I had been in the bedroom in question. I said no.

Anjelica and I were taken in separate cars to the West Los Angeles police precinct on Purdue Avenue. I should have been handcuffed, but I wasn't. When we arrived, I was booked by the detective who'd arrested me. The form was filled in by a uniformed desk sergeant seated behind a grille – another flash of déjà vu. I'd watched this happening to others; now it was happening to me.

It was a busy night in the precinct. A youthful alcoholic was led in, handcuffed. Something inside him seemed to snap as he vaguely gathered where he was, because he let out a series of high-pitched, hysterical screams so spine-chilling that even his escorts were impressed and sat him down gently in a chair. His terror was too extreme and irrational to be anything but the product of DTs.

The desk sergeant said to me, 'What in hell do you think you're doing, going around raping people?' I didn't reply.

I was fingerprinted, then asked if I'd like some coffee. Just a glass of water, I said. I was also dying for a pee. They took me along a corridor, where I saw Anjelica waiting. She shrugged. I felt awful. 'Sorry about this,' I said, though it sounded rather inadequate.

Now was the time to call my lawyer. I got through to Wally Wolf. Although it was around 1:30 a.m., he didn't seem surprised to hear my voice. I later learned that Frank Simon had called Maurice Azoulay, a hairdresser friend of mine, who'd called Andy Braunsberg, who'd called Wally and asked him, cryptically, 'Has Roman been in touch? Is he in trouble?' I told Wally where I was being held.

I sat waiting for him on a chair near two desks occupied by

uniformed policemen. They'd obviously had a tough week. One of them said to his buddy, 'Know what I'm gonna do this weekend? I'm gonna sleep and fuck and eat and sleep and fuck and eat.'

Wally showed up with a friend of his, a television producer. Not being a criminal lawyer, Wally didn't have any bail bondsmen on tap. He'd phoned his friend in the knowledge that he always kept a large amount of ready cash at home. Bail was set at $2,500. Once Wally had handed over the money, I was released.

I got into Wally's car – his friend had come separately – and we headed back to the Beverly Wilshire. Wally turned on the radio; every station was carrying a news flash reporting my arrest for rape. 'The hotel will be swarming with news-hounds,' Wally said. We turned around and drove instead to Maurice Azoulay's house on Coldwater Canyon. Listening to those news flashes, I knew my world was in ruins.

All through the rest of that night I talked things over with Maurice. He did his best to reassure me, but I now knew how much trouble I was in.

I needed a criminal lawyer. On Sunday Wally Wolf drove me downtown to a tall building on Flower Street. There, in a big, bleak office with cold, modern furniture and traffic crawling thirty-three stories below, I was introduced to the man who had agreed to represent me.

I got to know Douglas Dalton well in the ensuing weeks and to appreciate his human as well as his professional qualities. At first sight, though, he didn't seem brimming with the milk of human kindness. He was a dour man who seldom smiled and spoke in a dry, flat, expressionless voice. Initial contact with him did no more to boost my morale than the sight of his cheerless office.

As the three of us reviewed the facts of the case to the extent that we knew them, the full force of the catastrophe overwhelmed me. I couldn't come to terms with it; nothing in my life had prepared me for the idea that I might be a criminal. It was like learning that I was the victim of a fatal but lingering disease, one from which there would be no merciful release. I was grateful, just the same, for Dalton's straightforward, down-to-earth exposition of the course the law would probably take: arraignment; grand jury; indictment; trial. It gave me something to focus on.

From his own experience of such cases, Dalton advised me to try to carry on working as normally as possible, discussing the case with no one. It was possible, he said, that I might be kept under surveillance.

I holed up at Maurice Azoulay's for the next two weeks, concealing my whereabouts from all but my closest friends. Hercules packed my things and brought them over from the hotel. I could think of nothing but the case and what lay in store for me, but I also had to finish the script. Wherever Hercules and I worked on it – indoors, beside the swimming pool, inside the house – my mind would wander off. I found it almost impossible to concentrate. Lisa Rome came to see me and often stayed the night. She did her best to console me, but I can't pretend that under the circumstances, I was the world's best lover. During those first few weeks after my arrest I spent much of each day closeted indoors, going out only to jog, to use public telephones – in case Maurice's phones were bugged – and to eat occasional, solitary meals in a dark little booth at the Hamburger Hamlet on the Strip.

My arraignment took place in a downtown L.A. court. The press turned out in force, and Jack Gotch, Doug Dalton's investigator, had to clear a way for me. He tried to prevent me from being mobbed by photographers, but all the pictures that were published made it look as if Gotch, a tough California ex-cop, were physically restraining me. The arraignment itself took only minutes. I remember a judge speaking into a microphone in a hoarse, gravelly voice. I was mesmerized by the allegorical figure on the State of California seal above him, a busty female holding a spear. I was in such a daze that I had to ask Dalton afterward what had actually happened. It seemed that the judge had assigned my case to a Santa Monica court.

The deputy DA, Roger Gunson, decided to convene a grand jury on March 24. This being an exclusively American

400

institution, Dalton had to explain to me what it entailed. I learned that it was a presentation of evidence to a jury, complete with witnesses, and that the hearing was designed to enable the DA to show that his case was sufficient to warrant my being brought to trial. No details of the proceedings were released except to the defense.

The star witness at this grand jury hearing, of course, was Sandra herself. Gunson put her gently through her paces. She testified that I had given her part of a Quaalude before having sex with her. Sandra admitted to two prior sexual experiences and to having sampled a Quaalude once before. On this occasion, she testified, the Quaalude had made her feel dizzy, and she had simulated asthma as a means of getting me to take her home.

The grand jury indicted me on six counts: furnishing a controlled substance to a minor; committing a lewd or lascivious act; having unlawful sexual intercourse; perversion; sodomy; and rape by use of drugs. Each accusation sounded worse than the last when Dalton ran through them for me. If the tinted plate glass windows of his thirty-third floor office hadn't been sealed, I might have jumped there and then.

At least, said Dalton, we now knew what we were up against. Reading the grand jury transcripts, he felt that my prospects were not, perhaps, quite as bleak as he'd originally thought. The DA's case would be weak without some supporting testimony from Anjelica Huston, who could place me in the house and the room where Sandra and I had made love. After several days of suspense we learned that Anjelica had been granted immunity on all charges of drug possession in return for undertaking to give evidence for the prosecution. I couldn't really blame her for accepting the deal, though it left me feeling slightly bitter.

The grand jury hearing was my first intimation that Jane had become aware of what had happened that fateful afternoon in a very roundabout way. Sandra had called her boyfriend and told him that she and I had made love. Tim overheard the conversation and told Jane. Jane then called her accountant, who advised her to go to the police. Although some ten witnesses were called, Bob wasn't among them. As far as the jury was concerned, he didn't exist.

Another surprising disclosure was that Sandra's asthma attack had been faked; she'd never suffered from asthma in her life. To ensure that her story wasn't blown, she'd hurried on ahead when I'd taken her home and told her mother, out of my hearing, 'If he asks, say I've got asthma.' Why she did so baffles me to this day.

The complete picture, I hoped, would emerge if it came to a trial. I knew I hadn't gotten Sandra drunk and that the bottle of champagne – not, as some reports stated, a magnum – had still been half-full when we left. Sandra's animated, unconstrained behavior during the drive home was proof that she hadn't been doped. Her sexual experience – if she'd been telling me the truth – was very different from what she admitted to before the grand jury.

I went to see Bruce Lee's *Enter the Dragon* one afternoon, alone. There were crowds outside the movie house – the picture was a smash hit – but Bruce, who had just died of a cerebral hemorrhage in Hong Kong, would never know it. I felt this was an apt commentary on Hollywood and fate in general. I recalled how desperate Bruce had been to break into pictures, recalled a letter he'd written me: 'If ever you want to direct a meaningful martial arts movie . . . ' Now he was dead, but the producers who had spurned him for so long were making millions.

As for me, I was a pariah. 'We can't have a rapist in our agency,' Sue Mengers was heard to declare. Although she later revised this judgment – swung to the other extreme, in fact – her initial attitude was shared by most of Hollywood. There was the inevitable crop of wisecracks: 'Heard the title of Polanski's next picture? *Close Encounters with the Third Grade*.' My real friends stood by me from the first. I didn't feel like seeing any of my girlfriends except Lisa Rome. She was someone I could talk to freely – a decent, sympathetic, intelligent girl.

I couldn't even go jogging anymore for fear of being recognized and accosted. Instead, an old friend from Poland, Stefan Wenta, used to take me off to his ballet school on Melrose and put me through my paces after his students had gone home for the day. No one else knew of these evening workouts at the exercise bar, not even Wally Wolf. I wondered how the public would have reacted to the idea of a suspected rapist perfecting his arabesques in a pair of black tights.

At the beginning of April, when interest in the case had waned a little, I moved into the Chateau Marmont. From there I started going to restaurants and other people's homes, though I knew that in most cases I'd been invited as an object of curiosity. Many people who appeared sympathetic were really only eager to boast of having met the notorious Hollywood rapist. Overnight I'd crossed the fine line between decent folks and scum. In all my many premonitions of disaster, one thought had never crossed my mind: that I should be sent to prison, my life and career ruined, for making love.

Temperamentally, however, I was on the side of law and order. I had a great admiration for American institutions and regarded the United States as the only truly democratic country in the world. Now, because of a moment's unthinking lust, I had jeopardized my freedom and my future in the country that mattered most to me. There were moments when I told myself it wasn't happening – it was all a bad dream. But it wasn't a dream. The banner headlines, the change of attitude noticeable in many of my friends, Columbia's abrupt abandonment of *The First Deadly Sin* project, even the curt refusal of an insurance company to renew its policy on my London house – all this, and much more, attested to the reality of my predicament.

My first brief appearance before the Santa Monica judge in charge of the case, Laurence J Rittenband, occurred on April 15. I had to run the gauntlet of a big posse of TV cameramen, photographers, and reporters, who charged at me like wild beasts. A party of local high school girls was also visiting the courthouse that day. They mobbed me with equal enthusiasm, squealing and clamoring for autographs. A ludicrous scuffle took place as schoolgirls and reporters jostled for position. I was formally charged on all six counts of the indictment and pleaded not guilty, after which my bail was renewed.

With the judge's consent I took temporary leave of absence from the United States. I'd decided to spend a few days at my London home, where I thought I should be less exposed to the press. I also wanted to consult *Vogue Hommes* in Paris, and that was when I made a chilling discovery.

When I tried to call Azaria – the same Azaria who had begged me for an interview and urged me to undertake the layout that had led to my troubles – he refused to come to the phone. I went to see Robert Caillé and explained how essential it was for Azaria to testify that I'd been working on a bona fide assignment. After hemming and hawing, Caillé finally said, 'He can't do that. You had no formal, written agreement.'

I certainly didn't, but then, I hadn't even had one for the *Vogue* Christmas issue until it was almost on the newsstands. I said everyone in *Vogue* knew I'd been offered the assignment.

'Look,' said Caillé, 'we've already been questioned by a man from Interpol. He came to ask about your assignment. We said we knew nothing about it.'

I felt betrayed. I knew why. *Vogue* thrived on chic, on the superrich, supersophisticated jet set. Almost all its articles were a form of publicity, overt or subliminal, for expensive jewelry, perfume, and couture firms; that was how it broke even. Now that the fat, glossy '*Vogue* by Roman Polanski' reposed on all the beautiful people's coffee tables, Caillé wanted to forget its very existence.

I gave up in disgust and returned to L.A. Soon afterward, Nastassia flew over accompanied by her mother. Ibrahim Moussa signed her up, as agreed, and went halves on her expenses with me. She started immediately on her English lessons and enrolled at the Lee Strasberg Institute. It was good to see Nastassia again. Although we'd ceased to be lovers by now, our ties of affection were strong. However much I might feel like an older brother toward her, Dalton warned me to be very careful never to be seen alone with her in the same hotel room. I knew I was under constant surveillance, certainly by the press and possibly by the law as well.

Then came my second appearance before Judge Rittenband. Dalton and I arranged to meet very early, around 7:30 a.m., at the International House of Pancakes. I knew it well, having often gone there with Sharon in the old days. Apart from being near the Santa Monica Courthouse, it wasn't far from the Aherne place. Dalton, who arrived first, tried to cheer me up by attaching a slip of paper to the menu. He wrote: 'Pancake of the Day: Polish sausage between two pancakes – $1.70.' I ordered one, but the waitress said I was nuts.

At this stage Dalton was uncertain whether to go for a trial or sentencing. If some of the charges could be dropped, he was for pleading guilty and accepting a sentence. If there was no possibility of eliminating the more serious charges, he was all in favor of my standing trial.

If there was to be a trial, the DA wanted it held as soon as possible. Sandra's appearance in court would be bound to dispose of any stories about her looking like a thirteen-year-old. It would be obvious to everyone present that she was a physically mature girl who could easily pass for eighteen. Gunson may have been worried that Sandra was growing and would soon be towering over me. 'She's getting older all the time,' he complained to Dalton.

'So is Polanski,' said Dalton.

Around this time an incident occurred that might have been brought up at the trial – if there had been one. Jane was summoned to the DA's office for questioning. Sandra and Bob, who came with her, remained outside in a waiting room. Through a crack in the door, one of Gunson's staff saw them locked in a steamy, passionate embrace. It wasn't the avuncular hug of a grown man comforting a young girl – it was more; her leg was between his legs. Gunson's subordinate was so taken aback by what he'd seen that he reported it to Judge Rittenband.

During the weeks that followed my second brief appearance, Dalton, Gunson, and Sandra's attorney met several times in Judge Rittenband's chambers. A consensus in favor of sentencing developed, with the prospect of the more serious charges being dropped. The family's legal advisers probably realized that if a trial were to take place and Sandra were cross-examined, the resulting testimony might reflect badly on her. 'If she's ever cross-examined,' one criminal lawyer told me, 'There's no way they can convict you, not even if she appears in court with her hair done up in braids, wearing white ankle socks and cuddling a doll.' Sandra's father, himself a lawyer, had taken her to live with him back East. I gathered that he was equally reluctant for her to appear in open court and might well keep her out of the state in the event of a public hearing. If a trial date had been set and Sandra failed to show up, the DA wouldn't have a case.

I also had no wish to see the girl take the stand at a public hearing. It wasn't just that a guilty plea would avert a trial and might secure me a better deal; I realized that I had already caused her considerable harm. I didn't want her exposed to a blaze of publicity that would sear her memory for life. There was no need for both of us to undergo that experience.

If the more serious charges against me were dropped, Dalton said, the likelihood was that I wouldn't go to jail if I pleaded guilty. The law, and its attendant penalties, varied from state to state. In Georgia, for example, 'Unlawful sexual intercourse' applied only to girls of twelve and under. In California the age of consent was eighteen. In 1976 some 25 percent of those found guilty of the crime in Los Angeles County had drawn probation, not jail, and they included schoolteachers and policemen – people with a direct responsibility for the welfare of minors. Even if I did have to serve a short term, the odds were against my being deported for

406

moral turpitude. This was vitally important because I'd already set my heart on living and working in the United States.

I now received the first good news I'd had in some time. After weighing the pros and cons, and fully appreciating the depth of the trouble I was in, Dino De Laurentiis nonetheless wanted me to direct a remake of *Hurricane*. Sue Mengers got me a million-dollar contract – my biggest to date. It was a welcome prospect. The sudden disappearance of my Columbia mirage had left me wondering how to make ends meet. My legal expenses were mounting fast.

Together with Dino and Lorenzo Semple, the writer whom he'd hired to work with me, I flew in Dino's Grumman jet to scout some possible locations in French Polynesia. With little hesitation, we plumped for the spectacular island of Bora-Bora.

My next requirement was some peace and quiet. After a few days in London, Semple and I tucked ourselves away in Tony Richardson's secluded house at La Garde-Freinet, near St-Tropez, where we set to work on the script. It presented considerable problems because John Ford's original movie and the novel itself were naïve in a way that would have been unacceptable to modern audiences. Though aiming at a period piece, we decided to render the story more plausible by making our principal characters young and ingenuous.

While still in France, I received some disturbing reports about Judge Rittenband. A bachelor in his early seventies and a pillar of the exclusive Hillcrest Club, he set great store by his Hollywood social contacts. Rittenband was clearly enjoying his first excursion into the limelight. He was peculiarly sensitive to the opinion of his fellow country clubbers, many of whom were in show business. According to Andy Braunsberg, who knew some of them and kept his ear to the ground, Rittenband apparently had no qualms about discussing my case at the club. It seemed that in the eyes of most Hillcrest members, I was no better than a child rapist. Rittenband came off as being extremely press-conscious; he liked to look and sound good in the papers. Despite all this, I felt heartened by the progress of behind-the-scenes negotiations – aimed at sentencing in return for the withdrawal of some charges – and doubly heartened now that Dino's faith in me showed I had ceased to be a complete Hollywood outcast.

I returned to L.A. for more preproduction work on *Hurricane*, using an office made available to me by Dino in his building on Canon Drive, and we started casting. I wanted Nastassia to play the female lead. Although Dino was bowled over by her looks, he doubted if she could acquire a sufficient command of English before shooting began. Impatient to put her to work, Moussa secured her a contract to appear in a German screen version of *Passionflower Hotel*. The money was adequate – more than enough to reimburse our outlay on her – but the picture was a low-budget, shoestring production that could only jeopardize her career. I would much have preferred her to wait and gamble on *Hurricane*.

August 8, the day before my next appearance in court, was the eighth anniversary of Sharon's death. I went to put some flowers on her grave at the Holy Cross. While I was kneeling there in the deserted cemetery, a man jumped out from behind some bushes and started snapping pictures. In the stillness, the click of his shutter sounded like machine-gun fire. I turned and walked away. So did the photographer, but the sight of him sauntering casually off transformed my pain and disgust into fury. Rounding on him, I demanded the film from his camera.

'Don't blame me,' he said. 'Magazine editors are always badgering us for pictures like this.' He had a strong German accent.

'I know,' I said, 'you were only obeying orders.' I ripped the camera from his neck and, after removing the film, left it with the cemetery attendant. The photographer went straight to the DA's office and lodged a complaint alleging grand theft property, misdemeanor, and assault and battery. Gunson rejected it, so he settled for a civil action instead.

408

The August 9 hearing was a crucial one. Much to the disappointment of the press, there wouldn't be a trial after all. The DA withdrew five of the six charges, leaving only one of 'unlawful sexual intercourse' – not necessarily a felony. I pleaded guilty.

My sentencing was set for September. In the meantime, Judge Rittenband called for a probation report. Because Sandra had been three weeks short of fourteen at the time of the offense, California law required a psychiatric evaluation to determine whether I was a mentally disordered sex offender, or MDSO. This would be carried out by two psychiatrists, one appointed by the prosecution and the other by the defense, and the probation officer would take their reports into account when recommending what sentence I should receive.

I had several long interviews with my probation officer and submitted myself, as ordered, to psychiatric examination. On the strength of his own findings and those of the two psychiatrists, as well as interviews with Sandra and her mother, the probation officer recommended that I should be fined and placed on probation.

Rittenband had fixed sentencing for September 19. Prior to that date, however, he told both Dalton and Gunson in chambers that he intended to see I spent some time in prison. This he proposed to do by deferring sentence until another psychiatric evaluation, or 'diagnostic study,' had been carried out in custody. The maximum period allowed for such a study was ninety days, though it seldom took more than fifty. After that, the judge implied, he would sentence me to probation.

As soon as I heard the news, I informed Dino and volunteered to step down from *Hurricane*. He provisionally rejected my offer on the grounds that a stay might be granted to enable me to complete preproduction work and that he could delay shooting for fifty days while I did my time in prison.

At the further hearing on September 19 Rittenband duly ordered me to the California Institute for Men at Chino for a diagnostic study but granted a ninety-day stay so that pre-production work could be completed.

Before going to Bora-Bora, I left for Europe at Dino's request to examine some casting possibilities and try to set up a distribution deal with Horst Wentlandt, the leading West German distributor. This European trip proved to be a disastrous turning point in the case – one used by Rittenband to justify his changed attitude toward it and me. My visit to Wentlandt coincided with the Oktoberfest, and I was photographed in a Munich beer hall, obviously enjoying myself.

The Santa Monica *Evening Outlook* ran this UPI picture on September 19, with the following caption: 'Film director Roman Polanski, who was given a stay of a Santa Monica Superior Court order that he undergo a 90-day diagnostic study at a State prison, puffs at a cigar as he enjoys the companionship of some young ladies at the Munich, Germany, Oktoberfest.'

The picture had been cropped so that only girls were visible around me. All, in fact, were accompanied by their boyfriends or husbands. There was Gloria, Sam Waynberg's wife; Vava Oiangen, Hans Möllinger's girlfriend; and Monika, the wife of another German friend, Thomas Datzmann, whose best man I'd been the year before. Rittenband, however, seemed uninterested in these facts. He told a reporter from the Los Angeles *Herald-Examiner* that 'Roman Polanski could be on his way to prison this weekend,' adding, 'I didn't know then that the movie would be impossible to finish in 90 days. I do feel that I have very possibly been imposed upon.'

I felt Judge Rittenband was being less than candid, to say the least. In chambers he had made no secret of his full awareness that shooting wouldn't start before January 1978 and had even – in private to Dalton – held out the possibility of a further ninety-day stay should this prove necessary. According to the timetable worked out in his chambers with Dalton, I would do the psychiatric evaluation in Chino Prison before the picture started, then begin shooting as soon as it was over. The implication was that evaluation would be followed by sentencing and that the latter would take account of the time I'd already spent behind bars. I would thus be able to start work on *Hurricane*, a free man once more.

I heard nothing about the rumpus until Dalton called me in London, where I'd taken Nastassia for a screen test which Dino had set up at Pinewood Studios, still with a view to her playing the lead in *Hurricane* after completing her German assignment. She was not only staying at the mews house but actually standing beside me when Dalton's call came through, though I didn't mention that to him. He said that Rittenband was furious, not least because of the adverse publicity he was receiving, and that an urgent hearing had been arranged to determine why I'd been 'enjoying myself' in Munich.

I returned at once to face the music. Dino testified that I'd been in Munich at his request. Although Rittenband allowed the stay to run, he made it very clear to Dalton that no further extension would be granted. One paper banner-headlined this latest development: 'Polanski Reprieve.' I flew to Bora-Bora to work on the sets and plan our shooting schedule, now knowing that come what might, Christmas would see me inside Chino, facing a possible three-month stretch.

Bora-Bora was a good place to be, under the circumstances. There were no newsmen, no photographers, no telephones. There was almost nothing to do but work. While the sets were being built, Lorenzo Semple and I were finishing the script. The film technicians stayed at the local Club Méditerranée. I preferred the seclusion of a little house at the other end of the island. Here I meditated on my veranda in the evenings, reveling in the utter tranquility of this picturebook South Seas paradise, with its limpid blue lagoon, waving palm trees and glorious sunsets. I led a solitary existence until the very end of my stay, when I met Aloma, a stunningly beautiful Tahitian girl who worked for the French Tourist Board in Papeete. Sadly, the one idyllic weekend we spent together was my last on the island.

I flew back to L.A., prepared to take my punishment in

relatively good spirits, my mind a little clearer than it had been. I'd decided to surrender two days ahead of time in order to escape the press. The night before I reported to Chino, Tony Richardson gave a dinner for me. It was attended by a few old friends – Jack Nicholson and Ken Tynan, among others – and I did my best to prevent the occasion from turning into a wake. I was scared stiff, of course, but determined not to show it. While the farewell party was in progress, newsmen and TV teams were staking out the prison and settling down to an all-night vigil. I suspect Judge Rittenband had tipped them off.

TWENTY-EIGHT

I was escorted to Chino by Doug Dalton, Wally Wolf, and Hercules Belville. We drove there in Dalton's silver gray Cadillac – as sinister a vehicle to me that day as any police car. On the way Dalton briefed me on prison regulations in his funeral parlor voice. Inmates, he warned me, were entitled only to cheap wristwatches. When we stopped for breakfast, I picked out a $15 Timex and gave my Rolex to Herky for safekeeping.

I'd hoped my arrival would go unnoticed, but reporters and photographers converged en masse as we pulled up outside the reception office, a clapboard building some distance from the penitentiary. They trooped in after me, jostling Dalton, who held the court order above his head to prevent it from being snatched. This stampede was the last straw; it totally destroyed my composure. I'd tried to put on a brave face, but I couldn't keep it up. I was disoriented, filled with foreboding, utterly ignorant of what to expect.

My sole recollection is of chaos: prison officers trying to keep the press at bay and vainly looking for some papers; my lawyers and Herky waving good-bye; my being hustled out of a back door and into a car. Two uniformed guards sat in front. One of them turned and spoke through the dividing grille. 'You got a shitty deal, that's all I want to say.' I didn't know whether he was referring to the press or the whole business of my going to Chino.

Scattered around the area were various barracks which Dalton had pointed out as places where prisoners in my category were usually housed. Instead, we headed for some-

413

thing that resembled a football stadium. The car pulled up outside what I came to know as the east gate. Striving to think about something unrelated to my predicament, I concentrated on the gateway itself, which had multicolored tiles set into the concrete around it. To the right of the gate was a watchtower with tinted glass windows. A guard leaned out of one and lowered a plastic bucket on a string. It seemed a curiously primitive arrangement for such an ultramodern setup. One of my escorts shouted, 'We don't have his papers. Polanski – he's expected.' The gate slid open.

We entered the 'yard,' an open space the size of a football field enclosed by a two-story building. Inmates were lolling on bleachers or lying around on the grass. As I made my way across this arena, still bemused, they started to wave and shout. 'Hey, Polanski!' I heard. 'Polanski, howya doin'?' My arrival at Chino had been televised live, and they'd been watching. Stepping through the gate and into the yard was an echo of my childhood theater experience. Like Gagatek, the clown, leaving the puppet stage to mingle with his audience, I'd stepped straight off a TV screen and come to life before an audience of convicts.

My first few hours in Chino were a kaleidoscope of impressions. I couldn't take in my surroundings, couldn't find my bearings. A scrawny black trusty in blue prison denims and a turban led me to a counter where a storeman took away my clothes and fitted me out with prison gear. He returned my sneakers – he'd run out of size 7½ regulation shoes – and my new Timex. Another trusty, white this time, hung a placard around my neck on a bit of frayed string. It read: 'CALIF PRISON B88742Z R POLANSKI 12 19 77.' Then he set up some lights and took a mug shot of me. Yet another trusty, a Chicano, started taking my fingerprints and palm prints. He made such a mess of the job, covering us both with ink in the process, that the supervising officer rejected his two attempts and ended up taking over himself.

Throughout these admission formalities, which lasted for more than an hour, I was getting a continuous stream of advice. Referring to the guard escorting me, the turbaned black muttered, 'He's all right – a fine dude.'

The guard, in his turn, said, 'Don't listen to any of these assholes. They'll con you if they can. Everyone's gonna try and be your buddy, but all they really wanna do is rip you off.'

The yard had emptied by the time I was shepherded across it to one of the cellblocks. My escort took me inside and handed me over to another guard, who signed for me. I was issued soap, a towel, toilet paper, and a book of prison regulations, then led down an empty corridor flanked by gray steel doors with small glass panels in them. The new guard slid one open, motioned me inside, and slammed it shut behind me. I was alone in a tiny concrete box filled with the blare of piped-in rock and roll. I stood there with the music boring into my head, wondering how much of it I could take.

Gradually I took stock of my surroundings. My cell, which was painted baby blue, had a narrow metal bunk with a thin mattress, a stainless steel stool, a table, and a shelf, all of them cemented into the wall. There was a metal washbasin with hot and cold running water controlled by push-buttons. Above the basin was a surprisingly large mirror, and beside it a flush toilet. At the head of the bunk was a slatted window, each strip of glass encased in steel. It looked out over an expanse of wasteland, featureless except for a single watchtower and an almost invisible barbed-wire fence on the horizon. I discovered that the window slats could be swiveled to admit more air by means of a knob. To my infinite relief, I found another knob on the wall below the shelf; the music could be turned off after all.

The whole cell was filthy. Laboriously and methodically I started to clean it with toilet paper. While I was busy doing this, the door slid open by remote control. I didn't know what I was supposed to do, so I waited. Then a voice called, 'Polanski, step outside.' I went into the corridor. The entrance was now sealed off by a sliding grille, and beyond this my guard was standing with two inmates. 'These guys here,' he said, 'want to give you something.'

I walked up to the grille.

One of the men held out a pack of Camels.

I said I didn't smoke.

'Chocolate?'

'Thanks.'

He passed me a candy bar. The guard brought me a mug of coffee. He explained that the two men were due for release, so they didn't have any ax to grind – unlike the rest of 'these snakes.' They just wanted to be nice to me on my first day inside. I learned that I would remain in solitary confinement on my empty 'tier' until the prison committee met and decided on my status. The guard and the two prisoners started talking among themselves, wisecracking and kidding around. After a while the guard told me I should go back to my cell. 'They'll come around nights and shine a flashlight on you through the window. It's only to make sure you're still breathing. You just give them a wave.' It happened the way he said, but I slept like a log despite the interruptions.

At 6:00 a.m. came a distant clatter. It drew nearer. Then my cell door slid open, and a voice said, 'Tea or coffee?' Someone thrust a tray into my hands. It was laden with a full meal, more lunch than breakfast: pork chops in gravy, bread and margarine, cornflakes, a little plastic bottle of milk. Everything had to be eaten with a spoon. The next meal was scheduled for 11:30. I realized that whatever other problems I met inside, undernourishment wouldn't be one of them. Though not really hungry, I decided to eat every crumb. I didn't want to seem uncooperative in any way. After breakfast the shower area was sealed off to everyone else until I'd used it. I was still in complete isolation.

'Wanna clean house?' asked a guard. He showed me where the brushes and mops were kept, and I regretted my earlier, rather futile efforts with toilet paper.

That afternoon I was taken in front of the prison committee. Its members weren't at all hostile or forbidding, but the news they gave me wasn't good. After talking things over, the superintendent announced, they'd decided to recommend protective custody for the duration of my stay. Allowing me into the yard might expose me to physical danger, not

416

because of the nature of my offense but because of my notoriety. 'You're a natural target,' the superintendent explained. 'This place is no different from anywhere else. People want publicity because it gives them status. To get status, someone might kill you.' I could appeal this recommendation, I was told, and my appeal would be considered; but I decided not to. I received formal confirmation the same day. It read: 'Polanski is aware he is a celebrity with the prison population and sees this as a problem to him should he be returned to the general population. By his own request he is being retained on a 'confined to unit' status.' This meant that throughout my spell in prison I would be denied not only yard but also library and gymnasium privileges. Protective custody did not, however, mean complete isolation. In view of my new status, I was transferred to the tier where protective custody prisoners were confined.

Little by little I got my bearings. My living quarters were in one section of the building enclosing the yard, which wasn't circular, as I'd originally thought, but octagonal. Each section had a dayroom, sparsely furnished with chairs, tables, and a TV set; a shower area; and, leading off this central section, the two tiers, each of which could be sealed off by metal grilles. All this could be seen from the guards' central vantage point, a glass booth containing a console manned twenty-four hours a day. The floor above was identical in layout to the ground floor and had its own glass booth, which was linked with the one below by a ladder.

My companions in protective custody included cop killers, prison gamblers who had welshed on their debts, informers, and others in danger from the ordinary prison population, together with inmates who had requested protective custody during their last few weeks in prison to ensure that their yard connections didn't jeopardize their release. Many were Chicanos and blacks. Like our ID cards, the prison notices and books of regulations were printed in Spanish as well as English.

Strange as it may seem, I was a happy man after a few days in Chino. For one thing, my long period of waiting was over;

for another, I was out of the public eye. I felt secure and at peace. There were moments of extraordinary serenity. I was reading a lot and thinking a lot. I grasped right away what it was about prison that made it so attractive to prisoners that they seemed to do all in their power to get back again. This was their world, their ingrained way of life. They missed it on the outside as a sailor misses the sea.

I worked out a routine that kept me active. Volunteering to clean up the dayroom and corridors, I learned to wield brooms and brushes to good effect, working early in the morning after breakfast and again when the others were back in their cells. It was Terry, one of the men who'd spoken to me on my first day, who suggested I team up with him and his partner. One advantage of being in the cleaning detail was that you could watch a film on TV to the end instead of having to return to your cell halfway through.

I resumed my jogging in prison – forty-five minutes daily, up and down the corridor. Some inmates thought I was crazy, but many joined in when I started doing workouts – only for the push-ups, though. They couldn't appreciate the need to work on one's leg and stomach muscles.

I penciled letters on cheap lined paper, which was freely available, and received a mass of mail. 'Polanski,' one of the guards said, 'you're a fucking post office.' There were sympathetic letters from Ken Tynan, Candice Bergen, and the Sylberts, gossipy letters from Sue Mengers, heartbreaking letters from my father. These the guards were supposed to censor, but when it came to Polish, they just gave up and let me have them anyway. There were letters from girls I'd dated, friends I hadn't seen since leaving Poland. There was even a letter from Alan Goodman, one of the two New York cops whose brains I'd picked for *The First Deadly Sin*. 'Dear Roman,' he wrote, 'Louie and I have been thinking about you and feeling badly about how this holiday season finds you in these surroundings. We both hope this New Year will bring an end to all this. We hate to see a friend in trouble.'

Prison routine was dull and predictable. The inmates used to sit in the dayroom, playing dominoes or watching TV. To my surprise, there weren't any real TV addicts among them. The majority watched the news, a movie, and not much else. For conversation, the main topic wasn't sex or freedom, as one might have expected, but prison gossip: who was getting out; who had shown up for another stretch; which guards were okay; who had been transferred from San Quentin or Central; what was happening in Folsom, reputedly the toughest penitentiary in California. Insignificant events assumed inordinate importance. I followed the progress of a fly across the wall, fascinated; I wouldn't have harmed it for anything. I came to appreciate small pleasures – little things transformed into treats by deprivation. There was rare value in the taste of a Hershey bar – and the sound of a woman's voice. I was astonished one morning to discover that some Chino guards were female. Strangely enough, they commanded more respect and civility than their male colleagues.

For Christmas, prisoners were allowed to receive packages. I sent Concepta, my secretary, a list of approved items, ranging from green chilies and tortillas to shampoo, though not after-shave lotion. But when my package arrived, I was informed that being a 'Z' prisoner, I couldn't have it. The 'Z' at the end of my inmate's number signified that I was in for psychiatric evaluation. For some reason the superintendent later relented and let me have it after all.

My first visitor, Doug Dalton, was shaken to find me in protective custody but reassured by my acceptance of the need for it. Dalton was allowed to come at any time. Other visitors such as Concepta and Hercules Belville were restricted to every fifth day except when it fell on weekends, which were reserved for next of kin. I quickly learned to submit to the routine search that occurred after any visit. The guards made you strip and looked everywhere, mainly for drugs. Not long before my arrival an inmate had swallowed a heroin-filled condom brought to him by a visitor. The condom burst with fatal results. Despite thorough searches, pot circulated inside Chino, as did some kind of hooch made from fermented fruit peel.

Although I initially looked forward to visiting days, I ended – like any other prisoner – by becoming almost indifferent. I had more requests for visits than I wanted, many from casual acquaintances and some from total strangers. When enterprising journalists tried to see me, posing as personal friends, I gave my counselor a list of the people I wanted to see and asked him to head off the rest. This didn't altogether protect me from press attempts to spy on me. Two prisoners from the yard made a habit of chatting with me through the dayroom window. Quickly suspecting that their pointed questions were being concocted by some newshound, I was always noncommittal. I later learned that my hunch was correct.

Dino De Laurentiis, who came to see me in the middle of January, told me that the sets of *Hurricane* were ready and the crew was complete. He also said he'd decided to hire a bankable female lead and was considering Farrah Fawcett-Majors. All this was secondary to his main piece of news. Not knowing how long I'd be staying in prison or what the outcome of my case would be, he'd been compelled to take me off *Hurricane* and hire Jan Troller, a Swedish director, in my place. I fully understood his decision.

It didn't take me long to realize that in common with anyone whose sole conception of life in prison is derived from movies, I knew nothing about the reality of it. Films tend to make convicts look big, tough, and menacing. Most of Chino's inmates were puny, undersize, and quite unremarkable in appearance. On the other hand, prison movies paled beside some of the real-life stories told to me by fellow prisoners in 'Lower Block No.2.'

Terry, one of the two men who had spoken to me on my first night inside, wasn't a habitual criminal. His had been a *crime passionel*, committed after finding another man in bed with his wife; he'd shot him. Another Terry, surname Koker, was more like the usual prison inmate. Heavily tattooed, with long hair, rotten teeth, and a straggling beard, he sported the kind of navy blue beanie worn to such effect by

Jack Nicholson in *One Flew over the Cuckoo's Nest* – the woolen egg cozy that really is conventional prison headgear. A petty criminal, Terry Koker was in this time for receiving stolen property.

His pet aversion was a gay black inmate named Beverly – in prison parlance, 'a girl.' Koker's prejudice against blacks was almost as intense as his hatred of homosexuals, and I broke up a number of fights between them. Part of the trouble was that Beverly kept pestering the guard in the booth to tune our piped radio to black stations, which didn't please the rest of the tier, Koker in particular.

At Koker's request, I autographed a photo for his little daughter.

He was released on parole shortly after I left Chino and wrote me several letters. The first of them, which opened with a rambling account of a new romance and trials and tribulations with his wife, went on: 'I stayed out of trouble just like you told me, Roman, cause you know how it was in Chino. It was very hard times for us two so I don't want Chino anymore.' Later, Koker approached a newspaper and sold them the story of my life in jail. The piece contained an allegation that I'd promised his daughter – age four – a part in a future movie and insinuated that my motives had been shady.

Lujan, a small, soft-spoken Mexican who came to our block shortly after I arrived, monopolized the whole tier where my own brief spell of isolation had been spent. A former hit man for 'M' or Emme, the Mexican Mafia, he'd killed sixteen men in various prisons on order from above. For some reason, Lujan had finally grown sick of his trade and decided to testify against his former associates. Emme had retaliated by killing every member of his family except his wife and small daughter, who lived in hiding under permanent police protection. He was in total isolation at all times, even his food being cooked separately to avoid the risk of poison. After his release, so a guard told me, Lujan would get facial surgery, a new identity, and a lump sum to enable him to settle in some remote spot, but the threat of death would follow him everywhere. 'Those mothers can smell a fink as far away as Taiwan.'

'Shotgun' had spent most of his adult life in jail. Muscular, good-looking, and not unintelligent, he'd been a petty criminal without a record until the night he was stopped for a traffic violation. Police who searched him found a stolen check for $80. He drew only a short sentence but was unlucky enough to be paired with a cellmate who tried to rape him. 'Shotgun' stabbed him to death and had been in and out of prison ever since. He wore the esoteric badge that distinguishes prison murderers: one teardrop tattooed on the cheek for every victim.

Fights and disturbances were frequent in Chino, though all the inmates agreed that it was less violent than Folsom. Much of the violence resulted from internal gang warfare between blacks and members of the so-called Aryan Brotherhood. While I was there, a member of the AB was stabbed in the yard by a black prisoner. His appointed bodyguard was blamed for not protecting him. Two fellow members of the same gang sneaked into the bodyguard's cell, where they skewered him several times with a sharpened screwdriver and rammed a pencil into his eye. He survived but refused to name his attackers. He was stabbed again in his hospital bed. That was when he started cooperating with the prison authorities.

The turnover in our block was brisk. Sometimes it was almost empty; sometimes the dayroom was crowded with new arrivals. Once, after I'd made some sarcastic remark about L.A.'s police chief, who'd just been interviewed on TV, a complete stranger sidled up to me. He was a thin, pale Chicano with sleek black hair. 'Want me to bump him off?'

'What do you mean?'

'I'm getting my parole next week. I'll take him out for you. Cost you five grand.'

Aside from being visited by some clergymen and a rabbi, I was interviewed as a matter of course by two psychiatrists and a psychologist – the purpose of my imprisonment. The psychologist, a woman, made me do all sorts of written tests with multiple choice answers. She also issued me two sheets of paper and asked me to draw a man and a woman. I'd attended life classes so often at art school in Krakow that habit prompted me to draw them naked. Doug Dalton's comment when I told him was 'Oh, shit!'

'What was I supposed to do,' I asked him, 'give them fig leaves?'

As time passed, its agonizing slowness dulled by the anesthetic of prison routine, I realized that many of the characteristics of American society were present on the inside, too. Bureaucracy was tempered with flexible individual responses and a practical approach to the penal system. The guards never engaged in beatings or even in verbal abuse. They tried to run the place as smoothly as possible, avoiding needless hassles and futile arguments with prisoners. All in all, they reflected the basic efficiency of the American way of life. Throughout this period, from the time of my arrest until I quit the United States, some of the nicest people I came across were policemen and prison officers. Neither hypocritical nor pruriently inquisitive, they refrained from passing judgment on me. They had a job to do, and they did it.

One of the toughest guards in Chino was assigned to our block during my time there. Schenck by name, he handled himself like a Marine Corps top sergeant. Although I couldn't quite gauge his attitude toward me from his manner, I suspected it might be hostile. Later I received a copy of his report on me:

Inmate Polanski has been under my supervision and has made the adjustment to prison life in a very efficient manner. He spends much of his time in his cell writing or reading. When he is out of his cell he exercises, watches TV or plays chess. Inmate Polanski has also volunteered for dormitory maintenance during the evenings and does a fast and efficient job. Inmate Polanski is an organizer and a leader and has not used his social status as a lever or

423

crutch and gets along well with both staff and inmates.

About halfway through my spell in Chino, a trusty tapped on my cell door and whispered, 'Roman, you'll be out on January 29.' I never found out how he knew, but he was right. On January 28, my counselor told me to get ready to leave, advising me at the same time to tell no one. On the morning of January 29 I packed my belongings in my Christmas carton, returned my prison gear to the store, and got back the clothes I'd arrived in. The guard who escorted me to the main gate grinned good-bye and said, 'Take it easy, tiger.'

Doug Dalton was waiting outside in his car with Wally Wolf. I felt almost as dazed coming out as going in, but happy that this time, at least, there were no photographers or TV cameras on hand. My uncut hair and the beard I'd grown would have made good page one material. I'd lost weight, too. Wally Wolf wanted to know if I was hungry. Not just hungry, I told him – ravenous for some nonprison chow.

Dalton stopped at a delicatessen on South Fairfax. It was midmorning, and there were few other customers in the place. Sitting at the long counter, I felt confident that my beard made me quite unrecognizable. I ordered borscht and lox. When the counterman brought my order, he said, 'Will that be all, Mr Polanski?'

I didn't feel like seeing anyone, oddly enough, but I did call Dino De Laurentiis. He came around the same afternoon and offered me my job back. He'd spoken to Jan Troller, who was prepared to stand down. If I wanted to come back on the picture, I could. Though touched and very tempted, I still didn't know what Judge Rittenband had in mind for me. Dalton was seeing him the following day, I told Dino, so the outcome of that meeting would enable me to give a definite answer.

Dalton's understanding throughout had been that my spell in Chino was all the time I would have to spend in prison. To his dismay, he found during a meeting with Rittenband on January 30 that the judge had changed his mind yet again. On

September 16 Rittenband had told Dalton in chambers that the diagnostic study in Chino would constitute my punishment. Now, after I'd done my time there, he announced that the report, which recommended probation, was the worst he'd ever seen – 'a complete whitewash' – and that he was determined to send me back inside. 'I'm getting too much criticism,' he confided to Dalton. 'I'll have to give him an indeterminate sentence.' He also expressed surprise that I'd spent only forty-two out of a possible ninety days in prison. This was almost absurdly disingenuous, since he knew as well as anyone that the average time for a diagnostic study in custody was around forty-seven days.

But Rittenband wasn't even prepared to sentence me to an additional forty-eight days, as the DA himself suggested, to make up the ninety he now said I should have served in full. He stated that the appearance of a state prison sentence must be maintained for the benefit of the press. 'You, Dalton, will argue for probation. You, Gunson, will argue for prison. I'll impose an indeterminate sentence and release him after ninety days if you make the motion.'

At the same time, however, Rittenband was singing the press a different song. He would release me after another forty-eight days, he said, but only if I agreed to voluntary deportation. It was not, of course, within the judge's discretion to decide whether or not I should be deported. In effect, he was employing a form of blackmail – compelling me to request deportation so as to cut short a prison term that could, depending on his whim, have dragged on for years.

After Dalton's meeting with the judge I reviewed the situation with him and Wally Wolf. They were both at a loss for words. Neither could offer any assurance that Rittenband would relent or that he would allow me to go free after serving a full ninety days. He had made it very plain that Hillcrest Club pressures mattered more to him than anything else. Giving me an indeterminate sentence would enable him to spin out the case for as long as he liked.

Since the judge seemed determined to prevent me from ever again living and working in the United States, and since it was clear that I had served my forty-two days in Chino for nothing, an obvious question arose: what had I to gain by staying? The answer appeared to be: Nothing.

Dalton's office was having a claustrophobic effect on me. I got up and walked to the door.

'Wait a minute,' Dalton said, 'where are you going?'

'It's okay,' I told him. 'I'll talk to you later.'

I left the two of them sitting there, looking glum.

I packed a bag and drove straight to Dino's office, where I told him what the judge had in store for me. 'I've made up my mind,' I said. 'I'm getting out of here.'

'That judge,' said Dino, '*che cazzo!*' He asked if I had money. I didn't. He summoned an aide. 'Anyone here got some cash?' The aide came back with $1,000, which Dino thrust into my hand. He hugged me. I hugged him back.

From Dino's I headed for Santa Monica airport. It would have taken me ten minutes to rent a Cessna 150 from Gunnel Aviation and another half-hour to pilot it across the border into Mexico. Then I thought better of it. I made a U-turn and drove to L.A.International. I got there with fifteen minutes to spare before the next British Airways flight to London and, with my American Express card, bought the last seat on the plane. I just had time to phone Concepta. 'I've left the car out front in the departure area,' I told her. 'There'll probably be a ticket.'

It was twilight when we took off. I could see Los Angeles sprawling endlessly below us, its sea of lights growing dimmer as we climbed above the smog. I didn't give a damn what happened now. I simply knew I'd rather do anything than go on living the way I had in the past year. I'd endured disgrace and press harassment, lost two director's jobs, and done time in prison. My exhilaration was almost manic. I didn't sleep a wink all the way.

London was damp and overcast. Depression set in even before I got to the mews house. Without unpacking my suitcase, I called Doug Dalton and told him I was in England.

He didn't have much to say and I knew why. I was putting

426

him in a spot. He'd never had a client skip the country before.

I wandered around the unheated rooms, trying to figure out my next move. There was something wrong. I felt I wasn't safe even now.

The same evening I flew on to Paris.

The next morning Dalton appeared in court to inform Judge Rittenband that I'd left the country. Though taken aback, Rittenband deferred sentencing until February 14. Dalton undertook to try to persuade me to return in the interim.

He flew over to Paris with Wally Wolf and did his best to talk me into coming back and facing Judge Rittenband. He enumerated all the disadvantages of my predicament and painted my future in the gloomiest colors, but my mind was made up. I waited till he was through. Then I said, 'Now you've gotten that off your chest, what else is new?' He and Wally left.

Rittenband was all set to sentence me *in absentia* and make a speech to the press when February 14 came. Meantime, however, at a series of interviews and press conferences he made his animosity toward me so plain that Dalton submitted a 'statement of disqualification' claiming bias, prejudice, and the manifest impossibility of my ever obtaining a fair and impartial hearing from him. This affidavit itemized the judge's fluctuations of mood and attitude, his successive decisions and counter-decisions, his statements to the press, his remarks about voluntary deportation, and other violations of the California code of judicial conduct, including his admissions to Dalton and Gunson that he was being deluged with mail and criticism from friends. The disqualification statement also recalled an incident witnessed by Dalton and Gunson in the judge's chambers. Rittenband had told them that according to a friend of his, I'd been in trouble before; a London newspaper had reported my involvement in a similar case some years previously. Gunson, who had already looked into the matter, informed the judge that his friend was mistaken. In the presence of both men Rittenband then made a

427

phone call. 'Helen,' he said, 'are you sure about that newspaper article?' Turning to the other two, he said, 'She's sure.'

Dalton lodged an immediate protest. 'Judge,' he said, 'you shouldn't even be talking to that lady.'

Rittenband was thrown by Dalton's affidavit, but even more so by the fact that the DA endorsed it. California law entitles a judge faced with a disqualification statement to publish a rejoinder within ten days. Although Judge Rittenband stated that Dalton's charges were unfounded, he never attempted to refute them in detail. He simply announced that 'for the sake of expediency,' he was stepping down.

The case was reassigned to Judge Paul Breckinridge. 'I've never sentenced anyone *in absentia* before in my life,' he declared, 'and I don't intend to do so now.' Breckinridge removed the case from the calendar, adding, 'If and when he returns, I'll ask for a new probation report, and we'll deal with it then.'

That is how things stand today. Were I to return to the United States, I should be arrested on arrival and held without bail. The reopening of the case would entail a new probation report and might even mean another diagnostic study in Chino. The fact of my having become a fugitive from justice would also be taken into account, but so, in all probability, would be the affidavit charging Judge Rittenband with bias, prejudice, and unprofessional conduct. In any case, my return itself would present a problem: soon after I arrived in Paris, my multiple-entry visa to the United States was declared invalid.

TWENTY-NINE

Across the street from me, some extensive renovation was in progress. The building opposite my third-floor apartment near the Champs-Élysées was a mass of scaffolding, and perched in it like crows were photographers with telescopic lenses poised to capture my every move. The more persistent of them nested up there, night after night, in sleeping bags.

I lowered the shutters and drew the curtains, turning the apartment into an artificially lit limbo. Life under such conditions was impossible. I felt even more hemmed in than I had in Los Angeles, just after my arrest. Knowing something of the press photographers' game, I guessed that one way of relieving the pressure would be to get a picture of me published as soon as possible.

I called Sveva Vigevono, a Swedish free-lancer who had taken some photoportraits of me in the past. Recently divorced, she had a small child to support and could use the money. I arranged to meet her off the premises. Then, accompanied by Paul Rassam, Jean-Pierre's brother, I took the elevator to the basement garage and got into the trunk of my car. Luckily the photographers hadn't yet discovered that the garage exit was in a side street around the corner.

Paul drove me to our rendezvous, a *café-tabac* on the Avenue Hoche. Sveva was already there at the counter. I sneaked up and put my hand on her shoulder. I still had my Chino beard and was wearing a cap and dark glasses. Failing to recognize me, she shrugged my hand off with obvious distaste. 'What's the matter?' I said. 'I thought you wanted a picture.'

Sveva's photos had the desired effect. Her competitors abandoned their vigil, but I kept up my cloak-and-dagger routine with Paul for a few days longer, taking over the wheel from him in another underground garage up the street. I discovered to my surprise that a stowaway in the trunk of a Mercedes can carry on a perfectly intelligible conversation with the driver.

By and large, the press and public opinion in France were kinder and less censorious than their counterparts in the United States. More or less left in peace after the first few weeks, I shaved off my beard and started leading the semblance of a normal life again.

I now took stock of my financial position. It was desperate. Many crisis meetings were held in my apartment with the two Rassams and their brother-in-law, Claude Berri. During one of these sessions we decided to make *Tess*.

It was less of a snap decision than it sounds. I'd been turning it over in my mind for many years. Sharon's comments on the book she'd left behind in London had lingered with me, sending me back to it again and again until I knew it almost by heart. At the height of my troubles in Los Angeles I'd asked Nastassia to read it, too, feeling that if the film were ever made, her looks and acting potential would fit her admirably for the name part. The project had been intermittently discussed with Claude Berri for the past two years or more, until it became a kind of joke: when are we going to make *Tess of the d'Urbervilles*? Now it was a joke no longer.

Claude Berri is a man of sudden but lasting enthusiasms and intensely loyal to his friends. My arrival in Paris as a fugitive from justice, not knowing if I would ever be able to work again, had transformed a vague idea into a firm intention: Claude wanted to produce the picture and have me direct it. He started talking money with European distributors – talking with as much conviction as if it were already in the can. Meanwhile, we had no script or cast or crew or any idea of where *Tess* would be filmed – except that it had to be in France rather than England, where I was extraditable.

*

Hardy's *Tess of the d'Urbervilles* is the story of innocence betrayed in a world where human behavior is governed by class barriers and social prejudice. It is also a study in causality. All the evils in Tess's life are the fortuitous products of the small but momentous coincidences that shape our destiny. Had there been no chance encounter between her drunken father and a parson who tells him he has aristocratic blood in his veins, there would have been no tragedy. Tess would have lived out her uneventful days as a Dorset peasant woman. She would never have met Alec d'Urberville, never have been raped by him, never have ended on the gallows.

To tell the story at all, it was essential to find the proper setting, a twentieth-century equivalent of Hardy's nineteenth-century Dorset. The only way to convey the rhythm of his epic was to use that setting as an integral part of the film, signaling the passage of time and the change in Tess herself by means of a visible, almost palpable change in seasons. Once our rural locations were chosen, we would have to film throughout the year from early spring, through high summer, to the depths of winter. This unusually long shooting schedule would inevitably make for a very expensive picture.

More than just a director-producer, Claude Berri headed a successful distribution company. Having recently bought the French rights to Francis Ford Coppola's *Apocalypse Now*, he pledged his future profits on the picture in order to raise preproduction money for *Tess*. At this stage, because of his friendly relations with Coppola, he thought that Coppola's own company, Zoetrope, might distribute *Tess* in the United States. For all his notional *Apocalypse* assets, Claude needed capital badly, even to get us started. Horst Wentlandt almost came in as a major partner, then backed out. This only reinforced Claude's determination to continue. He ended up borrowing heavily from banks and mortgaging everything he owned. I took Nastassia, who was visiting Paris, to see Claude at his home. He was so captivated by her looks, which were obviously right for Tess, that he barely listened to my remarks on her language problem.

Although *Tess of the d'Urbervilles* would be out of copyright by the end of the year, we knew we had to start right away or not at all. Claude paid the Selznick estate some $25,000 for the film rights of the book, which had been made into a silent movie in 1924. Still working furiously on the script with Gérard Brach, I took time off to photograph Nastassia in Fontainebleau Forest, wearing a romantic-looking nineteenth-century dress. Claude ran the picture as a huge double-page ad in *Variety* during the 1978 Cannes Film Festival, boldly and simply captioned 'Tess, by Roman Polanski.' Although this brought a spate of inquiries from would-be private investors, they either backed out – after protracted and futile negotiations – or proved to be complete fakes.

While we were writing *Tess*, I clocked up 18,000 miles looking for suitable places to film – and that after one of our assistants, who carried out the original search, had driven the production unit's Renault 4L into the ground. We were still looking for some minor locations when shooting began. Despite a remarkable 320-page 'breakdown file' compiled in record time by Thierry Chabert, my assistant director, there was no time for adequate preparation – just as well, perhaps, for had we known what we were getting into, we might never have gone ahead. None of us could have foreseen at this stage that shooting would continue for a full nine months.

It was logical that *Tess* should be an Anglo-French coproduction with a predominantly English cast and key technicians, so we brought in Timothy Burrill as coproducer. One of his first steps was to find an experienced writer to work with Gérard and me on an English version of the screenplay – an important factor, since Hardy often dispenses with dialogue at crucial moments in his story. Through the Society of Authors, Timothy found us John Brownjohn, whose home, by an extraordinary coincidence, was in Marnhull, the 'Marlott' where Hardy's heroine was born.

432

Casting presented few problems. I decided to send Nastassia to England to study with Kate Fleming, the National Theatre dialogue coach who had worked with me on *Macbeth*, and it was agreed that if Nastassia, mastered the Dorset dialect in time, she would get the part. With the aid of *Spotlight* and Mary Selway, my casting director, I chose Leigh Lawson and Peter Firth to play Alec and Angel, the two men in Tess's life. The vast resources of Britain's stage and screen directory were also enlisted to help fill the minor roles in the film.

The crew was a mixture of Claude's collaborators and my own. I was joined once again by Pierre Guffroy, my designer for *The Tenant*, and by Ludovic Paris and Didier Lavergne, the handsome pair who had done such a good job as hairdresser and makeup artist on the same picture. I was fortunate in getting Claude's usual production manager, Pierre Grunstein. Pierre's amiable disposition attracted a team of technicians as efficient and devoted as himself – men like Dédé Thierry, an exceptionally fine grip whose prizefighter's looks belied his great intelligence and professional skill.

My acquaintanceship with Geoffrey Unsworth, one of the world's greatest and most experienced cameramen, went back to *Vampire Killers*. After having seen him in operation on the set of *2001: A Space Odyssey*, I'd always wanted to work with him. Geoffrey was just finishing *Superman*, a long and grueling assignment, but he agreed to embark on *Tess* without the break he badly needed. He told me that the book was a lifelong favorite of his and that he'd dreamed of filming it for years. By another coincidence, it was one of the books required for his daughter's public examination in English that year.

I also needed a really outstanding costume designer, and Timothy Burrill suggested Anthony Powell, whose work had already won him two Oscars. Anthony flew over to Paris for a three-hour lunch at the Grande Cascade in the Bois de Boulogne, followed by a nap at my apartment. Although we barely touched on the film, it wasn't necessary. I knew at once that he was just the man for the job.

By the time we were ready to roll Claude Berri was head over heels in debt. Still without a British or American distributor, we would never have been able to start filming at all but for a contract Claude had secured from the Société Française de Production, or SFP. In return for a one-third stake in the picture, this subsidiary of the state-owned French TV network became our service organization.

In any film the first day's shooting sets the mood and pace of the whole operation. This makes it vitally important to achieve the right blend of speed and precision, humor and enthusiasm. On August 7, 1978, the first day of *Tess*, I got up before dawn, opened the window of my Fontainebleau hotel room, and found that it was pouring with rain.

It poured all day long. The scene to be shot was the one in which Alec d'Urberville feeds Tess a strawberry on a shimmering summer's day. Leaden clouds kept rolling across the sky, so we erected a canopy, more than 100 yards long, to keep the rain off the rose garden, the camera, and the actors. Little could be heard but the drumming of rain on plastic sheeting. The hothouse – an important feature – was badly in need of a coat of paint, but the painters supplied by the government-run SFP worked strictly to rule. They refused to leave their Paris base till 9:00 a.m., arrived just before 11, broke punctually for lunch, and took another regulation break before leaving in midafternoon so as to make Paris by the end of their prescribed working day. Once they had quit the set, hairdressers, continuity girls, production assistants, and everyone else around lent a hand with the painting. Despite the weather and union rules, the rose garden scene comes across with a luminous, magical midsummer quality that testifies to Geoffrey Unsworth's extraordinary skill.

It was because *Tess* took so long to shoot that our cast and crew became more than just a group of people temporarily banded together for the purpose of making a film. They developed a communal existence and rhythm of their own, with births and deaths, love affairs and divorces, moments of high comedy and deep tragedy. We were a movable feast that traveled from midsummer in Normandy, through fall and winter in Brittany, and back again to springtime in locations familiar to us from months before. The sheer beauty of the French countryside helped, but so did the fact that we were a close-knit, congenial team – a happy band of friends. Something of the idyllic atmosphere of those months may well be reflected in the film itself. For me, coming so soon after Chino, this was a peculiarly important episode in my life and an extraordinarily cleansing experience.

Eighteen whole days of our schedule went on traveling time alone, so we were fortunate in having a first-class mobile canteen manager who thought nothing of serving lunch in one village and the next meal forty or fifty miles away. Food being almost obsessively important to French film crews on location, our meals weren't the slapdash, stand-in-line-with-a-tray affairs they would have been in the United States, but substantial repasts consumed under canvas and washed down with good local wine. On our first night in Normandy, where seafood is staple fare, we sat down to a superb meal in Cherbourg's Café de Paris. Nearly 200 strong by then, we had taken over the entire restaurant. As a platoon of waiters carried in huge trays of oysters and crayfish, lobsters, and crabs, I nudged Claude Berri and uncharitably reminded him that everyone in sight was eating on his tab.

The opening sequence of the film was shot at a country crossroads that might have sprung straight from Hardy's imagination. I found it quite by chance. The production team had gotten together and bought me a racing bike – I thought it ironic that I'd had to wait this long to acquire such a marvelous machine. I took to cycling again like a duck to water, and it was during one of my after-hours excursions that I discovered this perfect spot and the adjacent field where the village maidens hold their 'club dance.' The crossroads were just outside a village called Omonville la Rogue, and we made a deal with the mayor to use the local football field as the village green. We needed to return to this location several times, however, and the mayor's undertaking to us landed him in serious trouble with the village. The football field issue, coupled with the fact that we had to mask the local team's changing room with a plywood representation of a Dorset village, complete with a church and thatched cottages, developed into such a full-scale political row that he was compelled to resign.

Another village, Leslay, made a perfect Emminster, Angel Clare's birthplace in the book. We altered the appearance of a whole street there by installing English-style sash windows and removing TV aerials and overhead power cables. The street remained that way for months, and we had to pay the residents handsomely for their trouble. Leslay's lovely little church was very English in style except for its steeple. This we concealed with a huge mirror. The sky it reflected perfectly matched the sky behind it, giving the tower the four-square appearance typical of English village churches. A similar device was employed on the large Normandy farm where all the dairy-farming scenes were shot. The cowshed wasn't big enough – its sole drawback – so I doubled the internal length with the aid of a mirror covering one entire end wall.

It was in Brittany that tragedy struck. One Sunday, in a small town called Morlaix, Geoffrey said he didn't feel well and complained of heartburn, so Timothy Burrill went off to buy him some indigestion tablets. That evening Geoffrey said he'd sooner have dinner in his room. I was getting ready to go down to the restaurant when Thierry Chabert hammered on my door. 'Come quick,' he called. 'Geoffrey's fainted.'

Geoffrey was lying sprawled across his bed, half on the floor, with his shoes off. His lips were blue, his eyes fixed and staring.

Desperate for some means of bringing him around, I sprinted to the makeup room for an ammonia popper of the type used to induce tears on the set. I broke it open under his nose. It had no effect; he'd stopped breathing. I couldn't find his pulse, so I put my ear to his chest: still nothing. My assistant started giving him mouth-to-mouth. Gaelle, a girl who happened to be with me at the time, suggesting massaging his heart. I did my best while someone ran to call an ambulance. The seven minutes it took to arrive were the longest in my life.

I realized how futile my own attempts at heart massage had been when the highly professional emergency team took over. After one look at Geoffrey, they dragged him onto the floor and put a wedge between his teeth. An ambulance man started pounding his chest with all his might, hitting it with the heel of his palm, five times in quick succession, then pausing, then repeating the process. 'You'll break a rib,' I told him.

'So much the better,' he replied, but his portable cardiac monitor continued to display an almost immobile red bead of light.

We sat around the hotel lounge, none of us able to sleep, none of us wanting to be alone. Our vigil continued long after word came that Geoffrey was dead. He was sixty-two.

The next day we were due to film the threshing scene. We decided to carry on shooting with the camera operator taking over on a temporary basis. I thought it best, even if what we shot had to be scrapped – Geoffrey would have wanted it that way. It was hard to get started without him. We felt as if half our team was missing, not just one man, but somehow we got through a full day's shooting.

So strong had been the impact of Geoffrey's personality, and so profound his understanding of this film version of his beloved book, that the entire crew and cast greeted his replacement, Ghislain Cloquet, with subconscious resentment. He was seen as an interloper, an alien officer coming in to lead troops deprived of a seasoned commander. Cloquet sensed but understood this feeling. Gradually, with just the right mixture of tact and discretion, he overcame it. The tragedy of Morlaix lost some of its immediacy, and we were able to work as a team once more.

The following month, November, we moved from Brittany to Boulogne for the scene where Tess and Angel, on the run from the police, spend their first and last night together. While driving there after dark with Jean-Pierre Rassam, I

437

thought I saw a strange white glow on either side of the freeway. 'Looks almost like snow,' I said. Jean-Pierre put another cassette in the tape deck and told me not to be absurd. I decided to stop for a closer look. It was snow all right.

'It's always milder near the Channel,' Jean-Pierre said soothingly. 'There won't be any in Boulogne.'

But the farther north we went, the thicker the snow got. As we drove up to the hotel where the crew were staying, I could see them in the restaurant, framed by a large bay window like something off a Christmas card.

Pierre Grunstein, my production manager and an incurable optimist, told me everything was going to be all right; he'd ordered some sweepers in. They went to work at dawn but the futility of their efforts soon became apparent. Undeterred, Grunstein sent for some gas-fired torches. As soon as they melted the snow, however, it started falling in earnest. Our hotel manager was bewildered. He'd been living in Boulogne for over twenty years, and he'd never seen anything like it. I seemed to have heard that before somewhere. We packed up and returned to Paris.

At $12 million, *Tess* was the most expensive film ever made in France. It cost as much as it did simply because shooting went on for so long. And the reason for that, in turn, was not just my need to mark the passage of time by recording the changing seasons. There were some eighty locations, and it took time to get to one, set things up, and move on to the next. Freak weather delayed us again and again.

The word in film circles was that my own extravagances had doubled the film's cost. This simply wasn't true. Even my biggest single so-called extravagance, Stonehenge reconstructed in a field some fifty miles north of Paris, cost less than transporting the crew to England would have done. All the authentic nineteenth-century farm machinery, early railroad cars, and other rare old props we used had been lent by collectors.

Our greatest and most annoying expense wasn't of our making. Throughout the shooting, the SFP was in dispute with the management of France's state-run TV network. Its members went on strike three times and we were their innocent victims. For four weeks they banned all work on their lot and locked up the warehouses containing the monoliths for our Stonehenge scene. By the time the strikes were over they had cost us more than a month's worth of working days. Our free-lance crew, who performed with incredible efficiency and enthusiasm, had to be laid off without pay whenever strikes interrupted shooting. With unprecedented loyalty, they all turned down other assignments to stick with *Tess*, even when this meant a considerable loss of income. But for them, the film would never have been completed at all.

Not unnaturally, as successive delays prolonged our shooting schedule and had inevitable repercussions on the budget, Claude Berri became more and more apprehensive. Having borrowed all the money he could reasonably expect to raise at the outset, he was now compelled to look around for more.

Because he wanted to keep the interest of potential British and American distributors alive, Claude insisted that Nastassia and I put in an appearance at the 1979 Cannes Film Festival. It would be good for the film, he felt, but he was wrong. Journalists weren't interested in writing about a picture still being edited – one we couldn't show them for months to come. All they wanted from me were comments on the Los Angeles affair, my private life, and how I was coping with both. The press conference became a pandemonium as scores of photographers, reporters, and curious fans stormed the lobby of the Carlton Hotel. It degenerated into an acrimonious shouting match between the minority that wanted to hear about *Tess* and the rest.

Another error, in retrospect, was Claude's pledge to Neue Konstantin Film, a West German distribution company, that it could give *Tess* a world premiere by October 31. He was equally adamant that the film must be released in France on November 1, to coincide with the All Saints holiday weekend. Finally, in his eagerness to sell it in the United States, he started showing potential buyers the rushes – always a mistake.

The sheer mass of rushes took me four hours' screening a day to get through, day after day for more than a month. I was fortunate in having the steadfast support and advice of Philippe Sarde, who wrote the music. The selected takes were as much a tribute to his judgement as mine, and I trusted his taste implicitly.

Tess was the first film mixed in France with stereo Dolby sound. Jean Nenni, a longtime idol of mine and the inventor of the rock and roll mixing system, was still a genius at gadgetry. Dolby is incompatible with homemade equipment, however; it calls for a superefficient installation and studio. Because Nenni's setup wasn't in perfect working order, the sound levels were never constant. As if that were not enough, Nenni had become an archconservative in his old age and hated the idea of using a novel system on principle. He was also going so deaf that he and his assistant had to shout along the console to communicate at three yards' range. I offended them both by making them a Boy Scout telephone out of two empty Coca-Cola cans and a piece of string.

Editing and mixing developed into a nightmare. Because we were racing against time, I had five cutting rooms working simultaneously and continuously. The supervising sound editor I brought over from London refused a black-and-white print, claiming that he could do a good job only with the original working print in color. He used to lock this up at nights, which prevented it from being used by anyone else and led to endless rows.

Because of our deadline, we were trying to do too many things at once. We needed an international sound version so the Germans could dub it. We were also working on a dubbed French version as well as the English original. All three versions had to conform, down to the last frame. It was very easy to go wrong, and one frame out of synch spelled disaster for the remaining footage. I had one film editor doing nothing but checking on the conformity of all three versions. We worked twelve-hour days at first, then eighteen-hour days, and finally, toward the end, around the clock. The Boulogne studio canteen stayed open all night for us.

Something of Claude Berri's tension showed through when I was at last able to run the film in a semifinished state. Everyone else who saw it was elated. Not so Claude, who hugged his plastic briefcase and said nothing. The storm didn't break till we were having a drink in a bistro opposite the Boulogne studio.

'It's too long!' he shouted. There was a sudden hush. 'It's too long!' he repeated at the top of his voice. 'It's got to be cut by an hour, and it's coming out on October thirty-first!'

I started to say something, but he shut me up. 'I'm only the moneyman, but the moneyman says it's too bloody long!'

Philippe Sarde tried to pacify him. We were all light-headed with strain and fatigue. I knew the film worked. I didn't consider the length a drawback – it gave *Tess* a special kind of quality – but I was too tired to marshal my arguments coherently. The tensions in the cutting room were such that our floor resembled a factory whose workers fought among themselves for tools and raw materials. It was insane. I could well understand the bafflement of potential foreign distributors, German film critics, and all whom Claude misguidedly, though with the best of intentions, had invited to see our work in progress.

Then Francis Ford Coppola entered the picture. Still toying with the possibility of distributing the picture, he turned up in Paris with a couple of Zoetrope executives. This time I was really on trial; Coppola was the knight in shining armor who was going to salvage *Tess* and Claude Berri's investment. After the screening came a dinner at Olympe, Claude's favorite restaurant. Coppola didn't choose to talk about *Tess* at all. The atmosphere at the table was so strained that I left after the first course, pleading another engagement. As I rose, one of Coppola's associates shook my hand and said, in a diffident undertone, 'Congratu-lations . . . ' The last two syllables trailed away. He couldn't bring himself to utter the word in full.

Tess had a disastrous German premiere. Nastassia, who phoned me afterward, told me that its reception had been so cold and hostile she'd wanted to hide under a seat. The reviews were snide. One critic called the film adequate only as a documentary about nineteenth-century dairy farming. Everyone regretted that I hadn't stuck to what I did best – horror movies. With no other reviews to guide them, the German critics decided to pan *Tess* en masse. It was almost as if they thought that releasing the picture in Germany first must mean there was something wrong with it.

The Paris opening drew good reviews and a lot of coverage. There were lines on the Champs-Élysées, but not the kind Claude Berri had hoped for. *Tess* ran for almost three hours; that meant only three daily showings instead of four and a corresponding reduction in box-office revenue. The mood in Claude's office was funereal. The German reviews had taken effect, and no firm U.S. offer was in sight. Claude blamed me for all this. I was held up as the villain of the piece – the man whose obstinacy was going to bankrupt his friends.

Claude and I had a heart-to-heart talk. I pointed out that his deadline hadn't given me time to fine-cut *Tess* as I would have liked. If allowed to do this, I could marginally shorten it without detracting from the atmosphere, but I wasn't going to remove the forty-five minutes that would squeeze in one more showing. Recalling what Sam O'Steen had done for *Rosemary's Baby*, I suggested that Claude hire him to edit nearly an hour out of the film. If anyone could do it successfully, he could.

Sam flew over. I didn't want to cramp his style while he worked on *Tess*. Preferring to be as far away as possible, I joined a small party of friends – none of them with movie-making connections – on a three-week trek and endurance test in the Himalayas.

As soon as our Sherpas hired the porters, what had started out as a leisurely walk became a serious climb. I was so obsessed with *Tess* I kept telling myself there couldn't be a better form of therapy than to concentrate on all the things I hadn't had time to think about for months. But as the going got tougher and we climbed ever higher through glorious rhododendron forests, heading for the snow line, all I could think of was how to put one foot in front of the other and what our cook was going to produce for the evening meal. After a while I realized that this was the finest possible therapy – to think of nothing at all, just to marvel at the extraordinary Himalayan panorama, with its plunging valleys and soaring mountain ranges.

At first we passed quite a few Nepalese, who greeted us with the customary *'Namaste,'* but the higher we climbed, the fewer we encountered. Three days out from the nearest village and one day short of a pass, we were supposed to camp for two days to get used to the altitude, but our Sherpa guide, Geljen, forecast snow. Although it very rarely snowed in November, he felt there was going to be a freak blizzard. We could either return to the village we'd come from or press on over the pass as quickly as possible.

The next few hours tested our powers of endurance to the limit. One of our party, a Thai architect named Sumet, couldn't go on. He just sat there in a stupor until Geljen went back for him and carried him over the snow-covered pass. I started having spells of altitude sickness myself – we were now at 19,000 feet – but managed it unaided. The Sherpas had fixed a rope on the other side. As I made my way down it, I could see our orange tents being pitched in the green valley below. Some loads were lost during the descent, however. The going had been too tough even for our porters, who had jettisoned them. When I reached our base, they were huddled together, crying.

I shared a tent with Nick, an English friend of mine. In the middle of the night I heard a gentle, persistent tapping on the canvas beside my head. I crawled out of my sleeping bag and unzipped the flap to investigate. Nick woke up and asked what it was.

'Snow.'

'It can't be.'

For the next two days we stayed put; further progress was impossible. Early each morning our Nepalese cook would come to the tent and call, 'Tea? Coffee?' It was like being back in Chino, though Chino, and even *Tess*, seemed a lifetime ago.

We resumed our trek. There was no more snow, but I had never known such cold. Our last major obstacle was a pass called Torong-la and to cross it, we got up at 3:00 a.m. and walked for ten hours nonstop. Then it was down to the first village we'd passed in days that had a rest house. The place was filthy, but it did have plank beds, bottled beer, and a hot spring. I'd seldom felt happier.

Returning to Paris, fit and clearheaded, I was shown the O'Steen version of *Tess*. For all of Sam's expertise, it was like watching a film with every other reel left out. However guilty I might feel about Claude Berri's impending bankruptcy, I couldn't let him show the abridged version of *Tess* in public – not, at any rate, without a fight. There was simply no doubt in my mind that the shorter version was inferior. *Tess* had a rhythm that didn't lend itself to drastic cutting. Besides, the film was now doing well in France. Though slow at first, box-office returns had steadily improved as time went by. Despite several nibbles, however, we still had no firm offer from any major U.S. distributor.

The film had now been released in other countries and was scoring a great success there. Those countries didn't include Great Britain, where George Pinches, longtime film buyer for the Rank circuit, declared that *Tess* would come out 'over his dead body.' As for America, I told Claude Berri I wanted to fine-cut the picture – do some of the careful editing that should have been done before it was released in the first place. Then, I suggested, we should preview my version alongside Sam O'Steen's. If the U.S. public preferred the shorter version, I would go with that.

Coppola's company organized the screenings and got a firm of specialists to analyze the audience reaction. The questionnaires, which were enthusiastic, gave the longer version a slight edge. Running time wasn't mentioned as a determining factor. The consultancy firm pronounced *Tess* a fine film to look at but declared that neither version gave 'an indication of significant commercial viability.'

Paul Rassam, who was in Los Angeles as Claude Berri's representative, called me to say that Coppola was very happy with the previews and definitely wanted Zoetrope to distribute the film. He was offering a $2 million distribution advance, but his condition was that further reediting be done. He wanted to talk to me in person. I asked what his specific requirements were. Paul hesitated. 'He wants to refocus the story on Tess.'

In my younger days I would have obeyed my immediate instinct and told him to stuff it. But I was now supposed to be mature. 'Ask him to come over,' I said, 'and we'll talk.'

Coppola was in no hurry to expose himself to my newfound maturity, however. It was several months before he showed up in Paris. We huddled over a cutting table and went through *Tess* together. He talked, I made notes.

His reaction to the opening titles was, 'What kind of picture is this? It could be a horror movie – audiences aren't to know. Anyway, how do we know it's a great book, a literary masterpiece? Why not do it the way they used to – open with a shot of the book and the pages being turned?' He suggested I cut the whole opening sequence, the village maidens' dance, Angel's first glimpse of Tess, the encounter between her drunken father and the parson on horseback. He wanted the film to open with Tess's mother telling her about the family's noble origins. He wanted the scene where Angel returns to find Tess living with Alec to open with a close-up of Tess. He wanted more close-ups of Tess in general and suggested we reshoot some. He wanted to dispense with the scene where Tess is arrested and led away at dawn by the mounted constables and end with a close-up of her falling asleep on her slab of stone. Last but not least, he wanted to rename the film *Tess of the d'Urbervilles*.

Obviously we weren't on the same wavelength.

When I ran through my notes with Claude Berri, I could tell he found them incredible, too. I pointed out that following Coppola's suggestions would put him another half million dollars in the red – without, in my opinion, doing anything for *Tess* except destroy its special quality.

There was no more talk of the Coppola solution or of Zoetrope's distributing the film.

At long last, more than a year after its release in Europe, Columbia began showing some interest. Studio representatives had seen some of the rushes at the editing stage and found them 'insufficiently romantic.' Their change of attitude may have been triggered by Charles Champlin, the Los Angeles *Times* film critic, for whom I'd screened *Tess* while he was serving on the jury of the 1979 Cannes Festival. 'The best film of the year,' he wrote afterward, 'hasn't found a distributor in the United States.' Columbia's thinking was that while *Tess* wouldn't make any money, it might win some awards. To be nominated for an Academy Award, it had to run commercially for at least a week in two U.S. movie houses before the end of the year.

People flocked to see the film as soon as it opened. They kept coming, too. The runs at both theaters were extended. *Tess* received six nominations. Thanks to belated critical acclaim and word-of-mouth recommendation, it became a commercial success after all. Claude Berri's nightmare visions of total ruin began to fade. I had deferred part of my fees, knowing how strapped he was. These payments were now resumed. I had my best ever U.S. reviews. The Los Angeles film critics named me best director of the year; Anthony Powell, Pierre Guffroy, Geoffrey Unsworth, and Ghislain Cloquet won Oscars; and *Tess* began making real money in the United States. It was now picked up by Columbia for other English-speaking countries. Despite Rank's boycott, *Tess* opened in a large London movie theater and ran for eighteen months.

The public's vindication came too late, however. By the time the earlier, disastrous trend reversed itself I was numb and somehow indifferent. Had *Tess* sunk without a trace, I would have felt the familiar urge to make another film right away, just to prove to myself that I still could. As it was, the nine months' bliss of making it, followed by two years of misery, had left me so disenchanted that I never wanted to make a film again. I began referring to myself as a 'former' film director.

THIRTY

It was a combination of circumstances that steered me back to the theater – the ordeal of making *Tess*, disappointment at not making *Pirates* – and a change in the political climate that took me back to Poland.

I had, over the past few years, turned down several invitations to direct films in Poland. Although my replies had always been noncommittal, my reluctance to work there was politically motivated: I knew I wouldn't be able to stand living in Poland for any length of time because of the regime. Now, thanks to the extraordinary chain of developments triggered by Lech Walesa's leadership of the Gdansk shipyard strike from August 1980 onward, the regime itself appeared to be undergoing a transformation. When invited by Tadeusz Lomnicki, my boyhood idol, to come and direct a play in Warsaw, I accepted right away. Professional considerations apart, I couldn't resist a chance to see for myself what was happening in Poland.

Deep down, I had always believed that freedom would someday return, not only to Poland but to the rest of the Soviet bloc. No totalitarian system of government, however brutal and repressive, could hold power indefinitely. I'd always felt, though, that the great awakening would have to start in the Soviet Union itself and that I couldn't expect to see it in my lifetime. In view of recent developments, I began to think I was wrong.

The press reports and TV newscasts we received in Paris were incredible. Walesa's strike leadership was an unprecedented phenomenon in a Communist country, as was the

448

virtual surrender of the Polish authorities to the Gdansk shipyard workers' demand for the establishment of a truly independent and democratic trade union.

The first inkling I had that the change was more than cosmetic came when I traveled to Poland in March 1981, for the Warsaw premiere of *Tess*. Knowing that the Polish film importing agency lacked the hard currency to pay for the rights, I'd persuaded Claude Berri to assign them for a nominal sum in zlotys. The opening was attended by a number of senior government officials – even by a cabinet minister or two. I was immediately struck by the change in their attitude toward the general public. They behaved less like the remote, unapproachable dignitaries of a totalitarian state and more like social democratic politicians. If they still maintained chauffeur-driven limousines, they certainly didn't parade them. 'I must go find my wife,' said Vice Premier Rakowski; 'she's got the car keys.' That remark alone would have made the occasion different from any Warsaw premiere I'd attended in the past.

Even during my few days in Poland I couldn't fail to notice major changes in the country's press and TV coverage. For the first time the media carried news – not the stodgy, official Commmunist propaganda and slanted reports that had been the Poles' unvarying diet since 1945 but genuine news, free from ideological bias, about Poland and the world at large.

For all these reasons, I accepted Lomnicki's invitation promptly and unhesitatingly. The play I chose to direct and act in was Peter Shaffer's *Amadeus*. What most attracted me to it was its marvelous theatricality. Whereas cinema has to be naturalistic, at least on one level, to succeed, theater depends on suggestion, illusion, convention. *Amadeus* possesses these qualities to an exceptional degree.

There were additional reasons for my choice. I found the theme – talent versus mediocrity – a compelling one. Equally compelling was Shaffer's brilliant demonstration that exceptional people do not have to match our preconceptions of them. A person could write music as sublime as Mozart's and still use swearwords and baby talk, still be childish and

449

sometimes gross. As an actor, the part appealed to me immensely, and my physical appearance was an asset. Liliana Cavani, the Italian film director, had once wanted me to play the composer on the screen, pointing out that we both were small, agile men with markedly similar profiles.

I bought the rights to *Amadeus* myself – Lomnicki's theater had no hard currency allocation – and began commuting regularly between Paris and Warsaw to work on a Polish text with him and Piotr Szymanowski, his literary director. Since I would be paid standard Polish theater fees in zlotys, artistic self-fulfillment was going to entail a year of considerable financial sacrifice. While staying with my old friends Kuba and Krystyna Morgenstern, who lived not far from Wajda, I began to appreciate the extent of the upheaval in Poland and the problems that freedom was bringing in its wake.

There was no doubt that Solidarity, now sweeping the country, had struck a chord in the hearts of the overwhelming majority of Poles. Their deep-seated craving for an end to cant, deception, and rule by pro-Soviet bureaucrats, for a new way of life and a new style of government, was universally apparent. It was detectable not just in the way current events were now being reported but in the general thirst for information about Poland's past.

Ever since the Communist takeover in 1945, blanket censorship had helped concoct a travesty of what had really happened to the country since the outbreak of World War II. Its dismemberment by the Germans and Russians was never mentioned; nor was the fact that the real strength of the Polish resistance movement resided in the Armia Krajowa, or Home Army, not in the Communist-led partisan units; nor, again, was it ever admitted that Poland's Communist regime had taken over without a popular mandate. Now the Polish people's newly awakened desire for facts, as opposed to official Communist interpretations of their country's recent history, burst forth in a wide variety of ways.

The Solidarity libraries were full of once-banned books. With a startling lack of constraint, Poles openly debated

450

topics that had been taboo in my youth: topics such as the Ribbentrop-Molotov pact that had paved the way for the partition of Poland; the Soviet invasion of September 17, 1939; Poland's extinction as a sovereign state; and the massacre of Polish officers at Katyn in 1940. May 1 was still celebrated as a workers' holiday, but for the first time since 1945 another date was celebrated too: May 3, the anniversary of Poland's first constitution – one of the first democratic constitutions in the world – put into effect in 1791. A documentary about the Gdansk Solidarity strike was released in an uncensored version. The movie houses showing it were so jam-packed that Poles stopped calling it *Workers 80* and referred to it simply as Sold Out. An exhibition of press photographs, held in Warsaw, displayed previously censored shots of the anti-Soviet and anti-Communist demonstrations of 1956, 1968, 1970, 1976, and 1980. Hundreds of thousands of Poles flocked to see them. In Krakow the official party newspaper started running a regular feature entitled 'Blank Spaces in Poland's History.'

The excitement of this summer of 1981, which was exceptionally hot, made some of the usual shortages more bearable. Filling up at a gas station was an interminable business, and people still waited outside food shops in the middle of the night. There were some mornings when my cast turned up for rehearsals in a state of utter exhaustion, after having stood in line since well before dawn.

The jokes told openly about the Soviet Union and Poland's Communist masters would have filled a book, but it wasn't just this explosion of humor that surprised me. I was struck by the articulate way in which workers negotiated with government representatives and even more so by the political sophistication of the young people I met. They hadn't, after all, been brainwashed by decades of Soviet imperialism and Communist indoctrination.

The system had left its mark, nonetheless, even on the staunchest of Solidarity supporters. At almost all levels of society the tremendous longing for a free enterprise system went hand in hand with total ignorance of what it entailed and with ingrained dependence on a welfare state, even of the appallingly inefficient Polish variety. Poles had been conditioned to expect the state to provide them with jobs, housing, telephones, medical services, and the rest. It was less important to them that their jobs didn't pay a living wage, that their apartments were cramped, jerry-built monstrosities, that their phones were tapped, their medical services grossly overburdened and inefficient, and their lives within such a system a wretched caricature of what life could be. They had almost forgotten what it meant to fend for themselves. In my young days we sought relief from Stalinism in mockery, farce, satire, the theater of the absurd, and, above all, jazz. Now, so it seemed, Poles solaced themselves with religion and alcohol.

Amadeus was affected by this new mood of emancipation and Solidarity's growing strength. Lomnicki, who was to play Salieri, found himself in trouble on account of his political background. A party member for the previous thirty years and a Central Committee member for the last eight, he was a pillar of the Polish cultural establishment, the rector of Warsaw's National Drama School, and a prolific stage and screen actor. All these things were now held against him. Our Na Woli Theater belonged to the Rosa Luxemburg Works and was situated in the working-class district of Wola. Lomnicki had turned it into one of the Polish capital's leading innovative theaters, with a list of productions that included plays by Pinter, Sartre, and Anouilh. The factory workers now claimed that they had never been consulted about this arrangement and wanted the Na Woli back for conversion into a movie theater. The many favors Lomnicki had done for others, using his influence to secure them apartments, telephones, and even cars, were forgotten overnight. Despite his professional and personal integrity, he came in for the same sort of criticism as any other member of the Communist establishment. Just as certain second-rate artists had gone far on the strength of their party allegiance, so some Solidarity opportunists were using the movement to further their own careers.

Lomnicki was highly sympathetic toward Solidarity and even showed a sensitive understanding of the reasons underlying certain individuals' opposition to him. To Lomnicki, the most remarkable feature of the continuing upheaval was the party's own revolt against the system. A third of all Communist party cardholders were Solidarity members, and the younger ones among them were calling for secret ballots, open nominations, and a genuine choice of candidates for public office. The latest trend was so revolutionary that only those who had spent a lifetime in Poland could appreciate its true implications.

As work on *Amadeus* entered its final phase, I shuttled between Warsaw and Paris, bringing back items like closed-circuit TV monitors, wigs, and other odds and ends unobtainable in Poland. One thing, however, was the same in Warsaw as everywhere else – the first night was preceded by frantic eleventh-hour crises and a dress rehearsal lasting into the small hours.

Amadeus was a sellout from the start and a critical success as well. I was relieved, knowing how warily some people regarded me and how much they secretly hoped to see me stuck with a flop on my hands. I played the title role for more than a month, and by the time I handed it over to an understudy my dressing room seemed to have been visited by everyone I'd ever known – not only filmmakers and production assistants, Lodz alumni and fellow players from *The Son of the Regiment*, but contemporaries from all the Polish schools I'd attended in my youth. *Amadeus* also attracted comment from the numerous foreign journalists in Warsaw. Poland was the current focus of world attention – and besides, they wanted to be on the spot if the Russians invaded.

During one of our few days off I returned to Krakow to immerse myself in the past – even in those aspects of it I'd done my best to forget for so many years. My pilgrimage took me to the Young Spectators' Theater, to the radio station where I'd first been hired by Billizanka, to the small apartment on Komorowski Street where I'd lived from the age of four, to the house where I'd almost been killed by a bomb in the closing stages of the war, to the Winowski apartment, where I'd first made love. Every cobblestone and street corner – every sound, sight, and smell – conjured up a different memory.

I steeled myself to cross the Vistula and roam the streets of what had once been the ghetto. On the site of the SS guardhouse was now a gas station. Plac Zgody, where the main gate had stood, was now called the Square of the Heroes of the Ghetto. I could still see traces of where the windows of our first ghetto house had been bricked up; I even thought I identified the spot where I'd crawled through the wire on my final exit.

I also made a sentimental journey to Wysoka. It was unrecognizable. Where once had stood a scattering of thatched peasant cottages, TV aerials sprouted from modern two-story houses and buses purred along asphalt roads. The fields were studded with telegraph poles. I found the Buchalas' house quite easily, though. It was abandoned and in ruins. When I called at the large modern farmhouse next door, introduced myself, and asked after my foster family, the farmer and his wife knew nothing about them but sent for some neighbors who did. Mr and Mrs Buchala were dead, and so was Marcin. Jaga had been institutionalized, and Ludwik was working somewhere in a Silesian coal mine.

I went to take a closer look at the cottage that had held all six of us. It was so tiny I wondered how we had ever managed to squeeze inside. The air was still thick with bees, heavy with the stench of manure. Returning to the house next door, I was pressed to stay for supper, then plied with vodka and questions. 'Is there rationing in France, too?' the farmer's wife wanted to know.

My thoughts kept straying to the ruined cottage. It had been while I was living in that wretched little hovel, miserably lonely, with only the bleakest of prospects ahead, that something had started me on the course my life had taken. What was it? What drove me to take my fantasy world and turn it into a real one?

Was it the sexual urge that had somehow been at the root of it all? Was it that I would never have met all the women I dreamed of possessing had I remained an undersize inhabitant of the Krakow ghetto or a peasant boy from Wysoka?

I didn't believe so. I don't believe so now.

Rather, I feel that my escapades, my wildness and strength have sprung from a sense of wonder at what life has to offer. My work, my fantasies have been motivated primarily by a desire to please, to entertain, to startle people or make them laugh. I enjoy playing the fool, strutting around on the world's stage. In fact, if I had my life to live again, I would devote more attention to acting and less to directing.

But it is as absurd to regret the past as it is to plan for the future. My father has always reproached me for overspending and failing to organize my life. I don't regret the substantial sums I've squandered. The notion of dying with a healthy bank balance is repugnant to me; life – and money – are there to be enjoyed.

Since Sharon's death, however, and despite appearances to the contrary, my enjoyment of life has been incomplete.

In moments of unbearable personal tragedy some people find solace in religion. In my case the opposite happened. Any religious faith I had was shattered by Sharon's murder. It reinforced my faith in the absurd.

I still go through the motions of being a professional entertainer, still tell funny stories and act them out to best effect, still laugh a lot and enjoy the company of people who laugh, but I know in my heart of hearts that the spirit of laughter has deserted me. It isn't just that success has left me jaded or that I've been soured by tragedy and by my own follies. I seem to be toiling to no discernible purpose. I feel I've lost the right to innocence, to a pure appreciation of life's pleasure. My childish gullibility and loyalty to my friends have cost me dear, not least in my relations with the press, but my growing wariness has been just as self-destructive.

I am widely regarded, I know, as an evil, profligate dwarf. My friends – and the women in my life – know better.

Many women seem irresistibly attracted by notoriety, and many – especially since the Los Angeles affair – are eager to meet me. When they discover that I'm not what they've been led to expect, a lot of them are disappointed. I have been on the receiving end of so many inaccuracies, misapprehensions and downright distortions that people who don't know me have an entirely false idea of my personality. Rumor, harnessed to the power of the media, creates an image of public figures that clings to them forever – a sort of caricature that passes for reality. I know what I am, what I have and haven't done, how things really were and are.

It was at Wysoka, while delving back into the past, that I first thought of putting down on paper what I felt to be the truth about myself. Although I realized that, however fully and frankly I tried to do so, some people would still prefer the caricature to the real thing, I would at least have given them something else to go on.

I had returned to Paris and was in the midst of rehearsals for the French production of *Amadeus* when the news from Poland broke. The imposition of martial law created another watershed in my life. Steeped in Polish history, like all my fellow countrymen, I saw it as one more episode in our national tragedy. This time, however, I had lived through some of Solidarity's finest hours in person, seen for myself how freedom still stirred in the hearts of the Polish people, witnessed their remarkable courage and endurance in the face of Communist tyranny.

It was an experience that triggered memories of my own early years, of the Stalinism we'd fought with mockery in Poland's real-life theater of the absurd. That story, too, deserved to be told.

Now was a good time to begin.